FIRE FORCE

03

ATSUSHI
OHKUBO

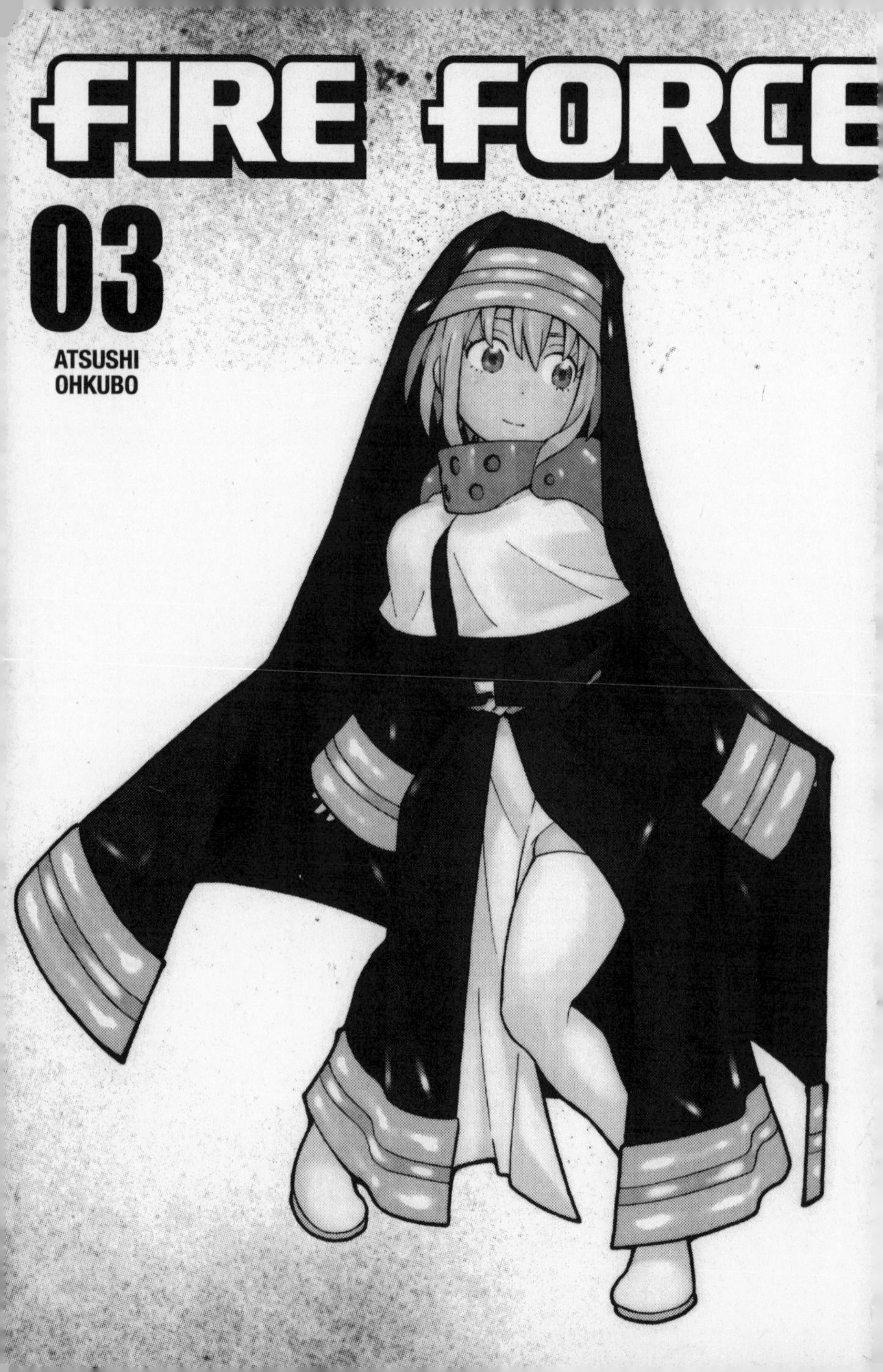

SPECIAL FIRE FORCE COMPANY 8

CAPTAIN (NON-POWERED)

AKITARU ŌBI

The popular and charismatic leader of the newly established Company 8. He has no powers, but uses his finely honed muscles as a weapon to accomplish at least as much as the pyrokinetics. Loves bodybuilding to an almost creepy extent.

SECOND CLASS FIRE SOLDIER (THIRD GENERATION PYROKINETIC)

ARTHUR BOYLE

Trained at the academy with Shinra. Although he follows his own personal code of chivalry as the self-proclaimed Knight King, he is incredibly stupid. But girls love him. He creates a fire sword with a blade that can cut through most anything.

WATCHES OUT FOR

TRUSTS

IDIOT!!

WATCHES OUT FOR

TRUSTS

STRONG BOND

SECOND CLASS FIRE SOLDIER (THIRD GENERATION PYROKINETIC)

SHINRA KUSAKABE

Since being accused of using his powers to cause the fire that took his family, his face's habit of tensing up into a bizarre smile when he gets nervous has earned him the derisive nickname of "devil." He joined the Fire Force to achieve his dream of becoming a hero and saving people from the fear of the flames.

A NICE GIRL

LOOKS AWESOME ON THE JOB

A TOUGH BUT WEIRD LADY

HANG IN THERE, ROOKIE!

TERRIFIED

STRICT DISCIPLINARIAN

LIEUTENANT (SECOND GENERATION PYROKINETIC)

TAKEHISA HINAWA

A dry, unemotional ex-military man. His stern discipline is feared among the new recruits, and he will even shoot them in response to their nonsense. He never allows the soldiers to play with fire. Has odd taste in hats.

FIRST CLASS FIRE SOLDIER (SECOND GENERATION PYROKINETIC)

MAKI OZE

A former member of the military, she is an excellent fighter who controls fire. Mad about love stories, her beauty is overshadowed by her "head full of flowers and wedding bells." She's friendly, but snaps when anyone comments on her muscles.

NUN (NON-POWERED)

IRIS

A sister of the Holy Sol Temple, she plays an indispensable role in extinguishing Infernals, reciting the prayers required to calm their souls. Personality-wise, she is no less than an angel. Her boobs are big. Very big. She is currently being held captive by Company 5.

THE GIRLS' CLUB

RESPECTS

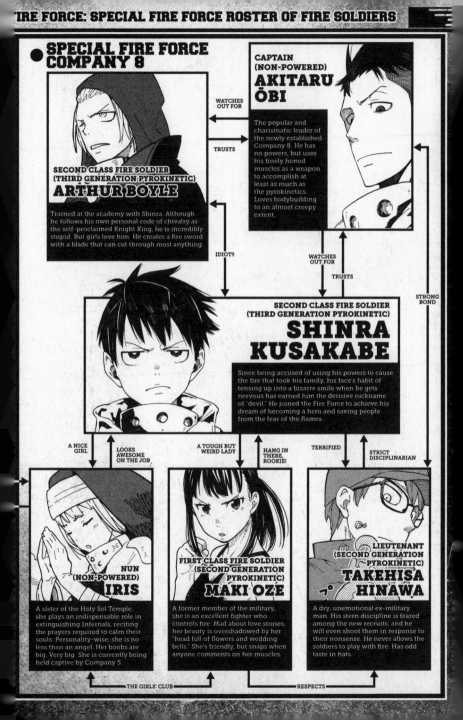

SPECIAL FIRE FORCE COMPANY 5

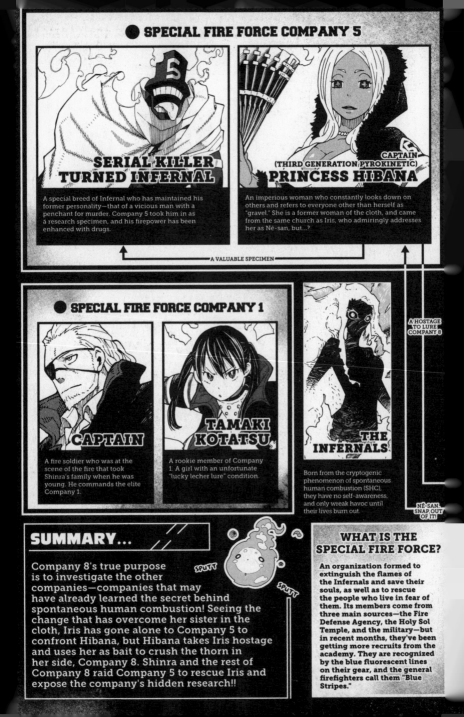

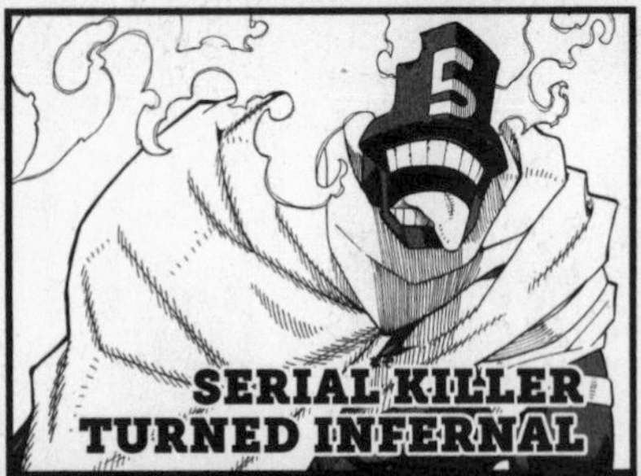
SERIAL KILLER
TURNED INFERNAL

A special breed of Infernal who has maintained his former personality—that of a vicious man with a penchant for murder. Company 5 took him in as a research specimen, and his firepower has been enhanced with drugs.

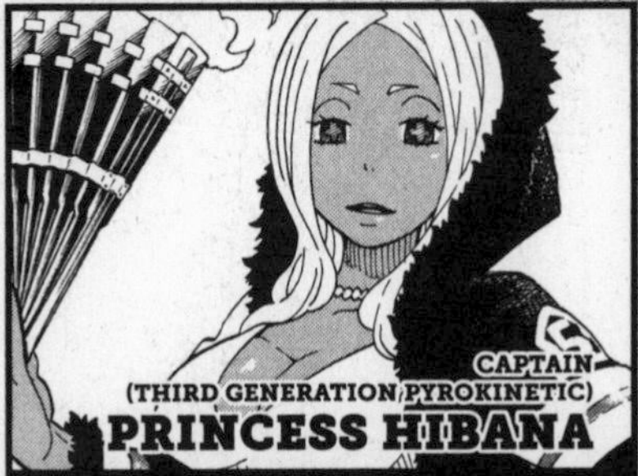
CAPTAIN
(THIRD GENERATION PYROKINETIC)
PRINCESS HIBANA

An imperious woman who constantly looks down on others and refers to everyone other than herself as "gravel." She is a former woman of the cloth, and came from the same church as Iris, who admiringly addresses her as Nê-san, but...?

A VALUABLE SPECIMEN

A HOSTAGE TO LURE COMPANY 8

SPECIAL FIRE FORCE COMPANY 1

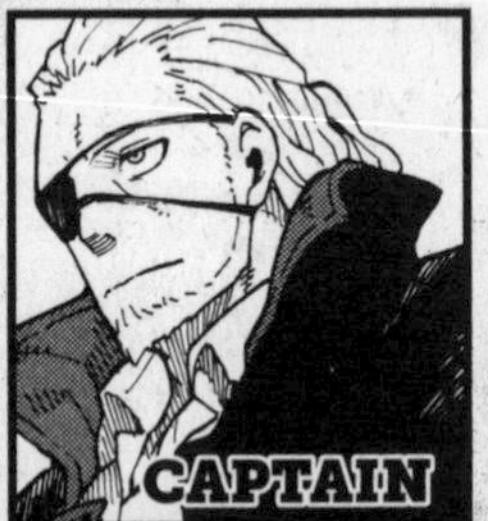
CAPTAIN

A fire soldier who was at the scene of the fire that took Shinra's family when he was young. He commands the elite Company 1.

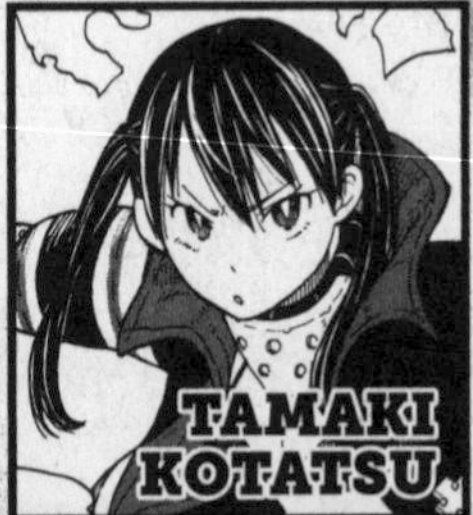
TAMAKI
KOTATSU

A rookie member of Company 1. A girl with an unfortunate "lucky lecher lure" condition.

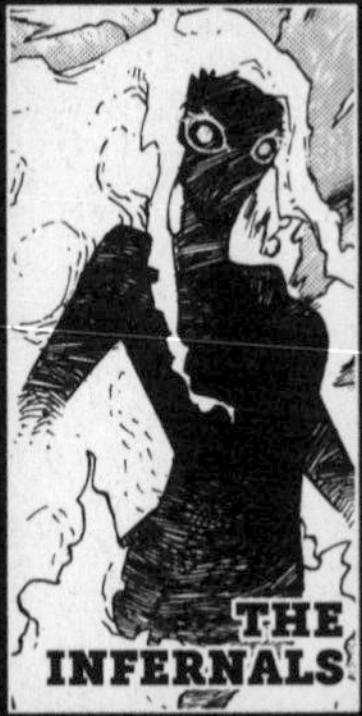
THE
INFERNALS

Born from the cryptogenic phenomenon of spontaneous human combustion (SHC), they have no self-awareness, and only wreak havoc until their lives burn out.

NÊ-SAN, SNAP OUT OF IT!

SUMMARY...

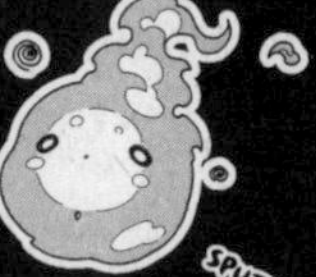
SPUTT
SPUTT

Company 8's true purpose is to investigate the other companies—companies that may have already learned the secret behind spontaneous human combustion! Seeing the change that has overcome her sister in the cloth, Iris has gone alone to Company 5 to confront Hibana, but Hibana takes Iris hostage and uses her as bait to crush the thorn in her side, Company 8. Shinra and the rest of Company 8 raid Company 5 to rescue Iris and expose the company's hidden research!!

WHAT IS THE SPECIAL FIRE FORCE?

An organization formed to extinguish the flames of the Infernals and save their souls, as well as to rescue the people who live in fear of them. Its members come from three main sources—the Fire Defense Agency, the Holy Sol Temple, and the military—but in recent months, they've been getting more recruits from the academy. They are recognized by the blue fluorescent lines on their gear, and the general firefighters call them "Blue Stripes."

FIRE FORCE 03
CONTENTS

FIRE FORCE

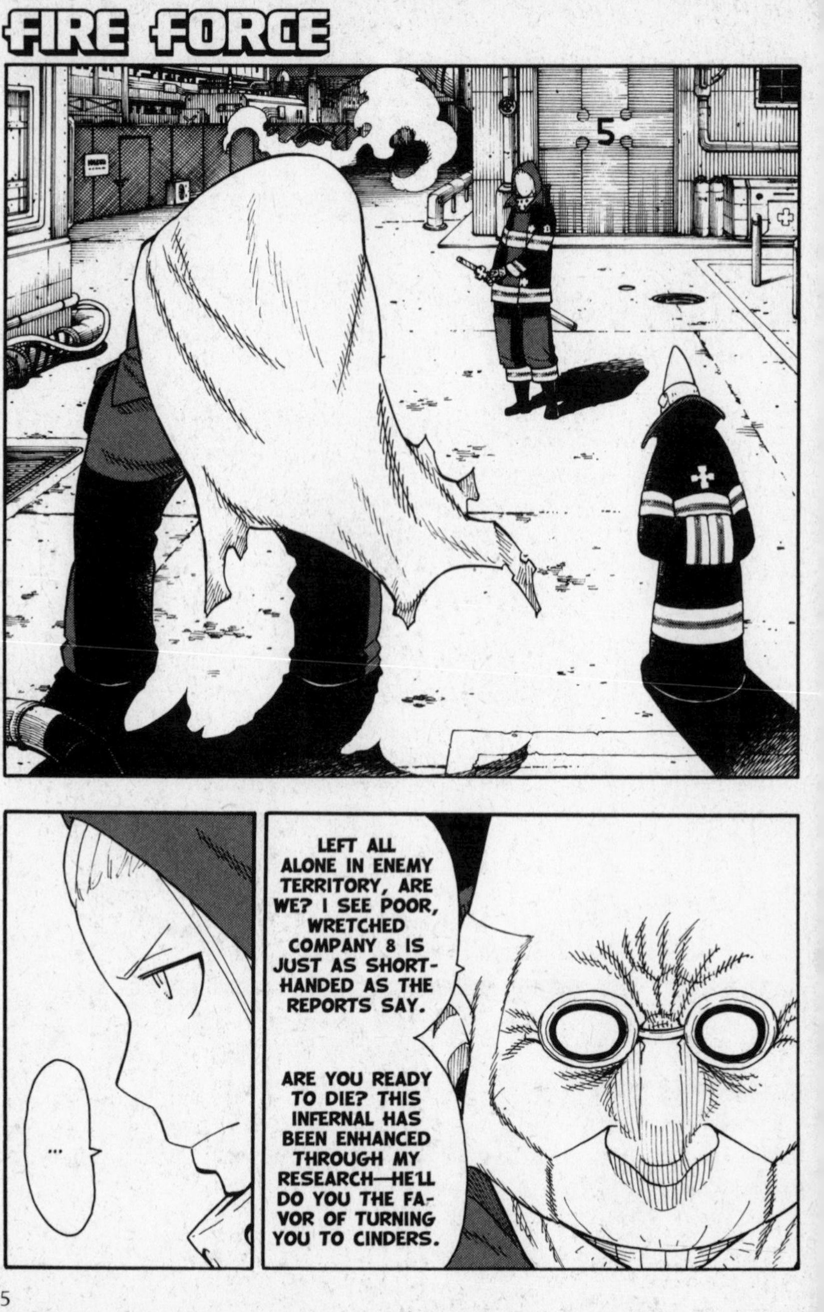
LEFT ALL ALONE IN ENEMY TERRITORY, ARE WE? I SEE POOR, WRETCHED COMPANY 8 IS JUST AS SHORT-HANDED AS THE REPORTS SAY.
ARE YOU READY TO DIE? THIS INFERNAL HAS BEEN ENHANCED THROUGH MY RESEARCH—HE'LL DO YOU THE FA-VOR OF TURNING YOU TO CINDERS.
...

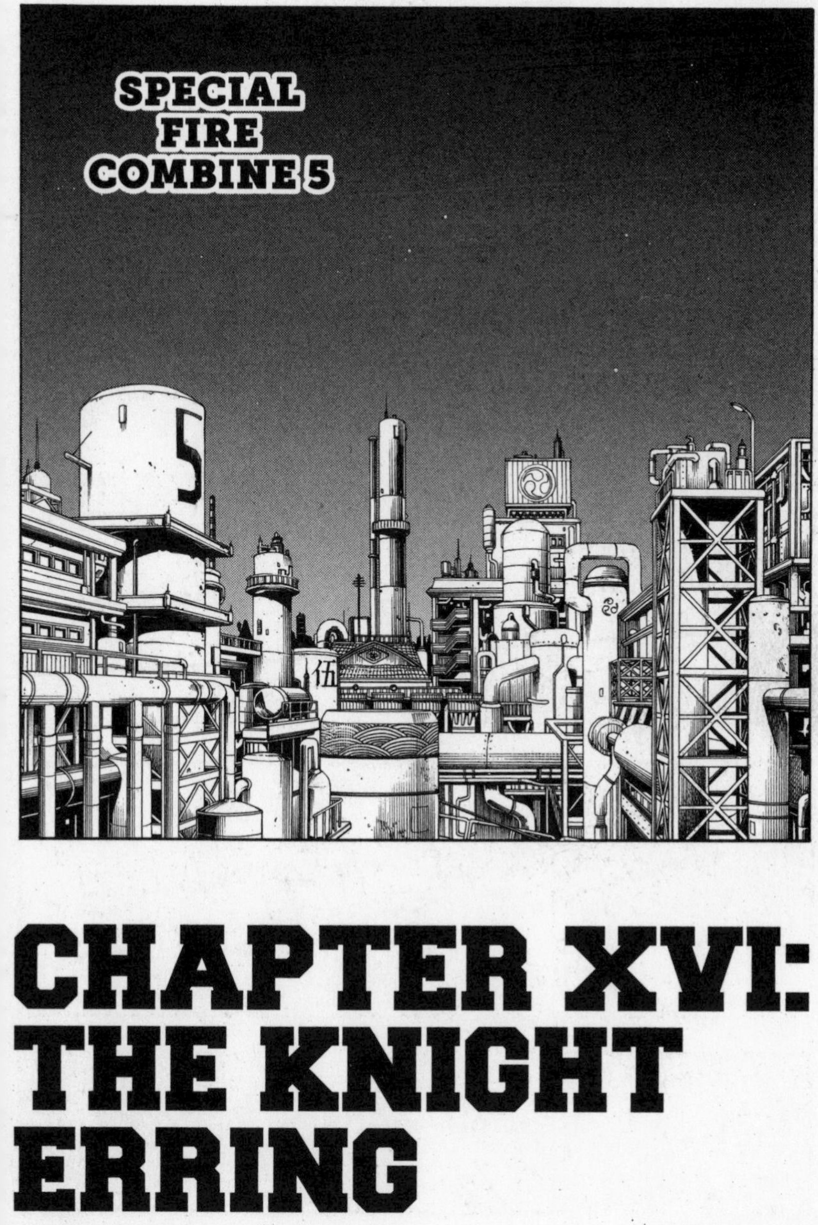
SPECIAL
FIRE
COMBINE 5

CHAPTER XVI: THE KNIGHT ERRING

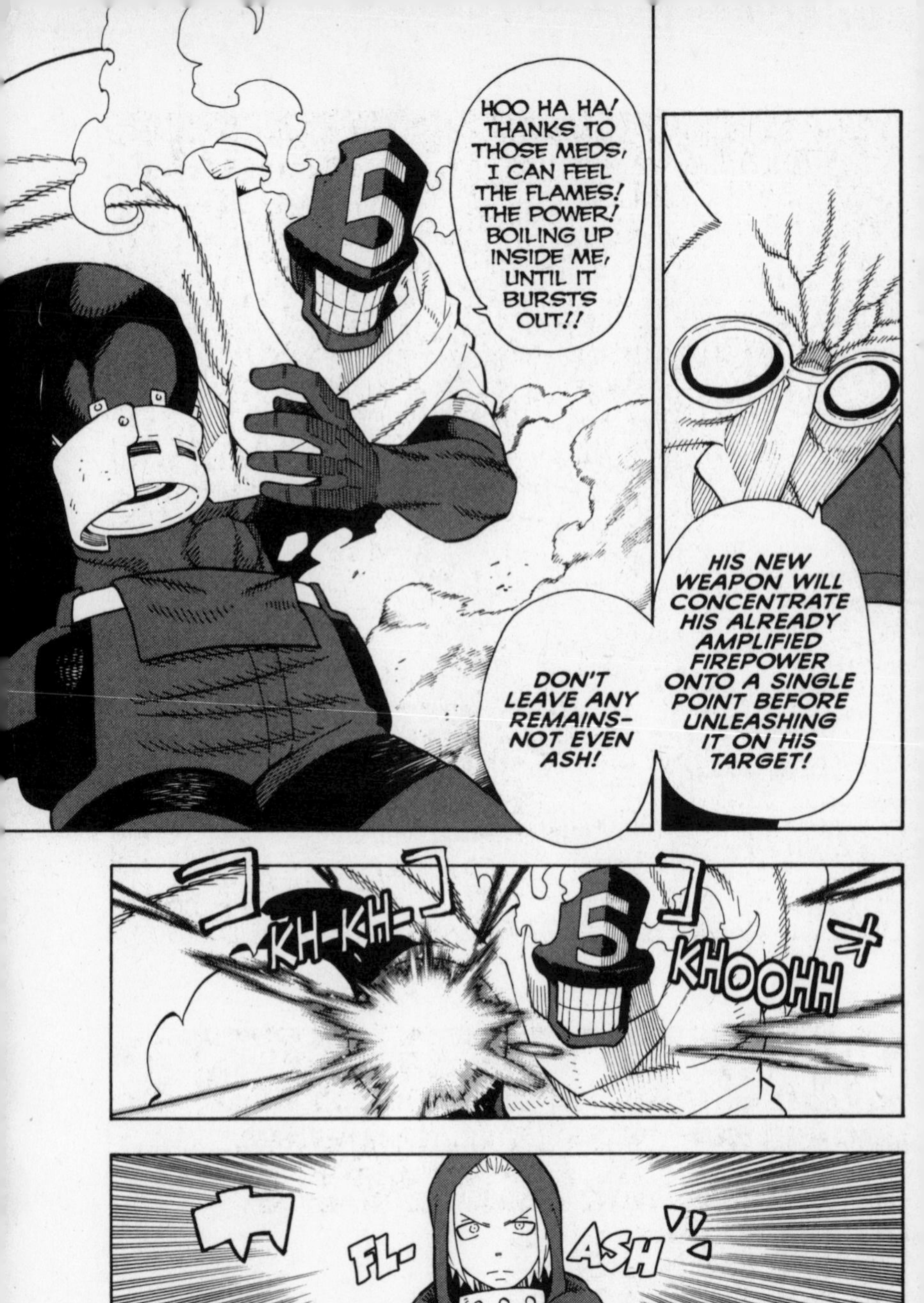
HIS NEW WEAPON WILL CONCENTRATE HIS ALREADY AMPLIFIED FIREPOWER ONTO A SINGLE POINT BEFORE UNLEASHING IT ON HIS TARGET!
HOO HA HA! THANKS TO THOSE MEDS, I CAN FEEL THE FLAMES! THE POWER! BOILING UP INSIDE ME, UNTIL IT BURSTS OUT!!
DON'T LEAVE ANY REMAINS-NOT EVEN ASH!
KHOOHH
KH-KH-
FL-ASH

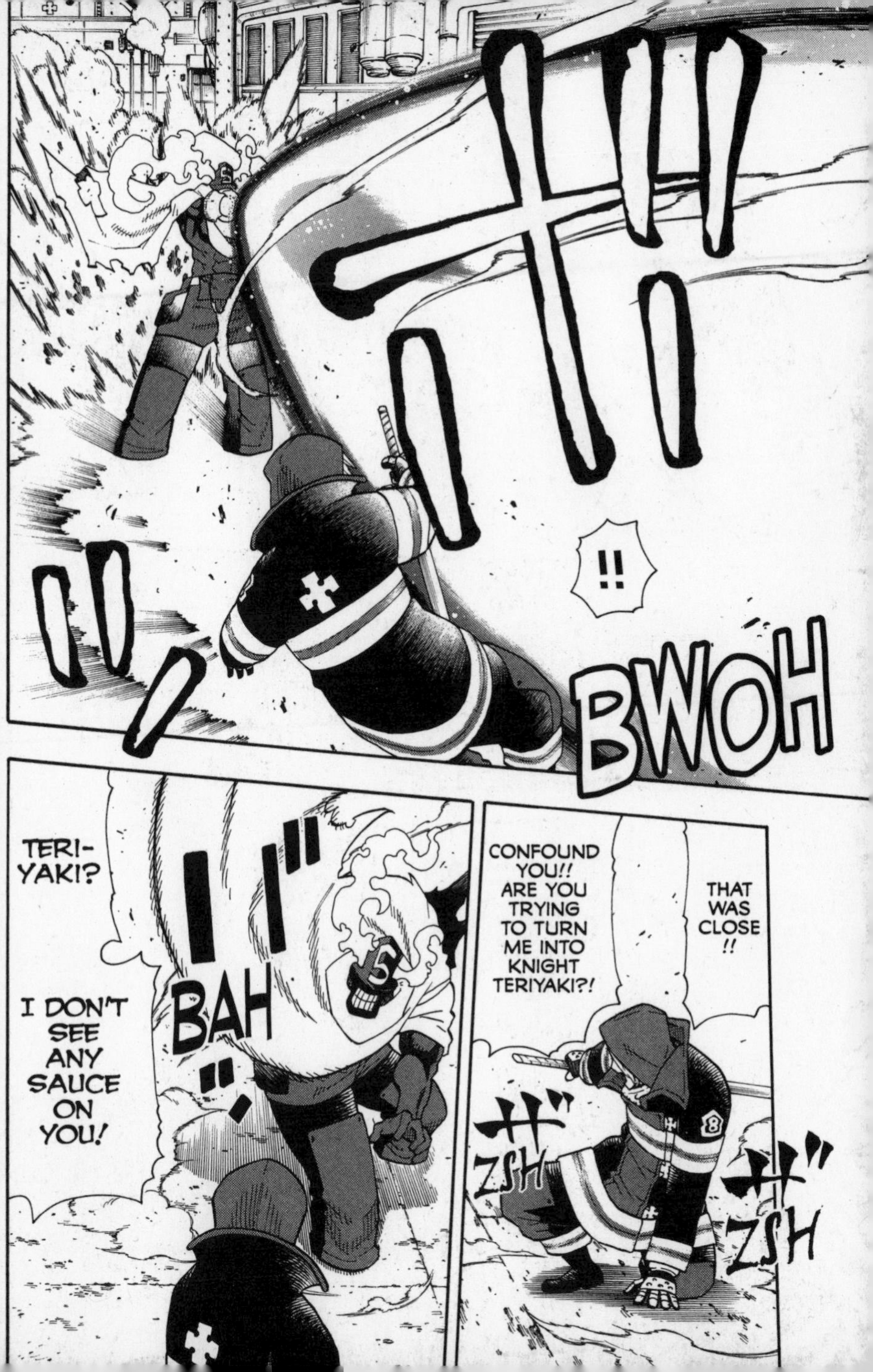
!!
BWOH
THAT WAS CLOSE!!
CONFOUND YOU!! ARE YOU TRYING TO TURN ME INTO KNIGHT TERIYAKI?!
ZSH
ZSH
TERI-YAKI?
BAH
I DON'T SEE ANY SAUCE ON YOU!

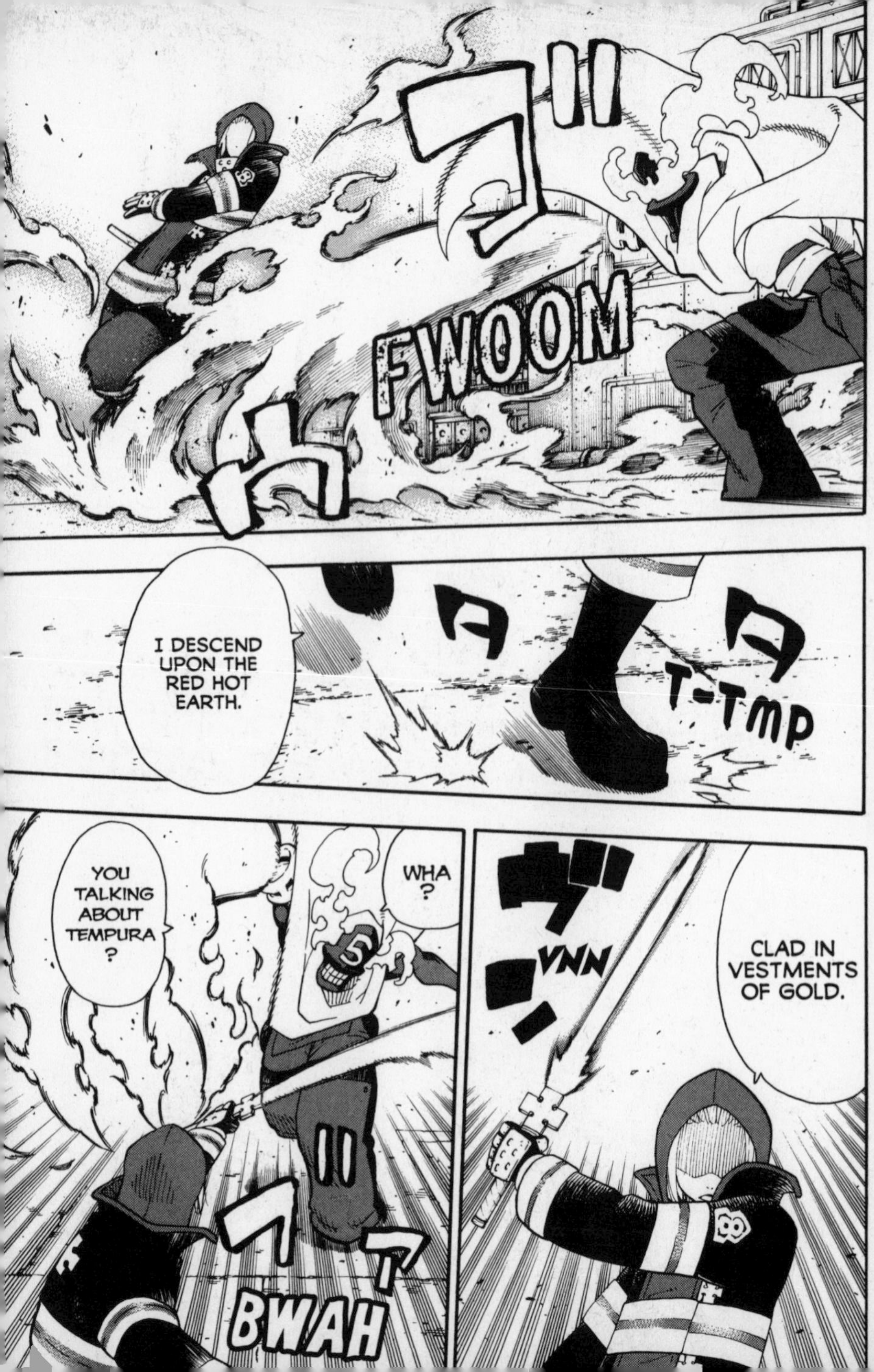
FWOOM
T-TMP
I DESCEND UPON THE RED HOT EARTH.
VNN
CLAD IN VESTMENTS OF GOLD.
WHA?
YOU TALKING ABOUT TEMPURA?
BWAH

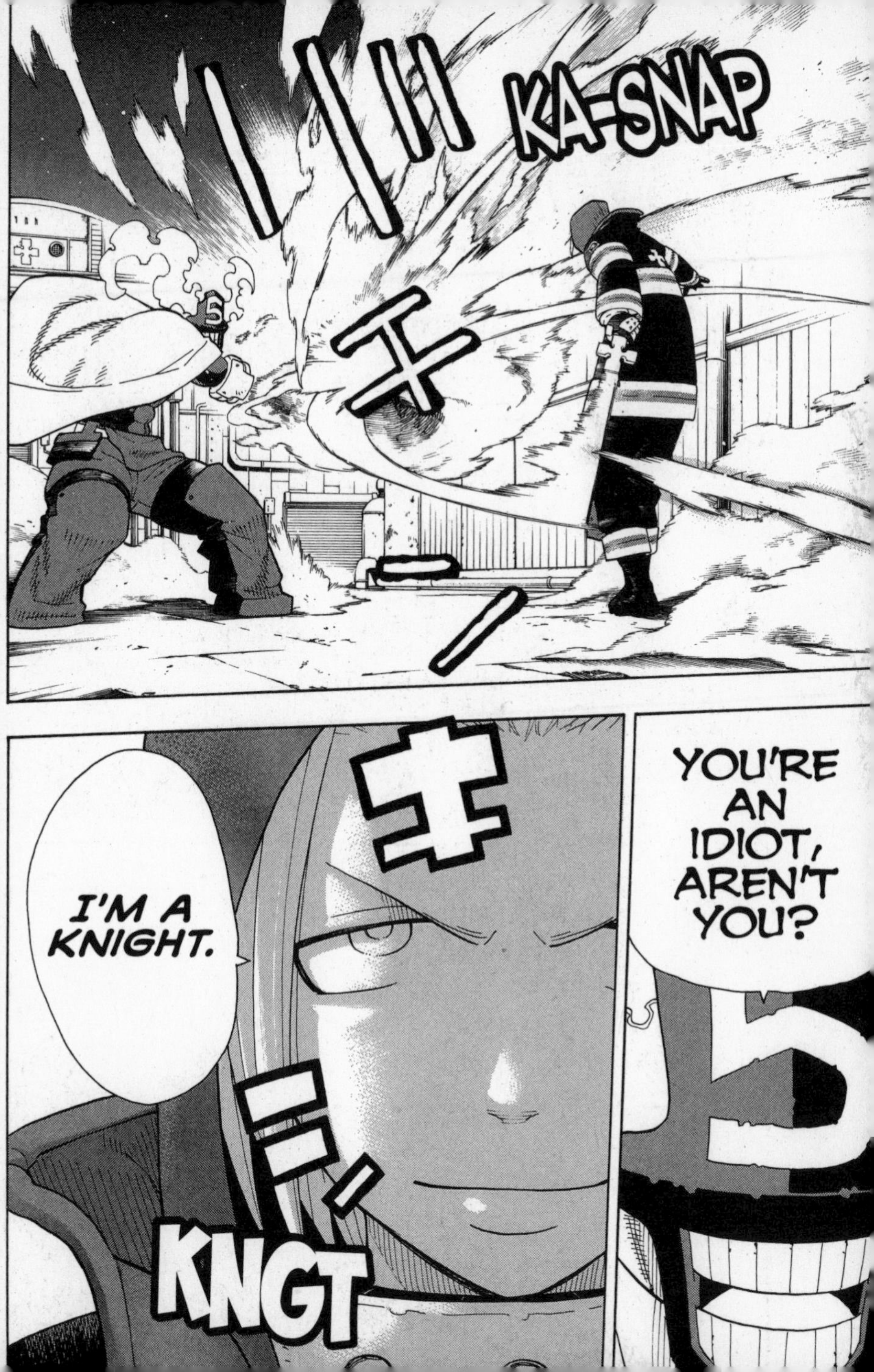
KA-SNAP
YOU'RE AN IDIOT, AREN'T YOU?
I'M A KNIGHT.
KNGT

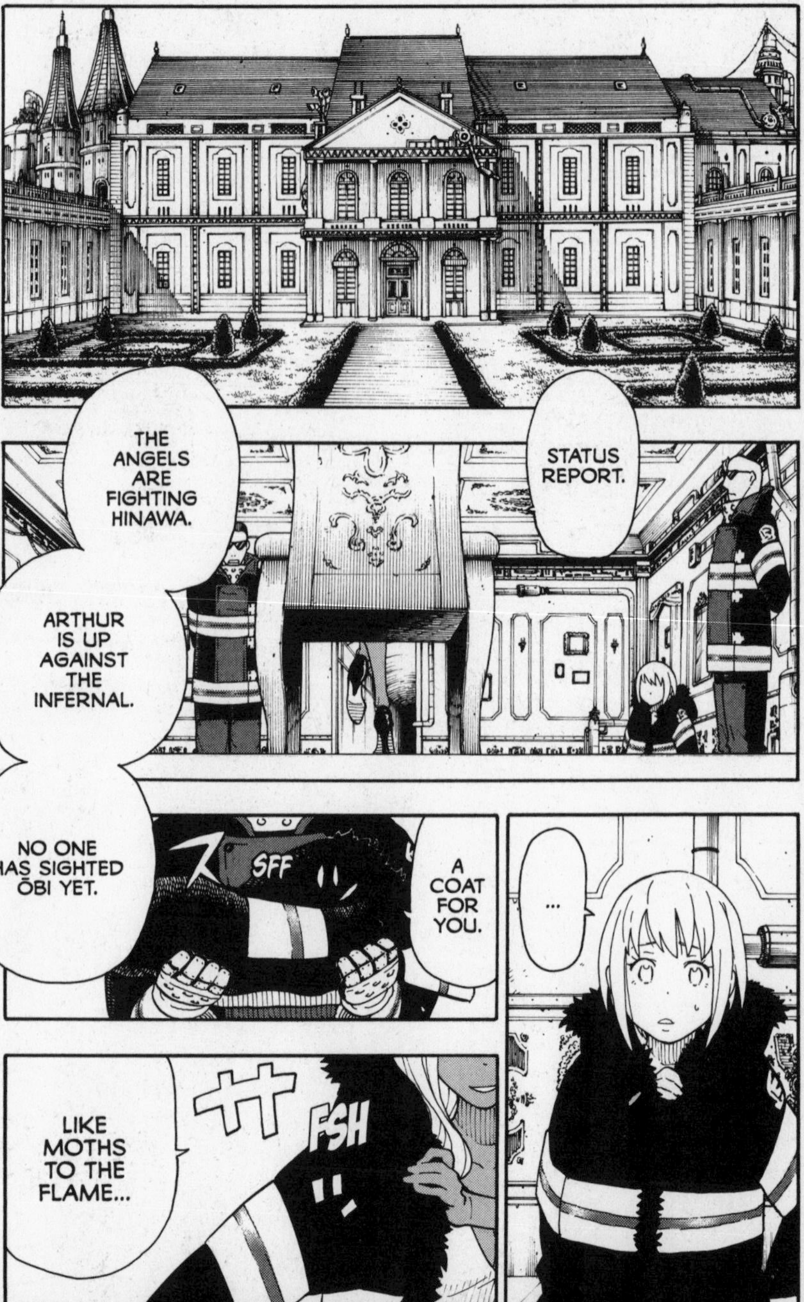
STATUS REPORT.
THE ANGELS ARE FIGHTING HINAWA.
ARTHUR IS UP AGAINST THE INFERNAL.
NO ONE HAS SIGHTED ŌBI YET.
...
A COAT FOR YOU.
SFF
LIKE MOTHS TO THE FLAME...
FSH

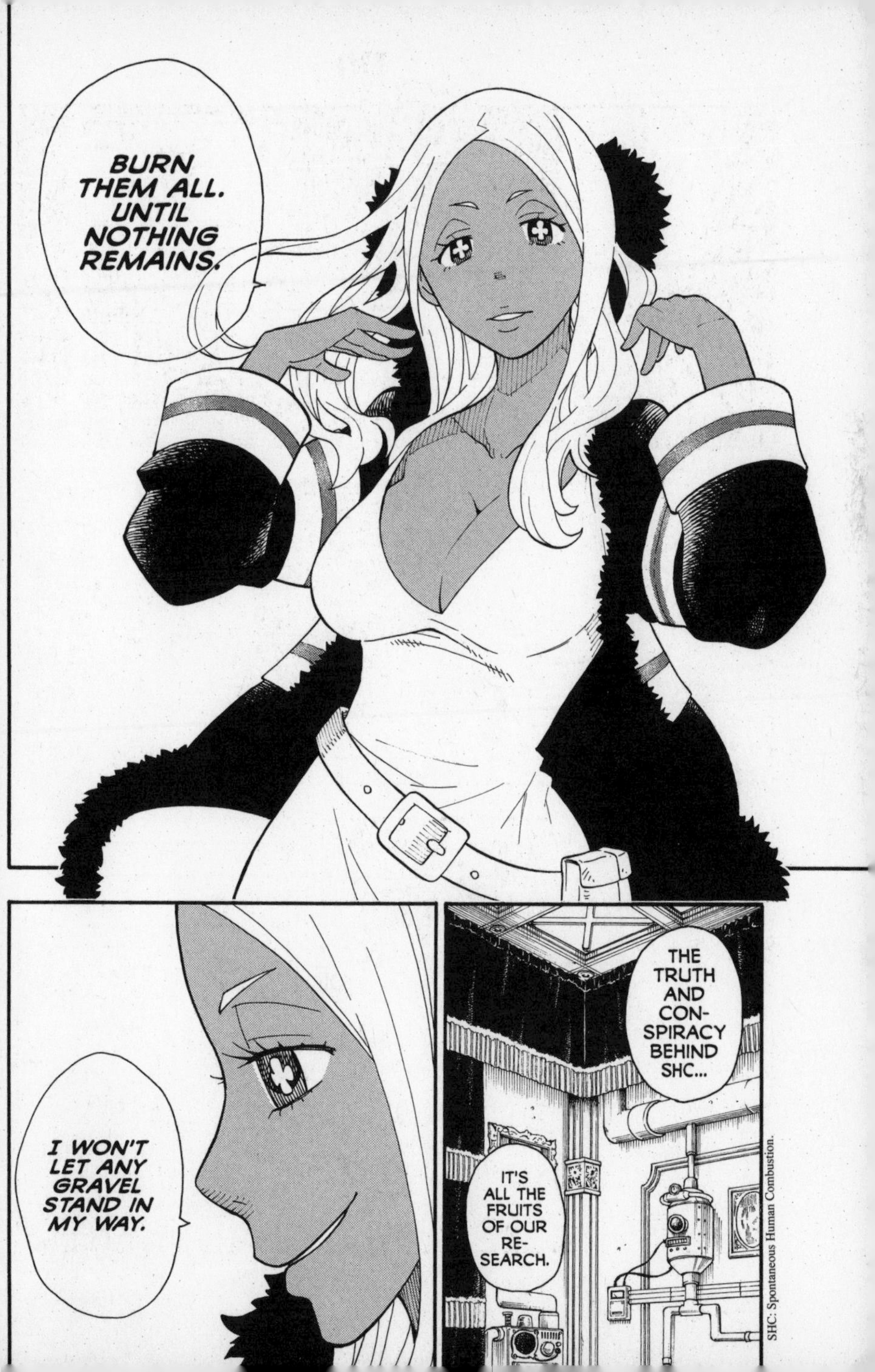
BURN THEM ALL. UNTIL NOTHING REMAINS.
THE TRUTH AND CON-SPIRACY BEHIND SHC...
IT'S ALL THE FRUITS OF OUR RE-SEARCH.
I WON'T LET ANY GRAVEL STAND IN MY WAY.

SHC: Spontaneous Human Combustion.

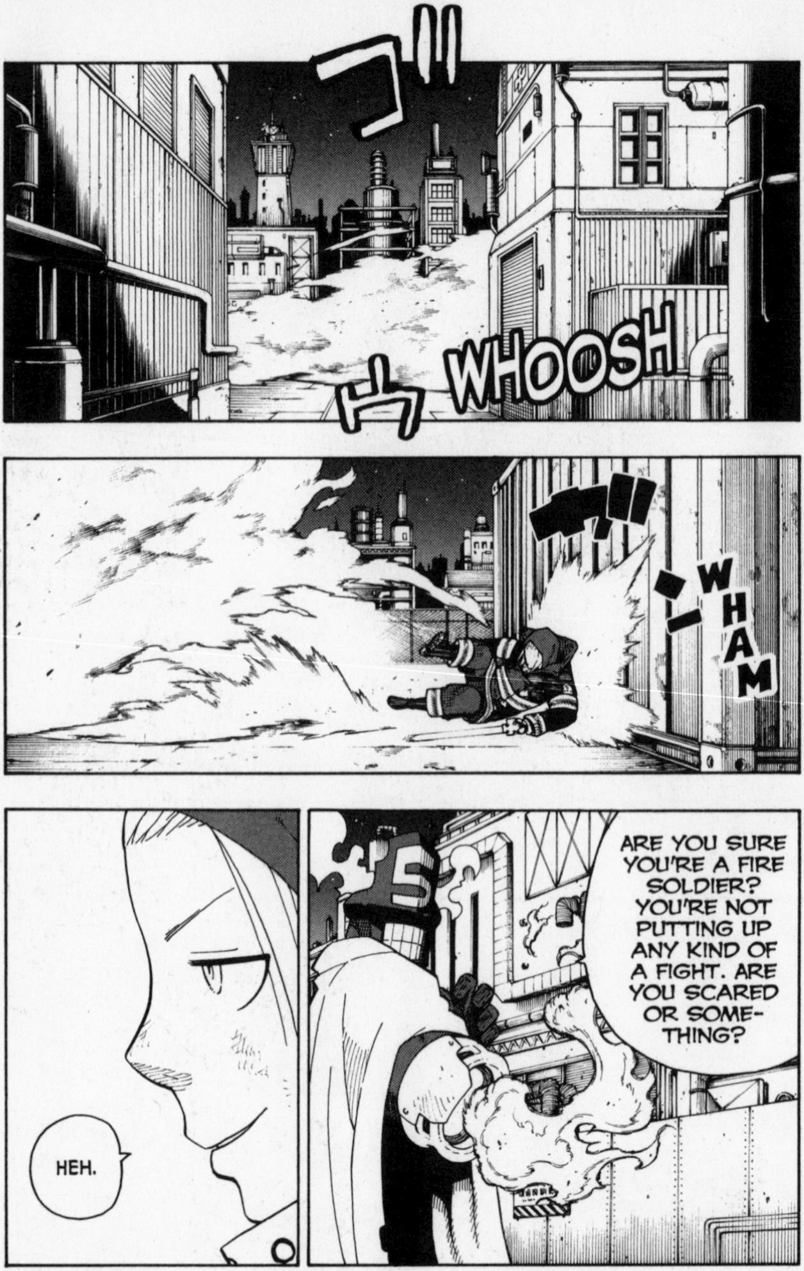
WHOOSH
WHAM
ARE YOU SURE YOU'RE A FIRE SOLDIER? YOU'RE NOT PUTTING UP ANY KIND OF A FIGHT. ARE YOU SCARED OR SOME-THING?
HEH.

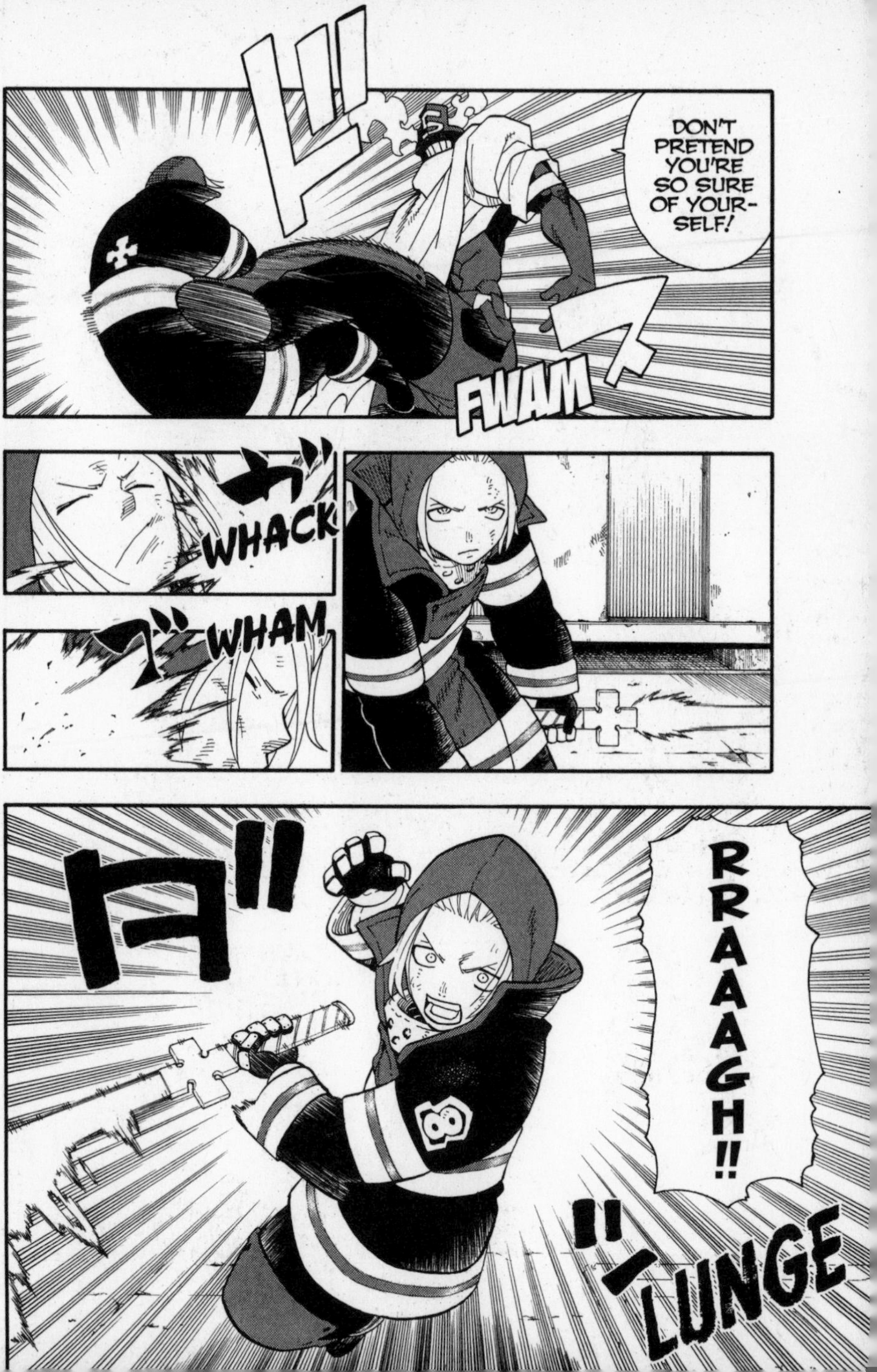
DON'T PRETEND YOU'RE SO SURE OF YOUR-SELF!
FWAM
WHACK
WHAM
RRAAAAGH!!
LUNGE

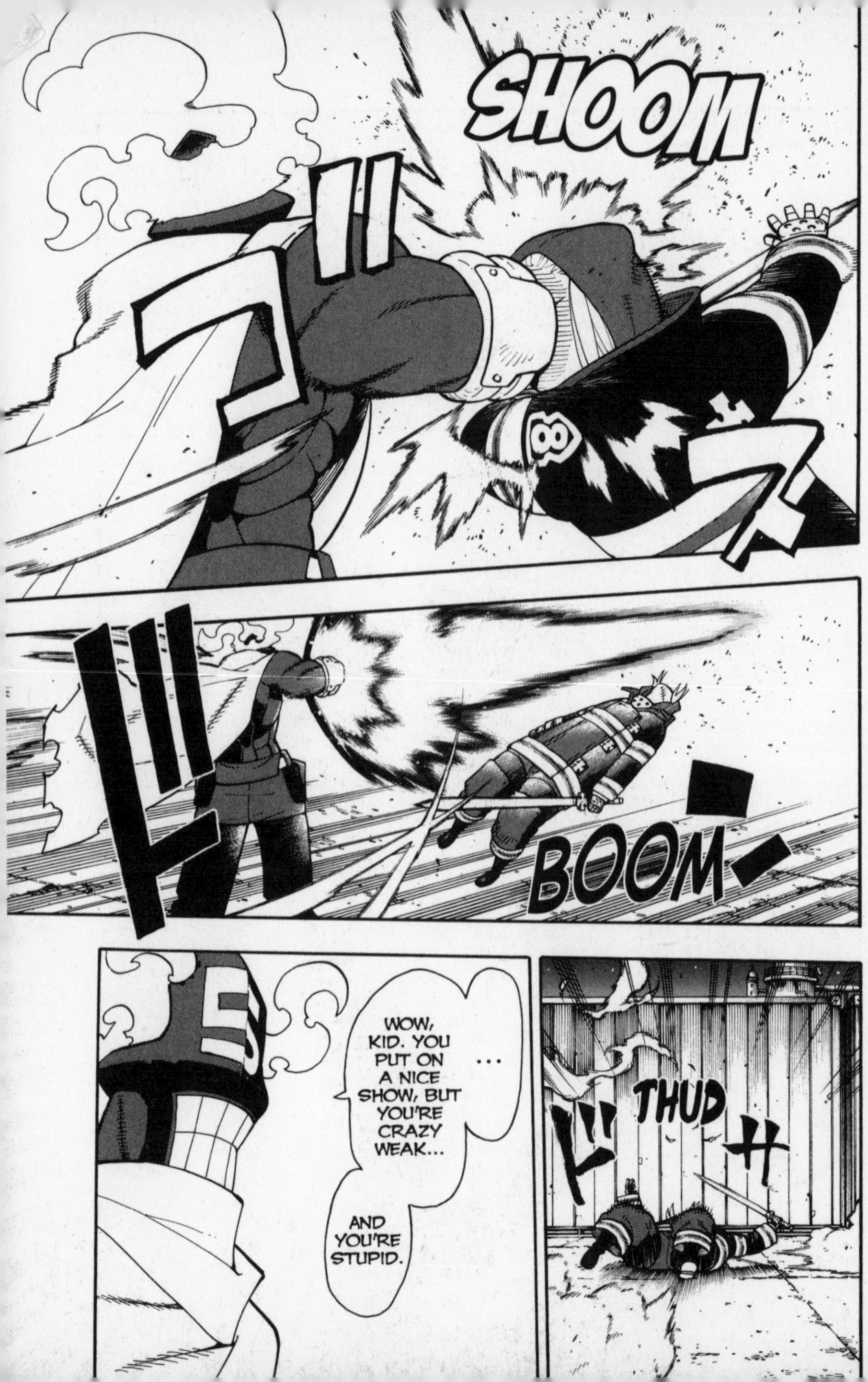
SHOOM
BOOM
THUD
...
WOW, KID. YOU PUT ON A NICE SHOW, BUT YOU'RE CRAZY WEAK...
AND YOU'RE STUPID.

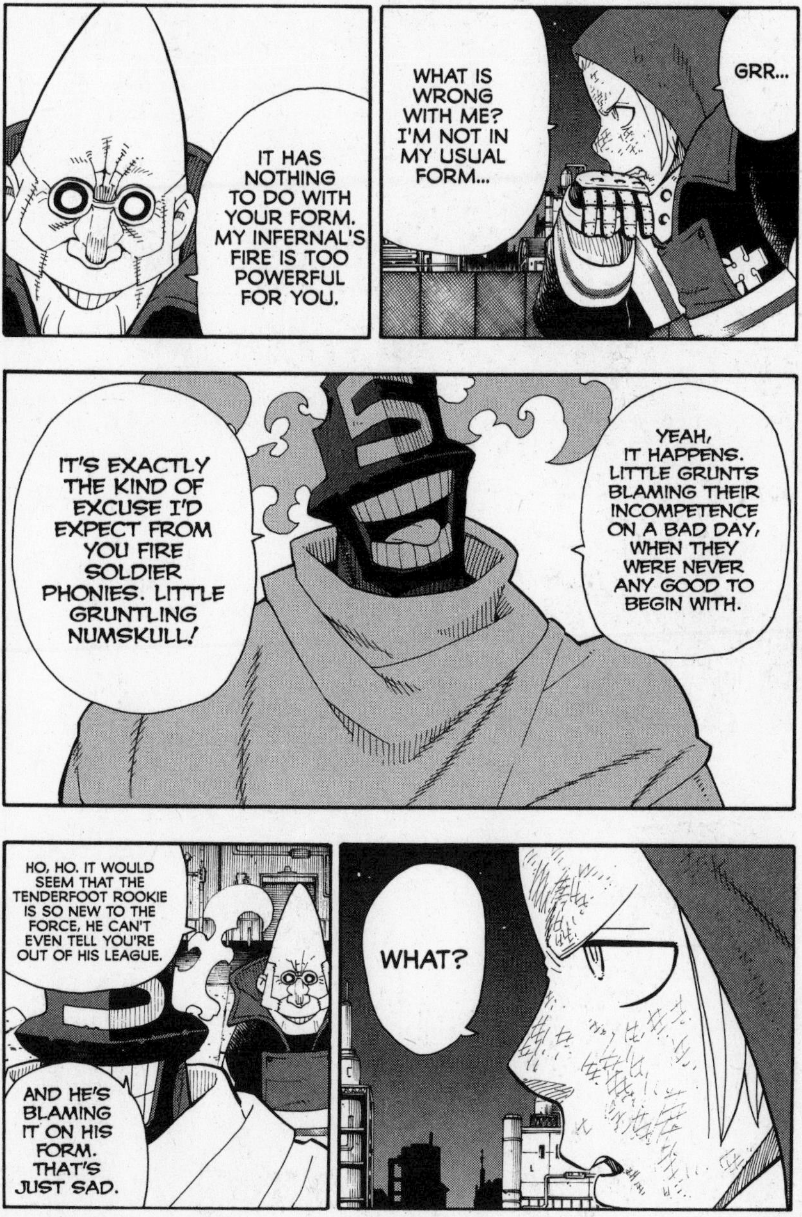
GRR...
WHAT IS WRONG WITH ME? I'M NOT IN MY USUAL FORM...
IT HAS NOTHING TO DO WITH YOUR FORM. MY INFERNAL'S FIRE IS TOO POWERFUL FOR YOU.
YEAH, IT HAPPENS. LITTLE GRUNTS BLAMING THEIR INCOMPETENCE ON A BAD DAY, WHEN THEY WERE NEVER ANY GOOD TO BEGIN WITH.
IT'S EXACTLY THE KIND OF EXCUSE I'D EXPECT FROM YOU FIRE SOLDIER PHONIES. LITTLE GRUNTLING NUMSKULL!
WHAT?
HO, HO. IT WOULD SEEM THAT THE TENDERFOOT ROOKIE IS SO NEW TO THE FORCE, HE CAN'T EVEN TELL YOU'RE OUT OF HIS LEAGUE.
AND HE'S BLAMING IT ON HIS FORM. THAT'S JUST SAD.

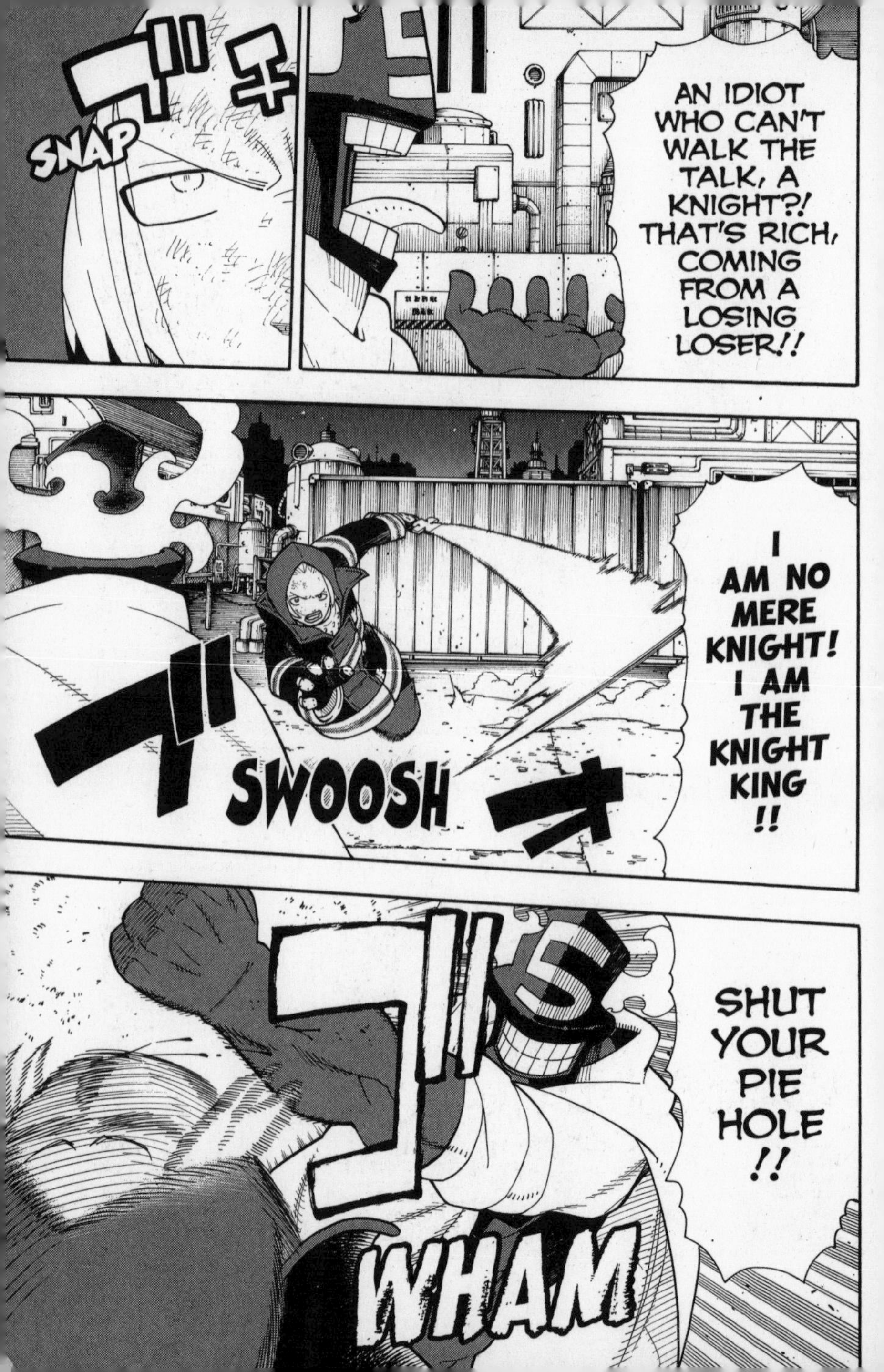
AN IDIOT WHO CAN'T WALK THE TALK, A KNIGHT?! THAT'S RICH, COMING FROM A LOSING LOSER!!
SNAP
I AM NO MERE KNIGHT! I AM THE KNIGHT KING!!
SWOOSH
SHUT YOUR PIE HOLE!!
WHAM

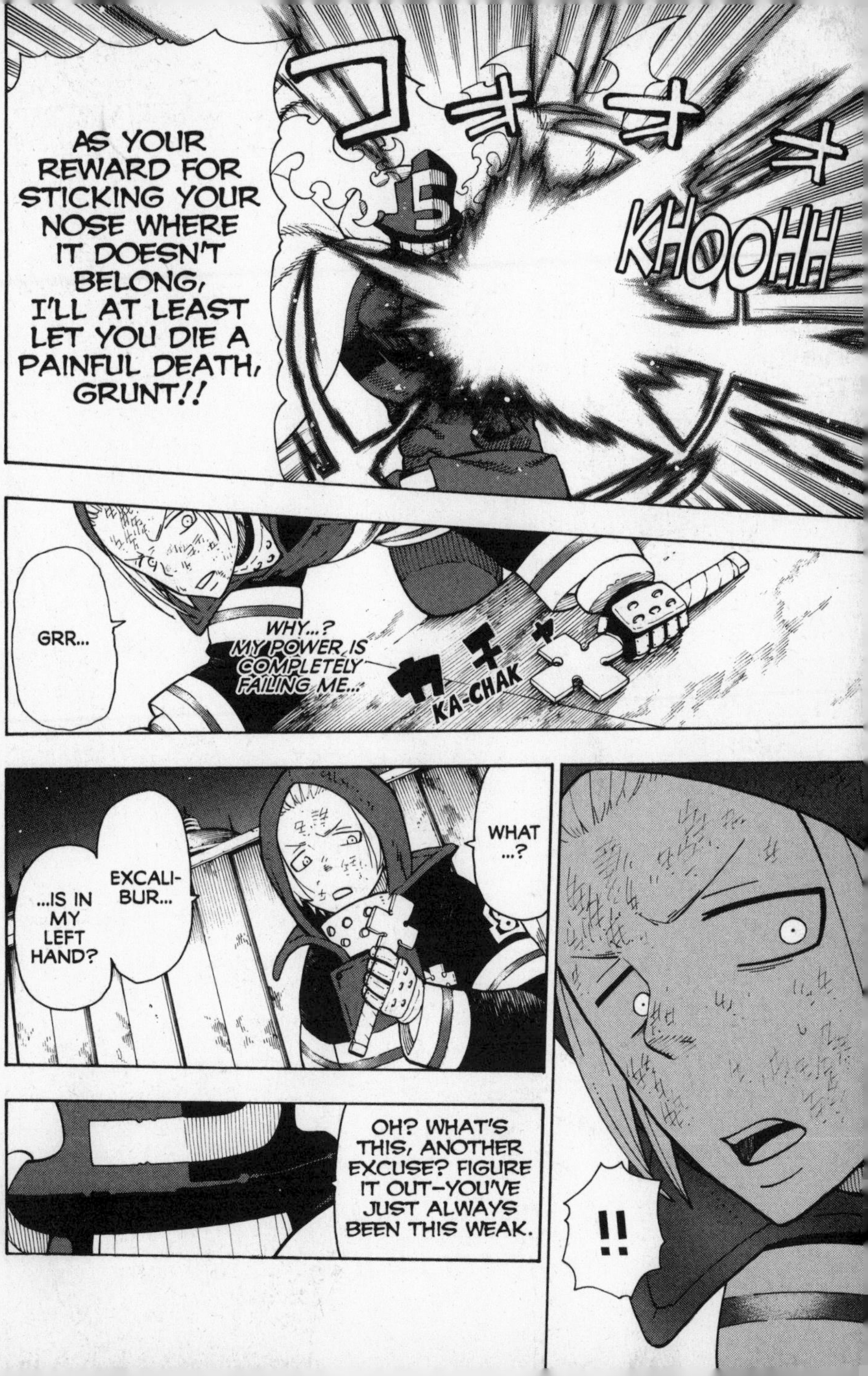
KHOOHH
AS YOUR REWARD FOR STICKING YOUR NOSE WHERE IT DOESN'T BELONG, I'LL AT LEAST LET YOU DIE A PAINFUL DEATH, GRUNT!!
KA-CHAK
WHY...? MY POWER IS COMPLETELY FAILING ME...
GRR...
!!
WHAT ...?
EXCALI-BUR...
...IS IN MY LEFT HAND?
OH? WHAT'S THIS, ANOTHER EXCUSE? FIGURE IT OUT—YOU'VE JUST ALWAYS BEEN THIS WEAK.

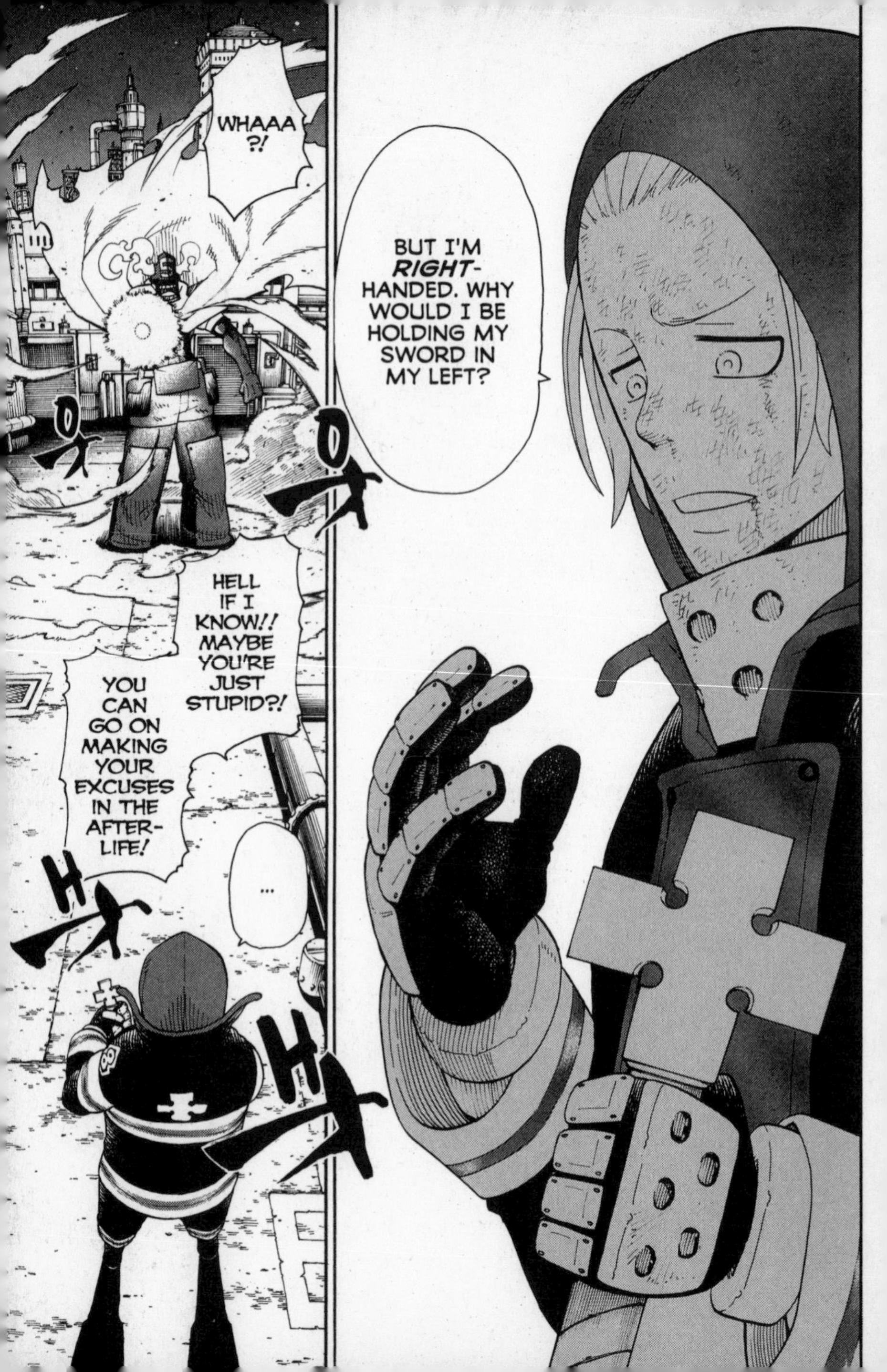
BUT I'M *RIGHT*-HANDED. WHY WOULD I BE HOLDING MY SWORD IN MY LEFT?
WHAAA?!
HELL IF I KNOW!! MAYBE YOU'RE JUST STUPID?!
YOU CAN GO ON MAKING YOUR EXCUSES IN THE AFTER-LIFE!
...

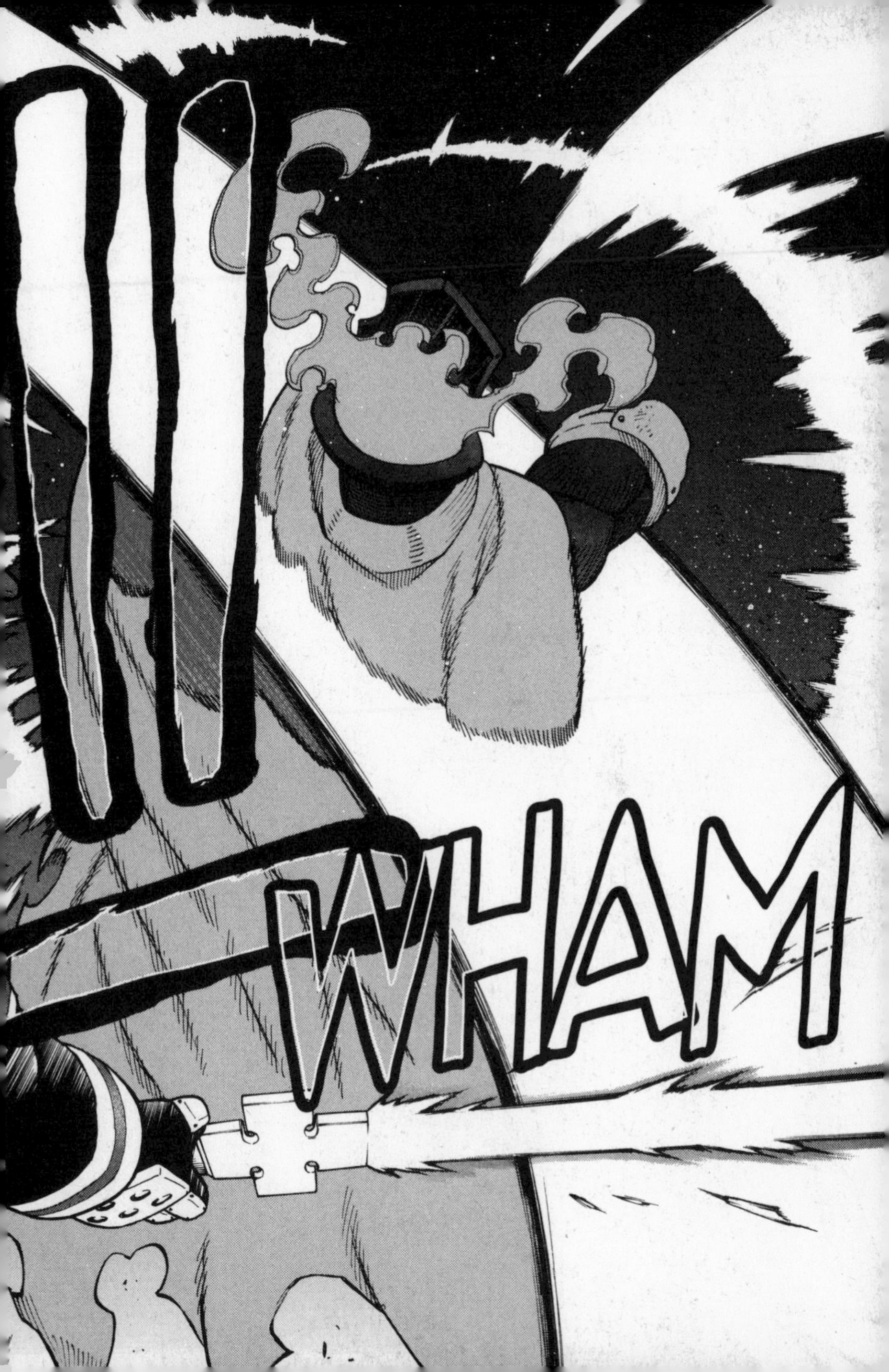
WHAM

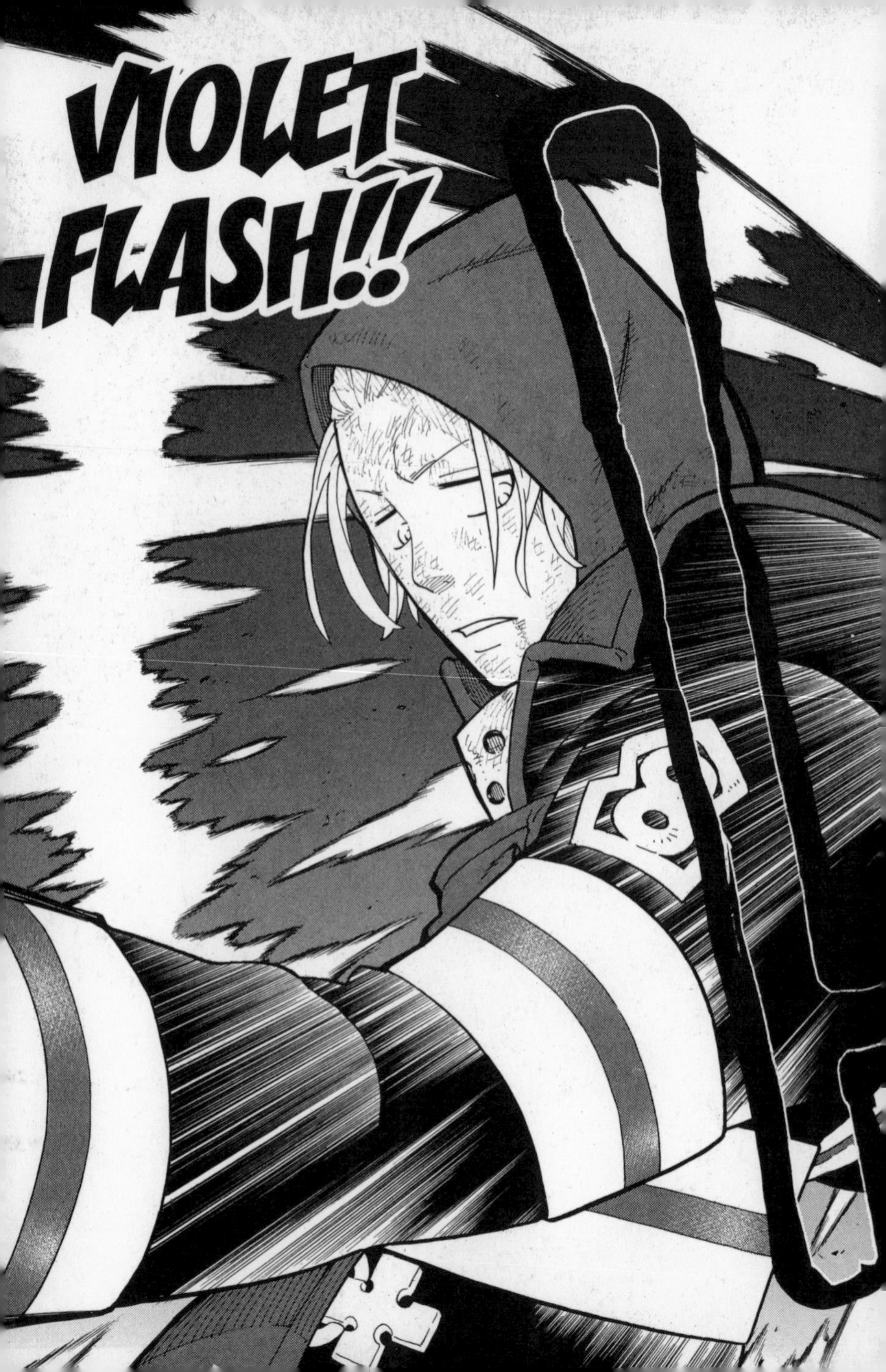
VIOLET FLASH!!

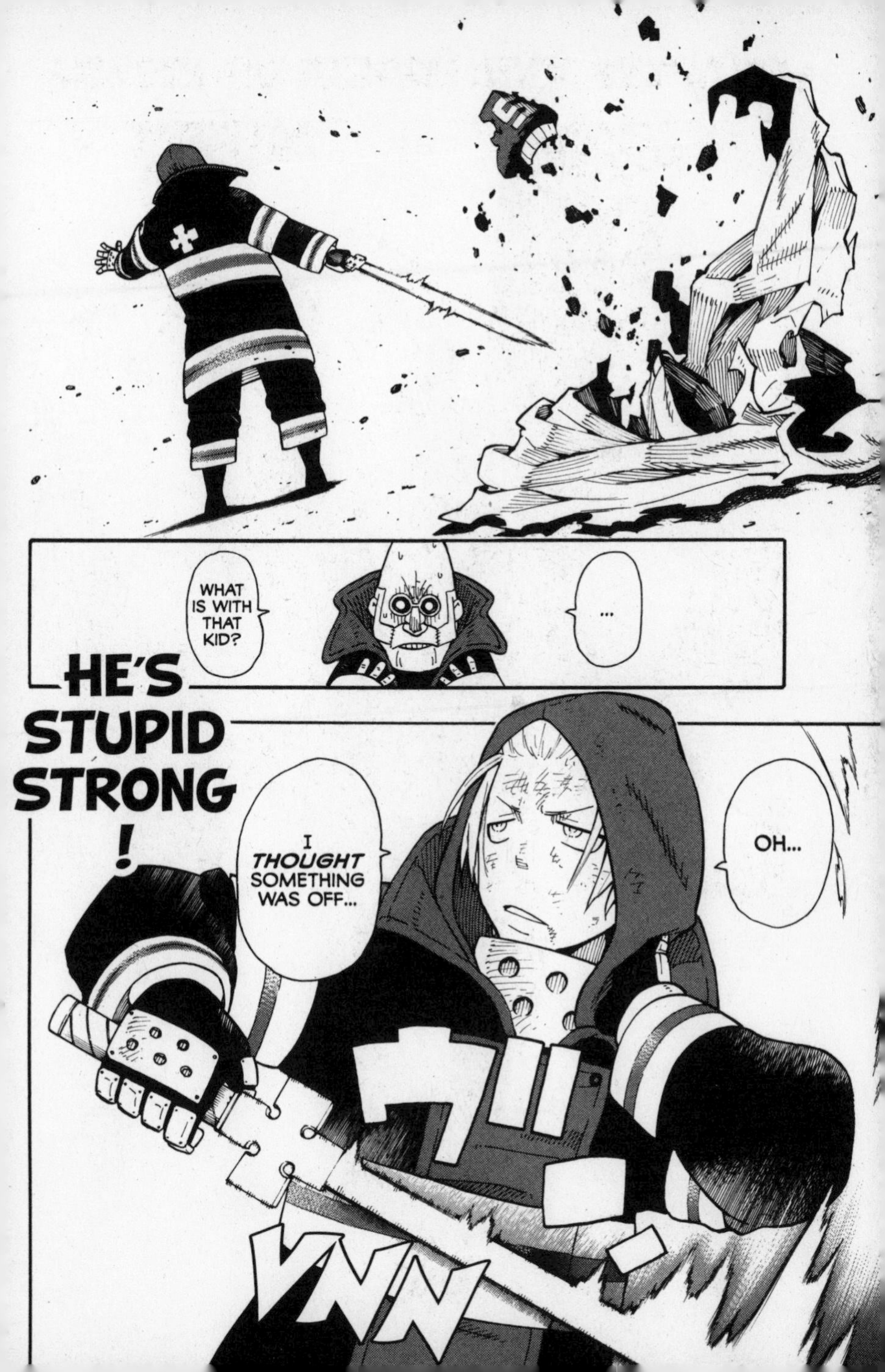
...
WHAT IS WITH THAT KID?
HE'S STUPID STRONG!
OH...
I *THOUGHT* SOMETHING WAS OFF...
VNN

CHAPTER XVII: SHINRA VS. HIBANA

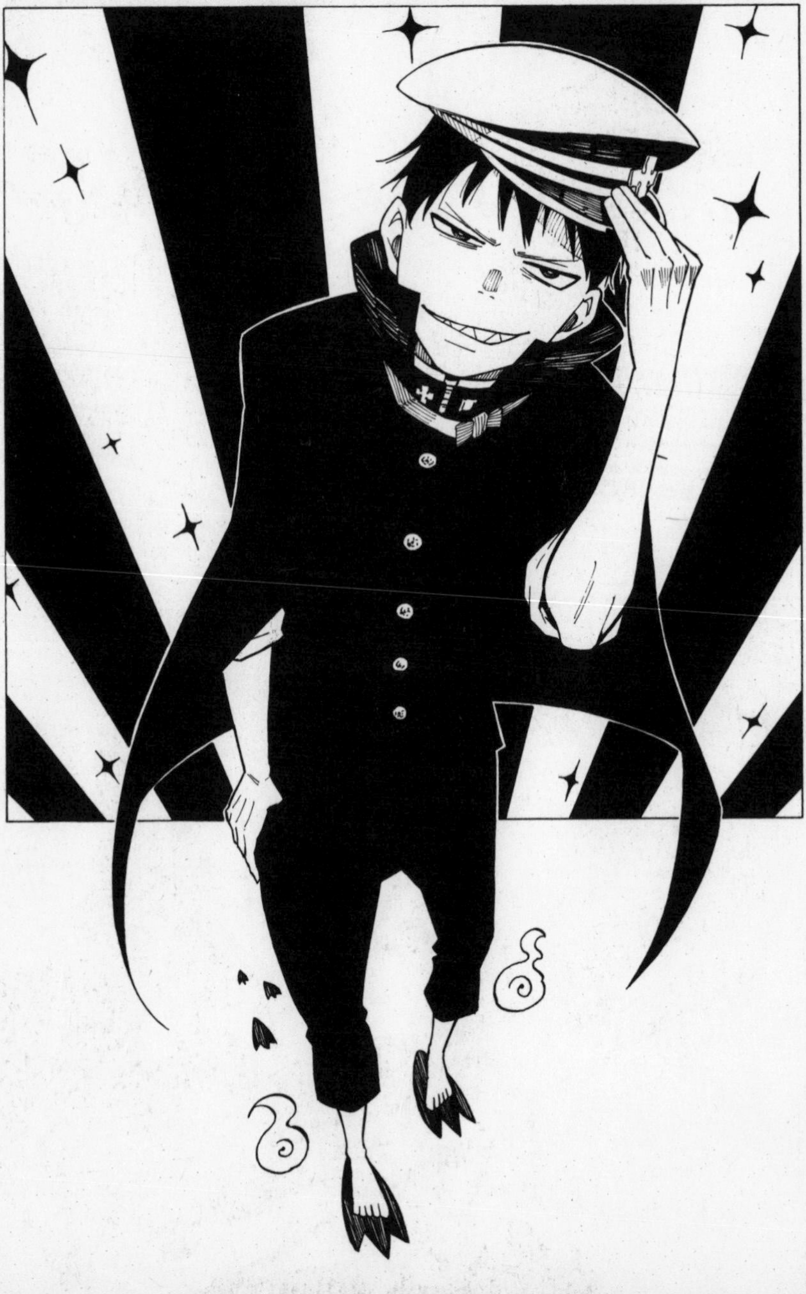

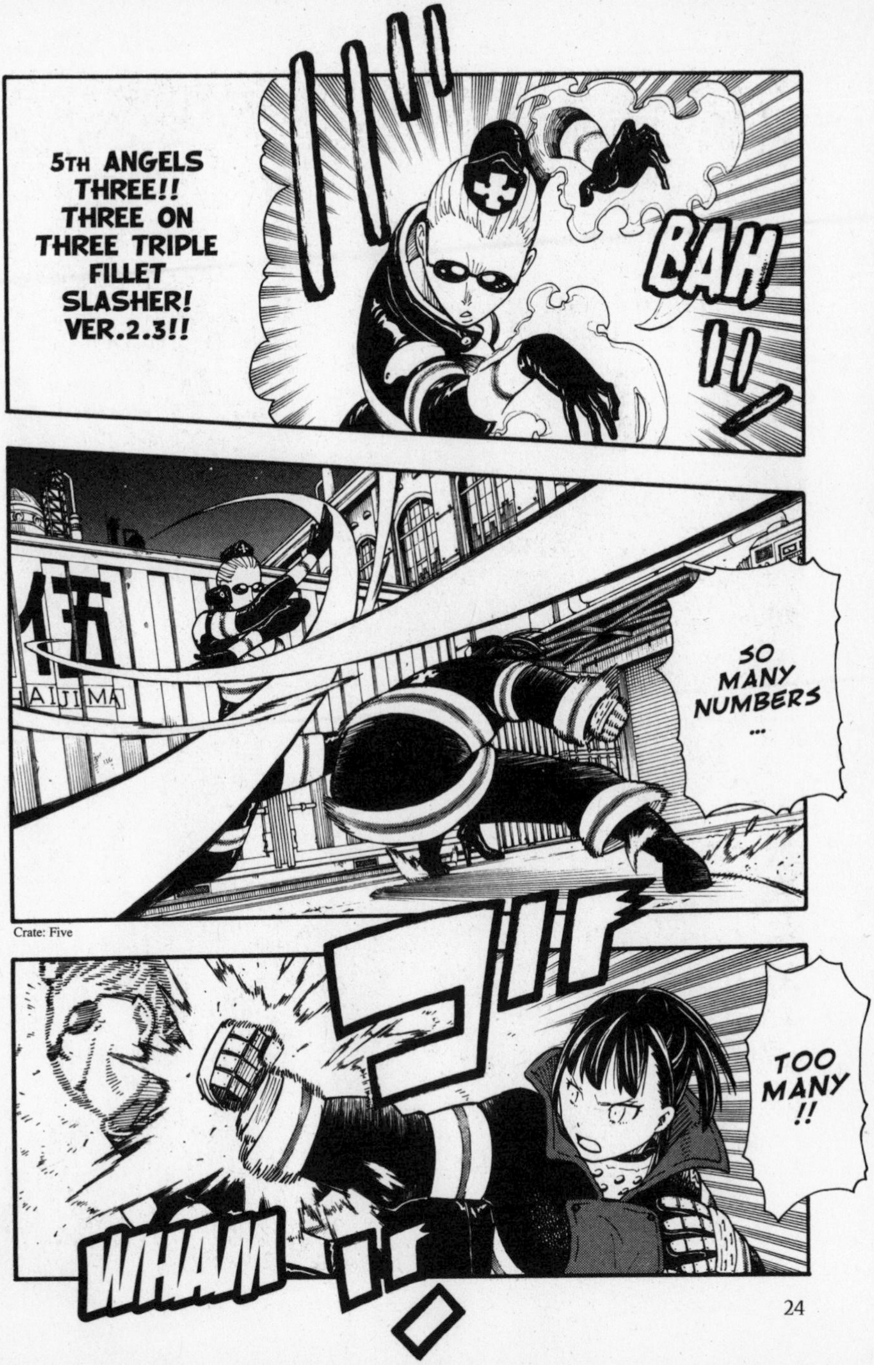
5TH ANGELS THREE!! THREE ON THREE TRIPLE FILLET SLASHER! VER.2.3!!
BAH!!
HAIJIMA
SO MANY NUMBERS...
TOO MANY!!
WHAM!!
Crate: Five

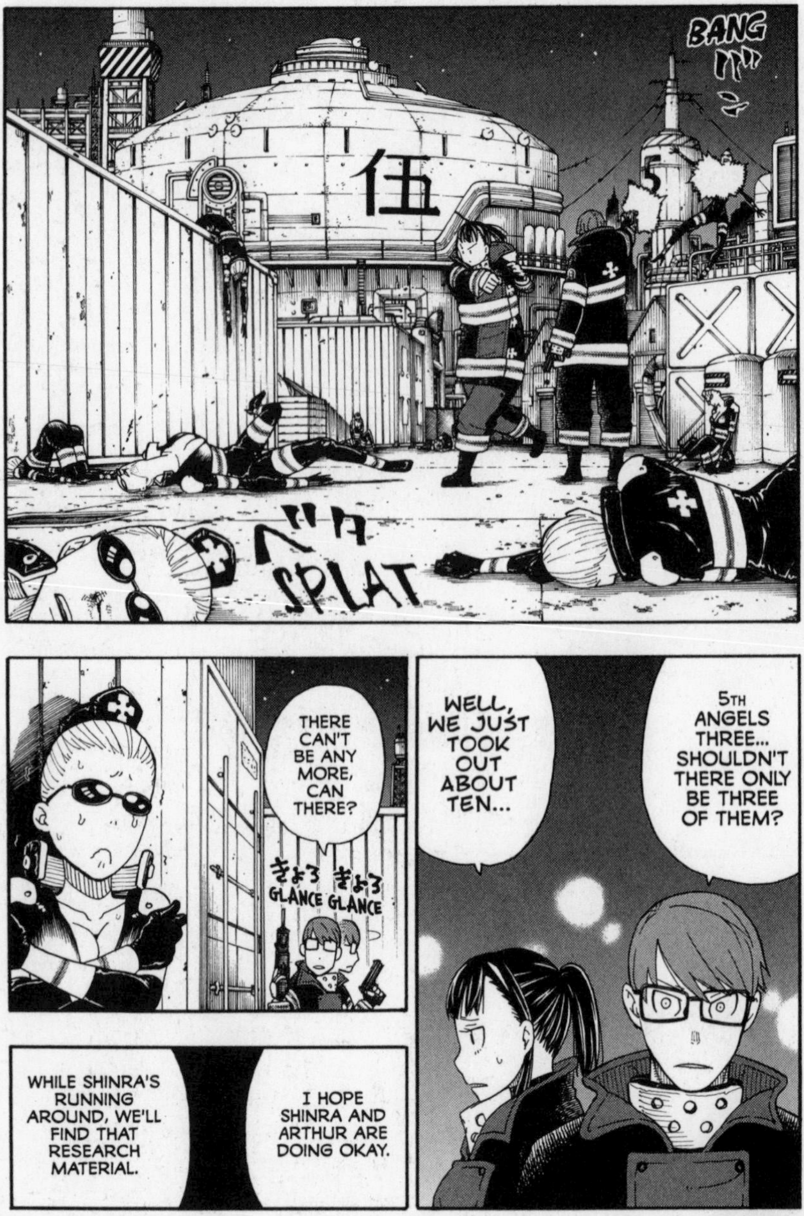
BANG
SPLAT
5TH ANGELS THREE... SHOULDN'T THERE ONLY BE THREE OF THEM?
WELL, WE JUST TOOK OUT ABOUT TEN...
THERE CAN'T BE ANY MORE, CAN THERE?
きょろ きょろ
GLANCE GLANCE
I HOPE SHINRA AND ARTHUR ARE DOING OKAY.
WHILE SHINRA'S RUNNING AROUND, WE'LL FIND THAT RESEARCH MATERIAL.

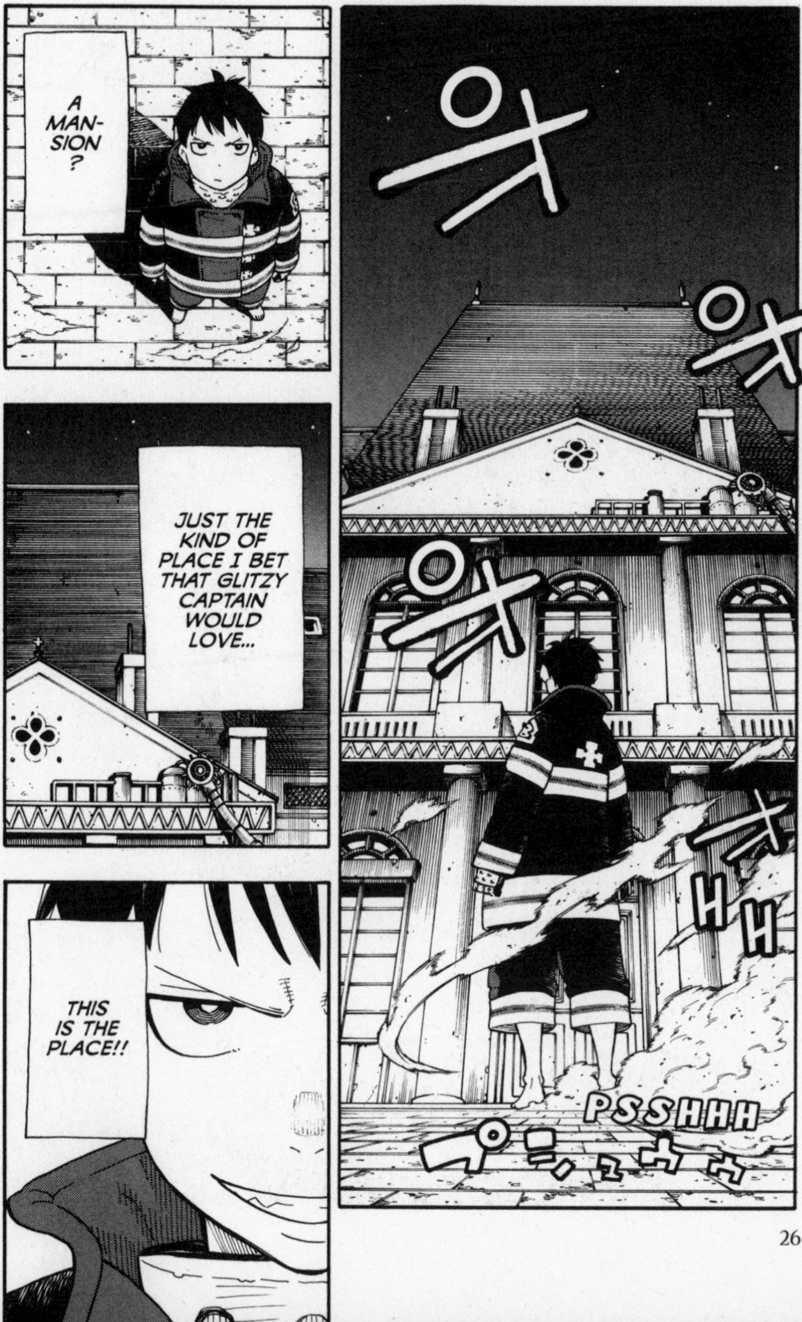
PSSHHH
A MAN-SION?
JUST THE KIND OF PLACE I BET THAT GLITZY CAPTAIN WOULD LOVE...
THIS IS THE PLACE!!

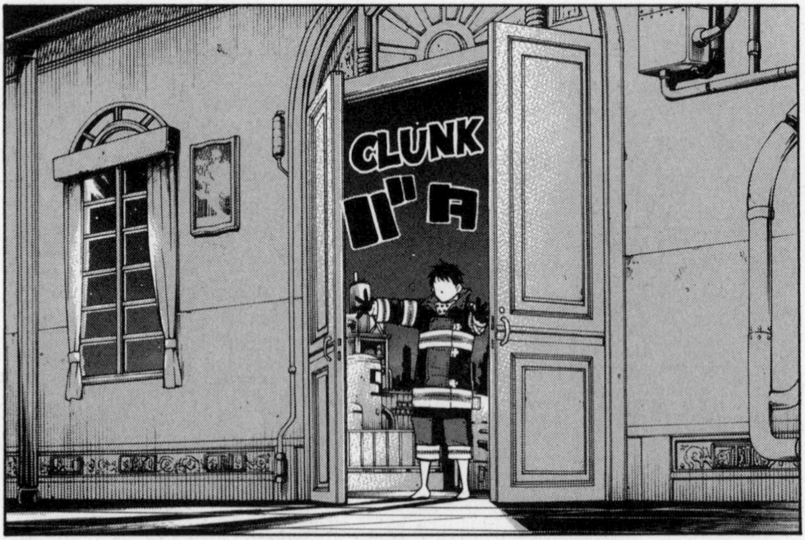
CLUNK

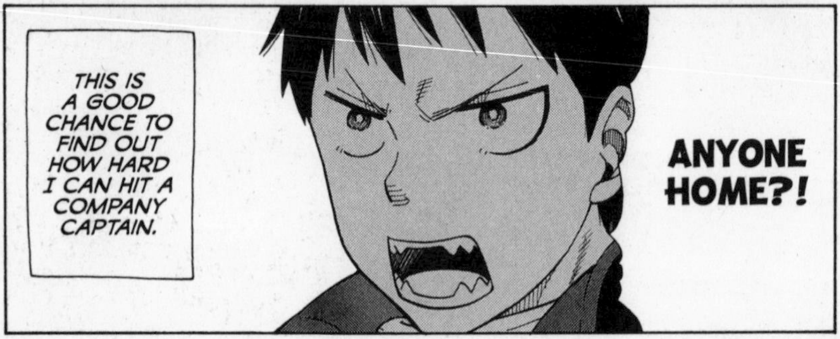
ANYONE HOME?!
THIS IS A GOOD CHANCE TO FIND OUT HOW HARD I CAN HIT A COMPANY CAPTAIN.

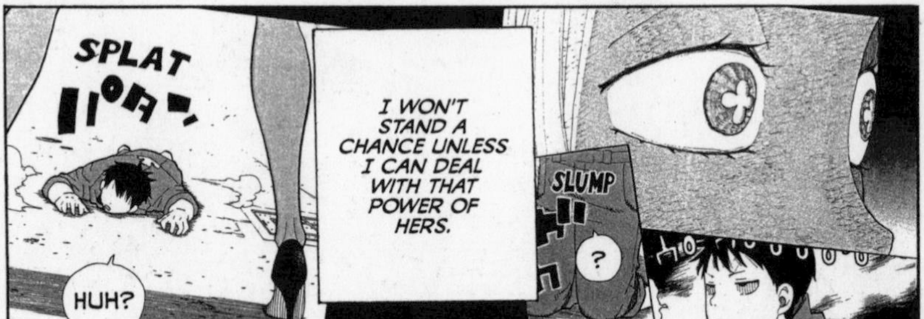
SLUMP
?
I WON'T STAND A CHANCE UNLESS I CAN DEAL WITH THAT POWER OF HERS.
SPLAT
HUH?

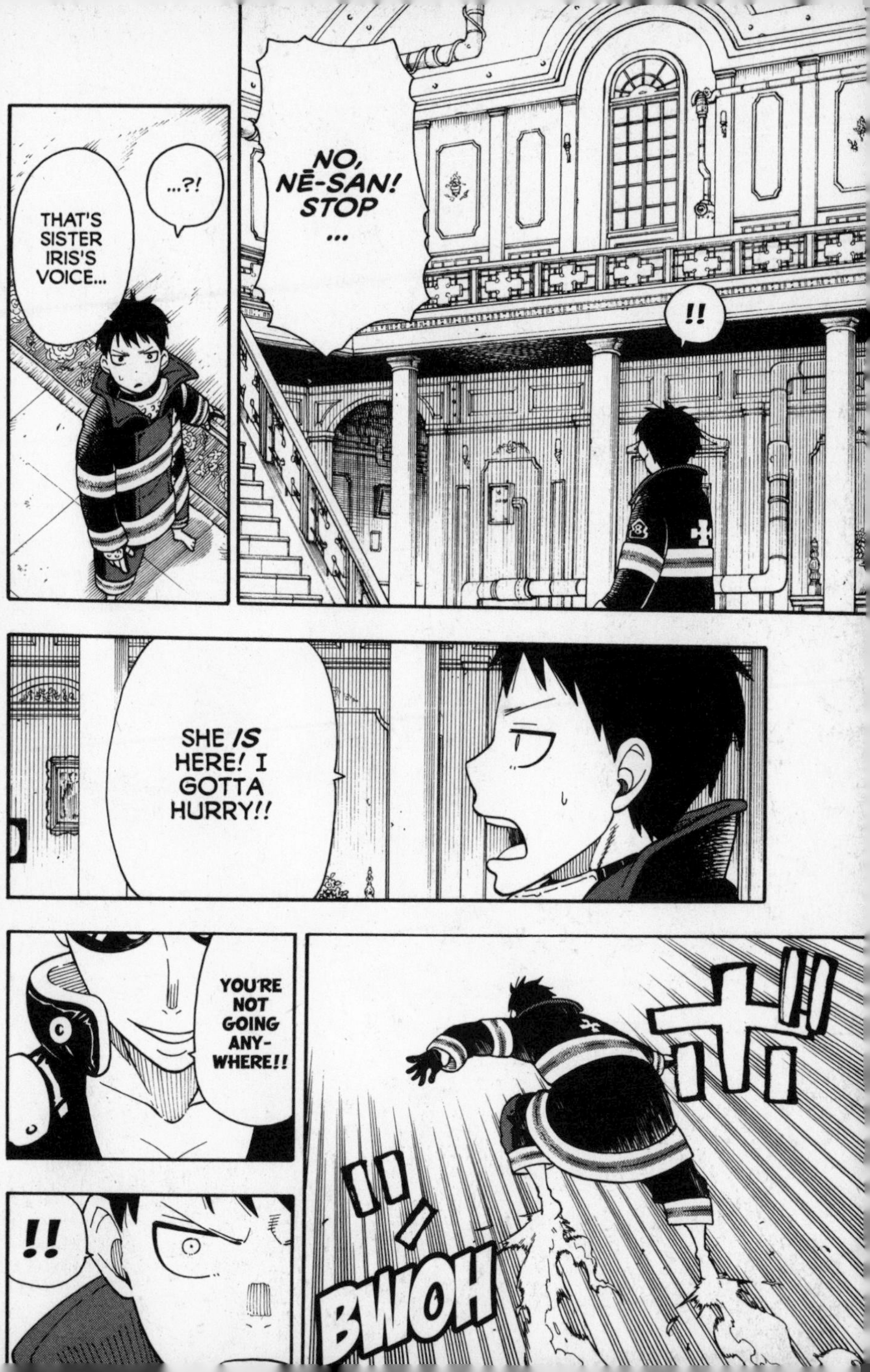
NO, NĒ-SAN! STOP ...
!!
...?!
THAT'S SISTER IRIS'S VOICE...
SHE *IS* HERE! I GOTTA HURRY!!
BWOH
YOU'RE NOT GOING ANY-WHERE!!
!!

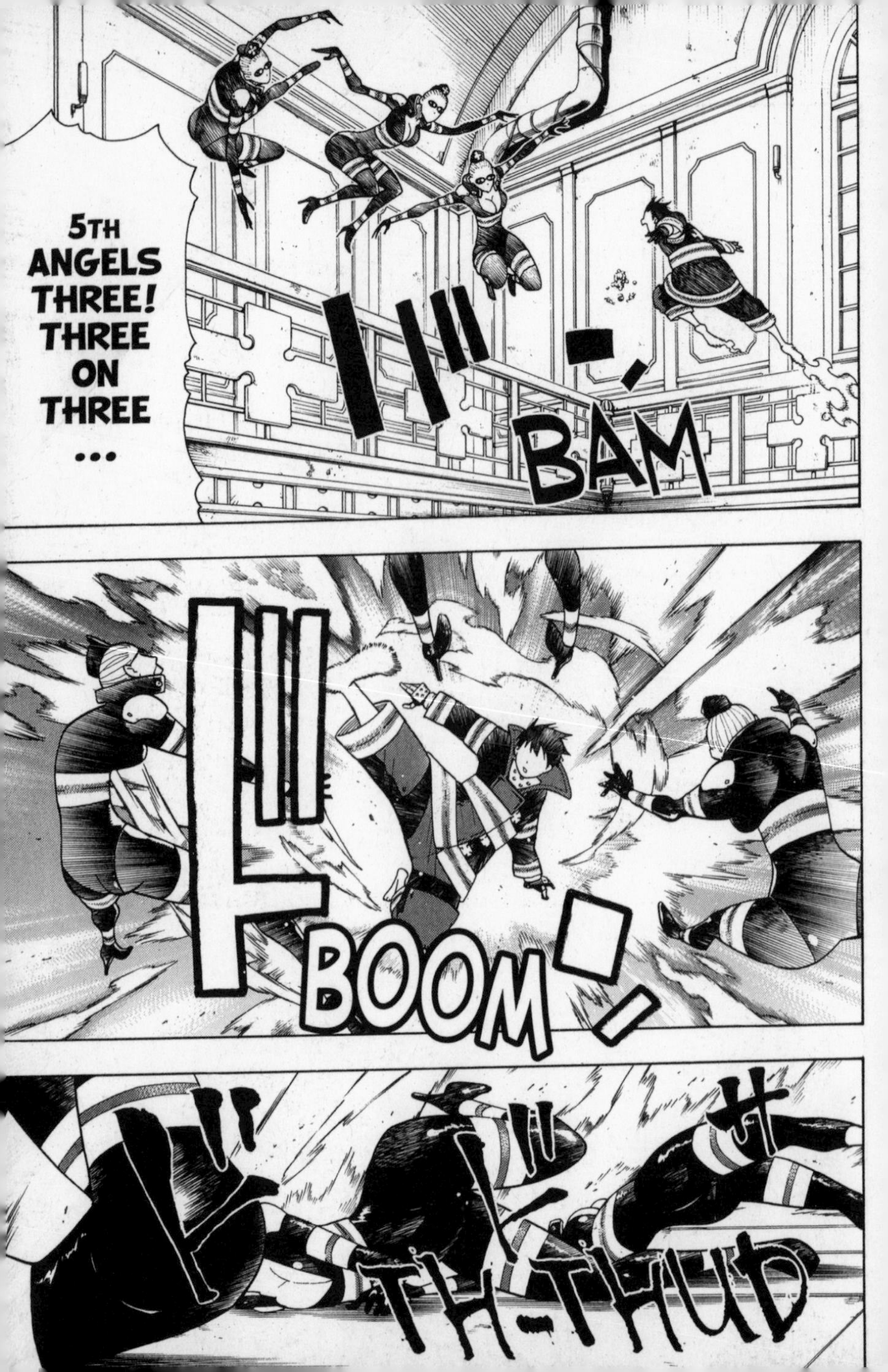
BAM
5TH ANGELS THREE! THREE ON THREE ...
BOOM
TH-THUD

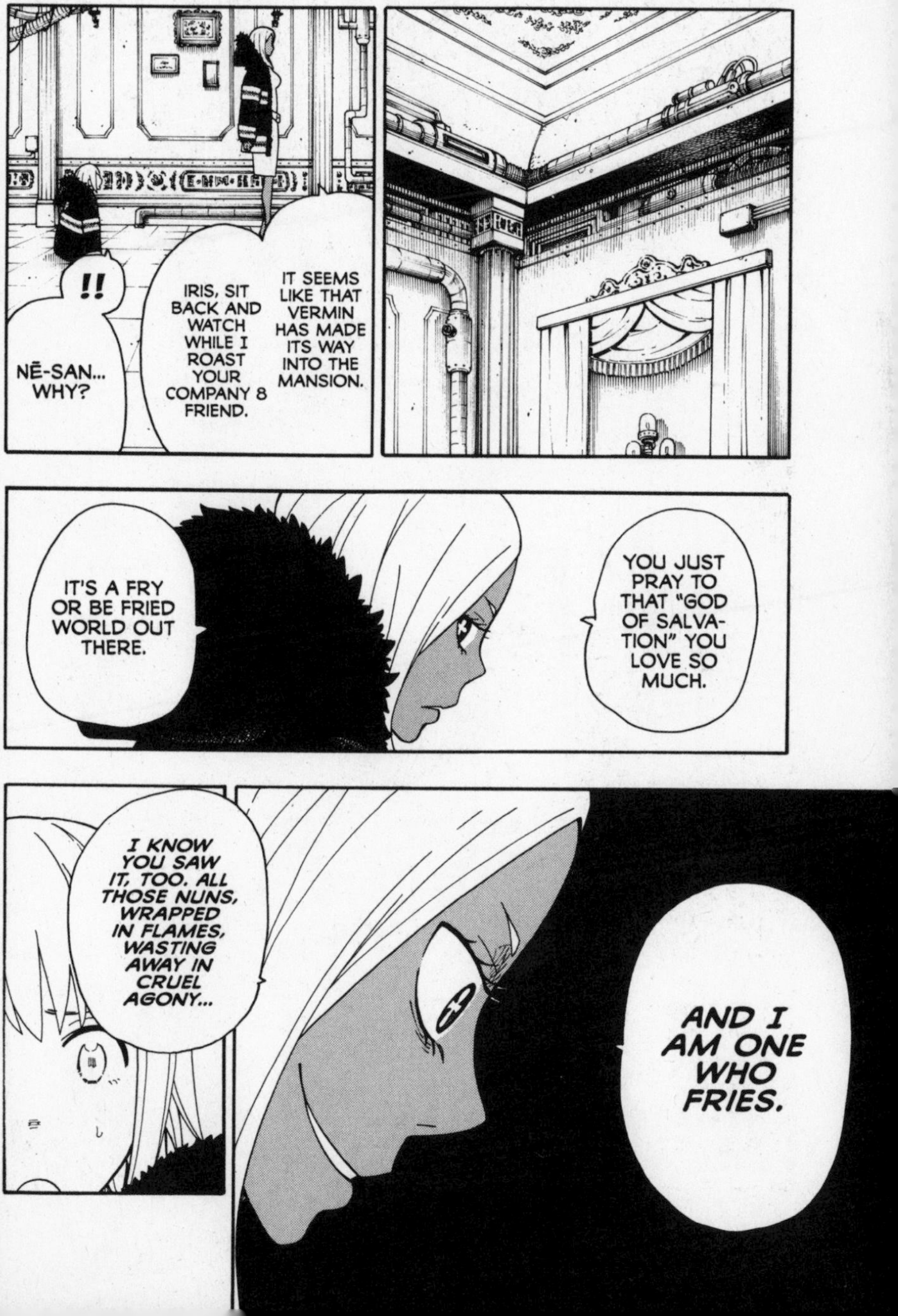
IT SEEMS LIKE THAT VERMIN HAS MADE ITS WAY INTO THE MANSION.
IRIS, SIT BACK AND WATCH WHILE I ROAST YOUR COMPANY 8 FRIEND.
!!
NĒ-SAN... WHY?
YOU JUST PRAY TO THAT "GOD OF SALVA-TION" YOU LOVE SO MUCH.
IT'S A FRY OR BE FRIED WORLD OUT THERE.
AND I AM ONE WHO FRIES.
I KNOW YOU SAW IT, TOO. ALL THOSE NUNS, WRAPPED IN FLAMES, WASTING AWAY IN CRUEL AGONY...

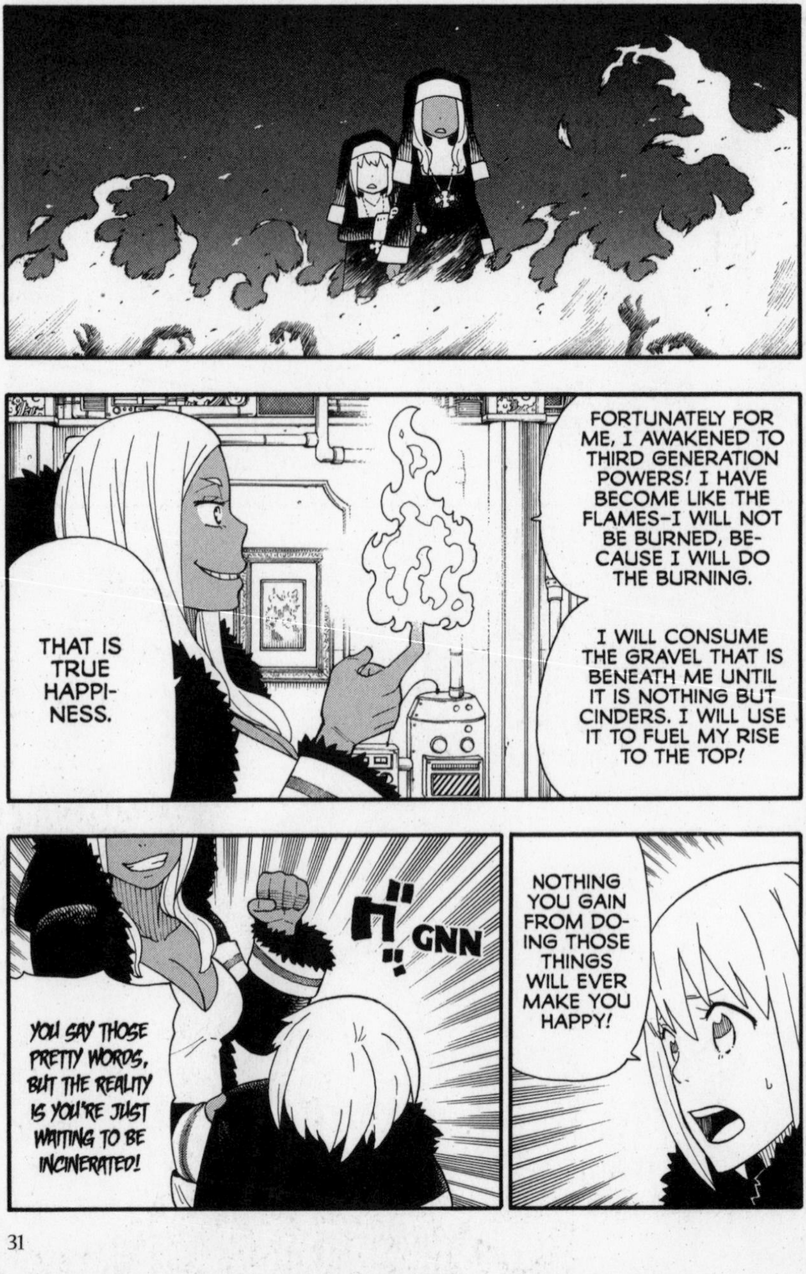
FORTUNATELY FOR ME, I AWAKENED TO THIRD GENERATION POWERS! I HAVE BECOME LIKE THE FLAMES–I WILL NOT BE BURNED, BECAUSE I WILL DO THE BURNING.
I WILL CONSUME THE GRAVEL THAT IS BENEATH ME UNTIL IT IS NOTHING BUT CINDERS. I WILL USE IT TO FUEL MY RISE TO THE TOP!
THAT IS TRUE HAPPINESS.
NOTHING YOU GAIN FROM DOING THOSE THINGS WILL EVER MAKE YOU HAPPY!
GNN
YOU SAY THOSE PRETTY WORDS, BUT THE REALITY IS YOU'RE JUST WAITING TO BE INCINERATED!

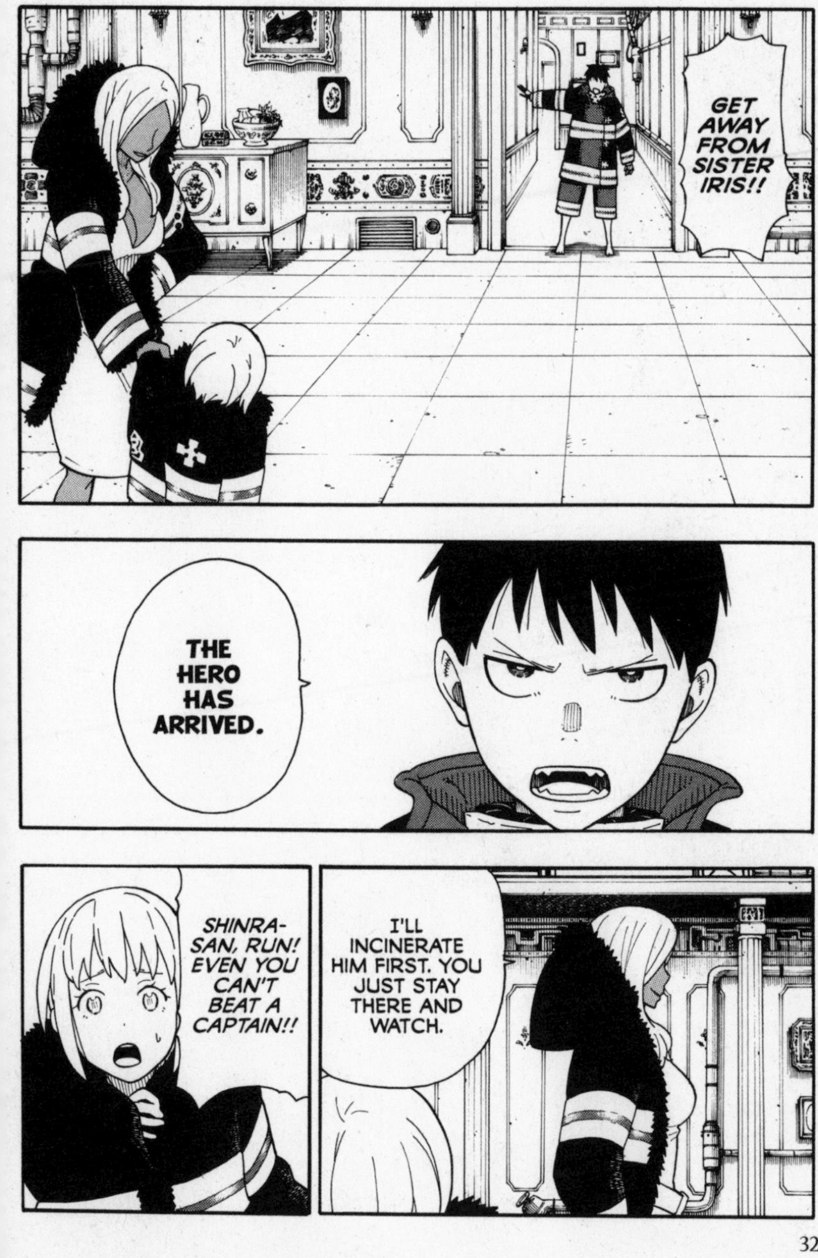
GET AWAY FROM SISTER IRIS!!
THE HERO HAS ARRIVED.
I'LL INCINERATE HIM FIRST. YOU JUST STAY THERE AND WATCH.
SHINRA-SAN, RUN! EVEN YOU CAN'T BEAT A CAPTAIN!!

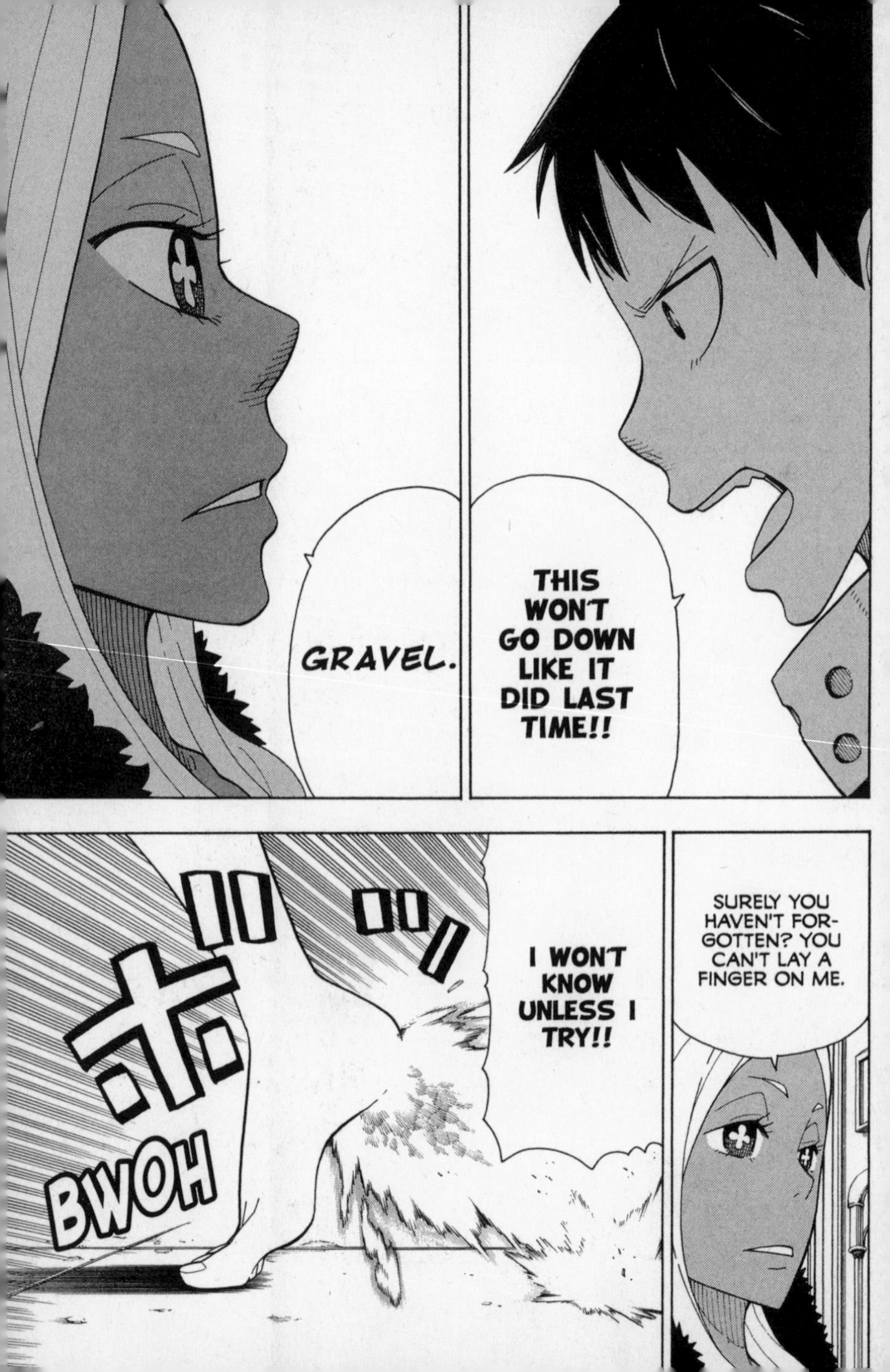
THIS WON'T GO DOWN LIKE IT DID LAST TIME!!
GRAVEL.
SURELY YOU HAVEN'T FORGOTTEN? YOU CAN'T LAY A FINGER ON ME.
I WON'T KNOW UNLESS I TRY!!
BWOH

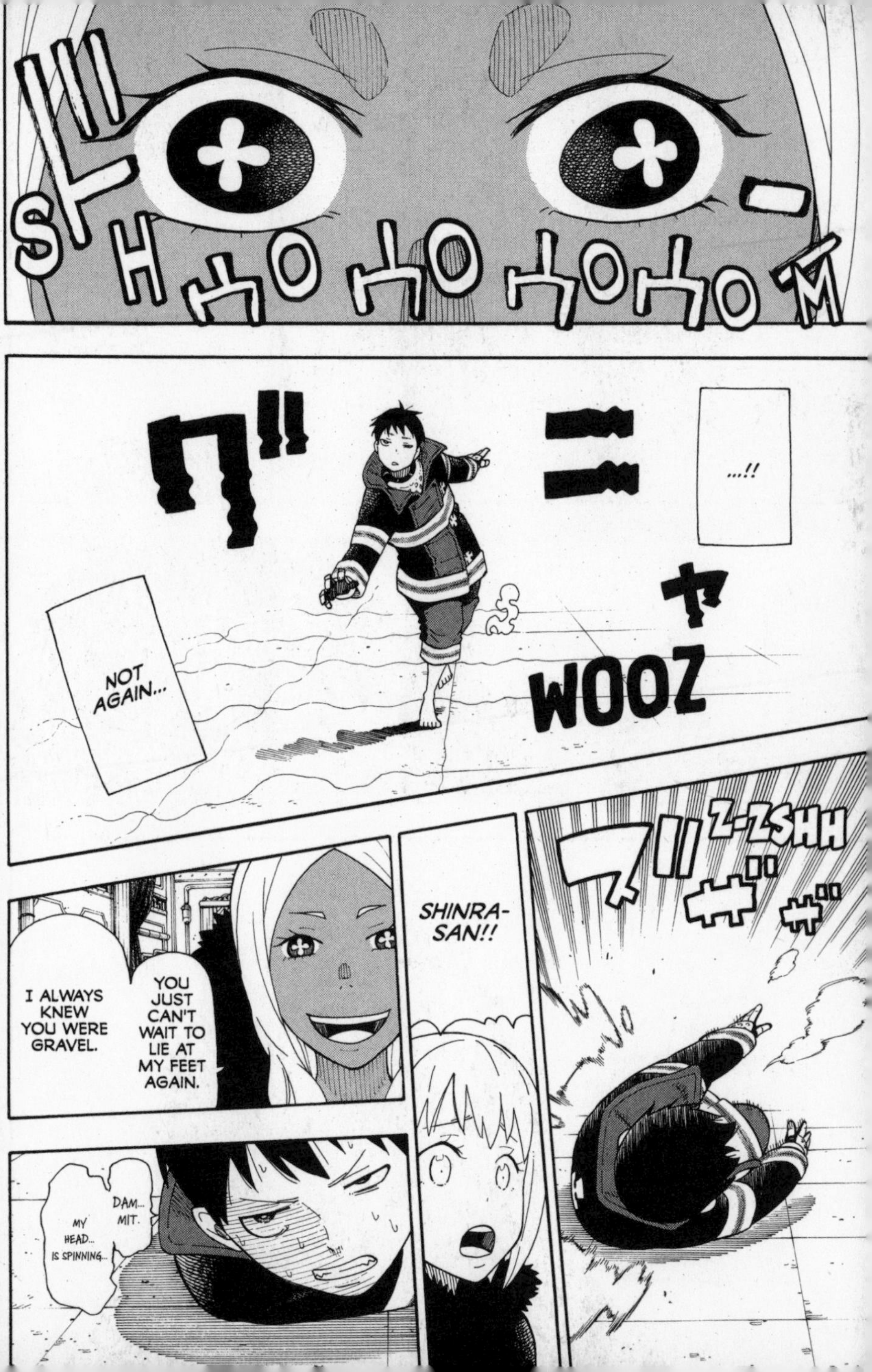

SHOOOOOOM
...!!
WOOZ
NOT AGAIN...
Z-ZSHH
SHINRA-SAN!!
YOU JUST CAN'T WAIT TO LIE AT MY FEET AGAIN.
I ALWAYS KNEW YOU WERE GRAVEL.
DAM... MIT.
MY HEAD... IS SPINNING...

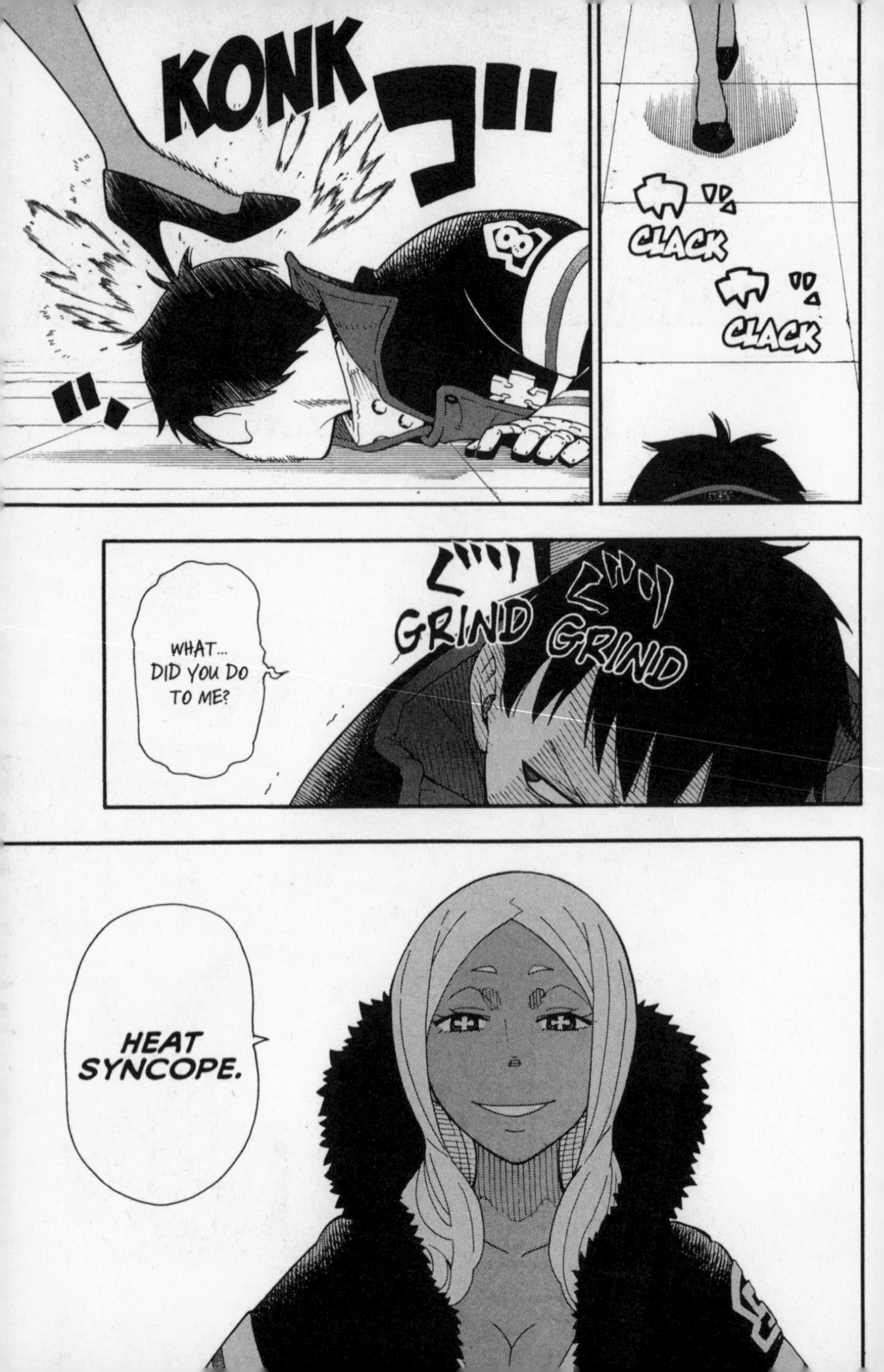
CLACK
CLACK
KONK
GRIND GRIND
WHAT... DID YOU DO TO ME?
HEAT SYNCOPE.

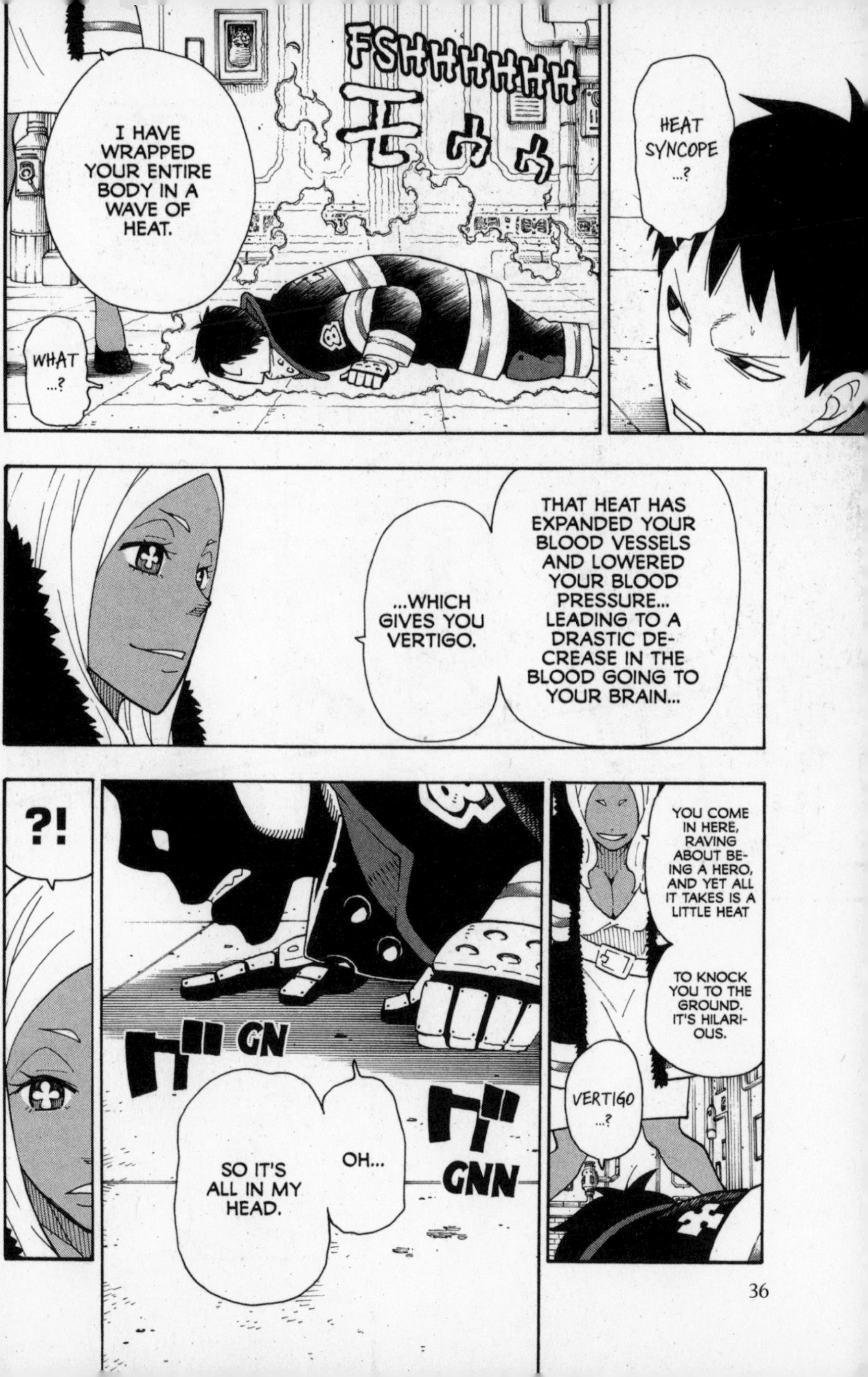
HEAT SYNCOPE ...?
FSHHHHHH
I HAVE WRAPPED YOUR ENTIRE BODY IN A WAVE OF HEAT.
WHAT ...?
THAT HEAT HAS EXPANDED YOUR BLOOD VESSELS AND LOWERED YOUR BLOOD PRESSURE... LEADING TO A DRASTIC DE-CREASE IN THE BLOOD GOING TO YOUR BRAIN...
...WHICH GIVES YOU VERTIGO.
YOU COME IN HERE, RAVING ABOUT BE-ING A HERO, AND YET ALL IT TAKES IS A LITTLE HEAT
TO KNOCK YOU TO THE GROUND. IT'S HILARI-OUS.
VERTIGO ...?
GNN
OH...
GN
SO IT'S ALL IN MY HEAD.
?!

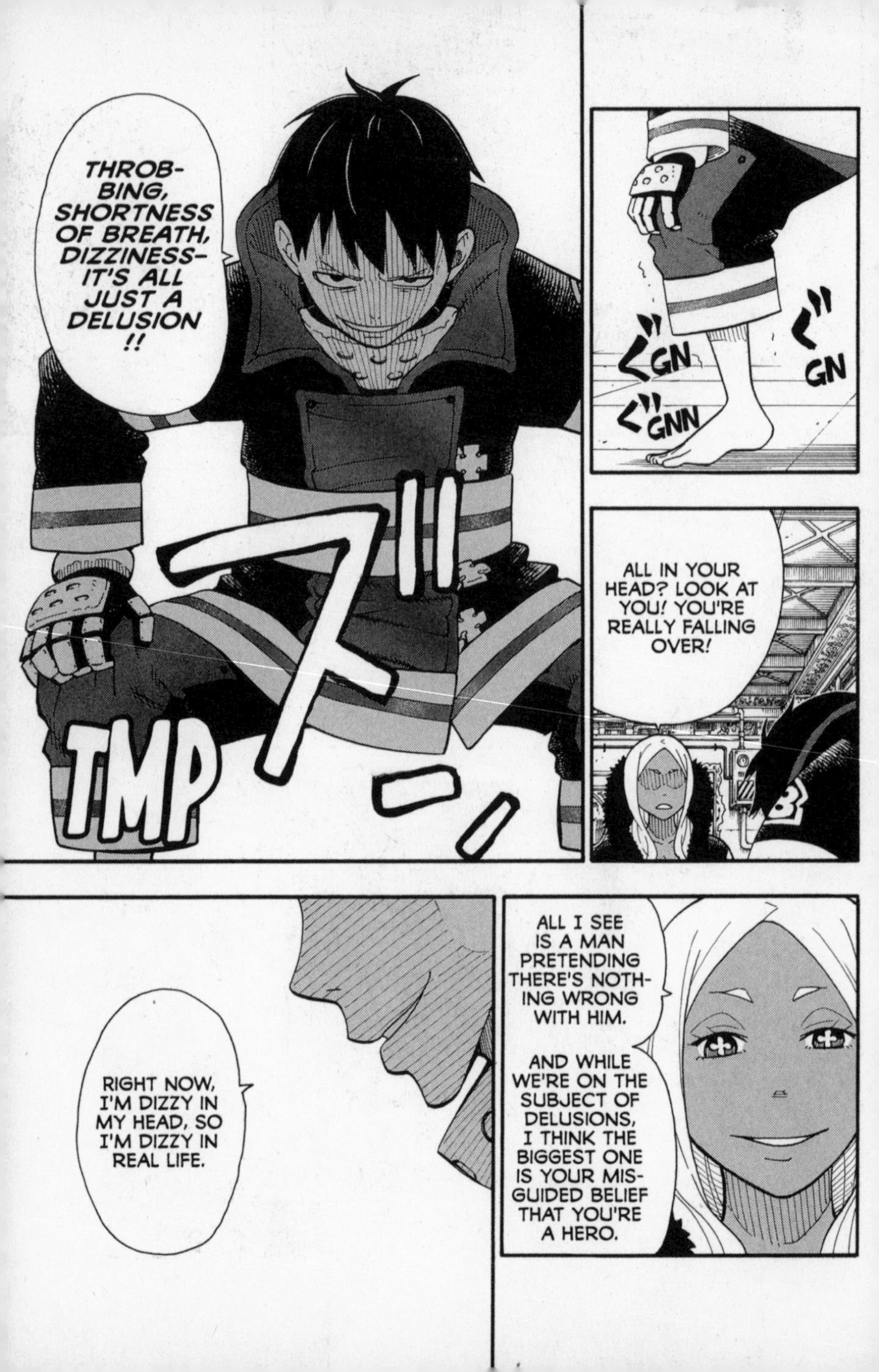
GN
GNN
GN
ALL IN YOUR HEAD? LOOK AT YOU! YOU'RE REALLY FALLING OVER!
THROB-BING, SHORTNESS OF BREATH, DIZZINESS-IT'S ALL JUST A DELUSION !!
TMP
ALL I SEE IS A MAN PRETENDING THERE'S NOTHING WRONG WITH HIM.
AND WHILE WE'RE ON THE SUBJECT OF DELUSIONS, I THINK THE BIGGEST ONE IS YOUR MISGUIDED BELIEF THAT YOU'RE A HERO.
RIGHT NOW, I'M DIZZY IN MY HEAD, SO I'M DIZZY IN REAL LIFE.

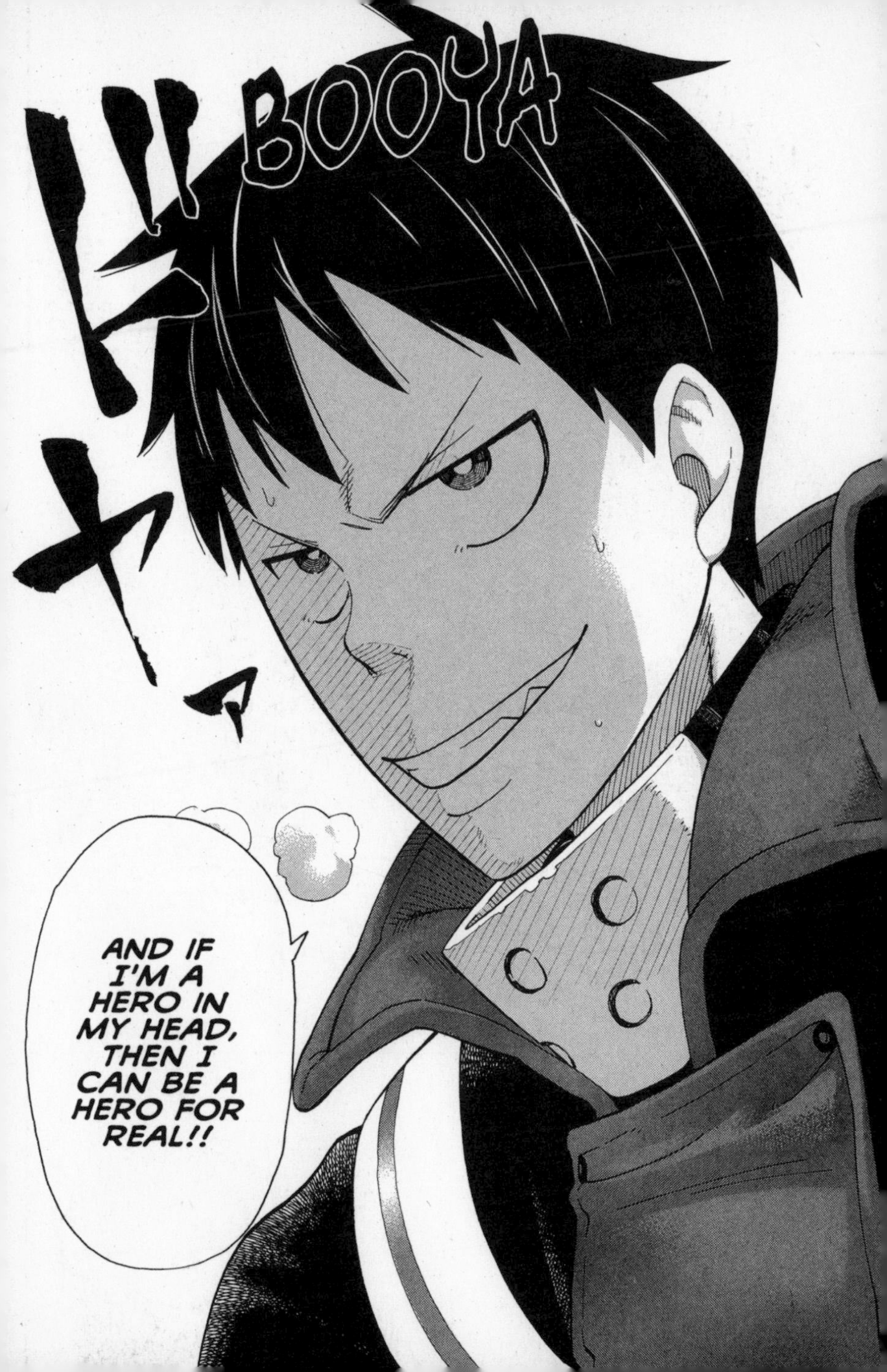
BOOYA
AND IF I'M A HERO IN MY HEAD, THEN I CAN BE A HERO FOR REAL!!

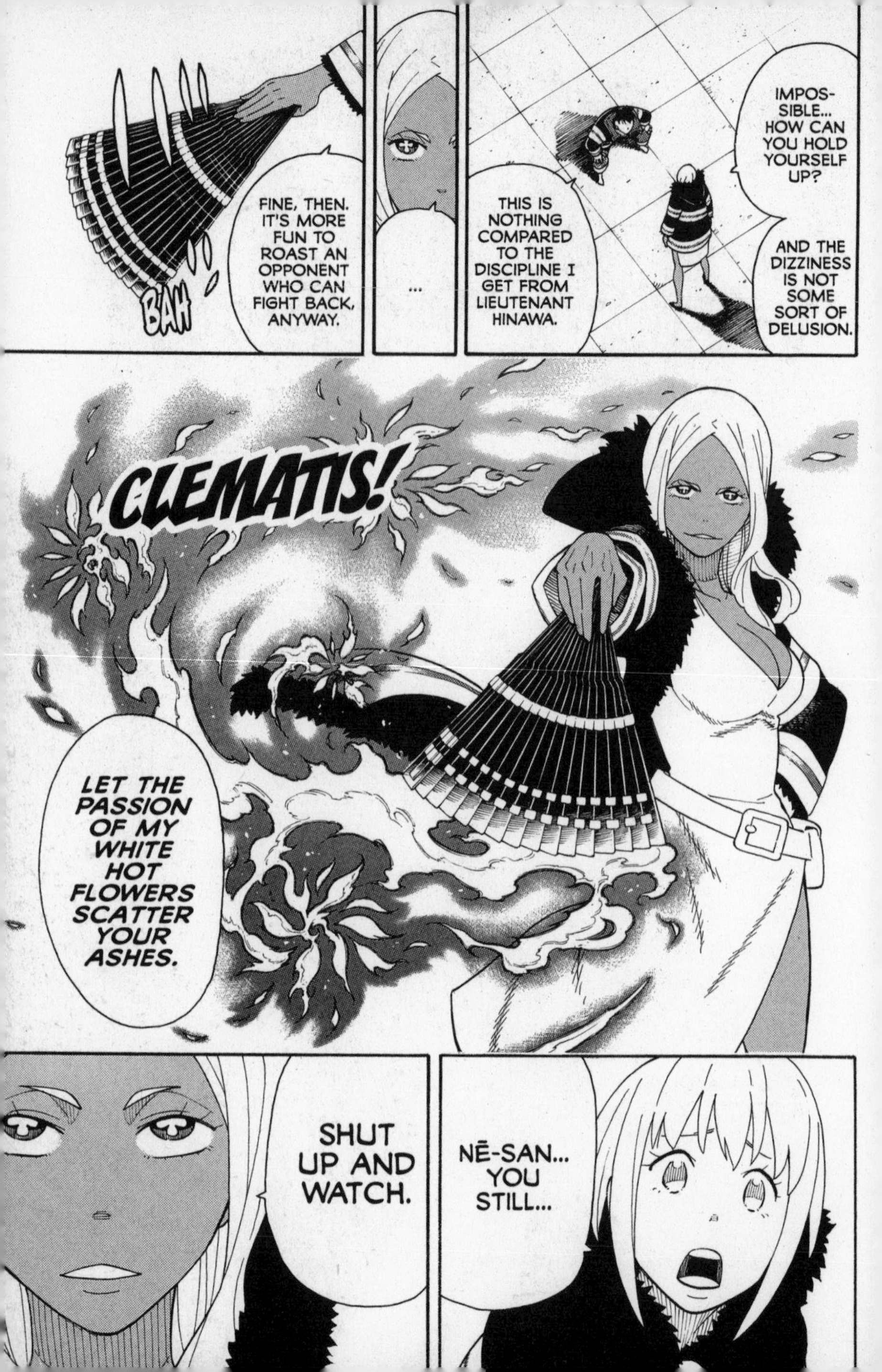
IMPOSSIBLE... HOW CAN YOU HOLD YOURSELF UP?
AND THE DIZZINESS IS NOT SOME SORT OF DELUSION.
THIS IS NOTHING COMPARED TO THE DISCIPLINE I GET FROM LIEUTENANT HINAWA.
...
FINE, THEN. IT'S MORE FUN TO ROAST AN OPPONENT WHO CAN FIGHT BACK, ANYWAY.
BAH
CLEMATIS!
LET THE PASSION OF MY WHITE HOT FLOWERS SCATTER YOUR ASHES.
NĒ-SAN... YOU STILL...
SHUT UP AND WATCH.

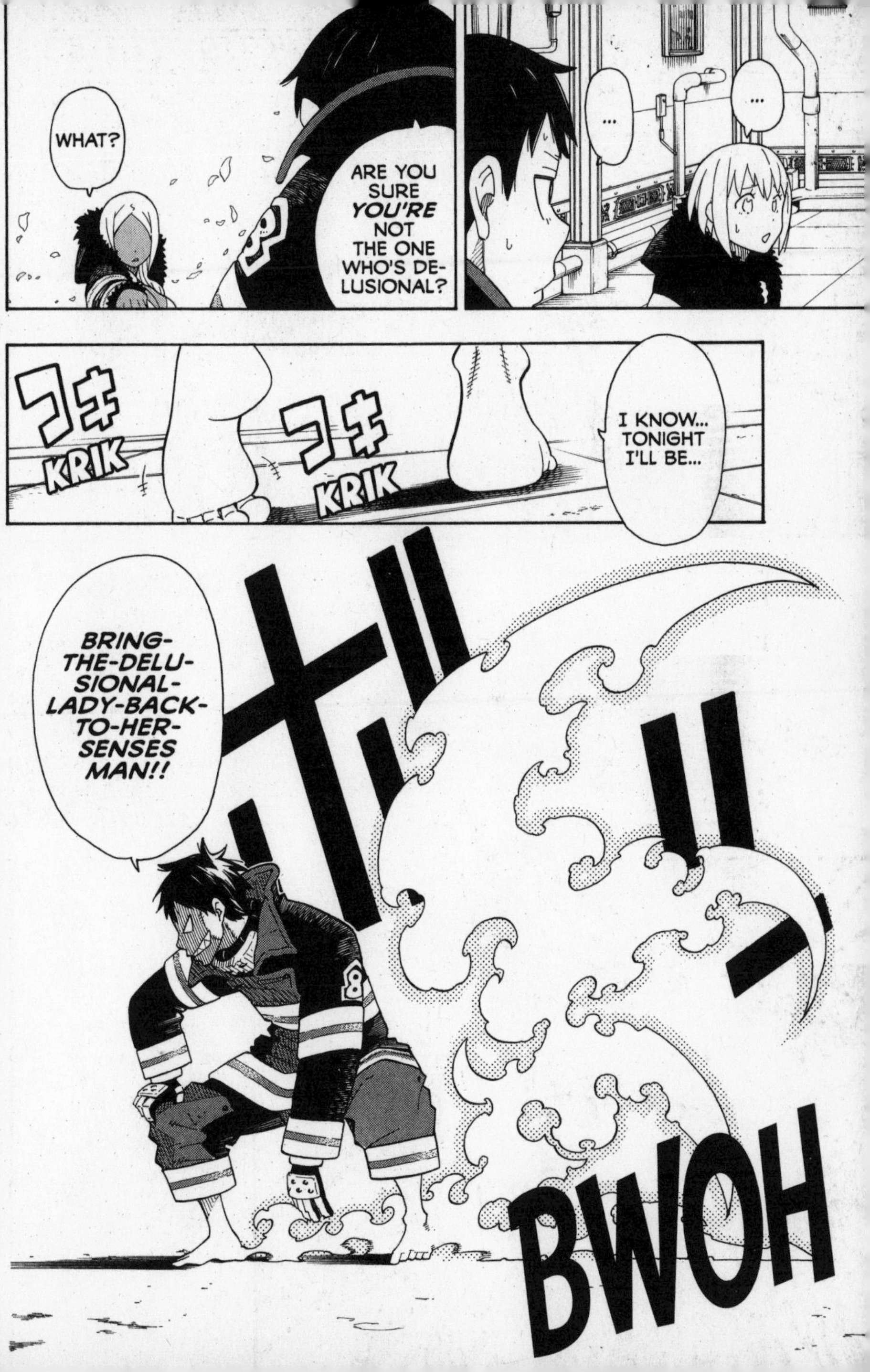
...
...
ARE YOU SURE *YOU'RE* NOT THE ONE WHO'S DE-LUSIONAL?
WHAT?
I KNOW... TONIGHT I'LL BE...
コキ
KRIK
コキ
KRIK
BRING-THE-DELU-SIONAL-LADY-BACK-TO-HER-SENSES MAN!!
BWOH

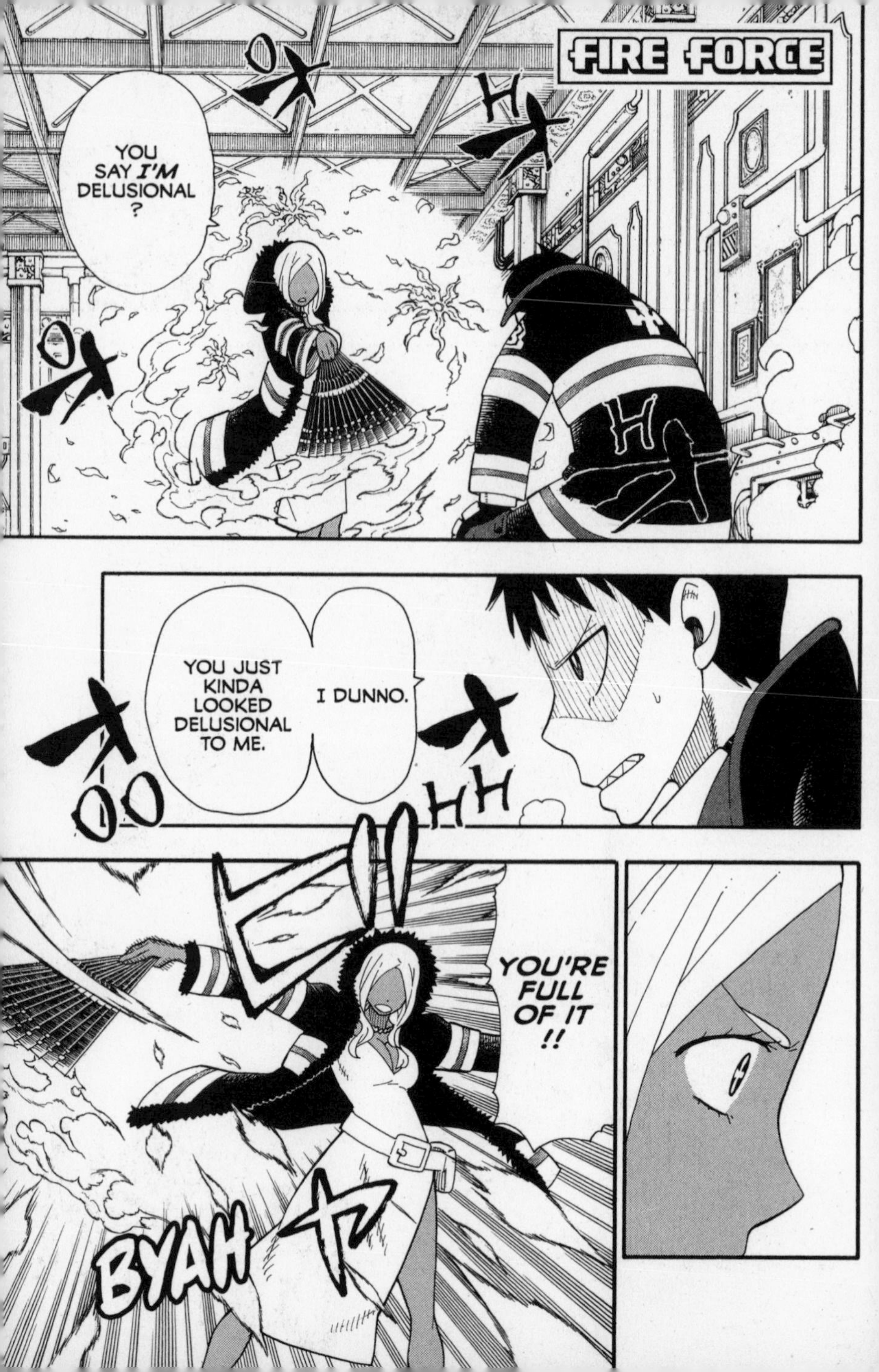
YOU SAY *I'M* DELUSIONAL ?
I DUNNO.
YOU JUST KINDA LOOKED DELUSIONAL TO ME.
YOU'RE FULL OF IT !!
BYAH

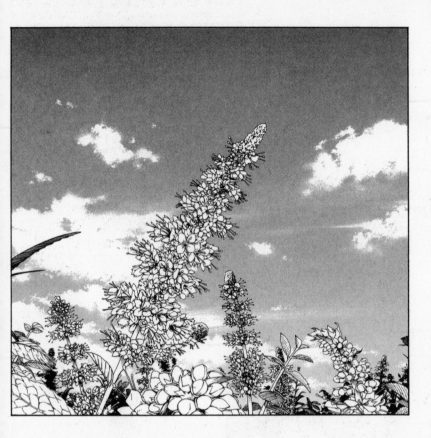

CHAPTER XVIII: CLASH

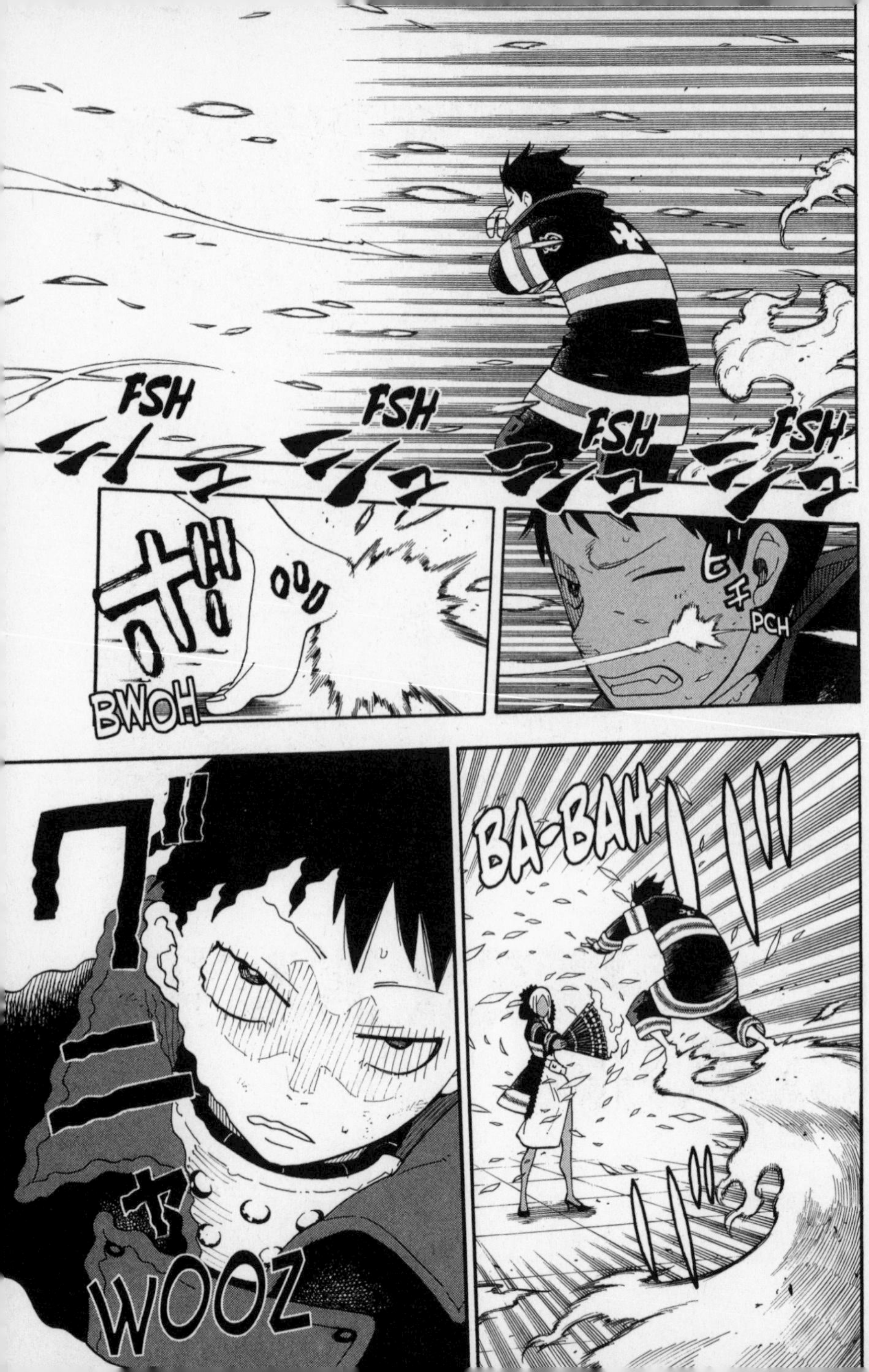
FSH
FSH
FSH
FSH
PCH
BWOH
BA-BAH
WOOZ

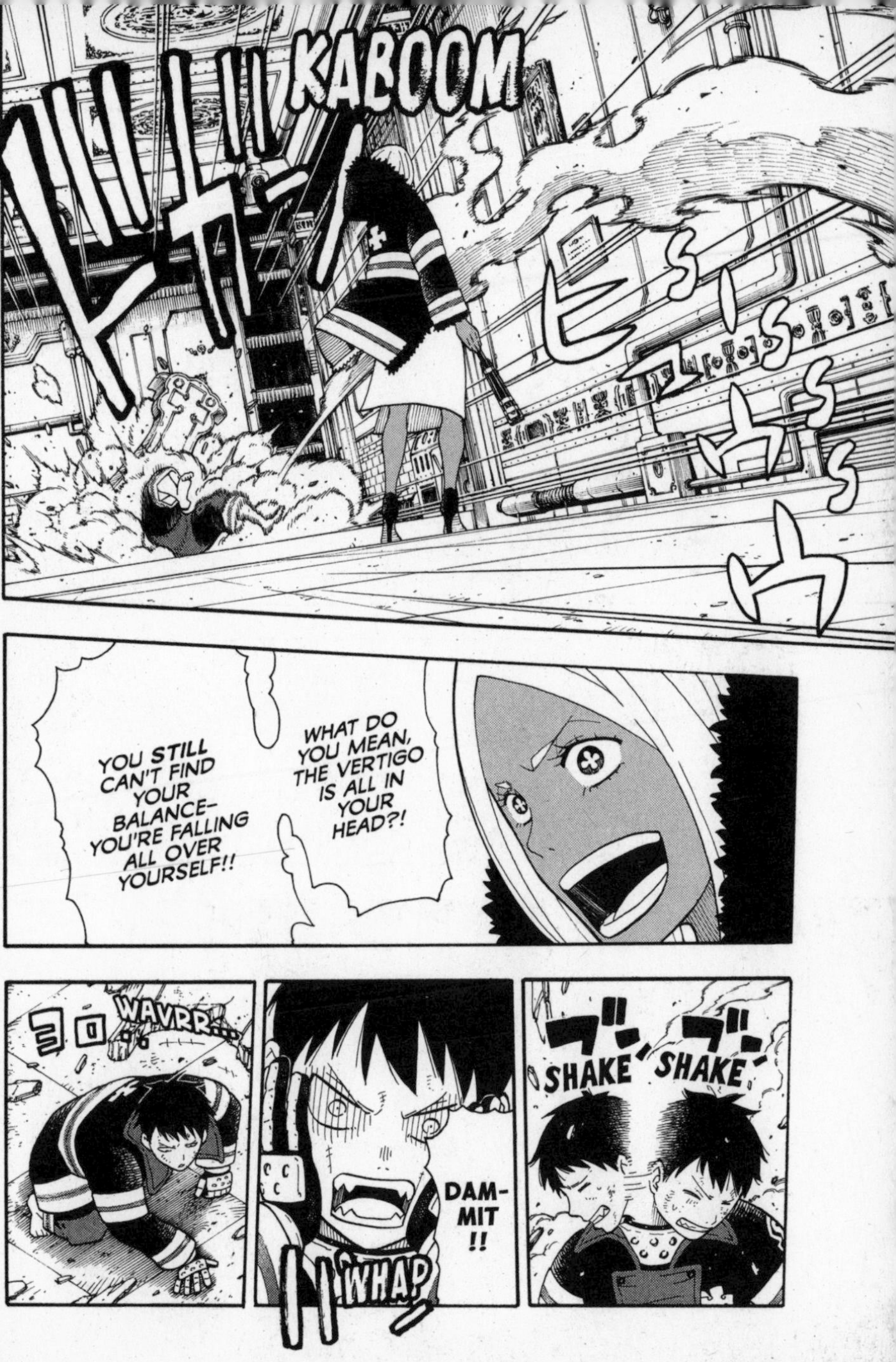
KABOOM
WHAT DO YOU MEAN, THE VERTIGO IS ALL IN YOUR HEAD?!
YOU STILL CAN'T FIND YOUR BALANCE- YOU'RE FALLING ALL OVER YOURSELF!!
SHAKE SHAKE
DAM-MIT!!
WHAP
WAVRR...

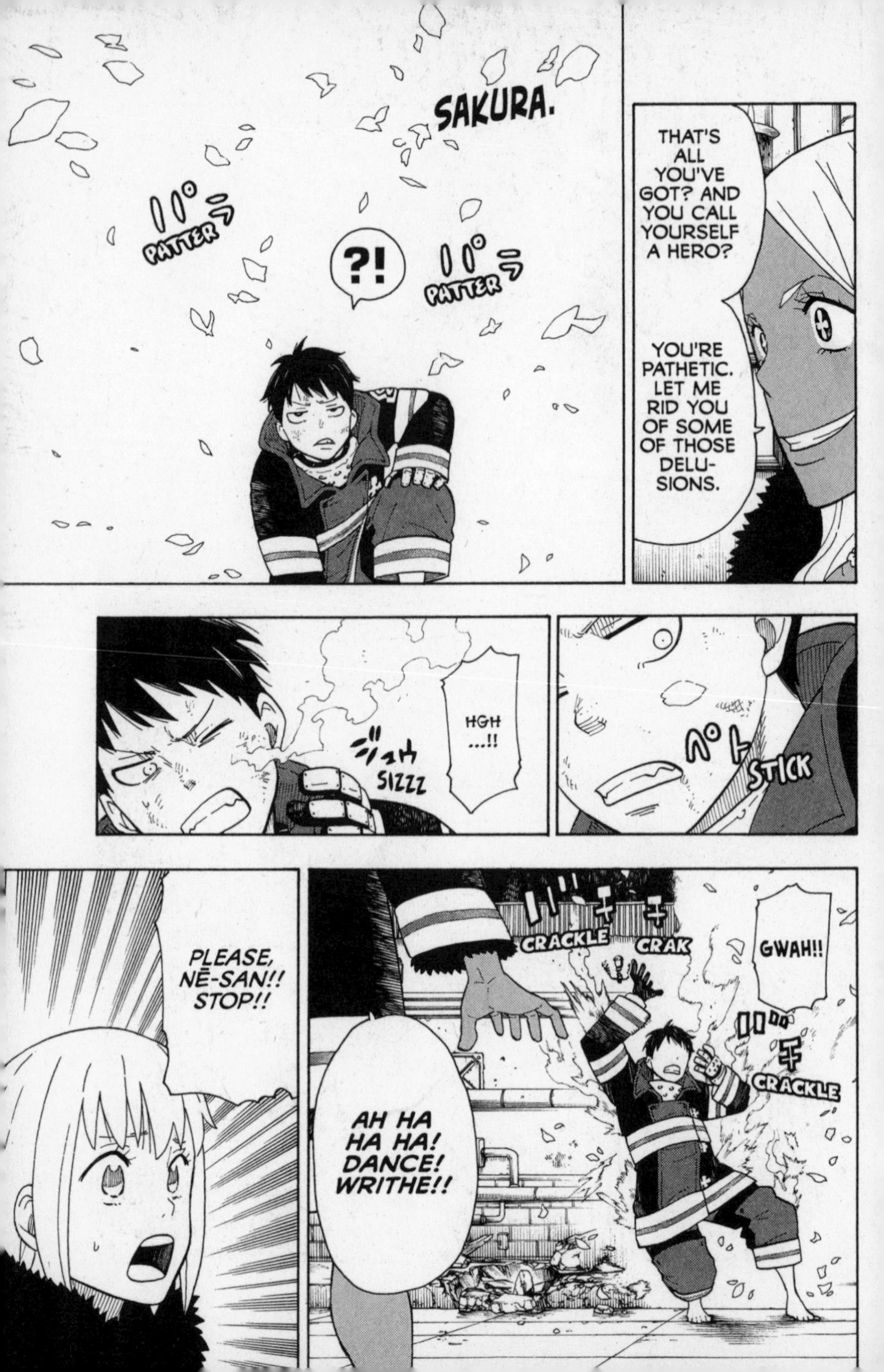
THAT'S ALL YOU'VE GOT? AND YOU CALL YOURSELF A HERO?
YOU'RE PATHETIC. LET ME RID YOU OF SOME OF THOSE DELUSIONS.
SAKURA.
PATTER
?!
PATTER
STICK
HGH ...!!
SIZZZ
GWAH!!
CRAK
CRACKLE
CRACKLE
AH HA HA HA! DANCE! WRITHE!!
PLEASE, NĒ-SAN!! STOP!!

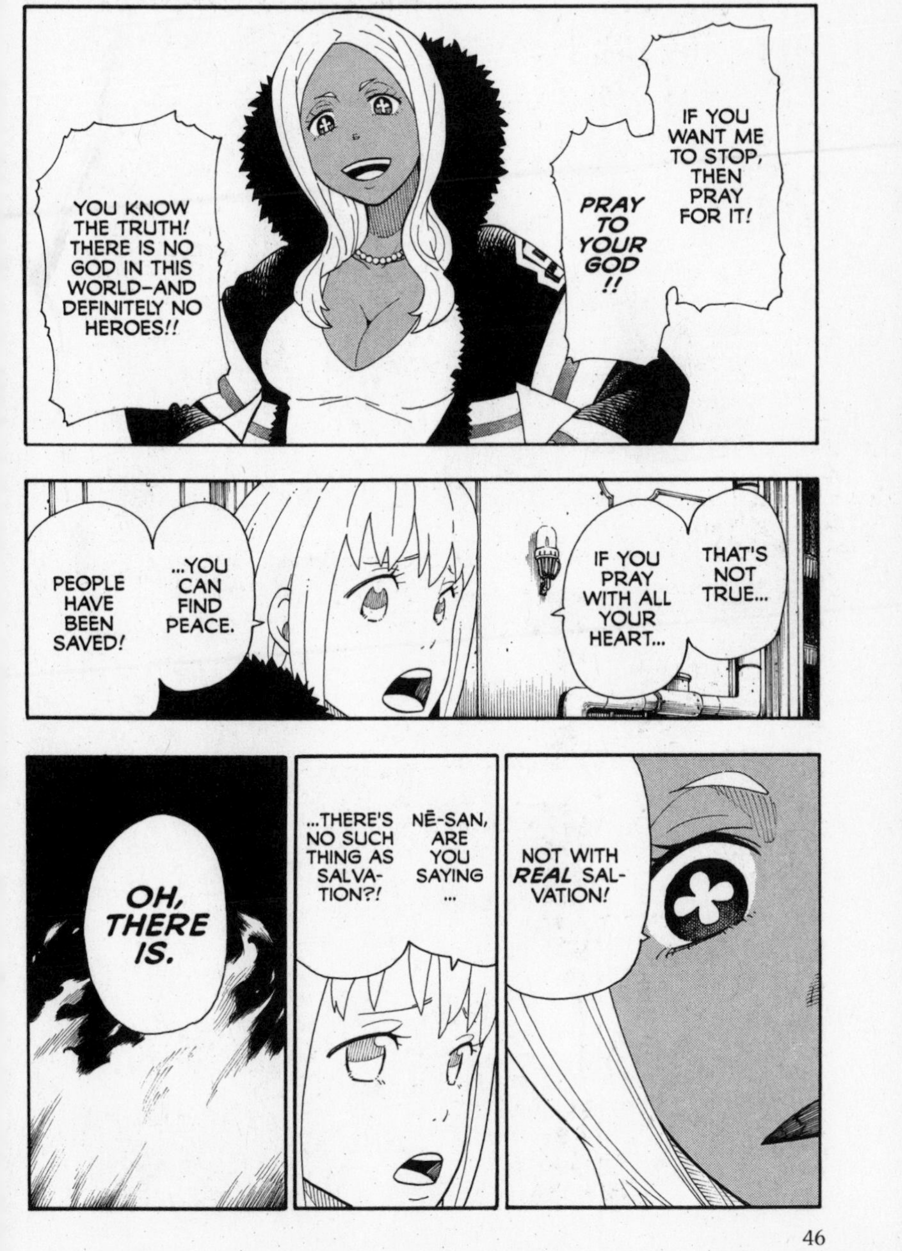
IF YOU WANT ME TO STOP, THEN PRAY FOR IT!
PRAY TO YOUR GOD!!
YOU KNOW THE TRUTH! THERE IS NO GOD IN THIS WORLD–AND DEFINITELY NO HEROES!!
THAT'S NOT TRUE...
IF YOU PRAY WITH ALL YOUR HEART...
...YOU CAN FIND PEACE.
PEOPLE HAVE BEEN SAVED!
NOT WITH REAL SALVATION!
NĒ-SAN, ARE YOU SAYING...
...THERE'S NO SUCH THING AS SALVATION?!
OH, THERE IS.

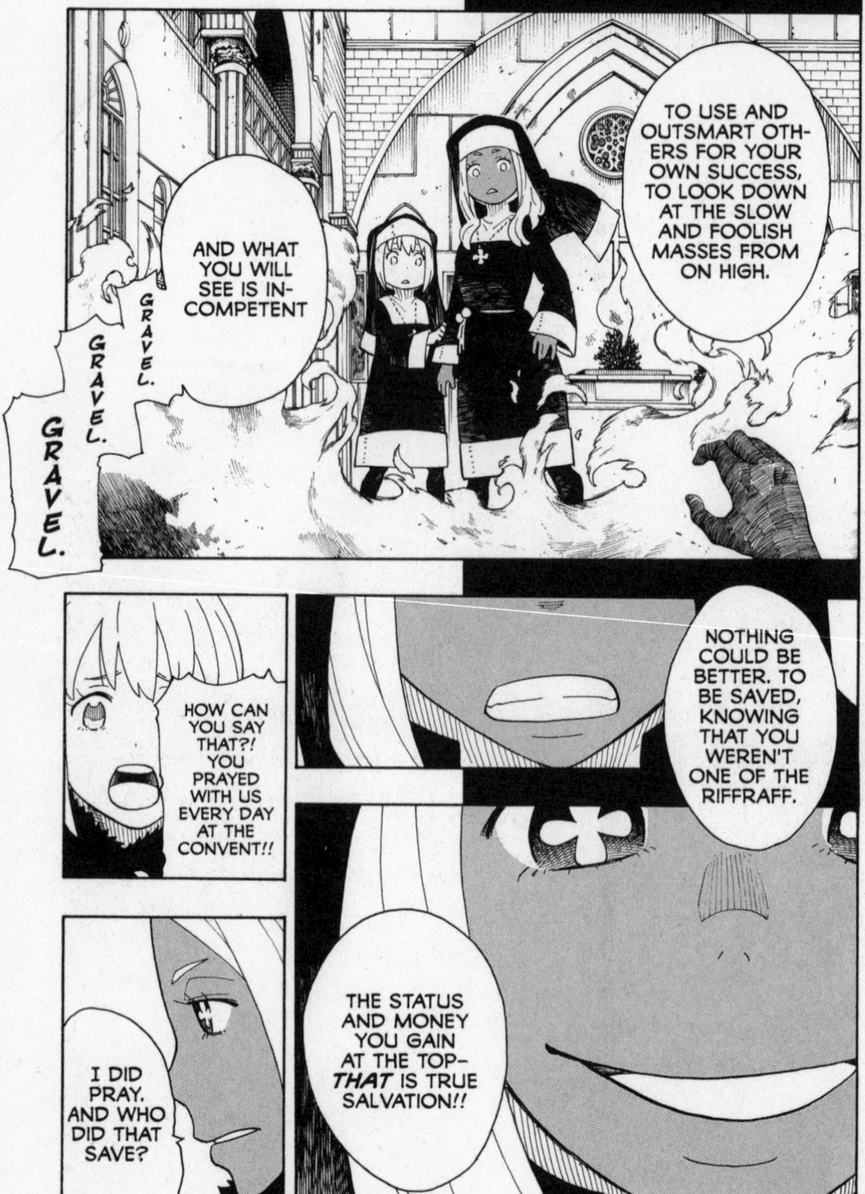
TO USE AND OUTSMART OTHERS FOR YOUR OWN SUCCESS, TO LOOK DOWN AT THE SLOW AND FOOLISH MASSES FROM ON HIGH.
AND WHAT YOU WILL SEE IS INCOMPETENT
GRAVEL.
GRAVEL.
GRAVEL.
NOTHING COULD BE BETTER. TO BE SAVED, KNOWING THAT YOU WEREN'T ONE OF THE RIFFRAFF.
HOW CAN YOU SAY THAT?! YOU PRAYED WITH US EVERY DAY AT THE CONVENT!!
I DID PRAY. AND WHO DID THAT SAVE?
THE STATUS AND MONEY YOU GAIN AT THE TOP—*THAT* IS TRUE SALVATION!!

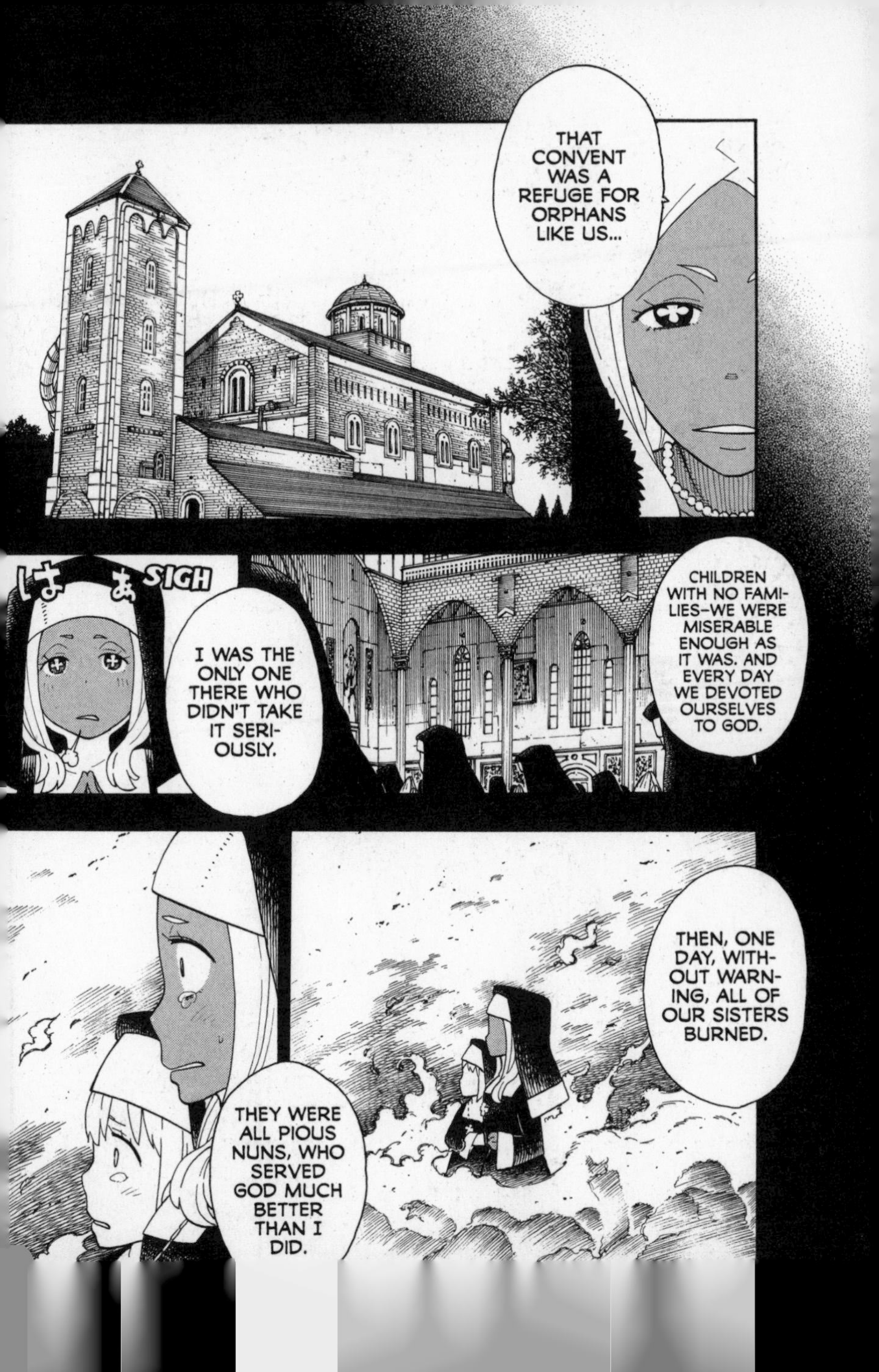
THAT CONVENT WAS A REFUGE FOR ORPHANS LIKE US...
CHILDREN WITH NO FAMILIES—WE WERE MISERABLE ENOUGH AS IT WAS. AND EVERY DAY WE DEVOTED OURSELVES TO GOD.
はぁ SIGH
I WAS THE ONLY ONE THERE WHO DIDN'T TAKE IT SERIOUSLY.
THEN, ONE DAY, WITHOUT WARNING, ALL OF OUR SISTERS BURNED.
THEY WERE ALL PIOUS NUNS, WHO SERVED GOD MUCH BETTER THAN I DID.

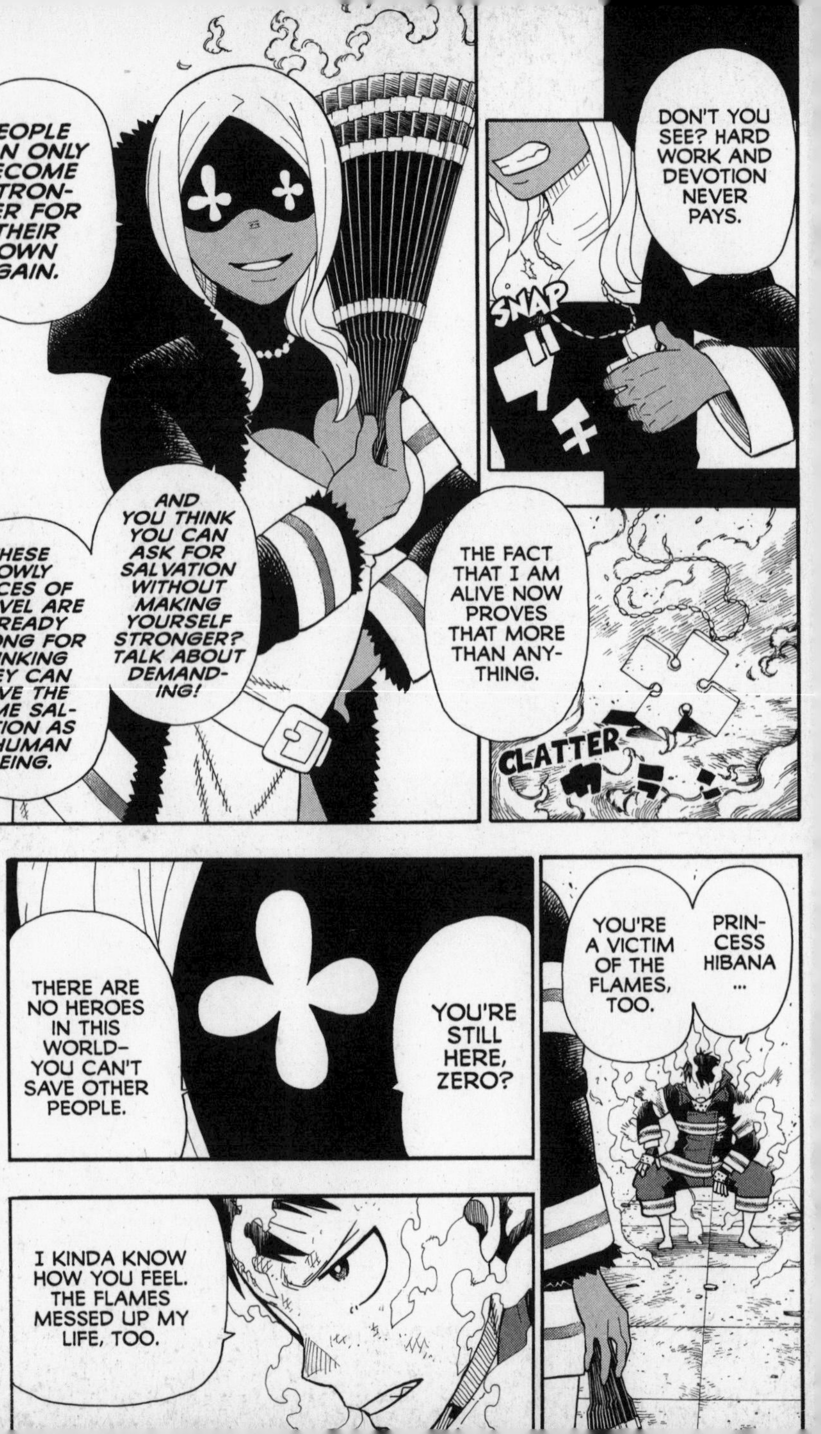
DON'T YOU SEE? HARD WORK AND DEVOTION NEVER PAYS.
SNAP
THE FACT THAT I AM ALIVE NOW PROVES THAT MORE THAN ANY-THING.
CLATTER
PEOPLE CAN ONLY BECOME STRONGER FOR THEIR OWN GAIN.
AND YOU THINK YOU CAN ASK FOR SALVATION WITHOUT MAKING YOURSELF STRONGER? TALK ABOUT DEMAND-ING!
THESE LOWLY PIECES OF GRAVEL ARE ALREADY WRONG FOR THINKING THEY CAN HAVE THE SAME SAL-VATION AS A HUMAN BEING.
PRIN-CESS HIBANA...
YOU'RE A VICTIM OF THE FLAMES, TOO.
YOU'RE STILL HERE, ZERO?
THERE ARE NO HEROES IN THIS WORLD- YOU CAN'T SAVE OTHER PEOPLE.
I KINDA KNOW HOW YOU FEEL. THE FLAMES MESSED UP MY LIFE, TOO.

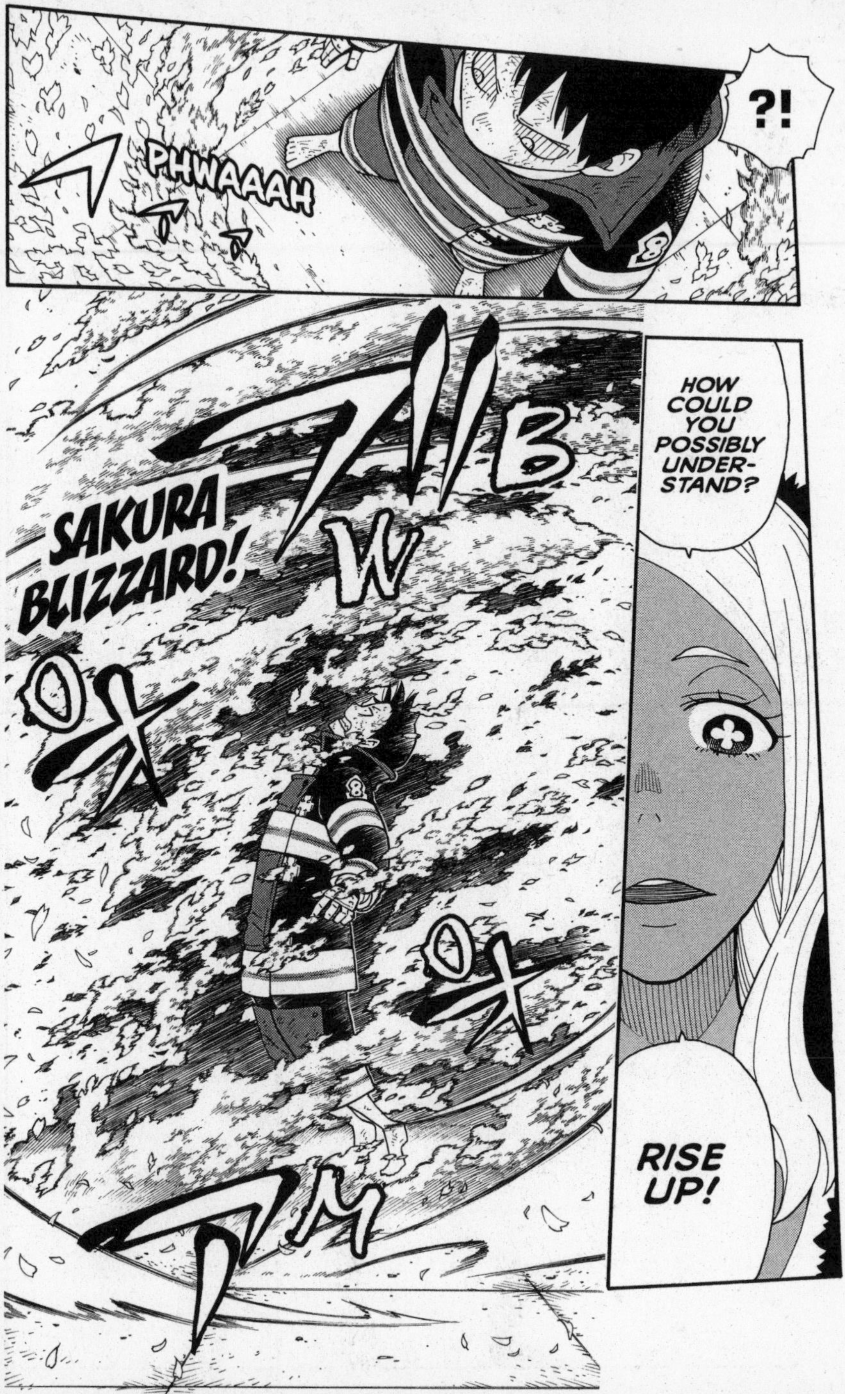
?!
PHWAAAH
HOW COULD YOU POSSIBLY UNDERSTAND?
RISE UP!
SAKURA BLIZZARD!

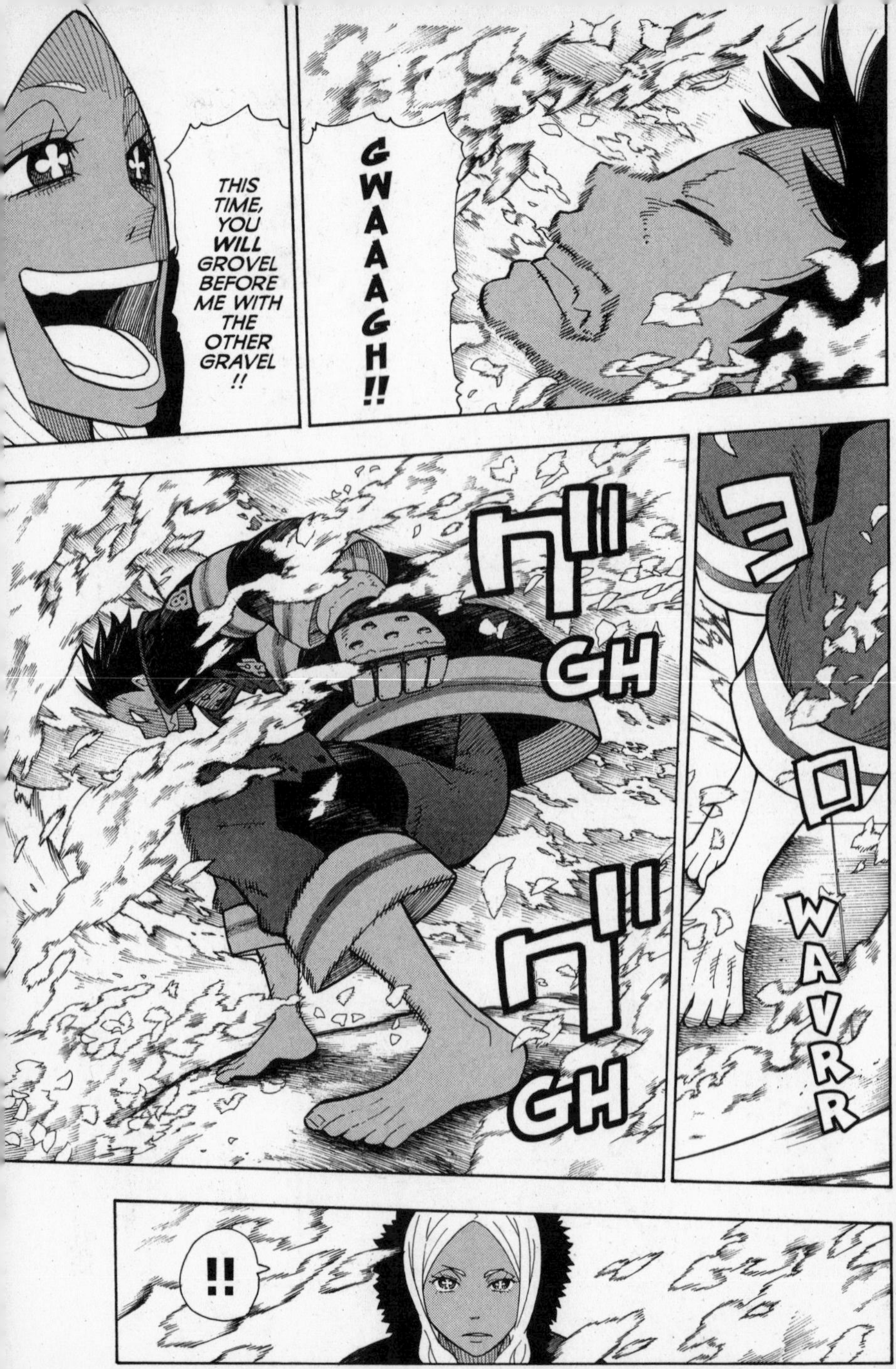
GWAAAAGH!!
THIS TIME, YOU WILL GROVEL BEFORE ME WITH THE OTHER GRAVEL!!
ヨロ
WAVR
ガ
GH
ガ
GH
!!

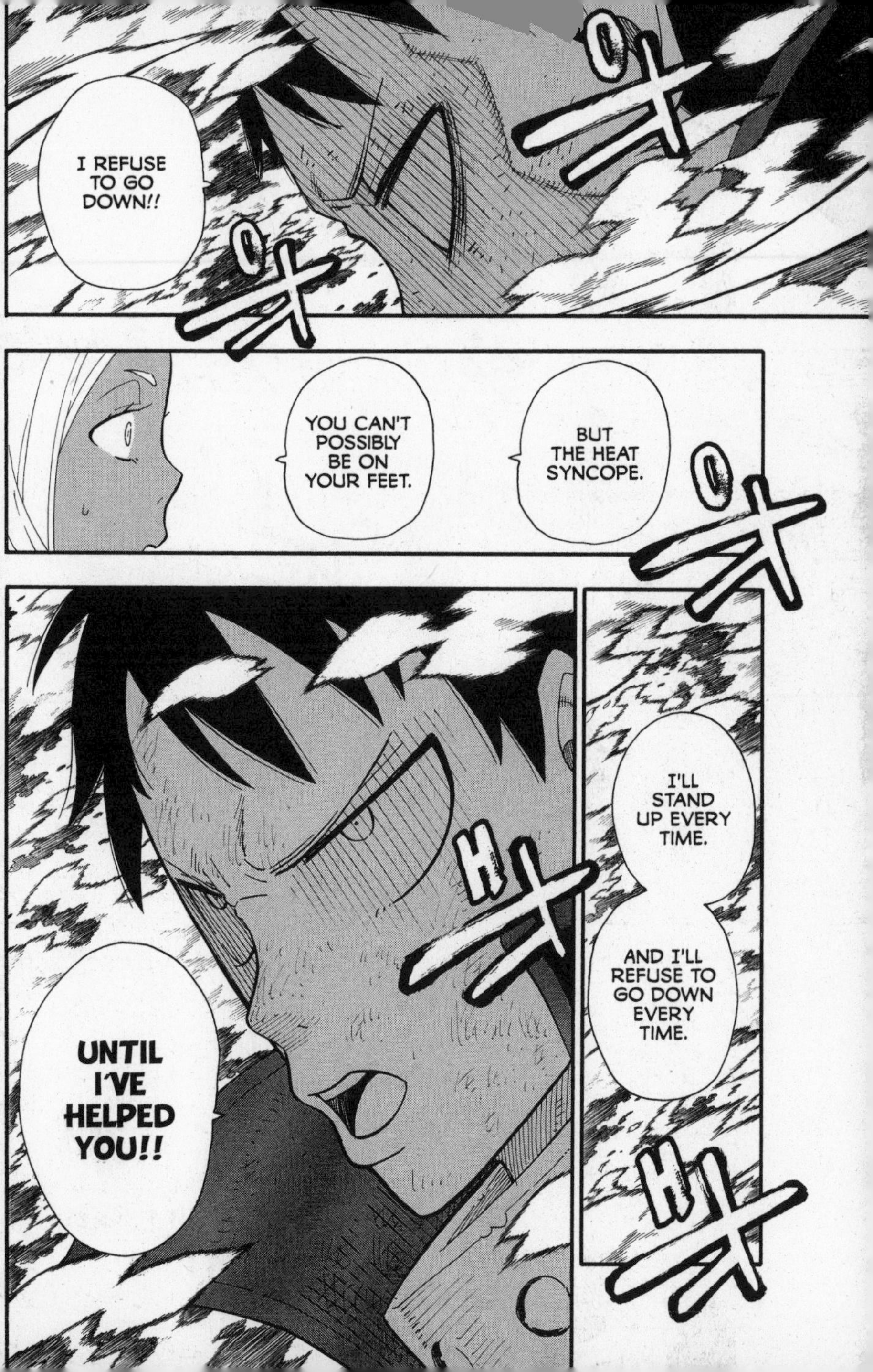
I REFUSE TO GO DOWN!!
BUT THE HEAT SYNCOPE.
YOU CAN'T POSSIBLY BE ON YOUR FEET.
I'LL STAND UP EVERY TIME.
AND I'LL REFUSE TO GO DOWN EVERY TIME.
UNTIL I'VE HELPED YOU!!

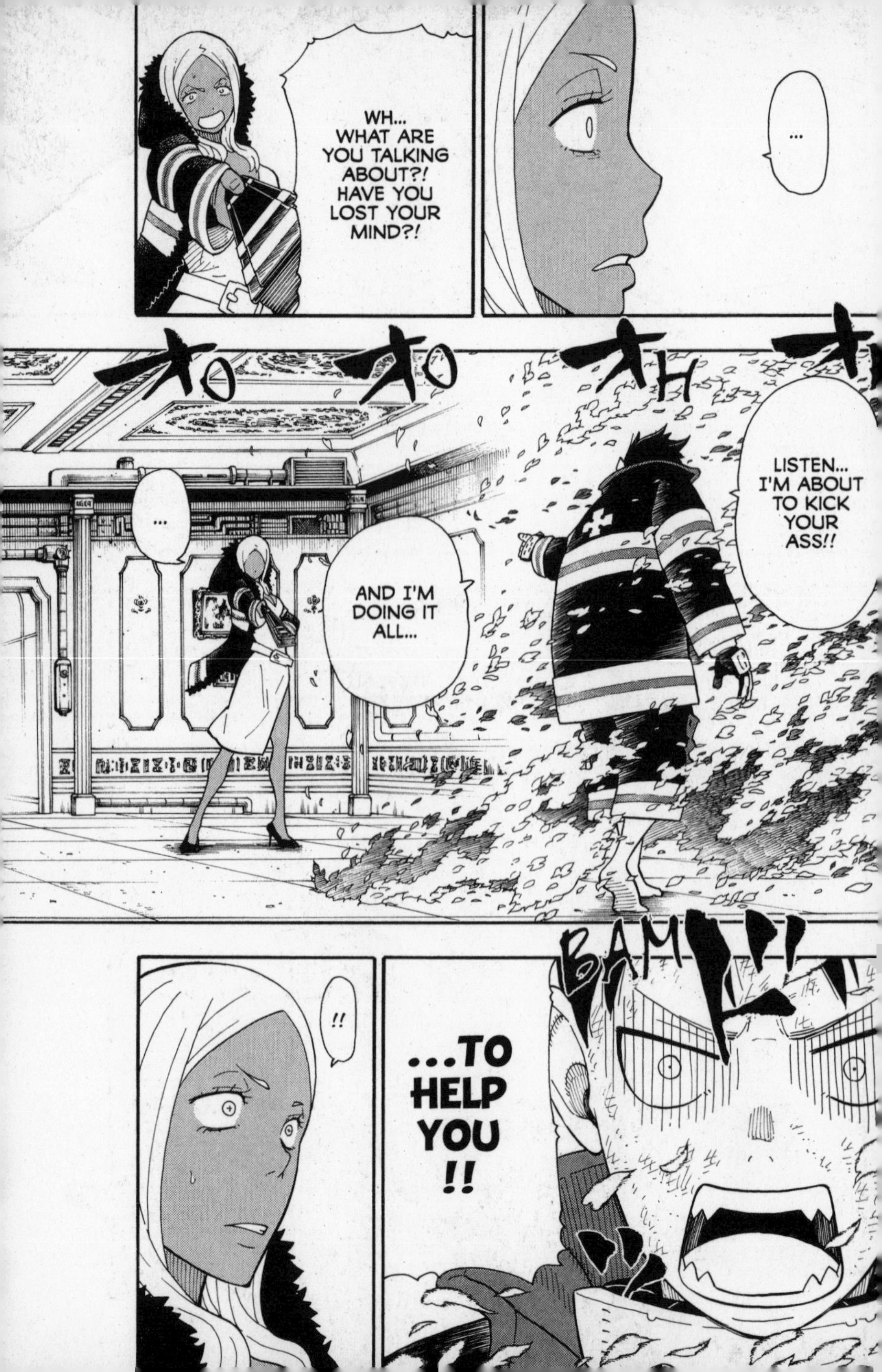
...
WH... WHAT ARE YOU TALKING ABOUT?! HAVE YOU LOST YOUR MIND?!
LISTEN... I'M ABOUT TO KICK YOUR ASS!!
AND I'M DOING IT ALL...
...
BAM!!
...TO HELP YOU !!
!!

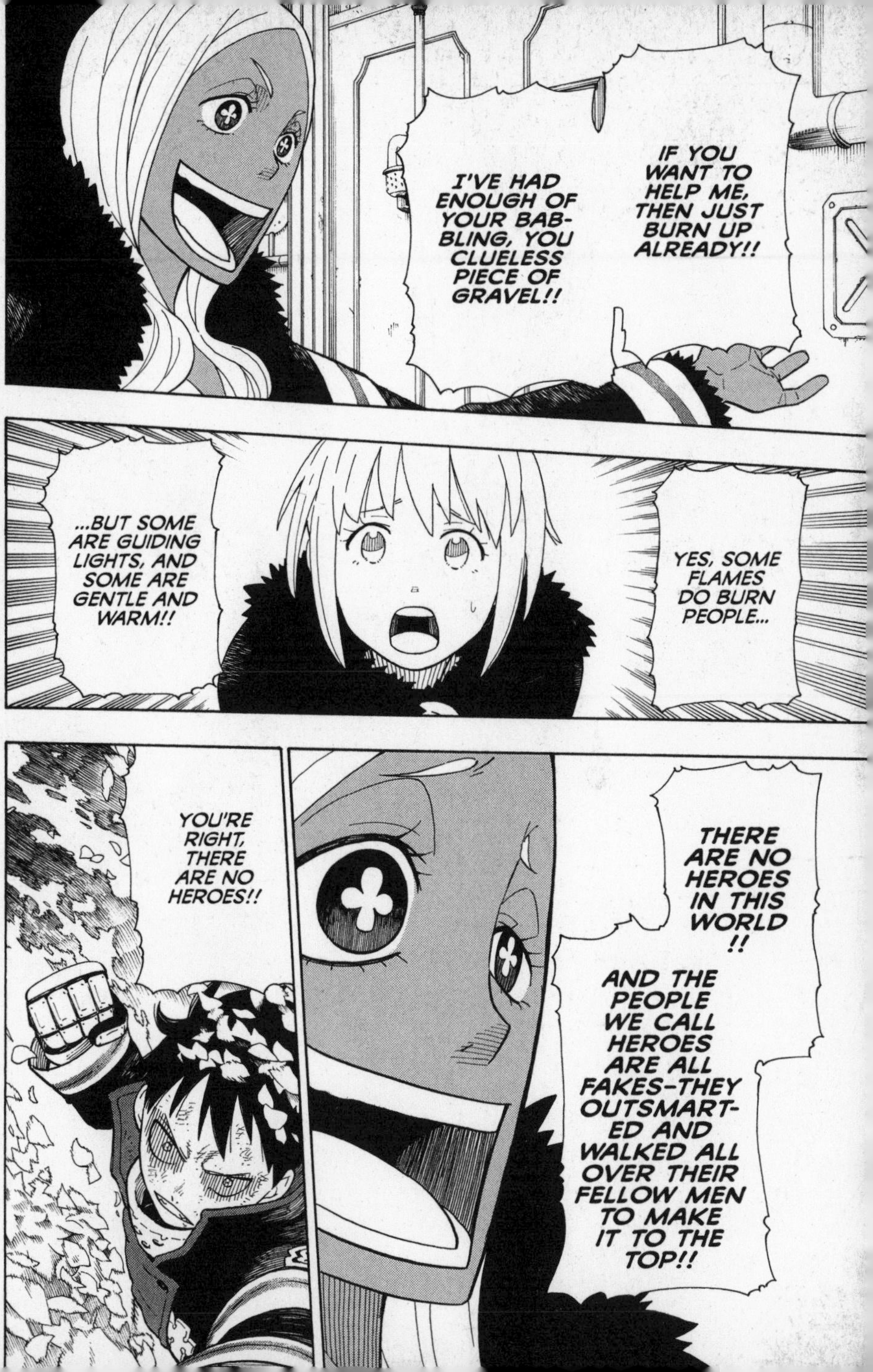
I'VE HAD ENOUGH OF YOUR BAB-BLING, YOU CLUELESS PIECE OF GRAVEL!!
IF YOU WANT TO HELP ME, THEN JUST BURN UP ALREADY!!
YES, SOME FLAMES DO BURN PEOPLE...
...BUT SOME ARE GUIDING LIGHTS, AND SOME ARE GENTLE AND WARM!!
THERE ARE NO HEROES IN THIS WORLD!!
AND THE PEOPLE WE CALL HEROES ARE ALL FAKES–THEY OUTSMART-ED AND WALKED ALL OVER THEIR FELLOW MEN TO MAKE IT TO THE TOP!!
YOU'RE RIGHT, THERE ARE NO HEROES!!

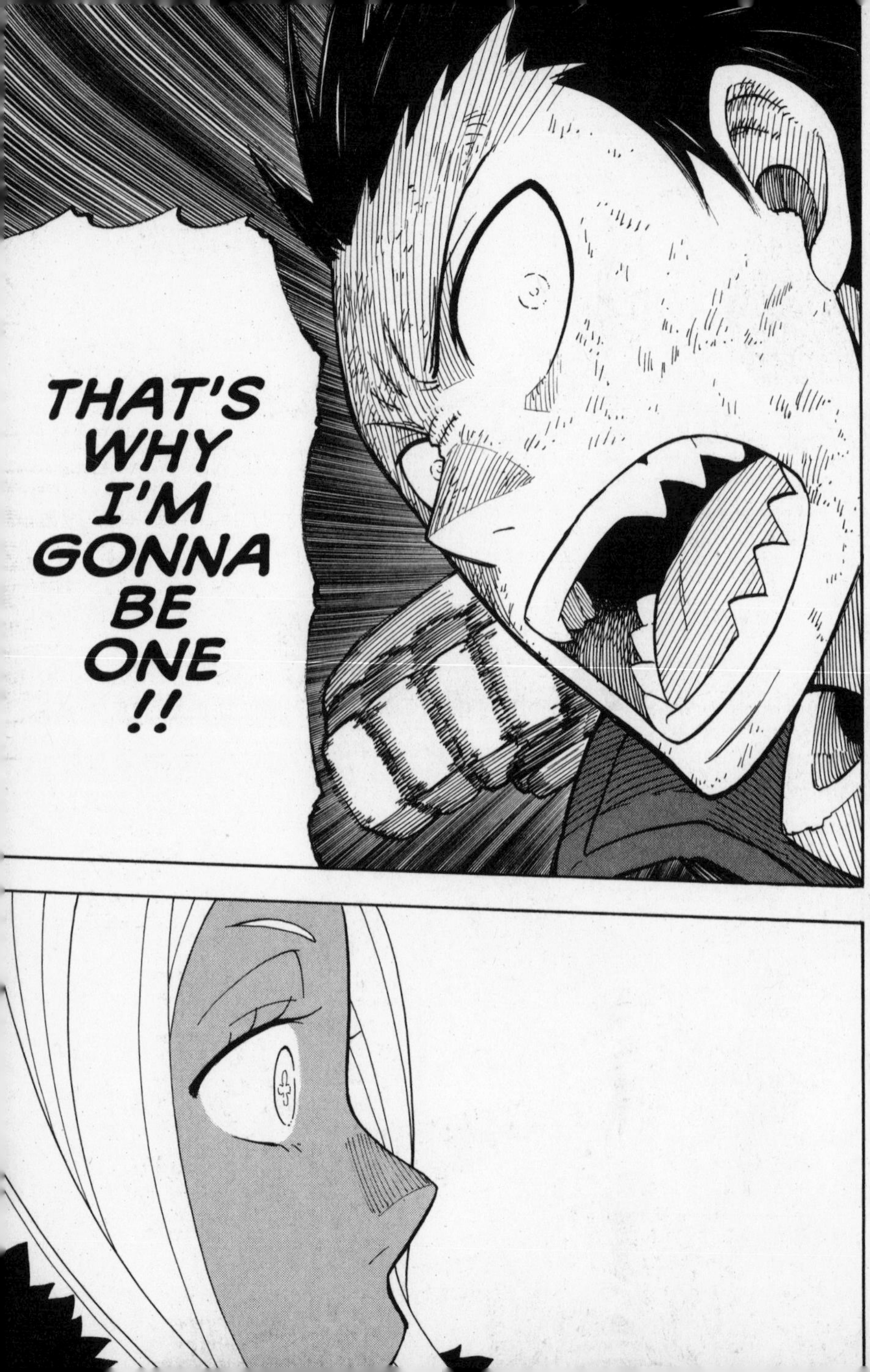
THAT'S WHY I'M GONNA BE ONE !!

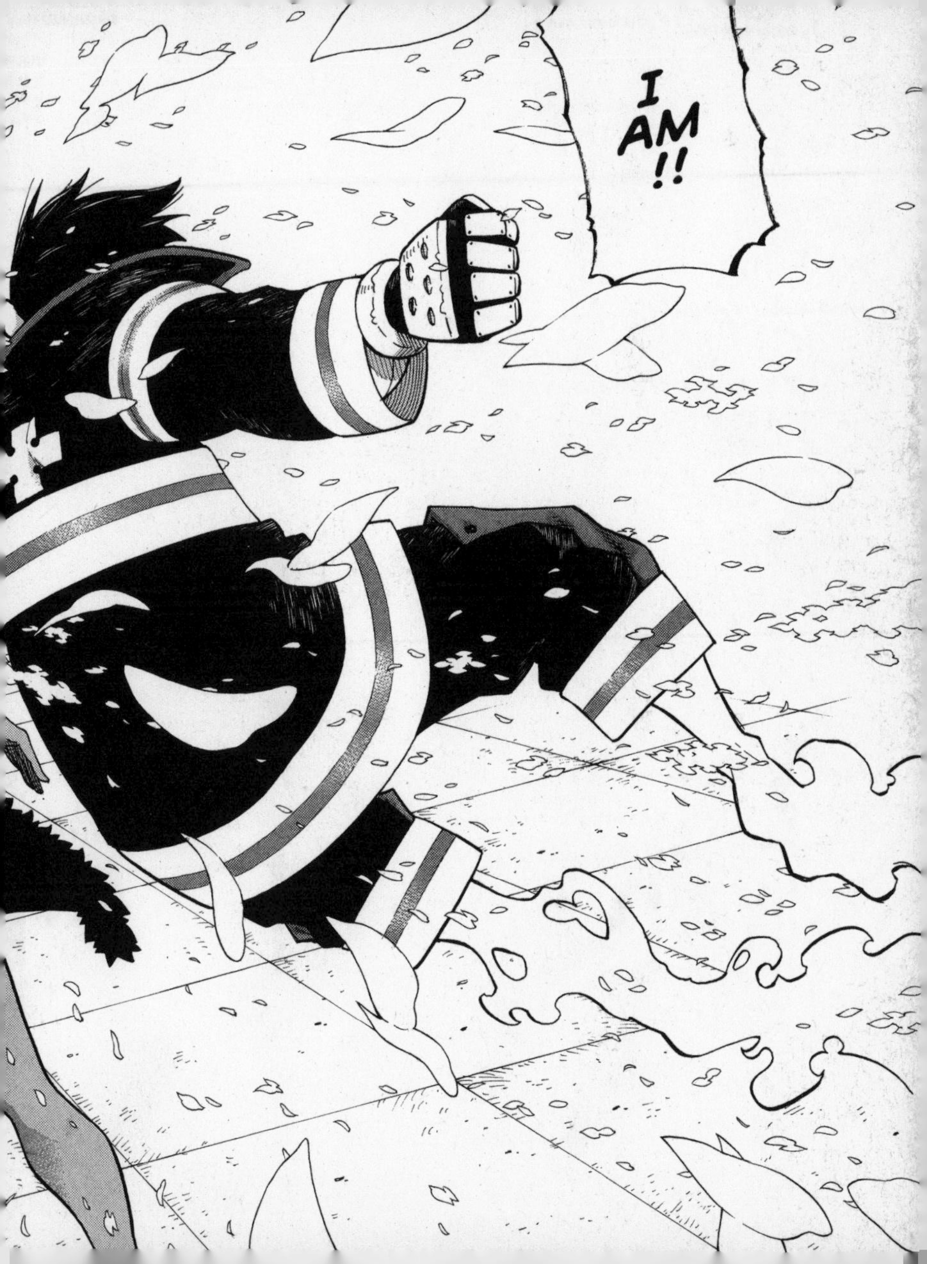
I AM!!

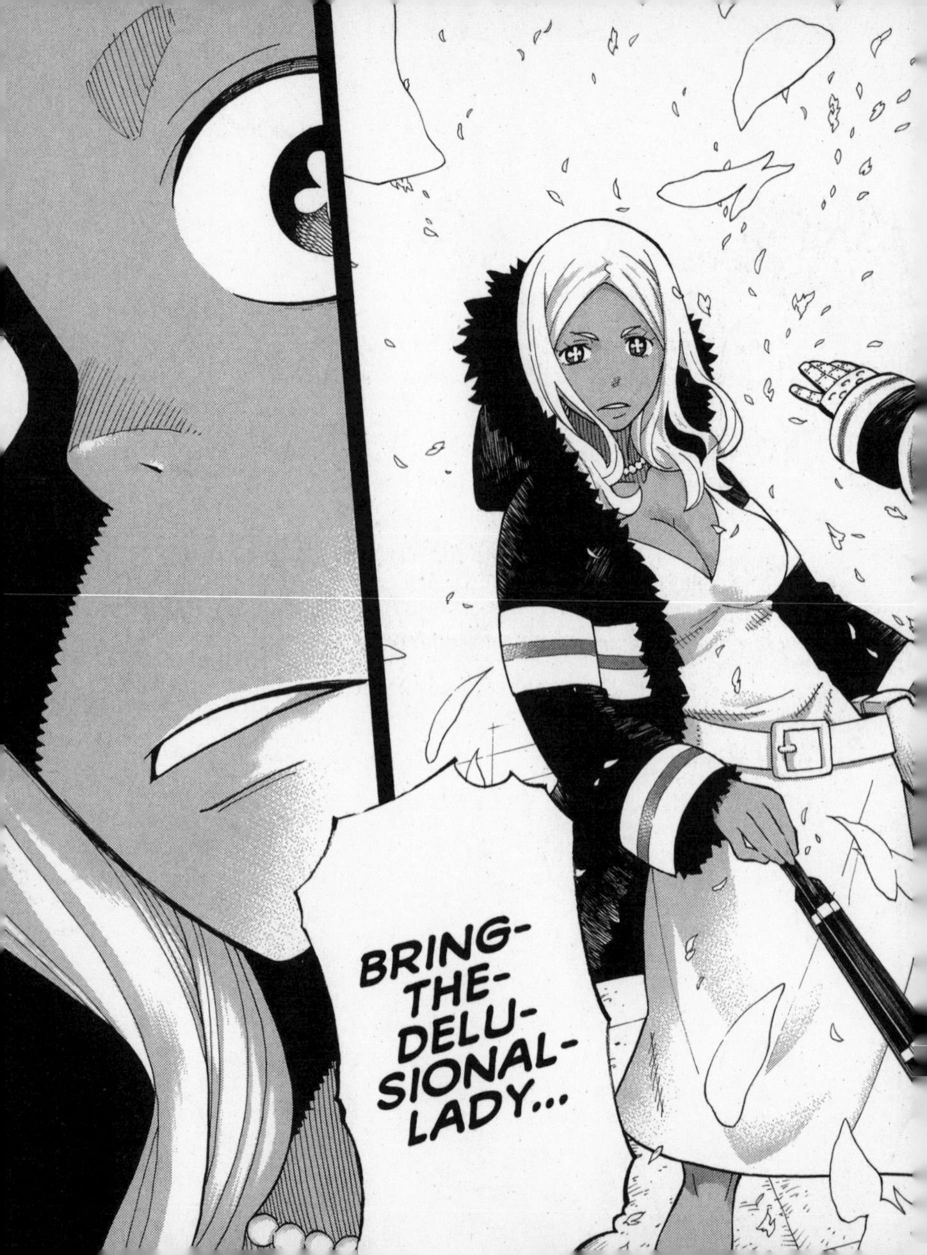
BRING-THE-DELU-SIONAL-LADY...

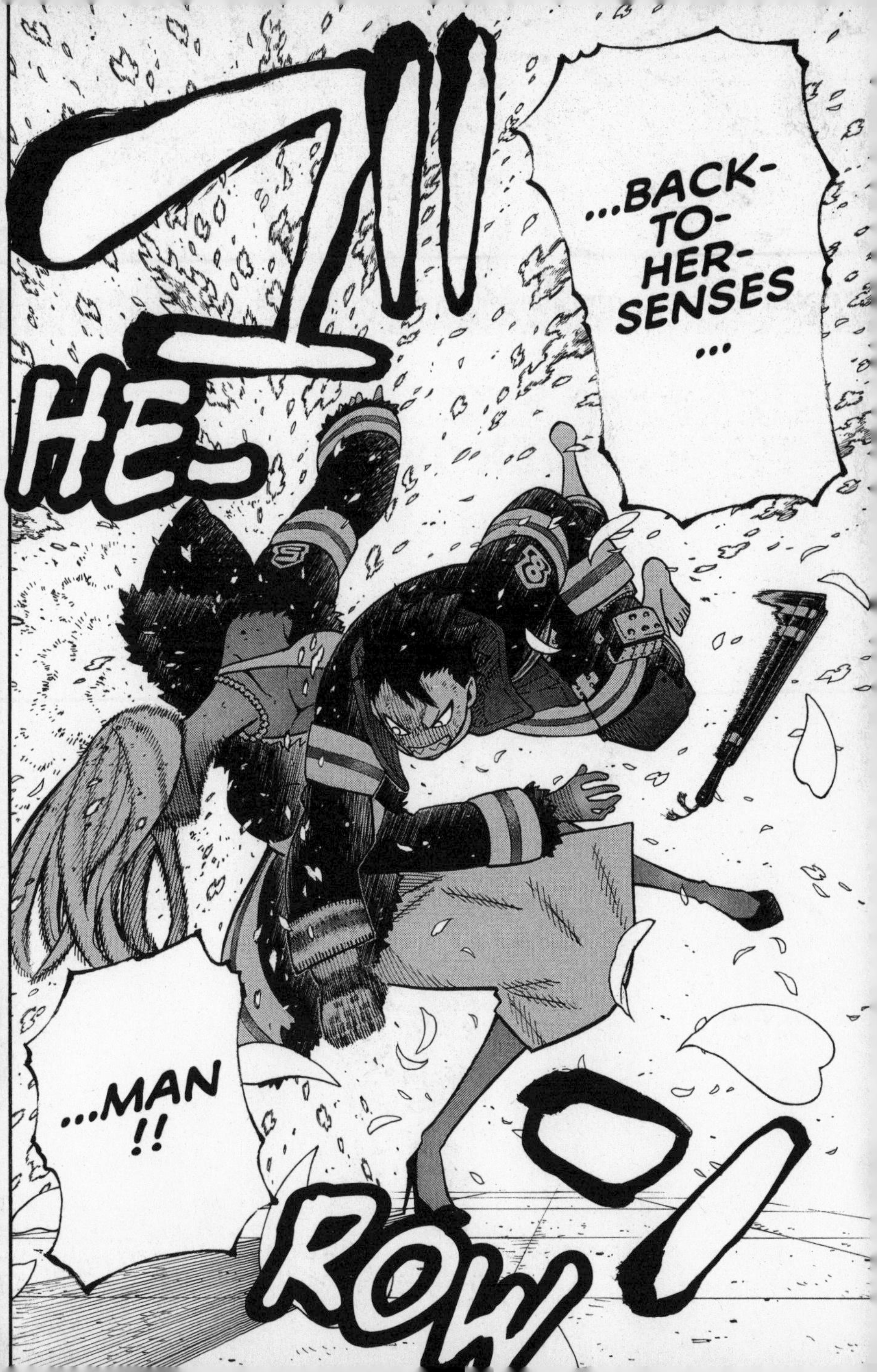
...BACK-TO-HER-SENSES...
HE-
...MAN!!
ROW

CHAPTER XIX: THE FLOWER OF PROMISE

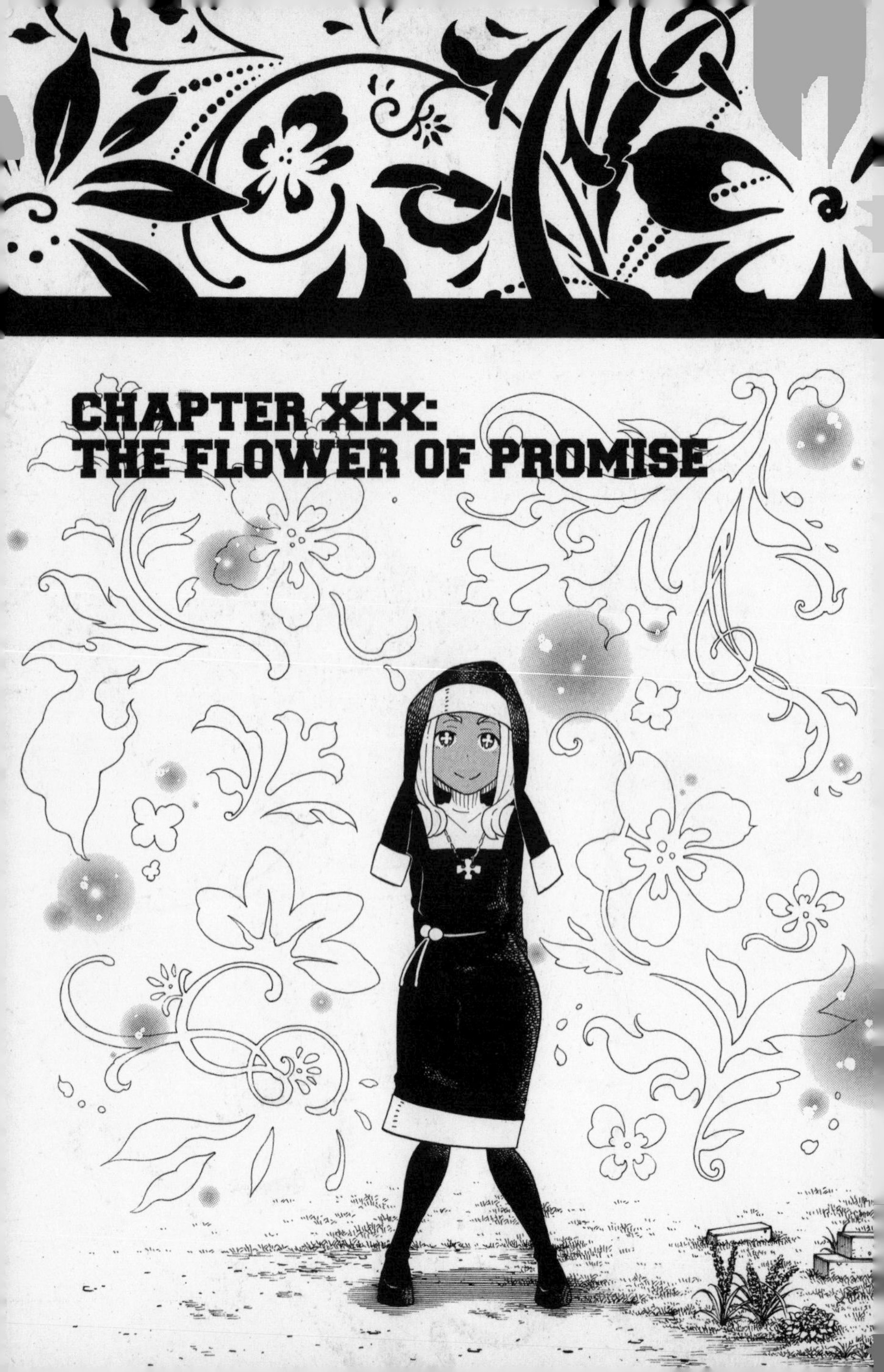

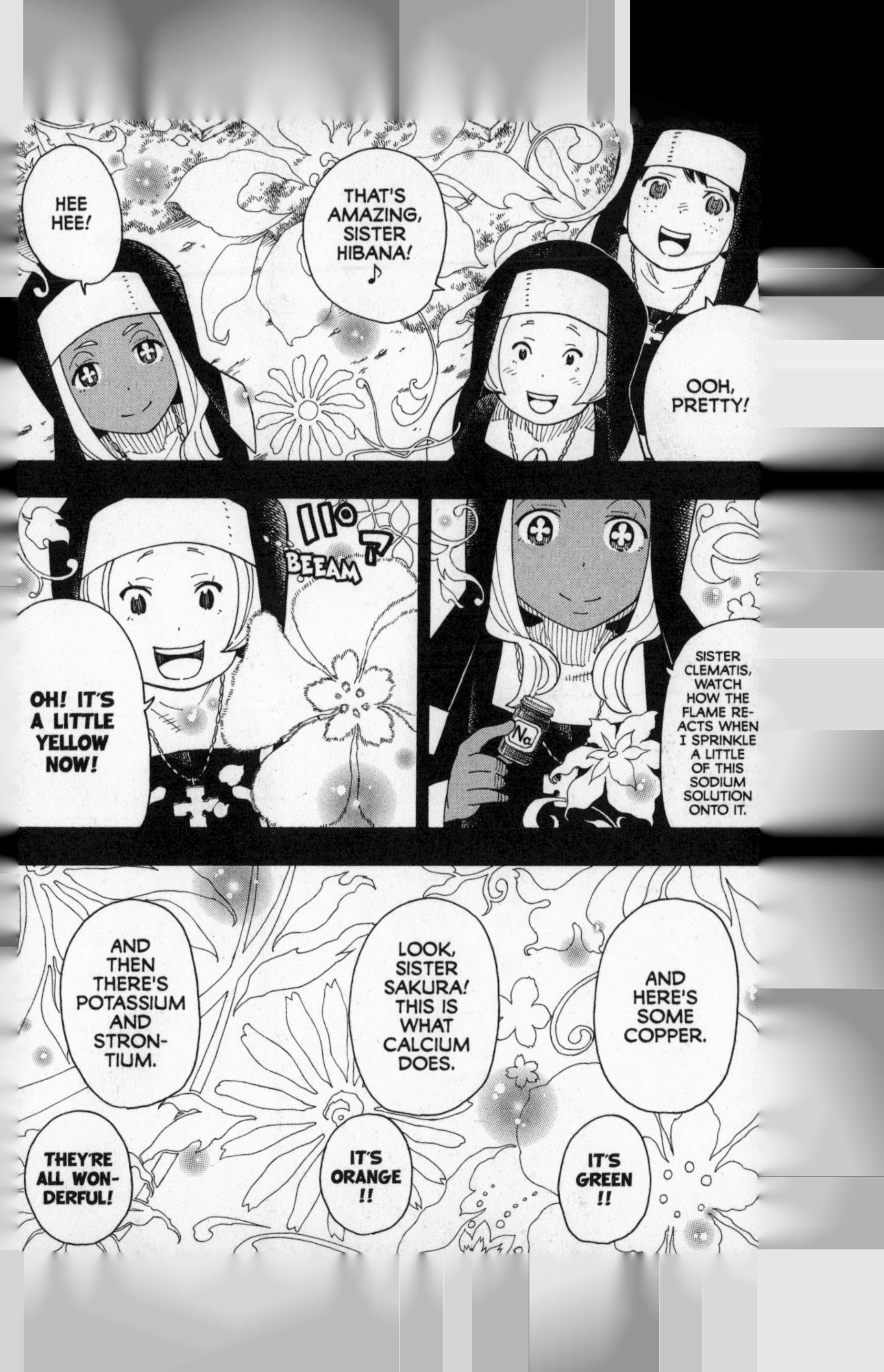
OOH, PRETTY!
THAT'S AMAZING, SISTER HIBANA! ♪
HEE HEE!
SISTER CLEMATIS, WATCH HOW THE FLAME REACTS WHEN I SPRINKLE A LITTLE OF THIS SODIUM SOLUTION ONTO IT.
Na
BEEAM
OH! IT'S A LITTLE YELLOW NOW!
AND HERE'S SOME COPPER.
IT'S GREEN !!
LOOK, SISTER SAKURA! THIS IS WHAT CALCIUM DOES.
IT'S ORANGE !!
AND THEN THERE'S POTASSIUM AND STRONTIUM.
THEY'RE ALL WONDERFUL!

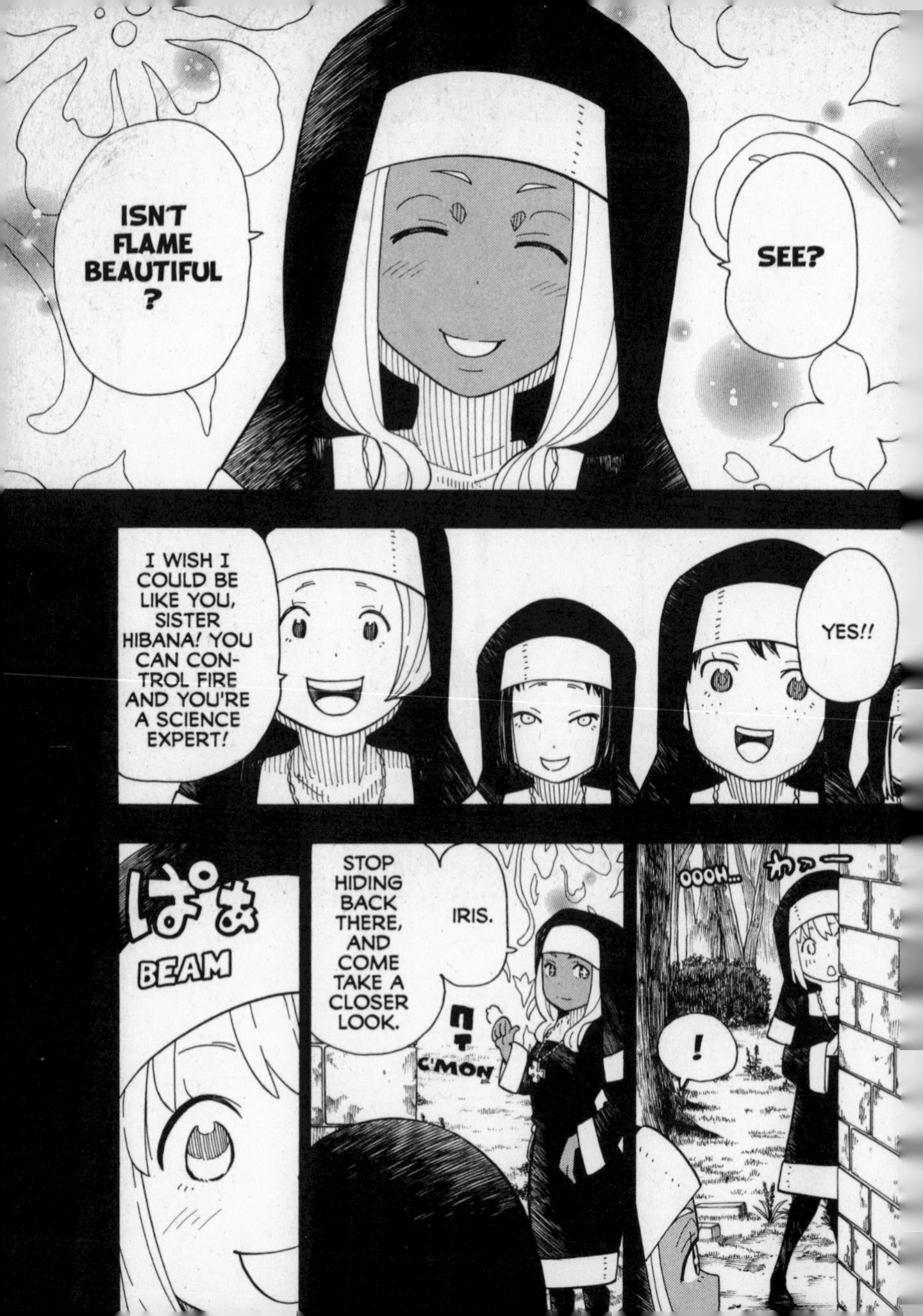
SEE?
ISN'T FLAME BEAUTIFUL ?
YES!!
I WISH I COULD BE LIKE YOU, SISTER HIBANA! YOU CAN CON-TROL FIRE AND YOU'RE A SCIENCE EXPERT!
OOOH...
!
IRIS.
STOP HIDING BACK THERE, AND COME TAKE A CLOSER LOOK.
C'MON
BEAM

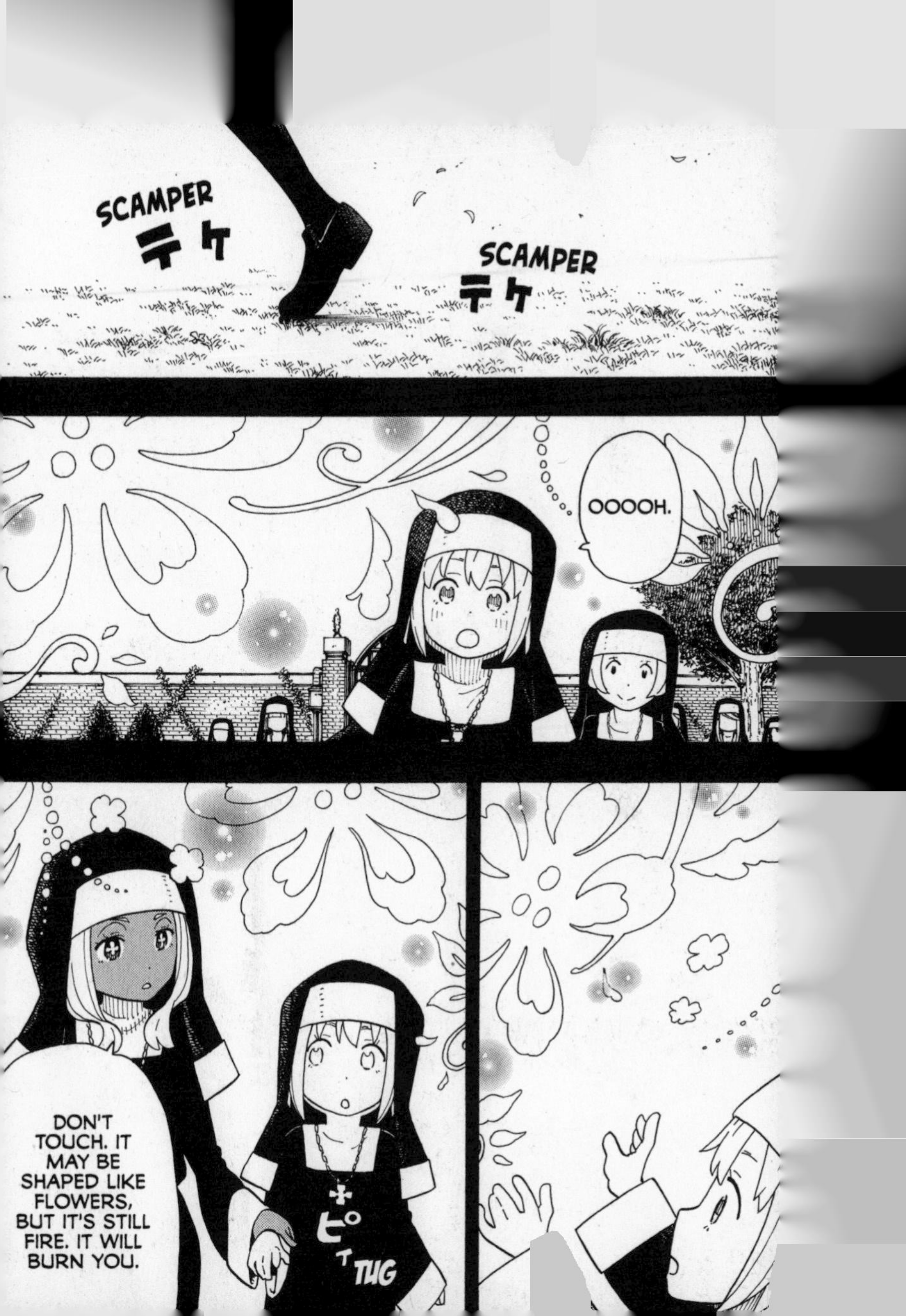
SCAMPER
テケ
SCAMPER
テケ
OOOOH.
ピッ
TUG
DON'T TOUCH. IT MAY BE SHAPED LIKE FLOWERS, BUT IT'S STILL FIRE. IT WILL BURN YOU.

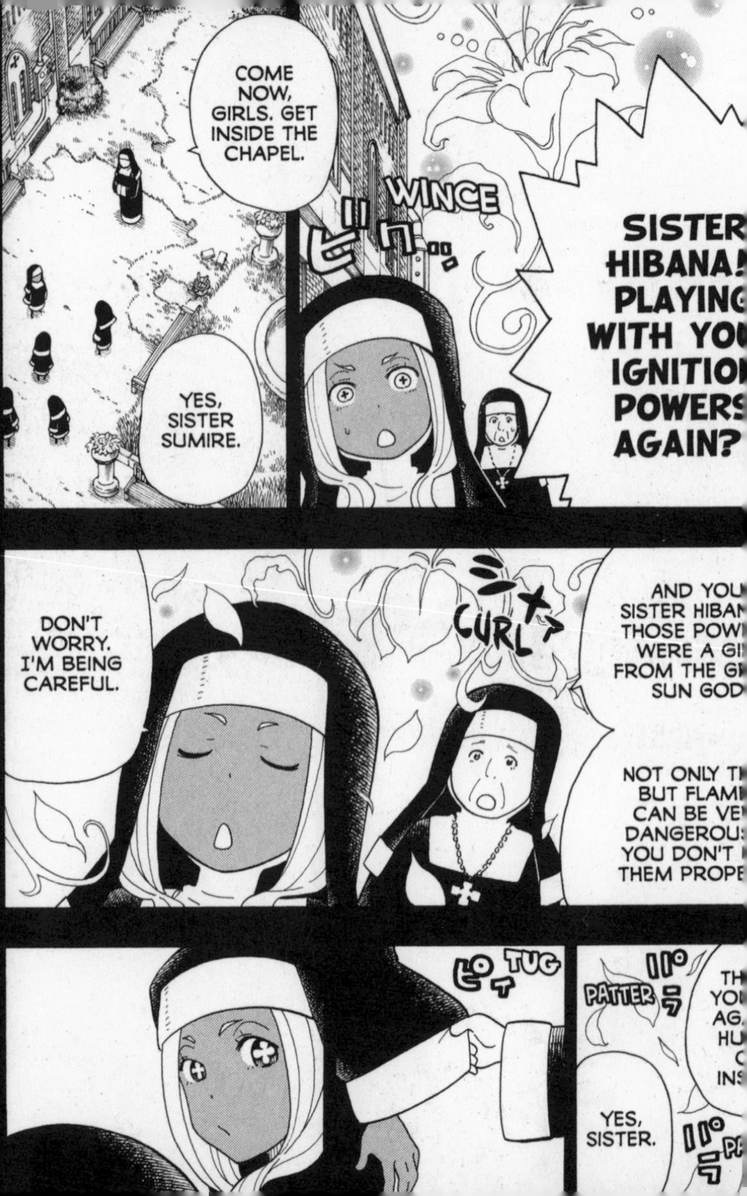

SISTER HIBANA! PLAYING WITH YOU IGNITIO POWERS AGAIN?
WINCE
COME NOW, GIRLS. GET INSIDE THE CHAPEL.
YES, SISTER SUMIRE.
AND YOU SISTER HIBAN THOSE POW WERE A GI FROM THE G SUN GOD
NOT ONLY T BUT FLAM CAN BE VE DANGEROU YOU DON'T THEM PROPE
CURL
DON'T WORRY. I'M BEING CAREFUL.
TH YO AG HU INS
PATTER
YES, SISTER.
TUG

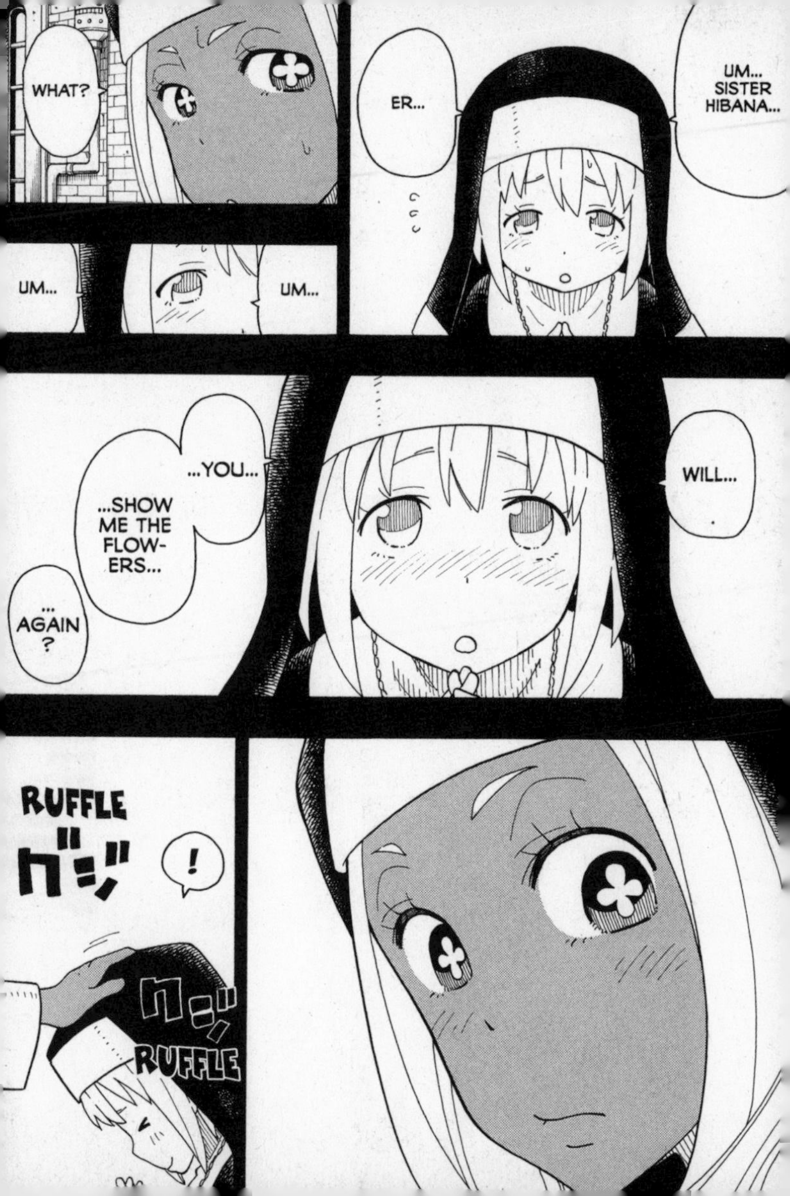
UM... SISTER HIBANA...
ER...
WHAT?
UM...
UM...
WILL...
...YOU...
...SHOW ME THE FLOWERS...
...AGAIN?
!
RUFFLE
RUFFLE

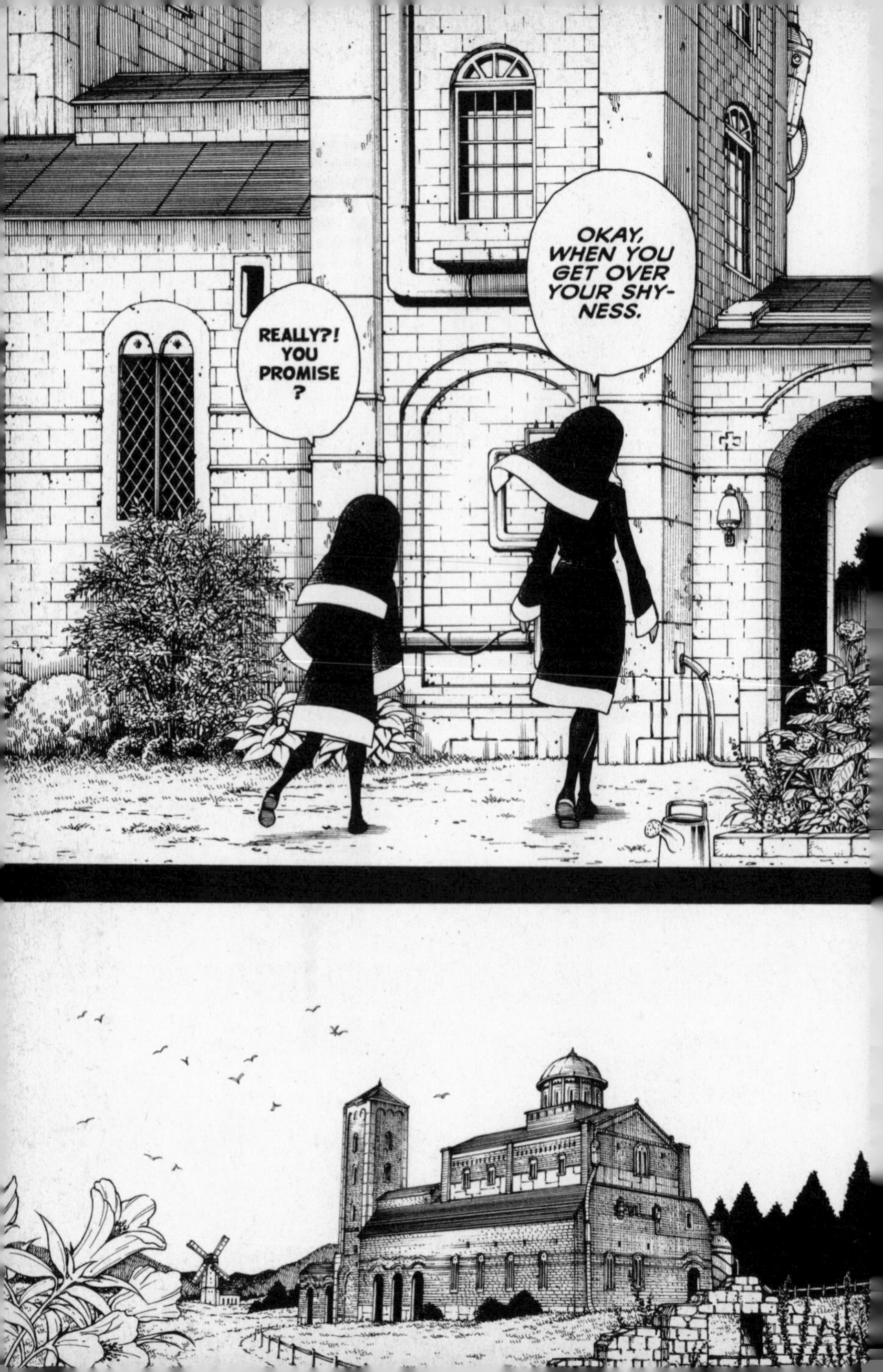
OKAY, WHEN YOU GET OVER YOUR SHY-NESS.
REALLY?! YOU PROMISE ?

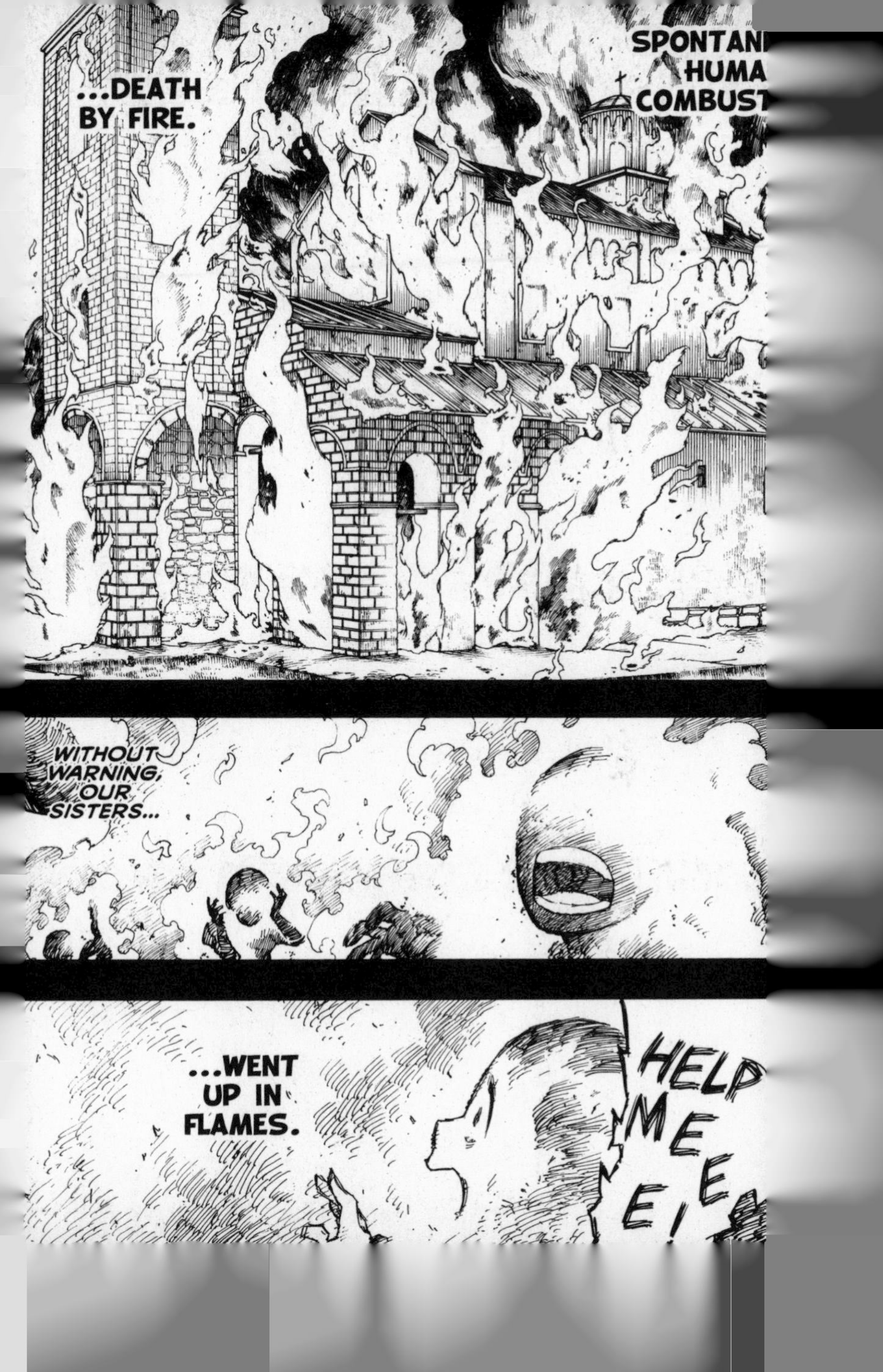
SPONTAN
HUMA
COMBUST
...DEATH BY FIRE.
WITHOUT WARNING, OUR SISTERS...
HELP MEEEE!
...WENT UP IN FLAMES.

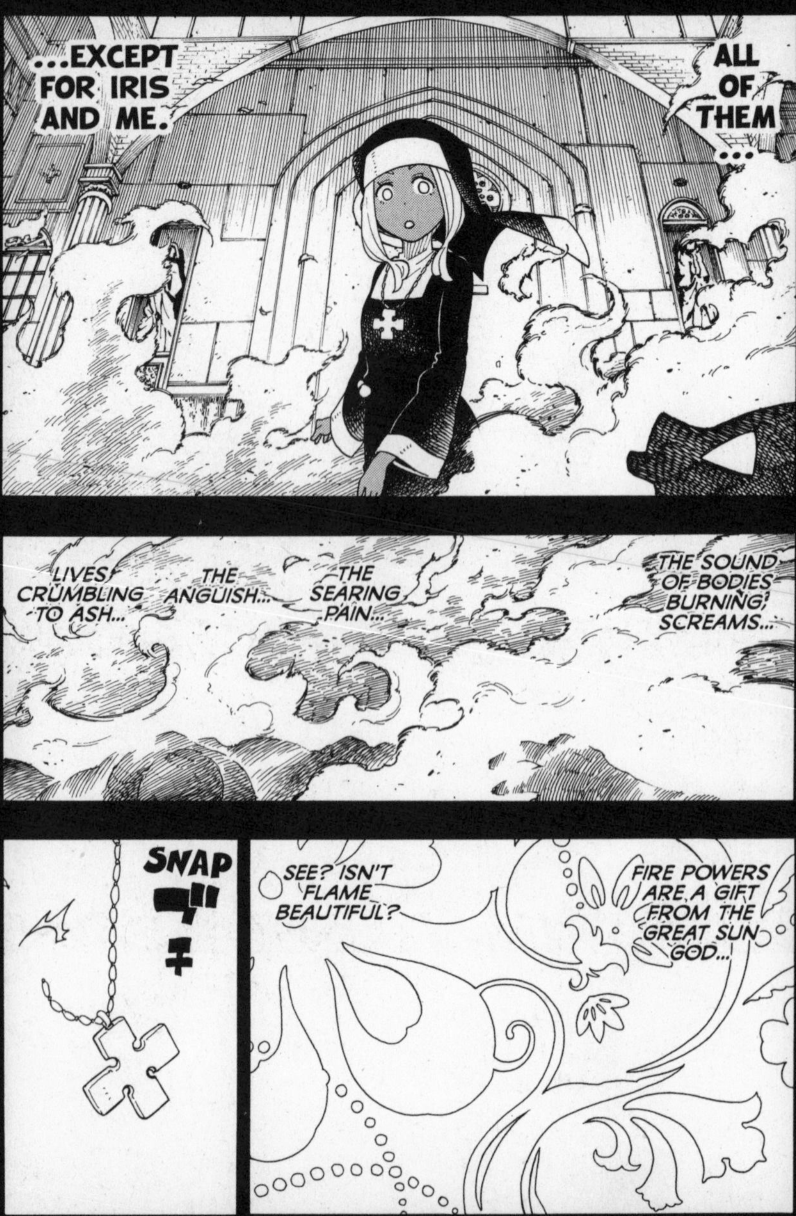
ALL OF THEM...
...EXCEPT FOR IRIS AND ME.
THE SOUND OF BODIES BURNING, SCREAMS...
THE SEARING PAIN...
THE ANGUISH...
LIVES CRUMBLING TO ASH...
FIRE POWERS ARE A GIFT FROM THE GREAT SUN GOD...
SEE? ISN'T FLAME BEAUTIFUL?
SNAP

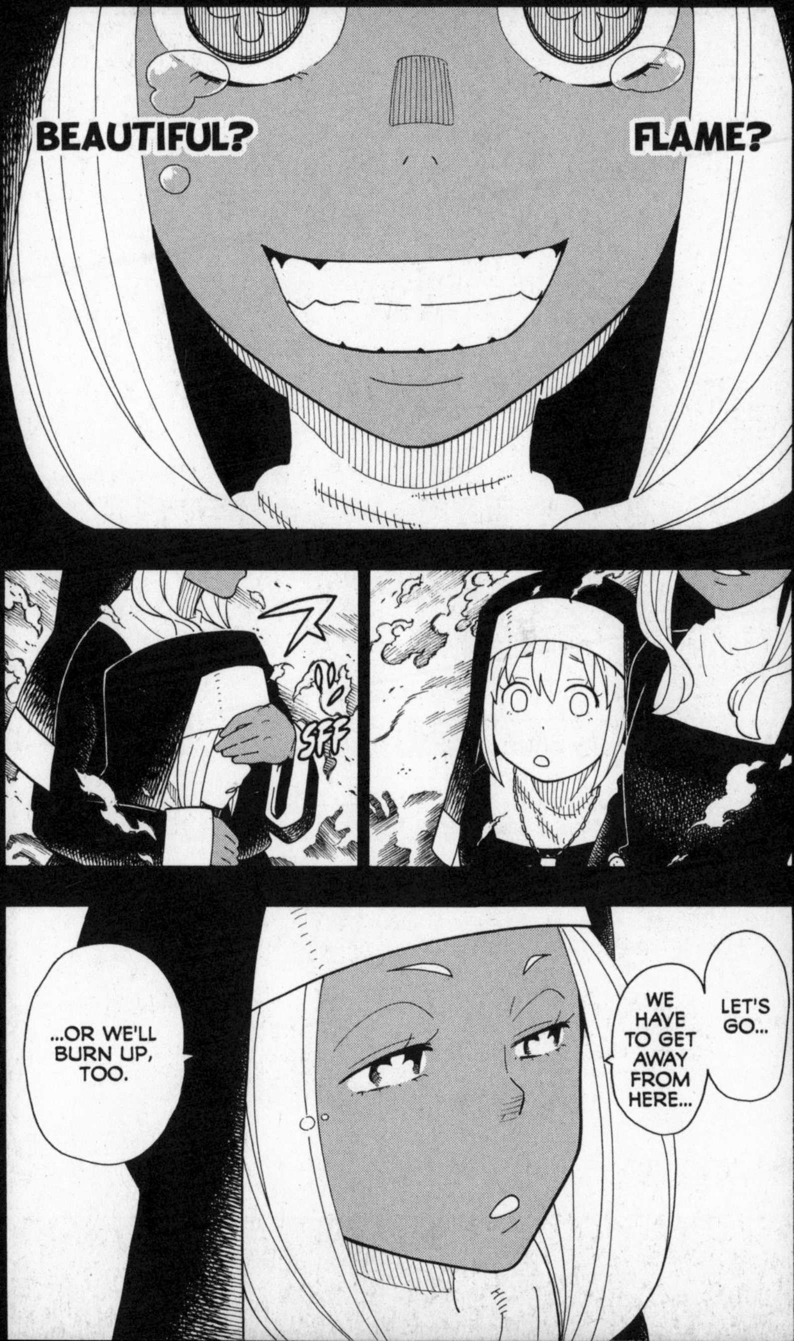
FLAME?
BEAUTIFUL?
SFF
LET'S GO...
WE HAVE TO GET AWAY FROM HERE...
...OR WE'LL BURN UP, TOO.

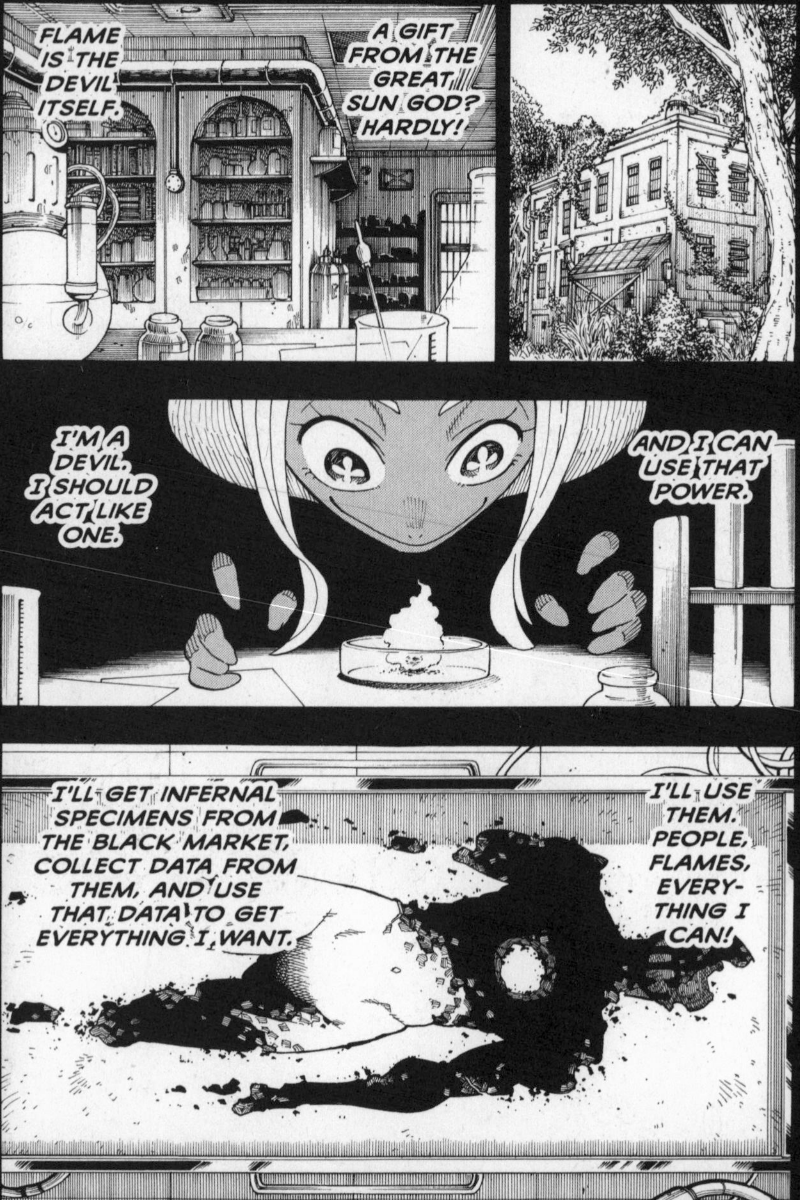
A GIFT FROM THE GREAT SUN GOD? HARDLY!
FLAME IS THE DEVIL ITSELF.
AND I CAN USE THAT POWER.
I'M A DEVIL. I SHOULD ACT LIKE ONE.
I'LL USE THEM. PEOPLE, FLAMES, EVERY-THING I CAN!
I'LL GET INFERNAL SPECIMENS FROM THE BLACK MARKET, COLLECT DATA FROM THEM, AND USE THAT DATA TO GET EVERYTHING I WANT.

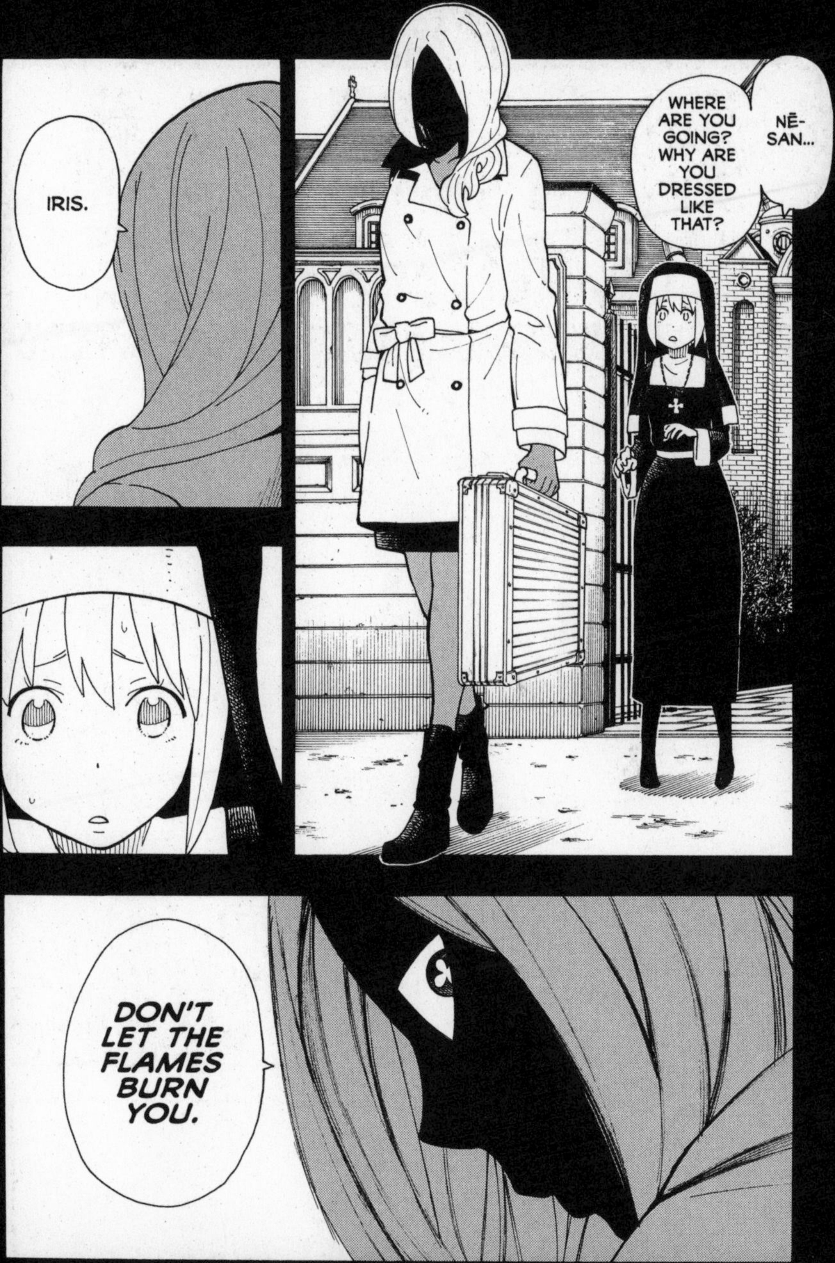
NĒ-SAN...
WHERE ARE YOU GOING? WHY ARE YOU DRESSED LIKE THAT?
IRIS.
DON'T LET THE FLAMES BURN YOU.

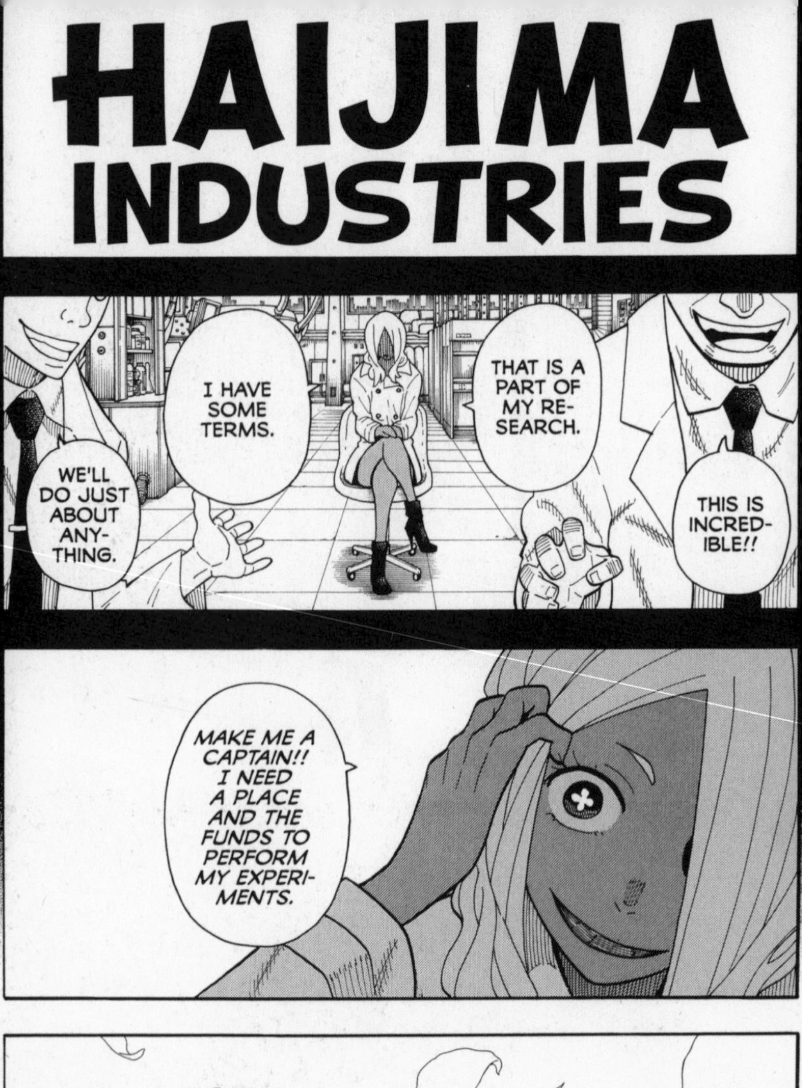
HAIJIMA INDUSTRIES
THIS IS INCREDIBLE!!
THAT IS A PART OF MY RESEARCH.
I HAVE SOME TERMS.
WE'LL DO JUST ABOUT ANYTHING.
MAKE ME A CAPTAIN!! I NEED A PLACE AND THE FUNDS TO PERFORM MY EXPERIMENTS.

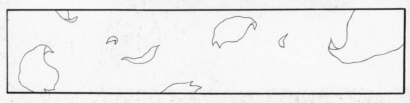

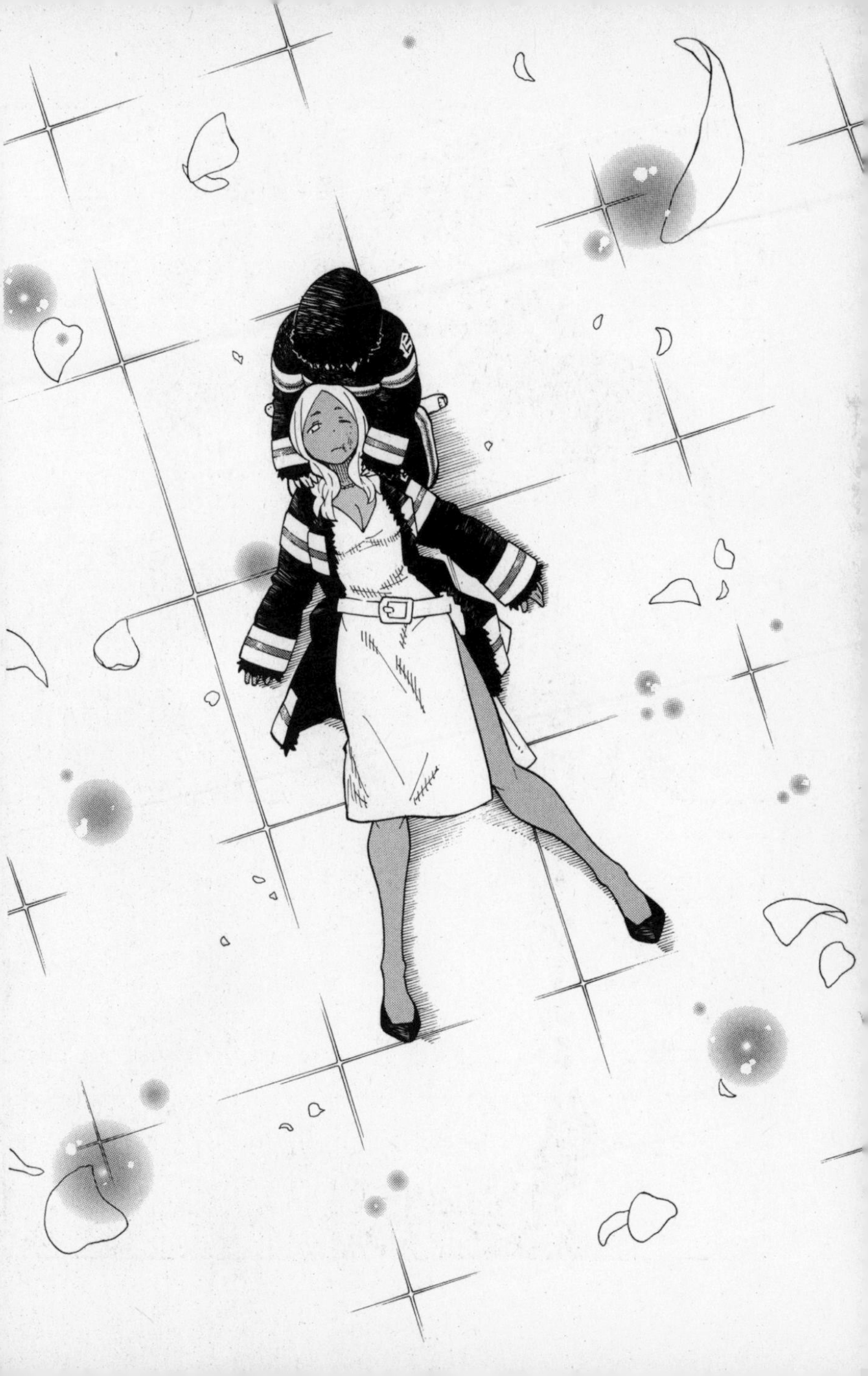

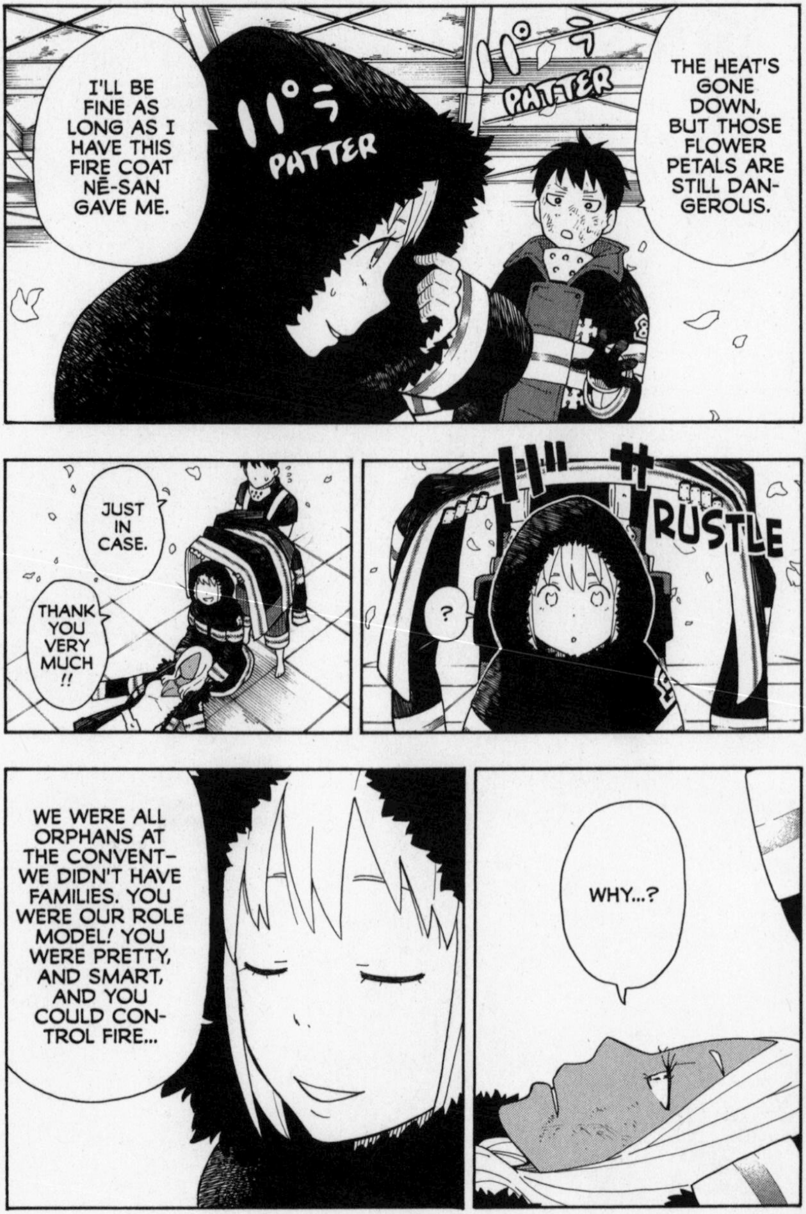
パラ
PATTER
THE HEAT'S GONE DOWN, BUT THOSE FLOWER PETALS ARE STILL DANGEROUS.
I'LL BE FINE AS LONG AS I HAVE THIS FIRE COAT NĒ-SAN GAVE ME.
パラ
PATTER
ドサ
RUSTLE
?
JUST IN CASE.
THANK YOU VERY MUCH!!
WHY...?
WE WERE ALL ORPHANS AT THE CONVENT—WE DIDN'T HAVE FAMILIES. YOU WERE OUR ROLE MODEL! YOU WERE PRETTY, AND SMART, AND YOU COULD CONTROL FIRE...

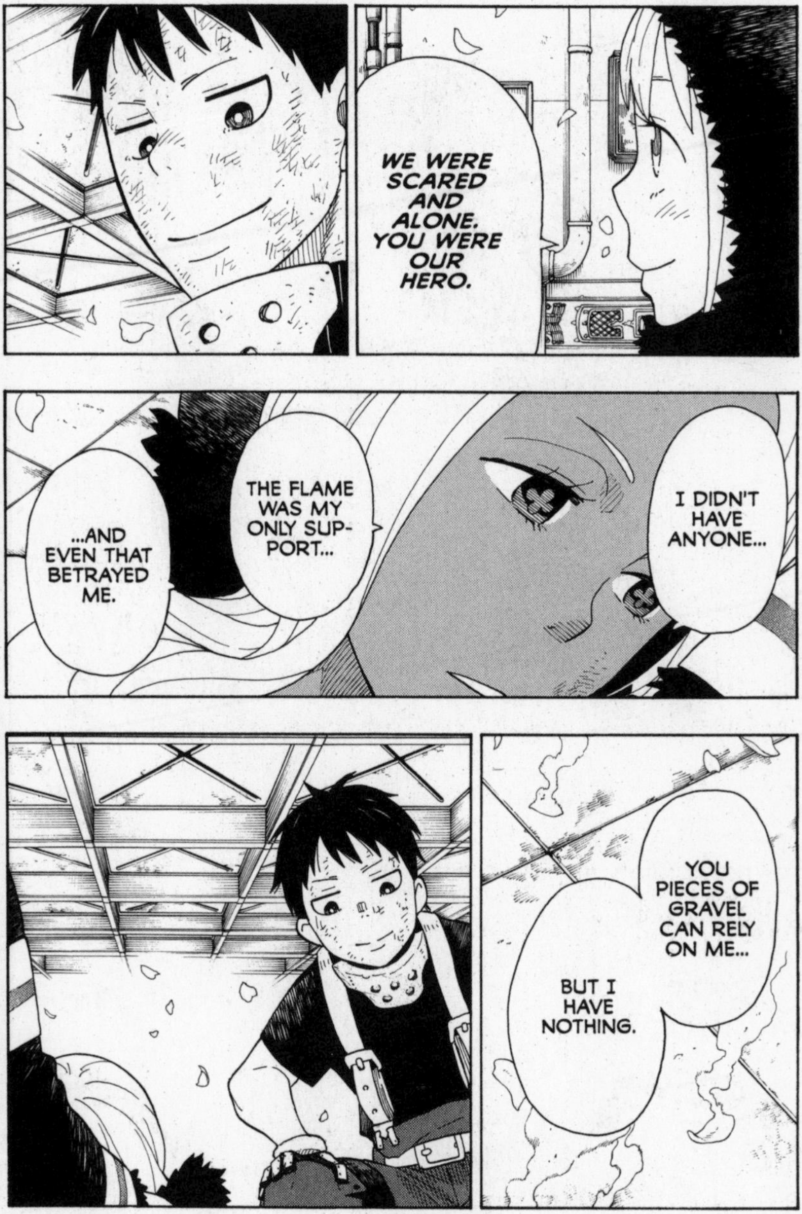
WE WERE SCARED AND ALONE. YOU WERE OUR HERO.
I DIDN'T HAVE ANYONE...
THE FLAME WAS MY ONLY SUP-PORT...
...AND EVEN THAT BETRAYED ME.
YOU PIECES OF GRAVEL CAN RELY ON ME...
BUT I HAVE NOTHING.

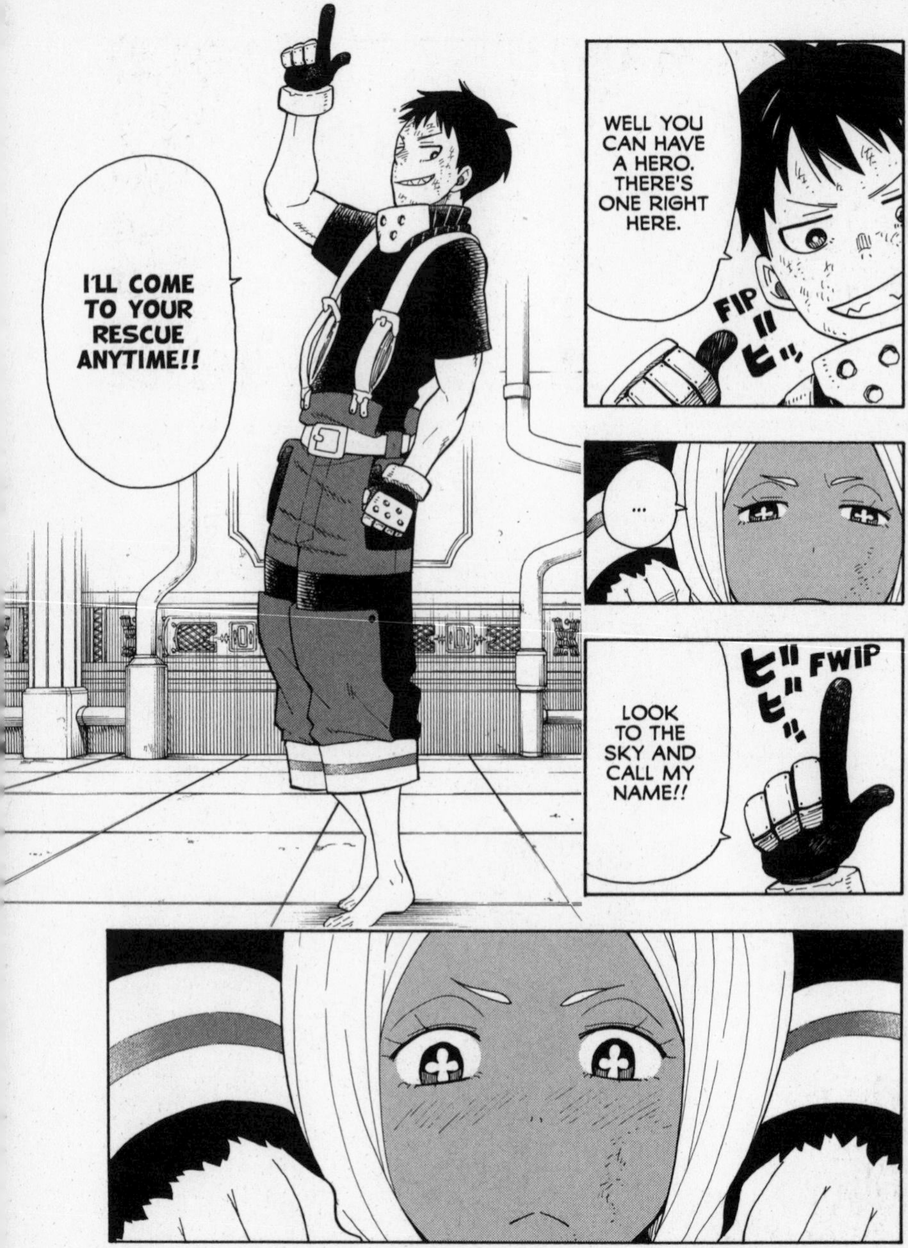
WELL YOU CAN HAVE A HERO. THERE'S ONE RIGHT HERE.
FIP
...
FWIP
LOOK TO THE SKY AND CALL MY NAME!!
I'LL COME TO YOUR RESCUE ANYTIME!!

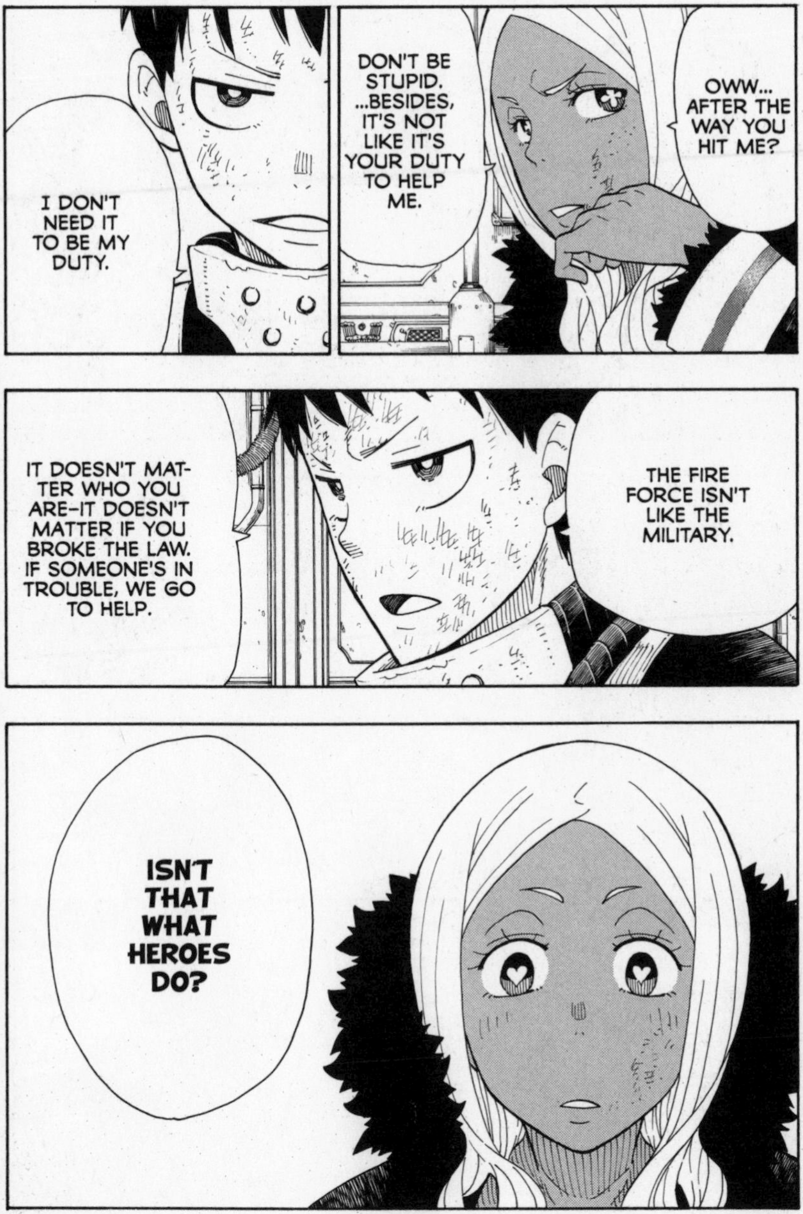
OWW... AFTER THE WAY YOU HIT ME?
DON'T BE STUPID. ...BESIDES, IT'S NOT LIKE IT'S YOUR DUTY TO HELP ME.
I DON'T NEED IT TO BE MY DUTY.
THE FIRE FORCE ISN'T LIKE THE MILITARY.
IT DOESN'T MAT-TER WHO YOU ARE–IT DOESN'T MATTER IF YOU BROKE THE LAW. IF SOMEONE'S IN TROUBLE, WE GO TO HELP.
ISN'T THAT WHAT HEROES DO?

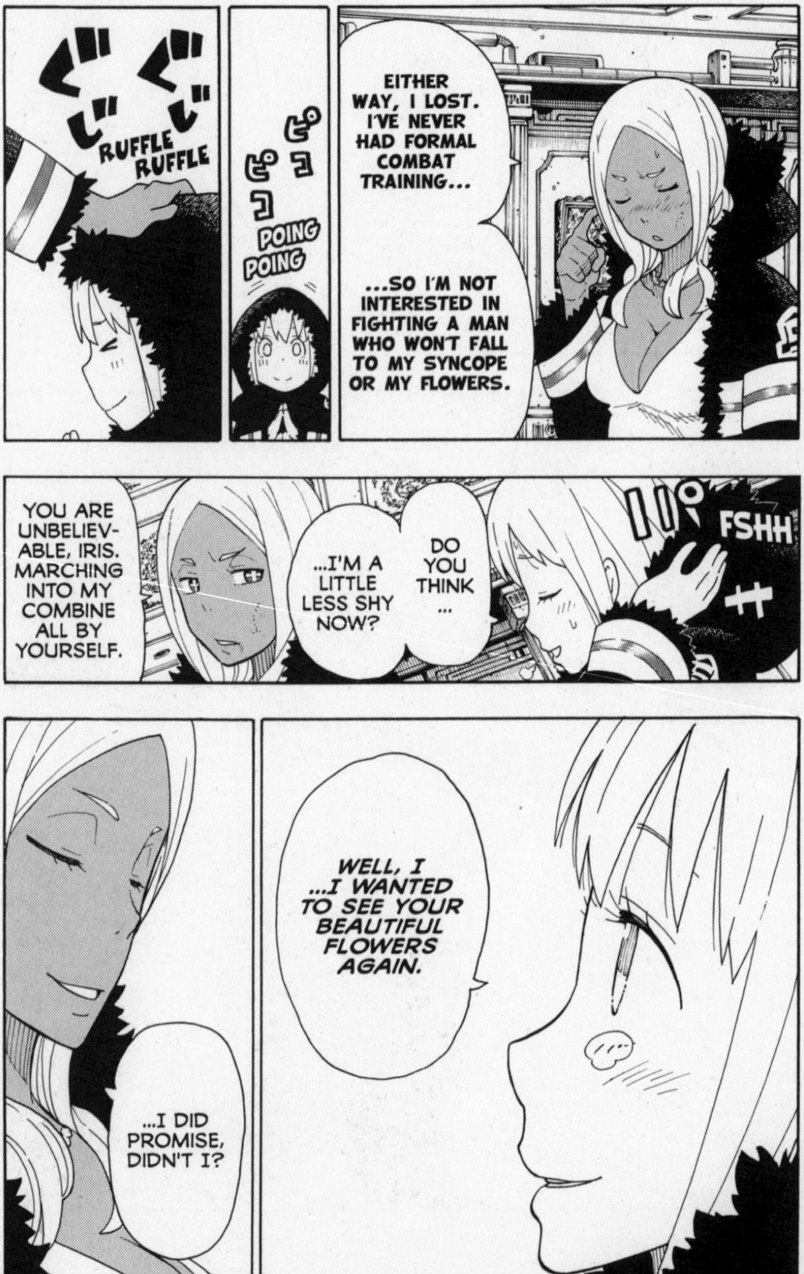
EITHER WAY, I LOST. I'VE NEVER HAD FORMAL COMBAT TRAINING...
...SO I'M NOT INTERESTED IN FIGHTING A MAN WHO WON'T FALL TO MY SYNCOPE OR MY FLOWERS.
ピョコ ピョコ
POING POING
RUFFLE RUFFLE
FSHH
DO YOU THINK ...
...I'M A LITTLE LESS SHY NOW?
YOU ARE UNBELIEV-ABLE, IRIS. MARCHING INTO MY COMBINE ALL BY YOURSELF.
WELL, I ...I WANTED TO SEE YOUR BEAUTIFUL FLOWERS AGAIN.
...I DID PROMISE, DIDN'T I?

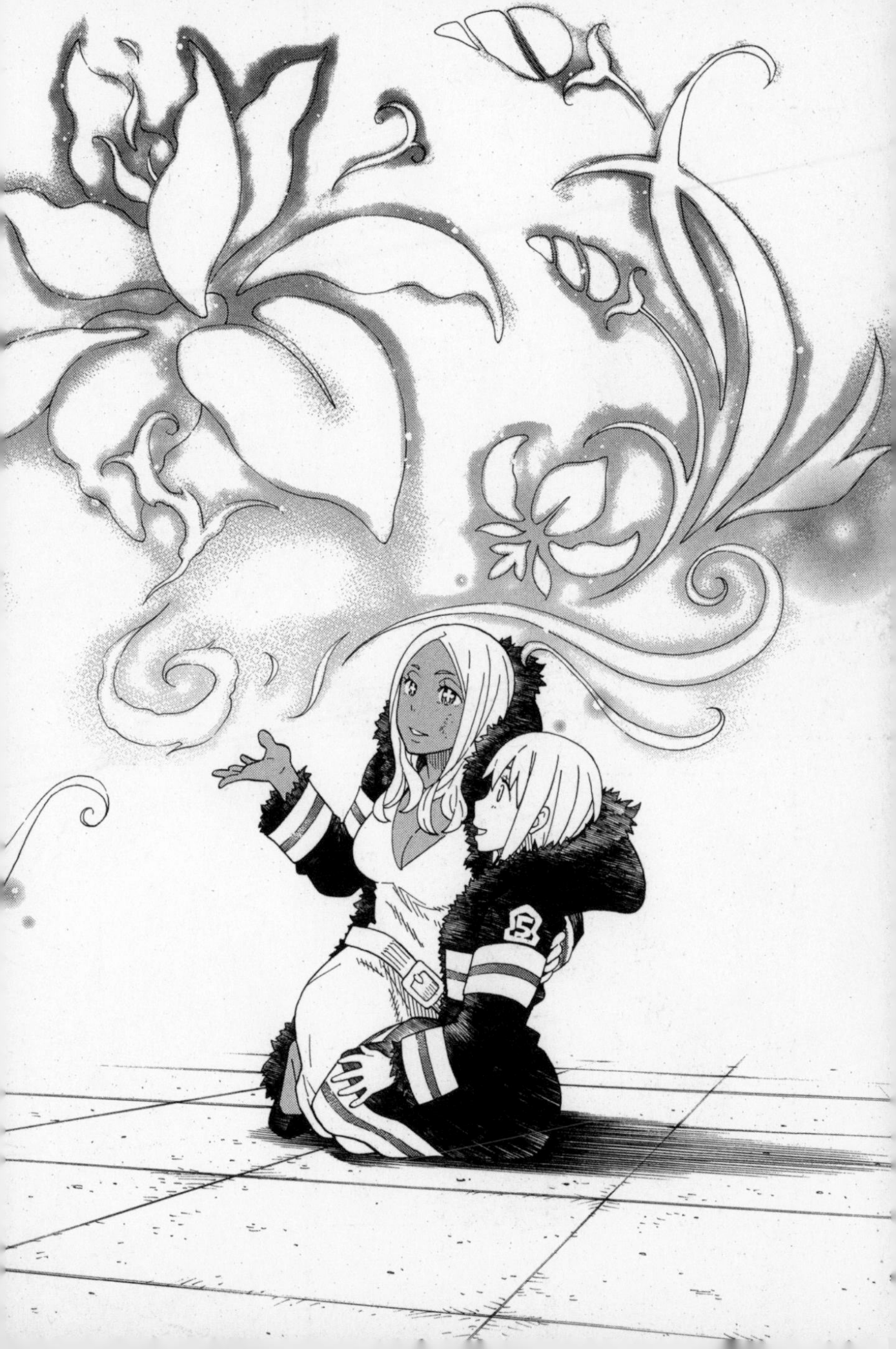

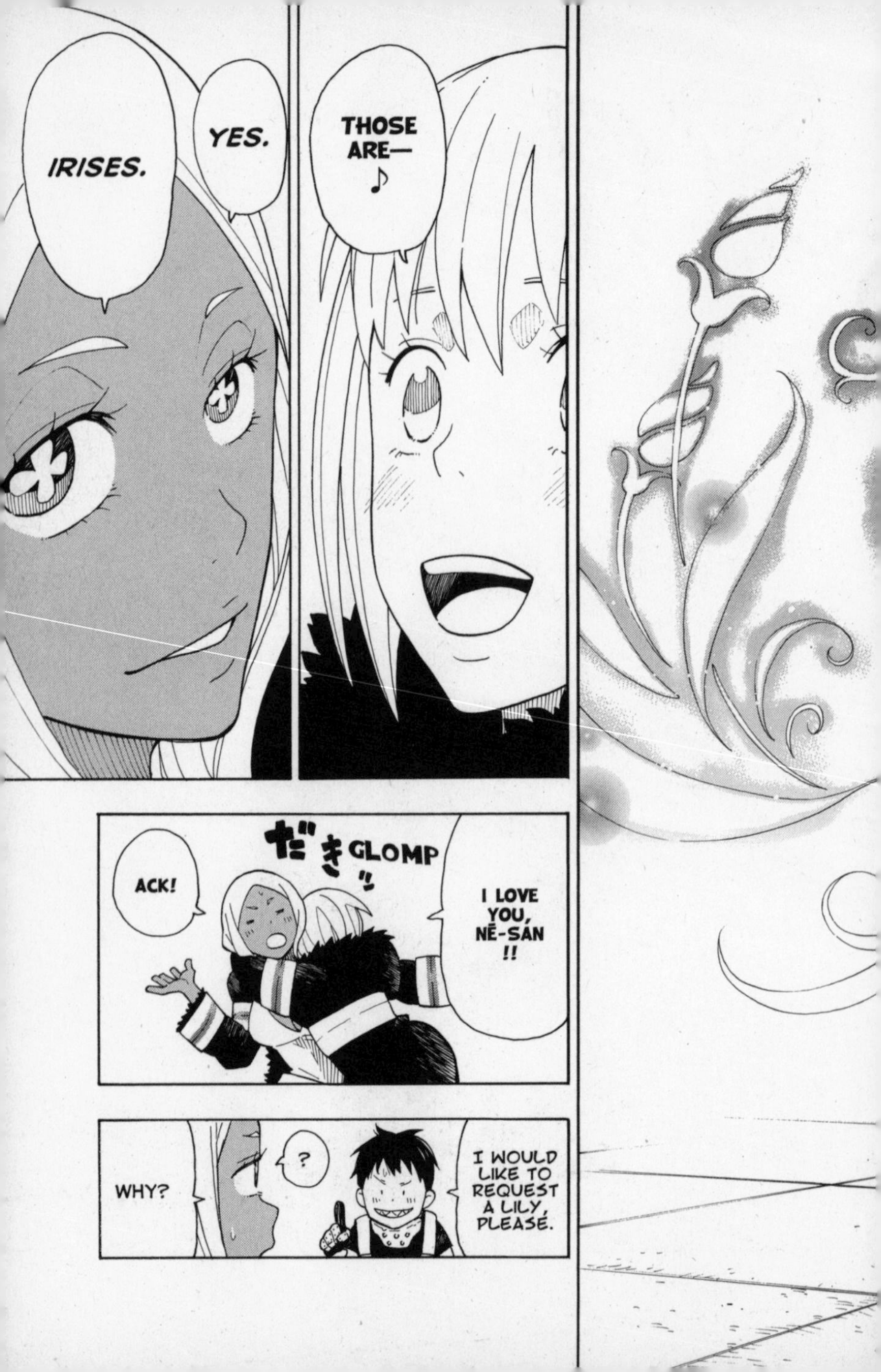
THOSE ARE—♪
YES.
IRISES.
I LOVE YOU, NĒ-SAN!!
だき GLOMP
ACK!
I WOULD LIKE TO REQUEST A LILY, PLEASE.
?
WHY?

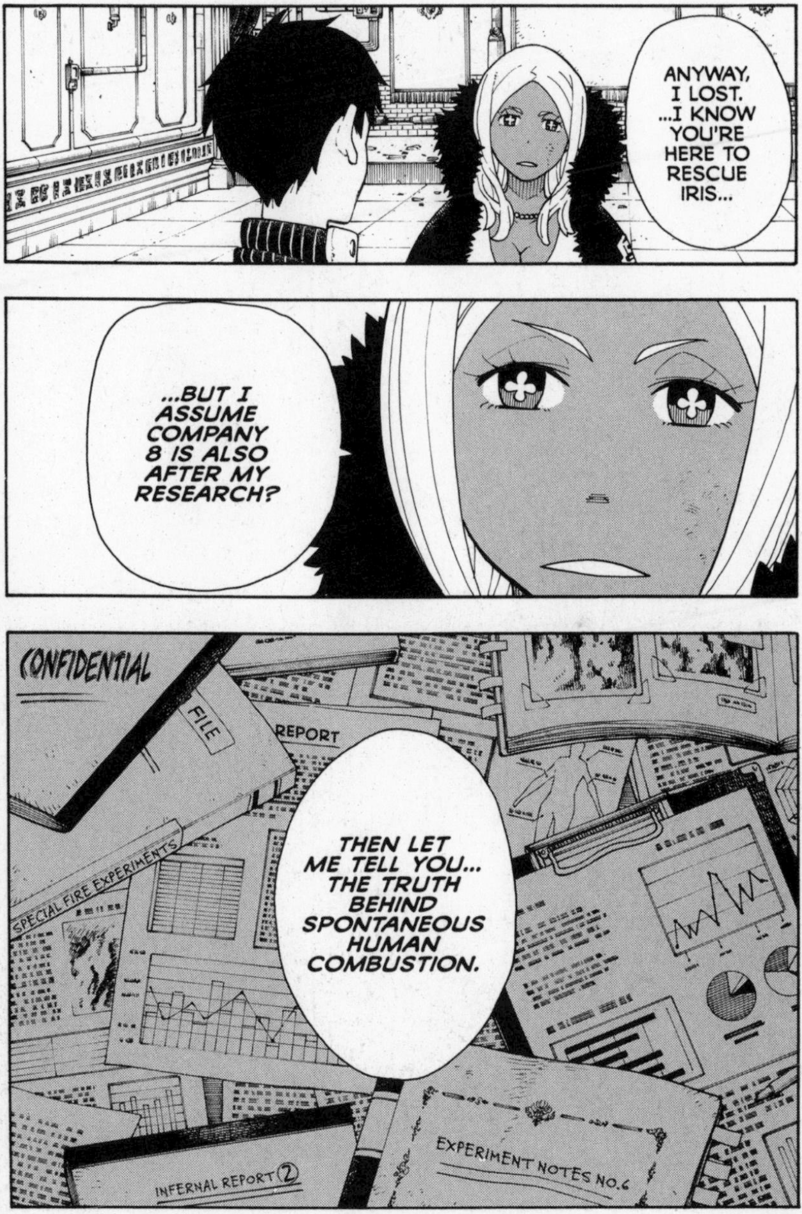
ANYWAY, I LOST. ...I KNOW YOU'RE HERE TO RESCUE IRIS...
...BUT I ASSUME COMPANY 8 IS ALSO AFTER MY RESEARCH?
CONFIDENTIAL
FILE
REPORT
THEN LET ME TELL YOU... THE TRUTH BEHIND SPONTANEOUS HUMAN COMBUSTION.
SPECIAL FIRE EXPERIMENTS
INFERNAL REPORT ②
EXPERIMENT NOTES NO.6

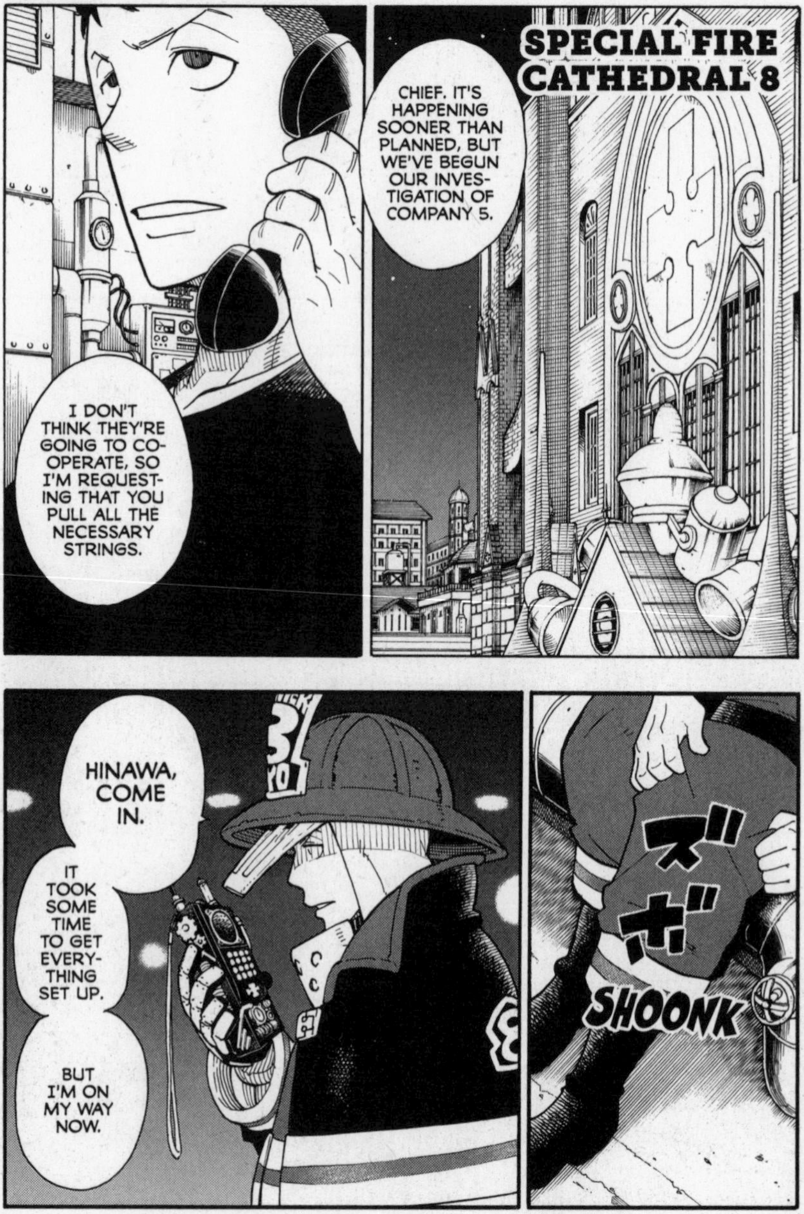
SPECIAL FIRE CATHEDRAL 8
CHIEF. IT'S HAPPENING SOONER THAN PLANNED, BUT WE'VE BEGUN OUR INVESTIGATION OF COMPANY 5.
I DON'T THINK THEY'RE GOING TO COOPERATE, SO I'M REQUESTING THAT YOU PULL ALL THE NECESSARY STRINGS.
ズボ
SHOONK
HINAWA, COME IN.
IT TOOK SOME TIME TO GET EVERYTHING SET UP.
BUT I'M ON MY WAY NOW.

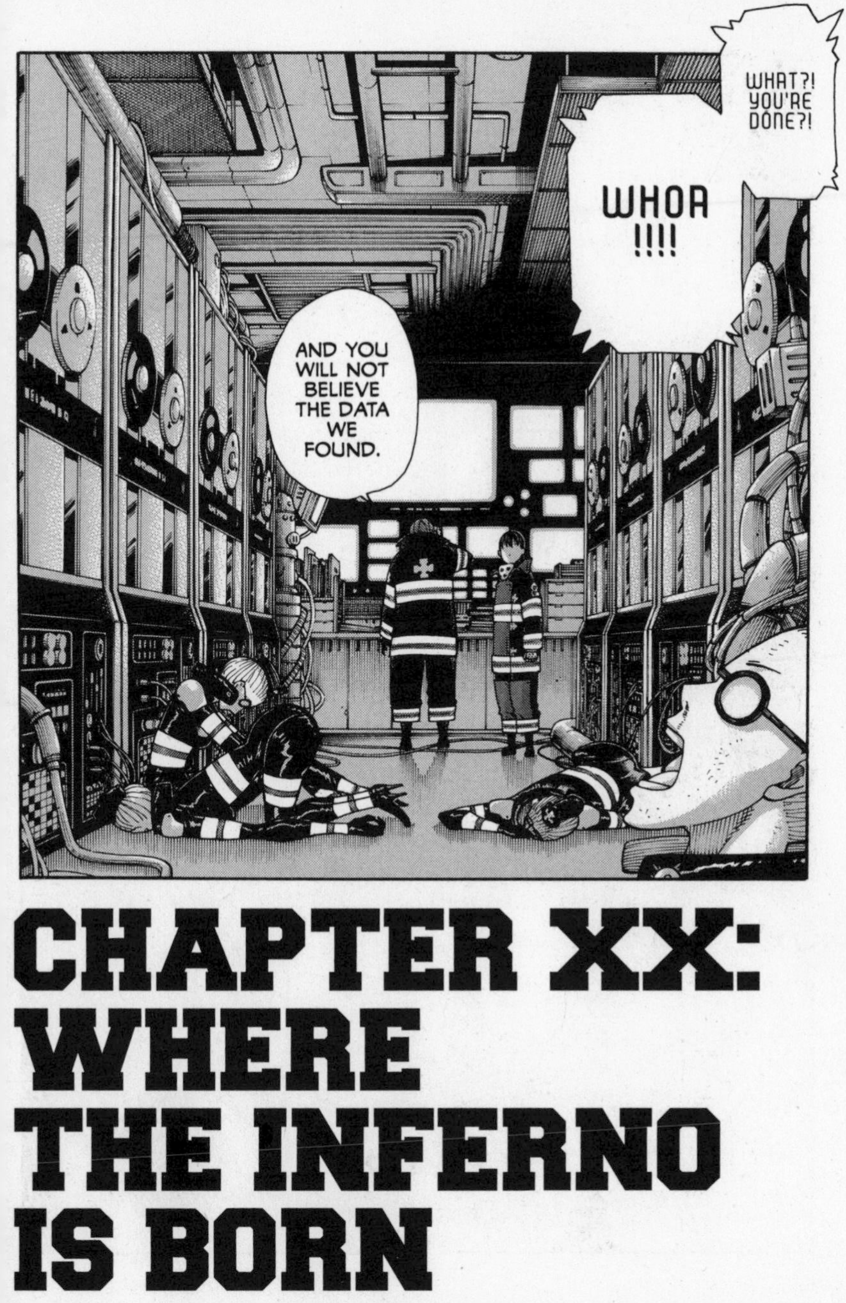
WHAT?! YOU'RE DONE?!
WHOA !!!!
AND YOU WILL NOT BELIEVE THE DATA WE FOUND.

CHAPTER XX: WHERE THE INFERNO IS BORN

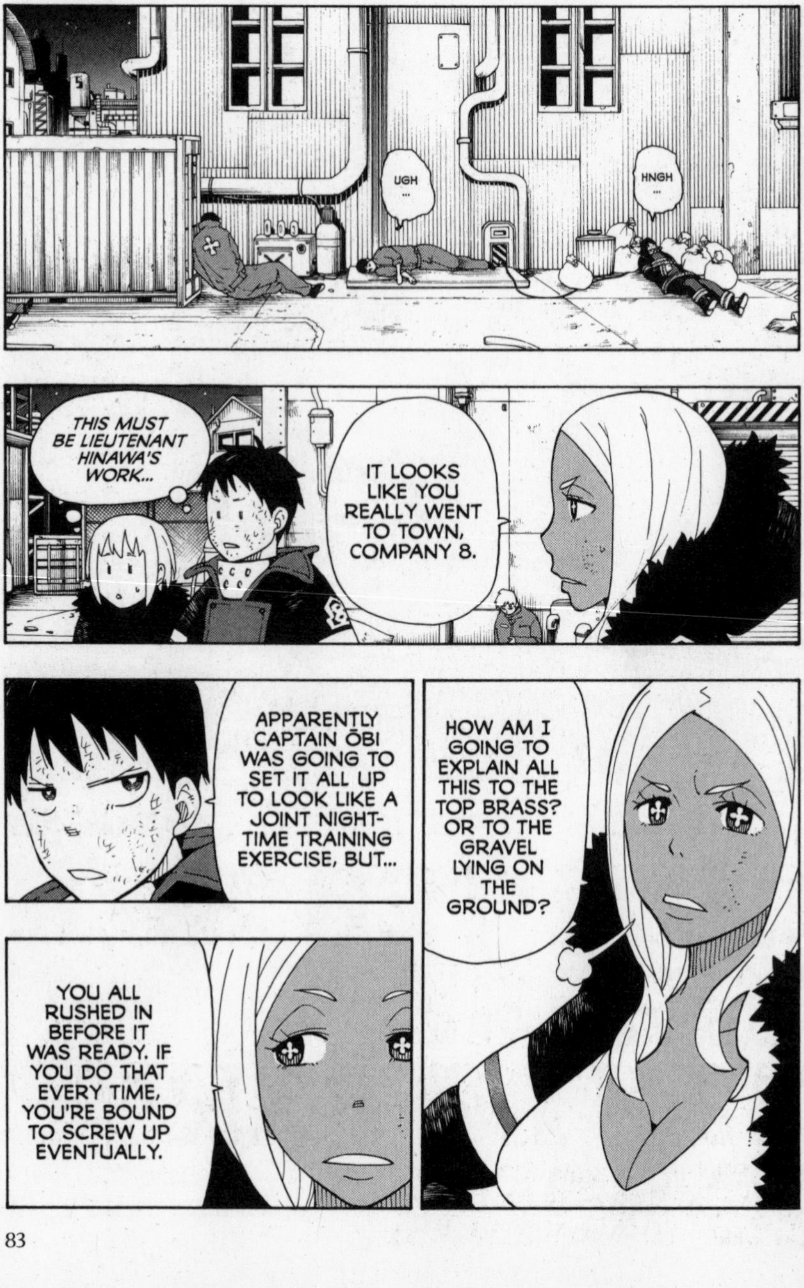
HNGH ...
UGH ...
IT LOOKS LIKE YOU REALLY WENT TO TOWN, COMPANY 8.
THIS MUST BE LIEUTENANT HINAWA'S WORK...
HOW AM I GOING TO EXPLAIN ALL THIS TO THE TOP BRASS? OR TO THE GRAVEL LYING ON THE GROUND?
APPARENTLY CAPTAIN ŌBI WAS GOING TO SET IT ALL UP TO LOOK LIKE A JOINT NIGHT-TIME TRAINING EXERCISE, BUT...
YOU ALL RUSHED IN BEFORE IT WAS READY. IF YOU DO THAT EVERY TIME, YOU'RE BOUND TO SCREW UP EVENTUALLY.

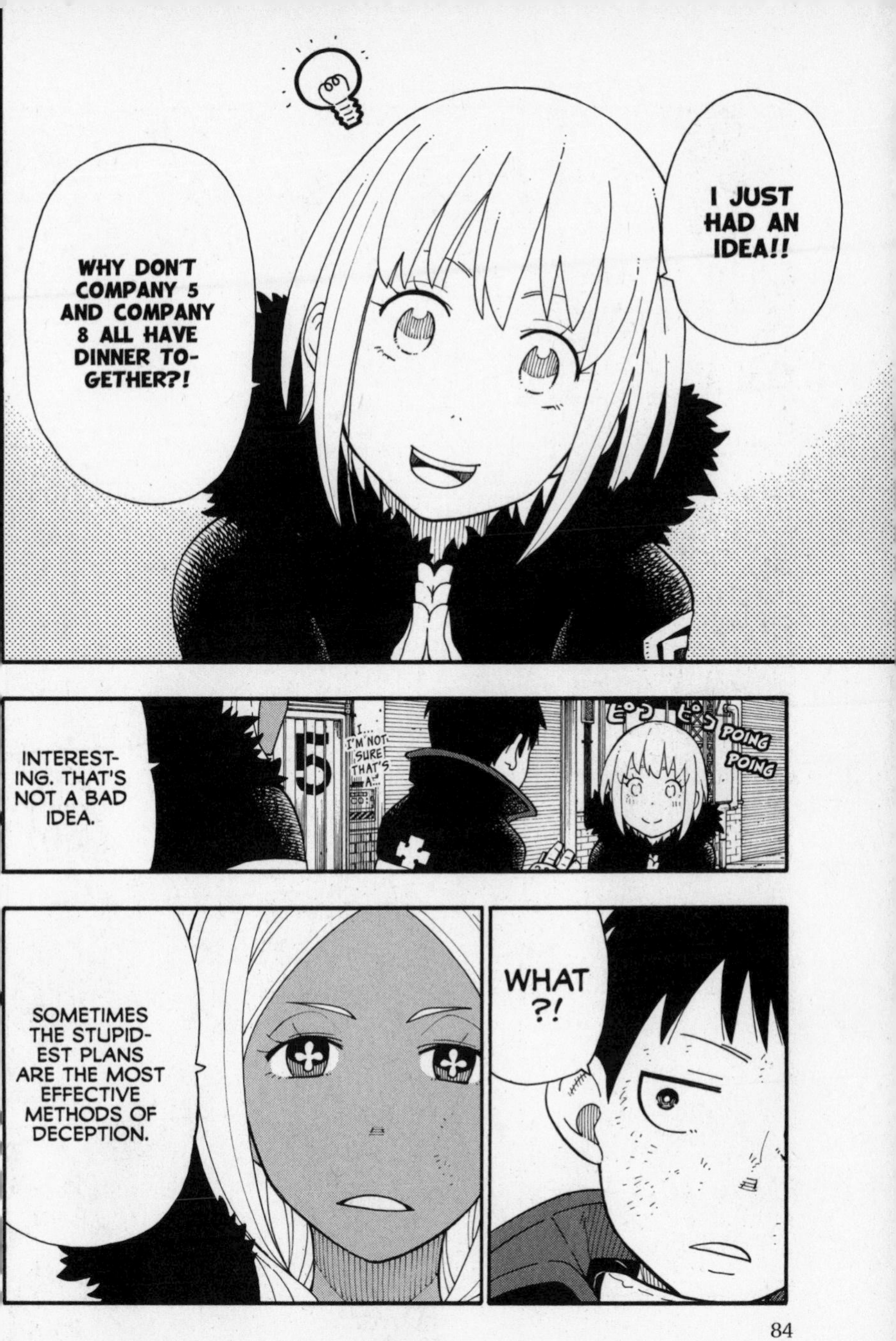
I JUST HAD AN IDEA!!
WHY DON'T COMPANY 5 AND COMPANY 8 ALL HAVE DINNER TO-GETHER?!
POING POING
I... I'M NOT SURE THAT'S A...
INTEREST-ING. THAT'S NOT A BAD IDEA.
WHAT?!
SOMETIMES THE STUPID-EST PLANS ARE THE MOST EFFECTIVE METHODS OF DECEPTION.

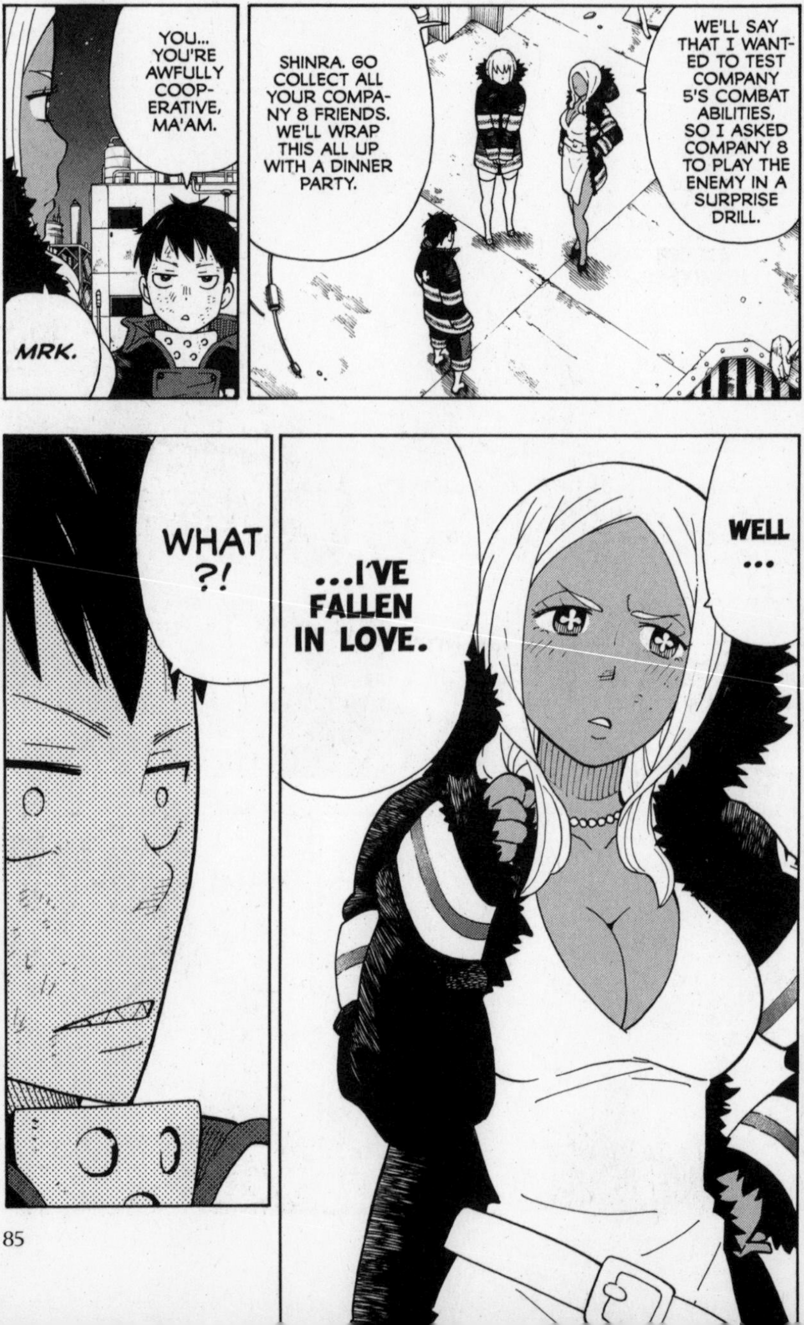
WE'LL SAY THAT I WANTED TO TEST COMPANY 5'S COMBAT ABILITIES, SO I ASKED COMPANY 8 TO PLAY THE ENEMY IN A SURPRISE DRILL.
SHINRA. GO COLLECT ALL YOUR COMPANY 8 FRIENDS. WE'LL WRAP THIS ALL UP WITH A DINNER PARTY.
YOU... YOU'RE AWFULLY COOPERATIVE, MA'AM.
MRK.
WELL...
...I'VE FALLEN IN LOVE.
WHAT?!

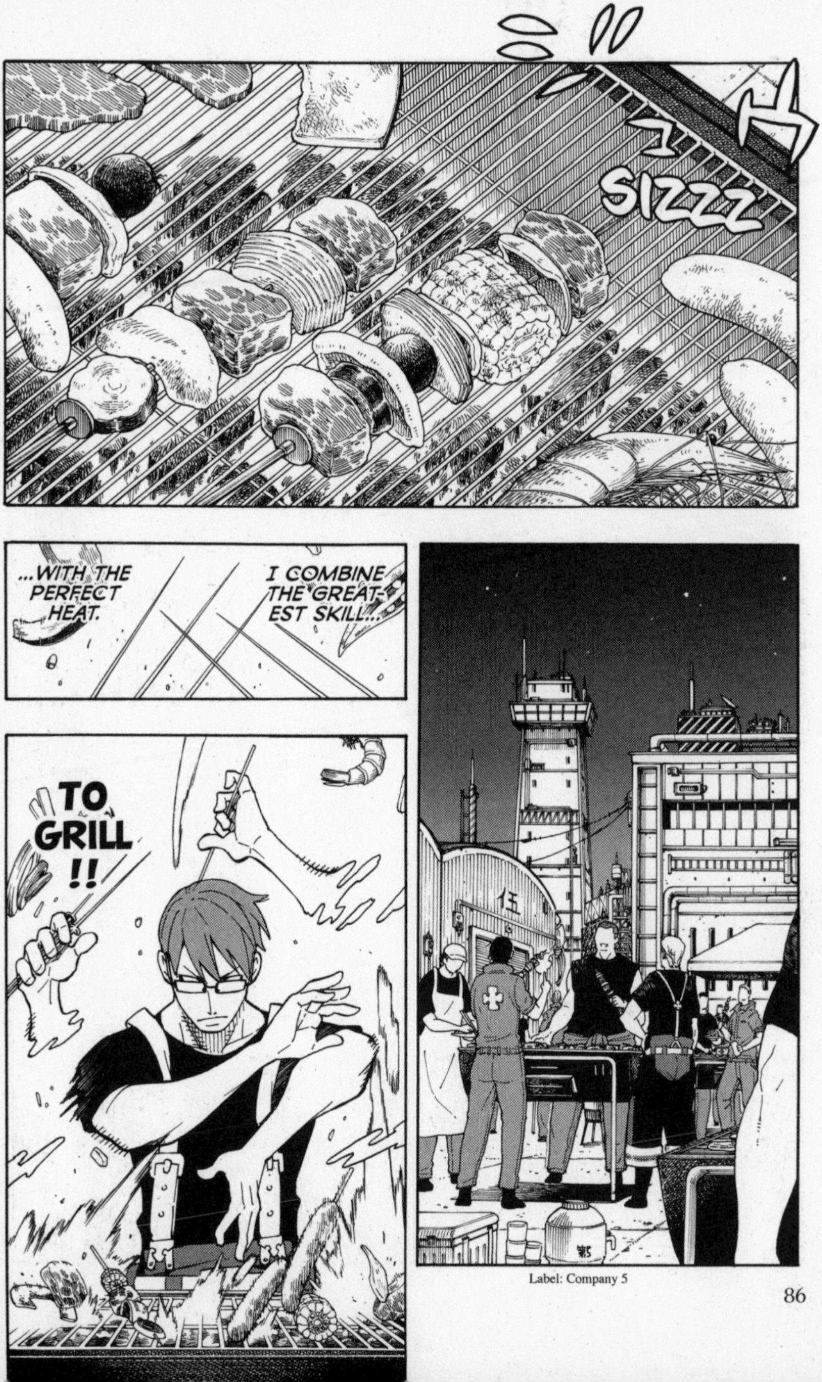
SIZZZ
I COMBINE THE GREATEST SKILL...
...WITH THE PERFECT HEAT.
TO GRILL!!
Label: Company 5

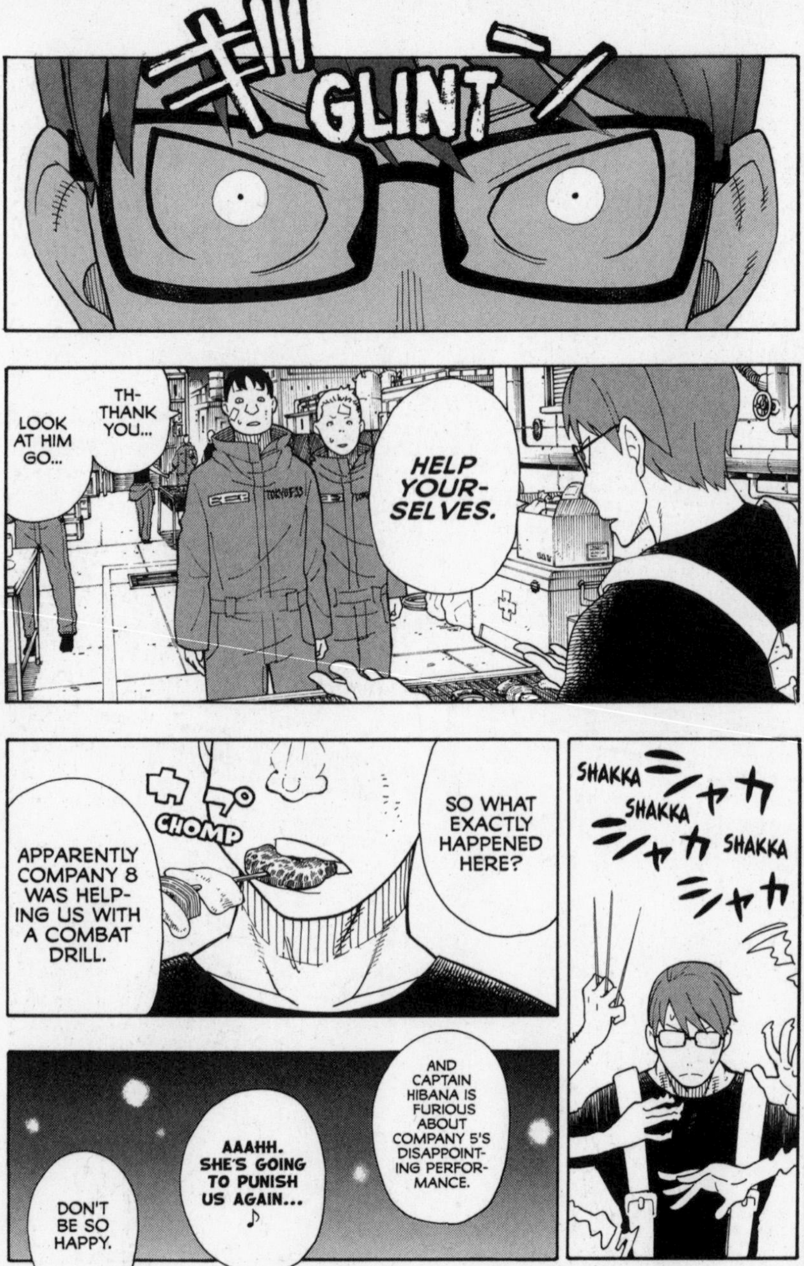
GLINT
HELP YOURSELVES.
TH-THANK YOU...
LOOK AT HIM GO...
SHAKKA
SHAKKA
SHAKKA
SO WHAT EXACTLY HAPPENED HERE?
CHOMP
APPARENTLY COMPANY 8 WAS HELPING US WITH A COMBAT DRILL.
AND CAPTAIN HIBANA IS FURIOUS ABOUT COMPANY 5'S DISAPPOINTING PERFORMANCE.
AAAHH. SHE'S GOING TO PUNISH US AGAIN... ♪
DON'T BE SO HAPPY.

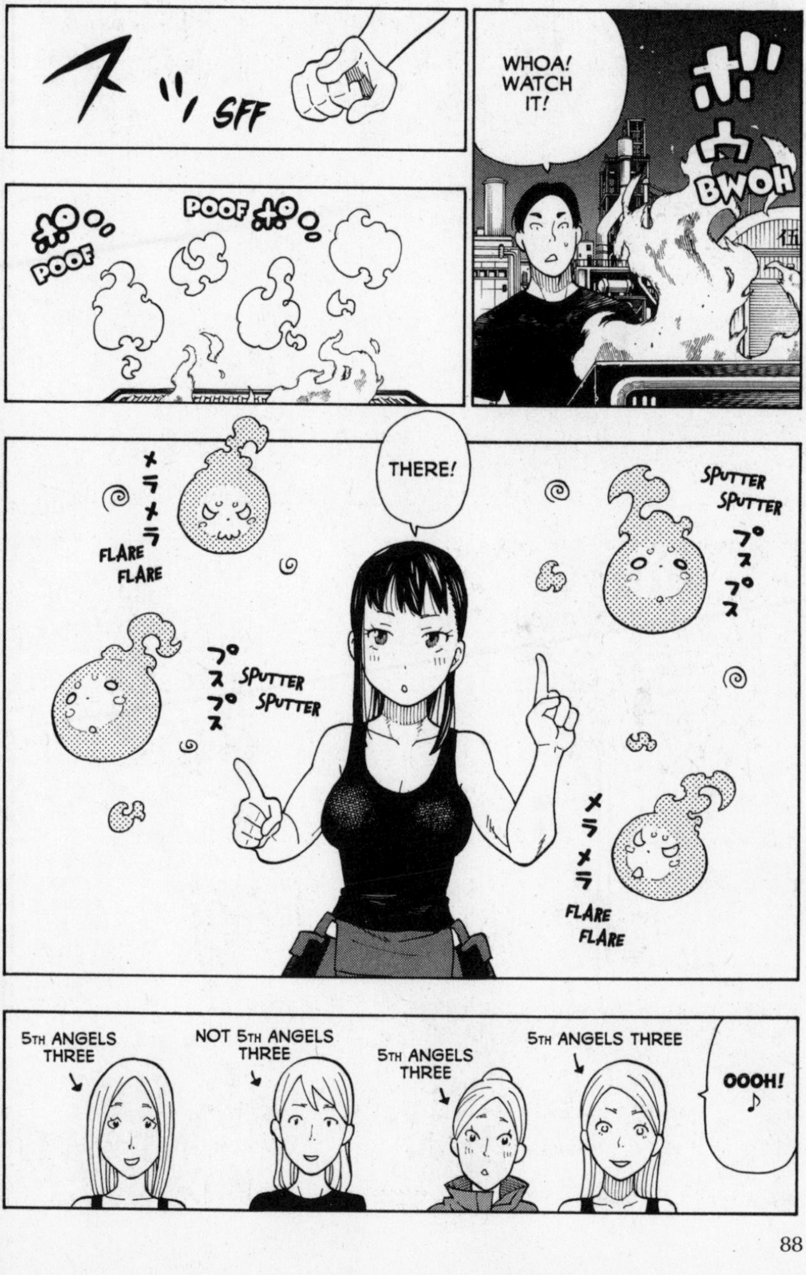
WHOA! WATCH IT!
BWOH
SFF
POOF
POOF
THERE!
SPUTTER SPUTTER
プスプス
メラメラ
FLARE FLARE
プスプス
SPUTTER SPUTTER
メラメラ
FLARE FLARE
OOOH! ♪
5TH ANGELS THREE
5TH ANGELS THREE
NOT 5TH ANGELS THREE
5TH ANGELS THREE

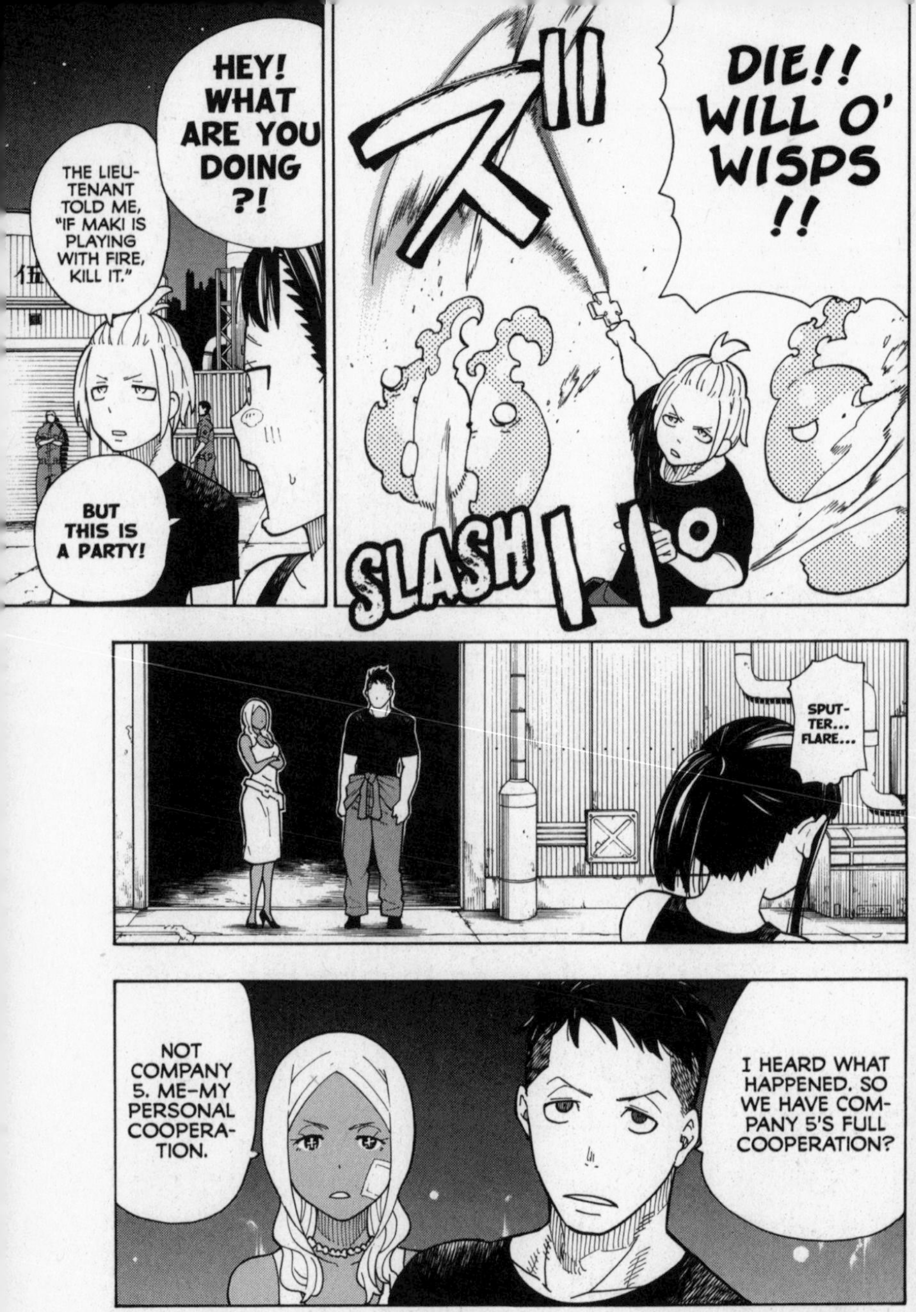
DIE!! WILL O' WISPS !!
ズ
SLASH
HEY! WHAT ARE YOU DOING ?!
THE LIEU-TENANT TOLD ME, "IF MAKI IS PLAYING WITH FIRE, KILL IT."
BUT THIS IS A PARTY!
SPUT-TER... FLARE...
I HEARD WHAT HAPPENED. SO WE HAVE COMPANY 5'S FULL COOPERATION?
NOT COMPANY 5. ME–MY PERSONAL COOPERA-TION.

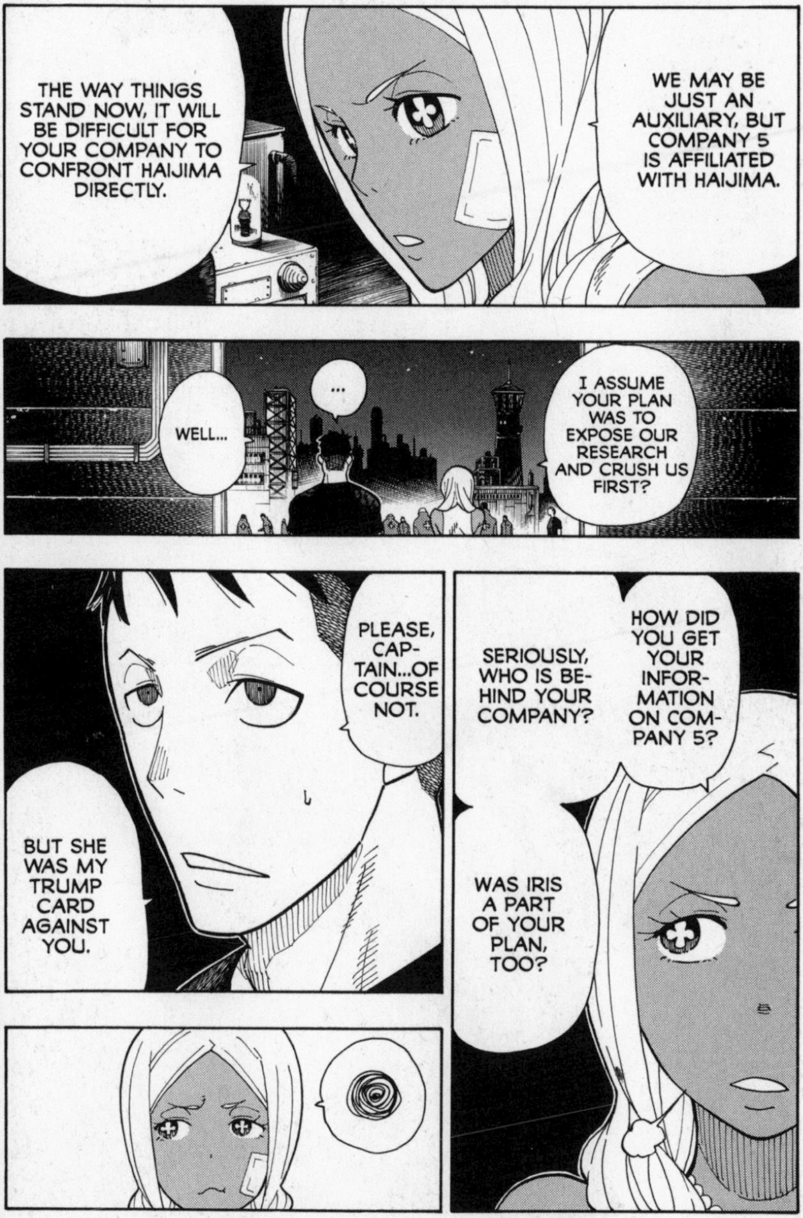
WE MAY BE JUST AN AUXILIARY, BUT COMPANY 5 IS AFFILIATED WITH HAIJIMA.
THE WAY THINGS STAND NOW, IT WILL BE DIFFICULT FOR YOUR COMPANY TO CONFRONT HAIJIMA DIRECTLY.
I ASSUME YOUR PLAN WAS TO EXPOSE OUR RESEARCH AND CRUSH US FIRST?
...
WELL...
HOW DID YOU GET YOUR INFORMATION ON COMPANY 5?
SERIOUSLY, WHO IS BEHIND YOUR COMPANY?
WAS IRIS A PART OF YOUR PLAN, TOO?
PLEASE, CAPTAIN...OF COURSE NOT.
BUT SHE WAS MY TRUMP CARD AGAINST YOU.

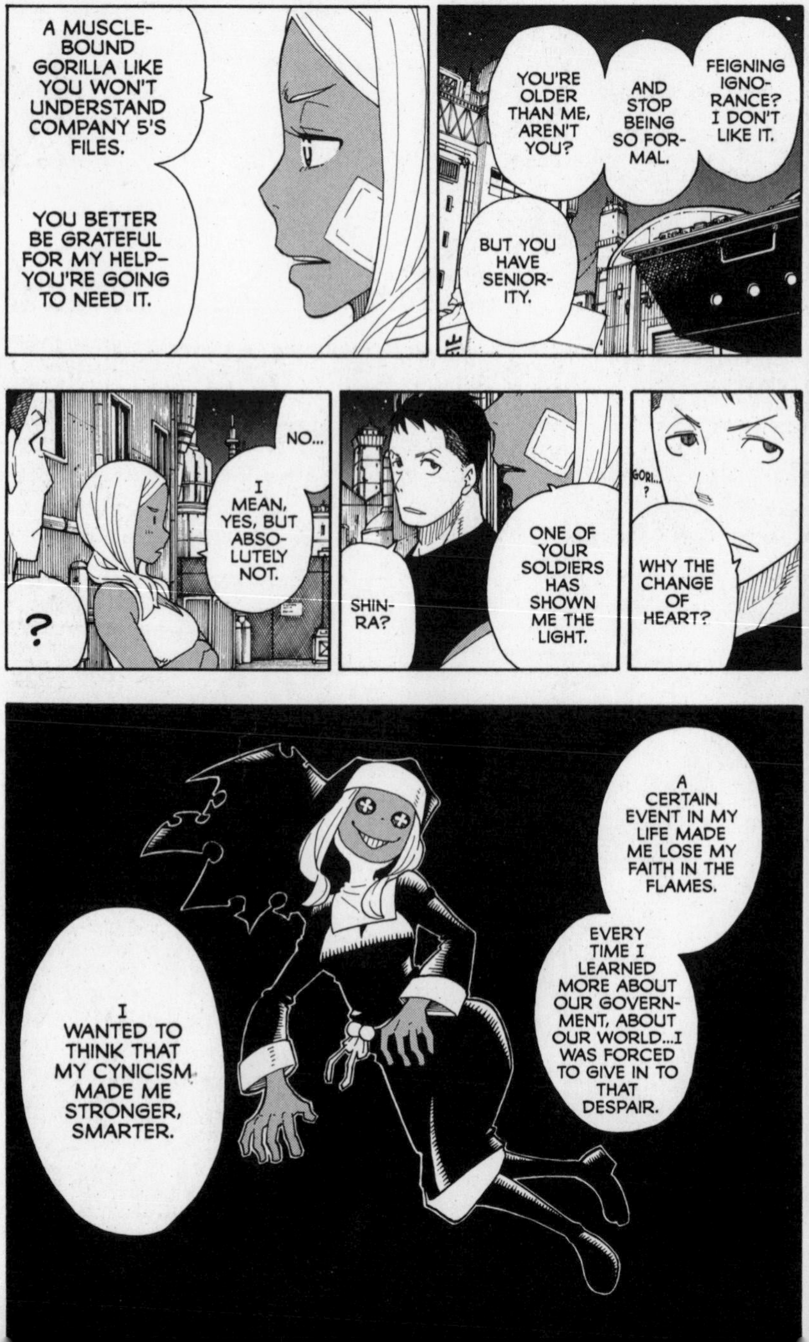

FEIGNING IGNORANCE? I DON'T LIKE IT.
AND STOP BEING SO FORMAL.
YOU'RE OLDER THAN ME, AREN'T YOU?
BUT YOU HAVE SENIORITY.
A MUSCLE-BOUND GORILLA LIKE YOU WON'T UNDERSTAND COMPANY 5'S FILES.
YOU BETTER BE GRATEFUL FOR MY HELP–YOU'RE GOING TO NEED IT.
GORI...?
WHY THE CHANGE OF HEART?
ONE OF YOUR SOLDIERS HAS SHOWN ME THE LIGHT.
SHINRA?
NO...
I MEAN, YES, BUT ABSOLUTELY NOT.
?
A CERTAIN EVENT IN MY LIFE MADE ME LOSE MY FAITH IN THE FLAMES.
EVERY TIME I LEARNED MORE ABOUT OUR GOVERNMENT, ABOUT OUR WORLD...I WAS FORCED TO GIVE IN TO THAT DESPAIR.
I WANTED TO THINK THAT MY CYNICISM MADE ME STRONGER, SMARTER.

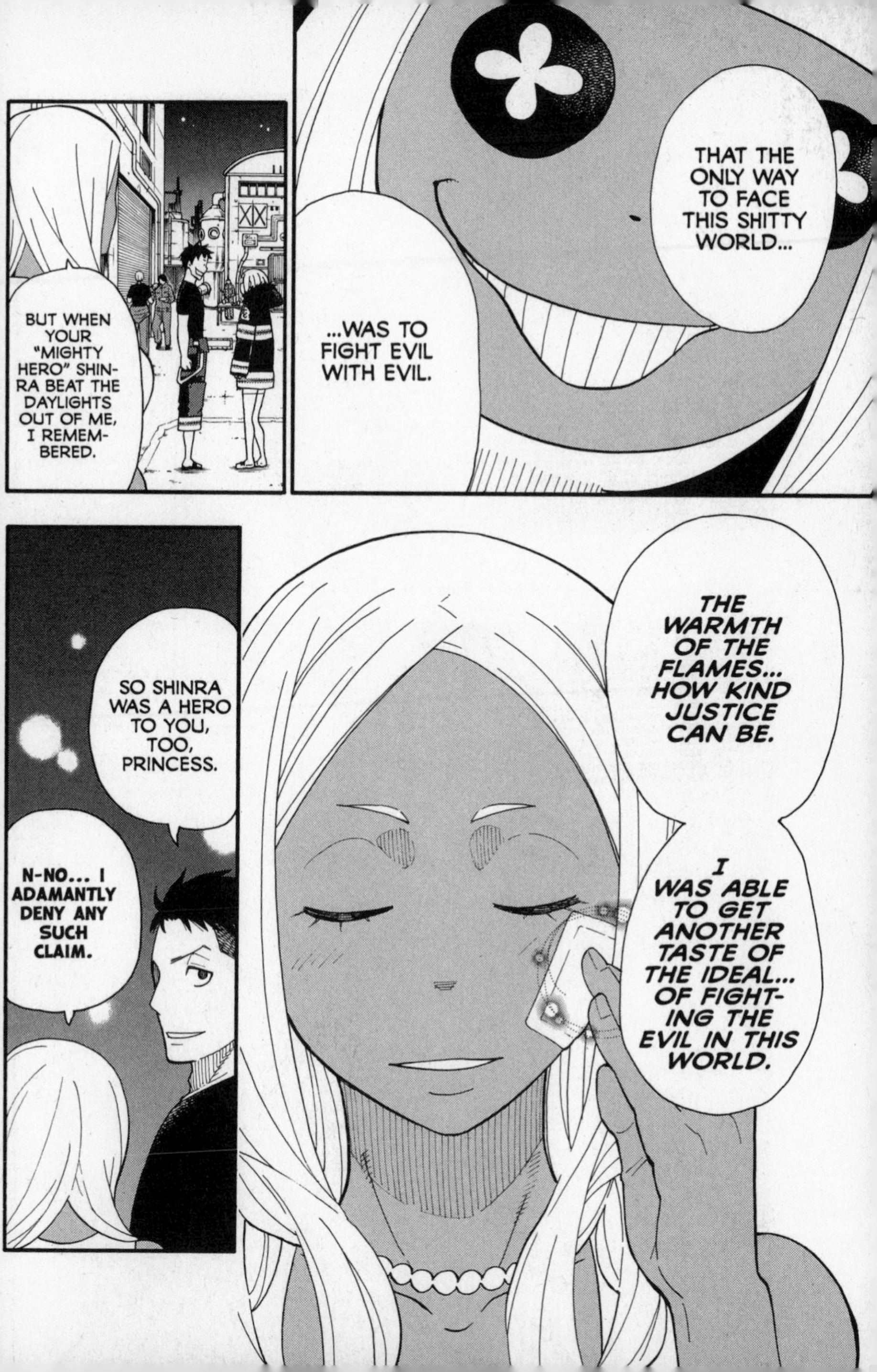
THAT THE ONLY WAY TO FACE THIS SHITTY WORLD...
...WAS TO FIGHT EVIL WITH EVIL.
BUT WHEN YOUR "MIGHTY HERO" SHINRA BEAT THE DAYLIGHTS OUT OF ME, I REMEMBERED.
THE WARMTH OF THE FLAMES... HOW KIND JUSTICE CAN BE.
I WAS ABLE TO GET ANOTHER TASTE OF THE IDEAL... OF FIGHTING THE EVIL IN THIS WORLD.
SO SHINRA WAS A HERO TO YOU, TOO, PRINCESS.
N-NO... I ADAMANTLY DENY ANY SUCH CLAIM.

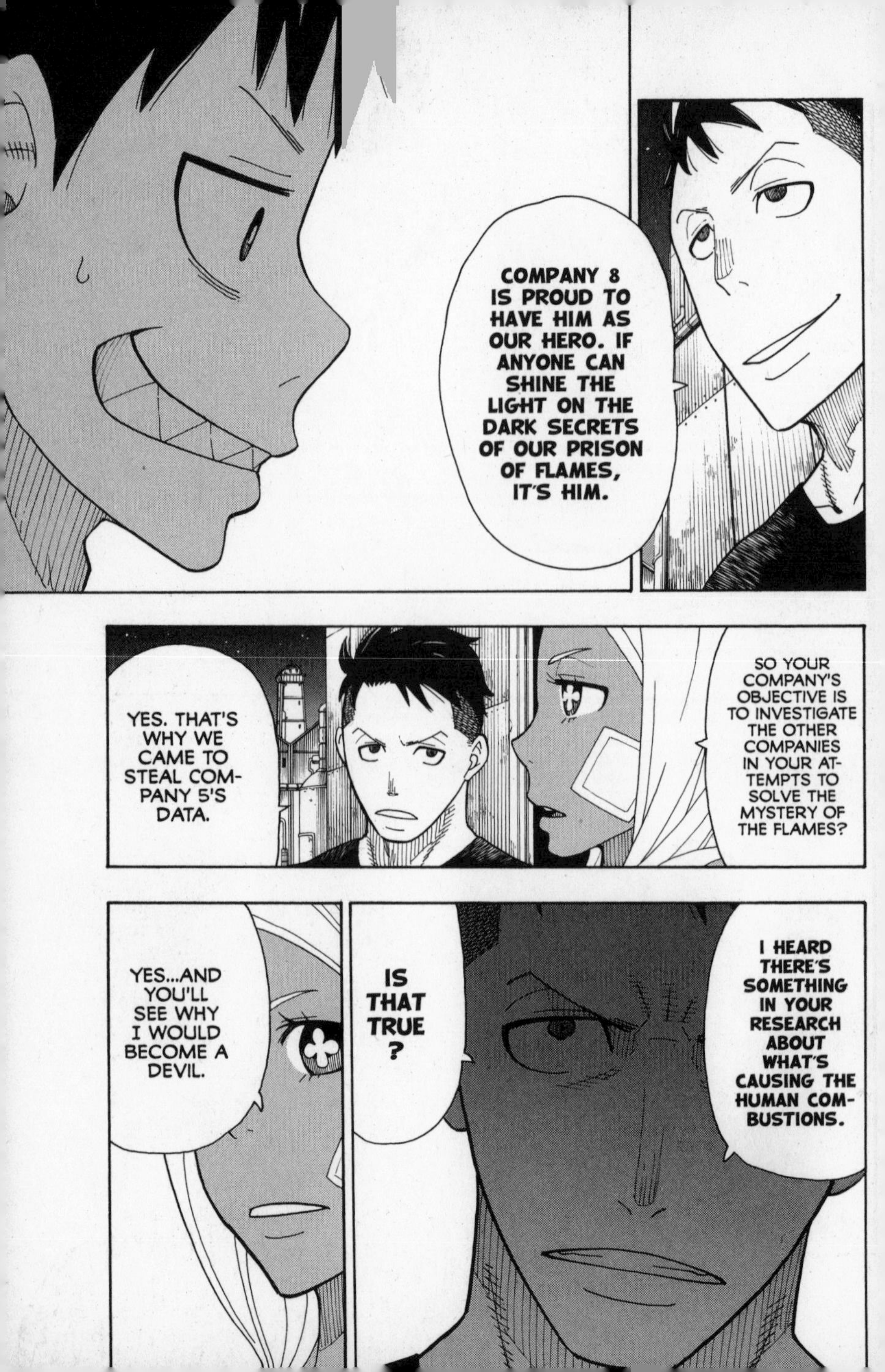
COMPANY 8 IS PROUD TO HAVE HIM AS OUR HERO. IF ANYONE CAN SHINE THE LIGHT ON THE DARK SECRETS OF OUR PRISON OF FLAMES, IT'S HIM.
SO YOUR COMPANY'S OBJECTIVE IS TO INVESTIGATE THE OTHER COMPANIES IN YOUR AT-TEMPTS TO SOLVE THE MYSTERY OF THE FLAMES?
YES. THAT'S WHY WE CAME TO STEAL COM-PANY 5'S DATA.
I HEARD THERE'S SOMETHING IN YOUR RESEARCH ABOUT WHAT'S CAUSING THE HUMAN COM-BUSTIONS.
IS THAT TRUE?
YES...AND YOU'LL SEE WHY I WOULD BECOME A DEVIL.

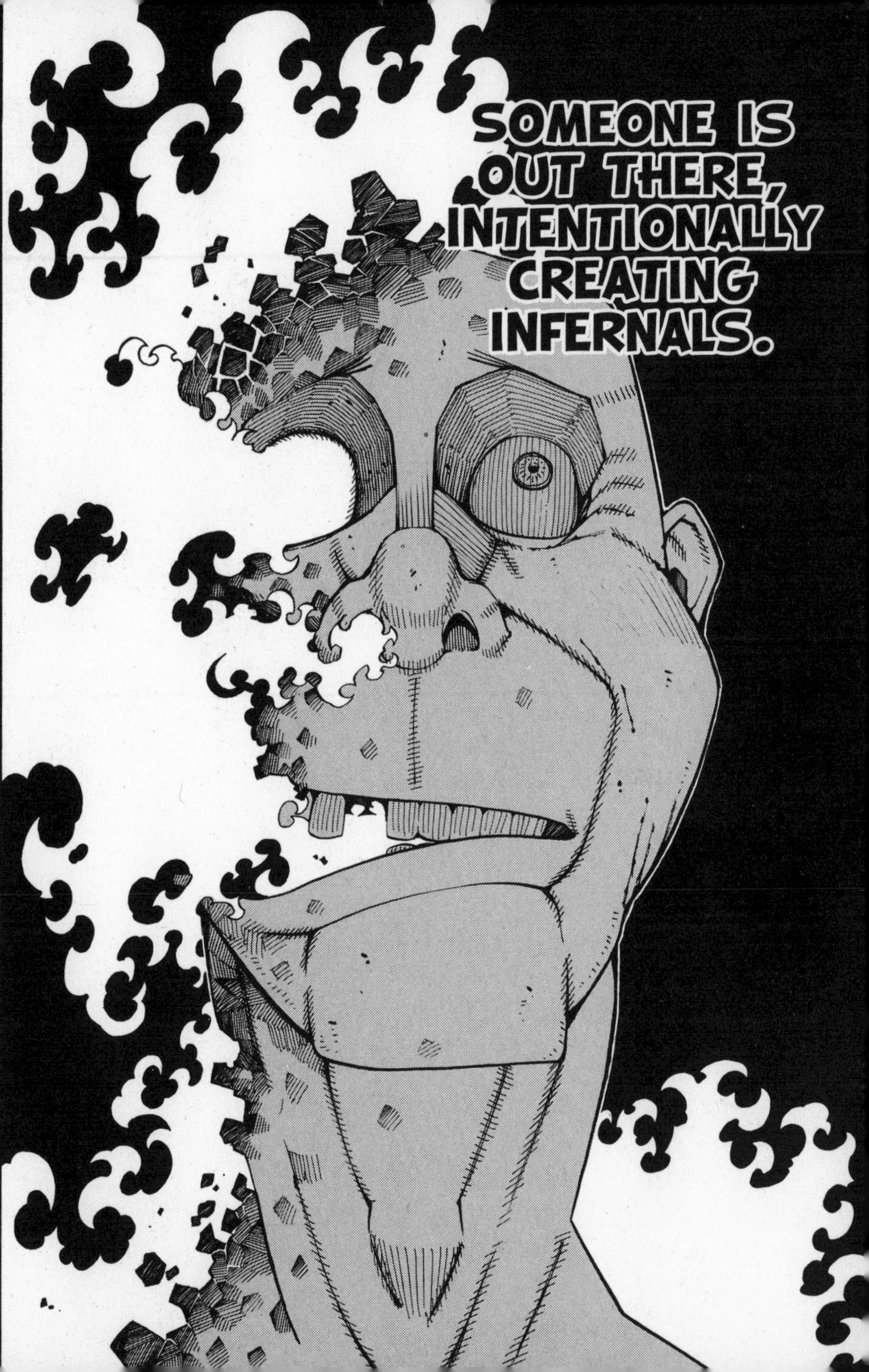
SOMEONE IS OUT THERE, INTENTIONALLY CREATING INFERNALS.

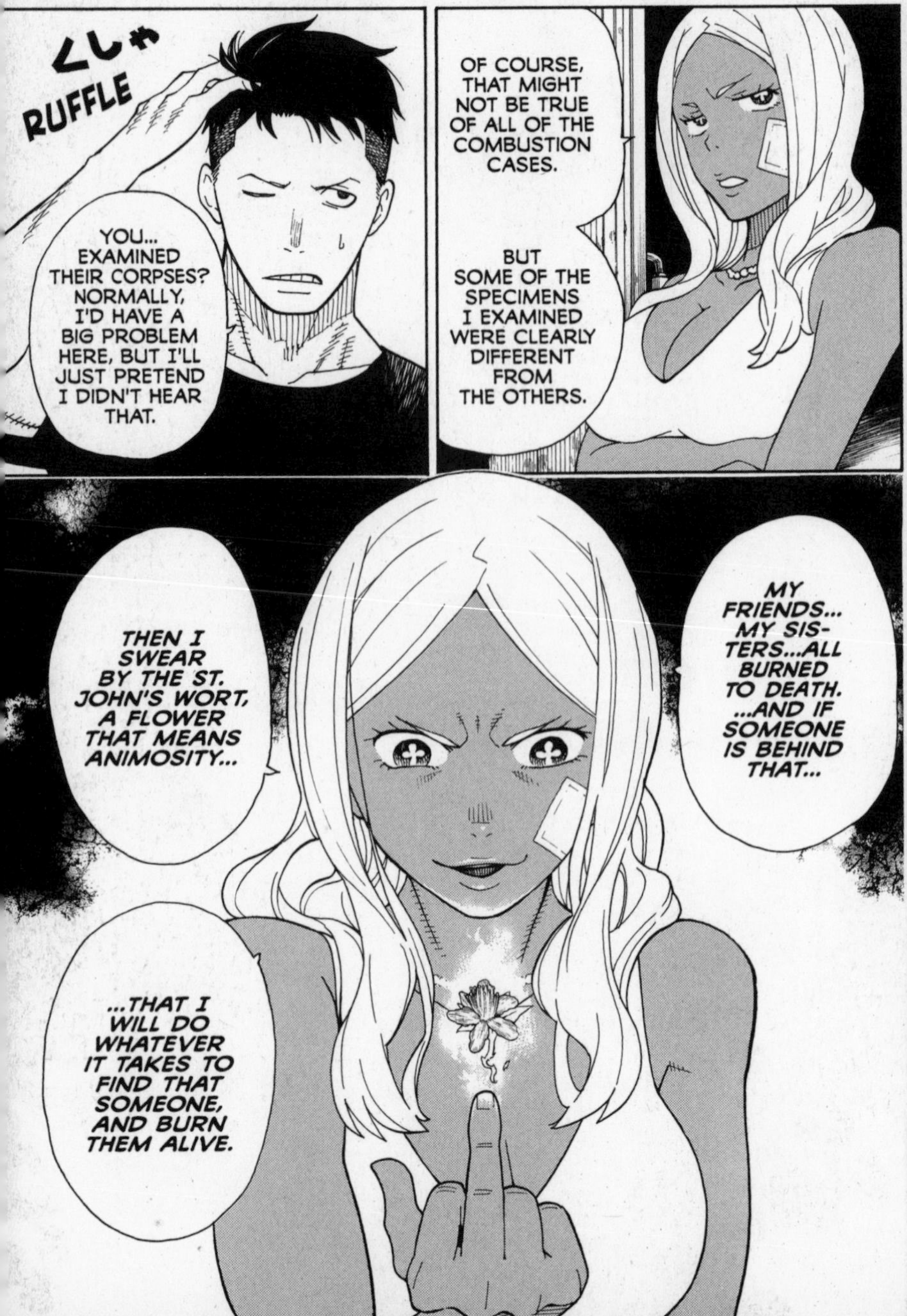
OF COURSE, THAT MIGHT NOT BE TRUE OF ALL OF THE COMBUSTION CASES.
BUT SOME OF THE SPECIMENS I EXAMINED WERE CLEARLY DIFFERENT FROM THE OTHERS.
くしゃ
RUFFLE
YOU... EXAMINED THEIR CORPSES? NORMALLY, I'D HAVE A BIG PROBLEM HERE, BUT I'LL JUST PRETEND I DIDN'T HEAR THAT.
MY FRIENDS... MY SISTERS...ALL BURNED TO DEATH. ...AND IF SOMEONE IS BEHIND THAT...
THEN I SWEAR BY THE ST. JOHN'S WORT, A FLOWER THAT MEANS ANIMOSITY...
...THAT I WILL DO WHATEVER IT TAKES TO FIND THAT SOMEONE, AND BURN THEM ALIVE.

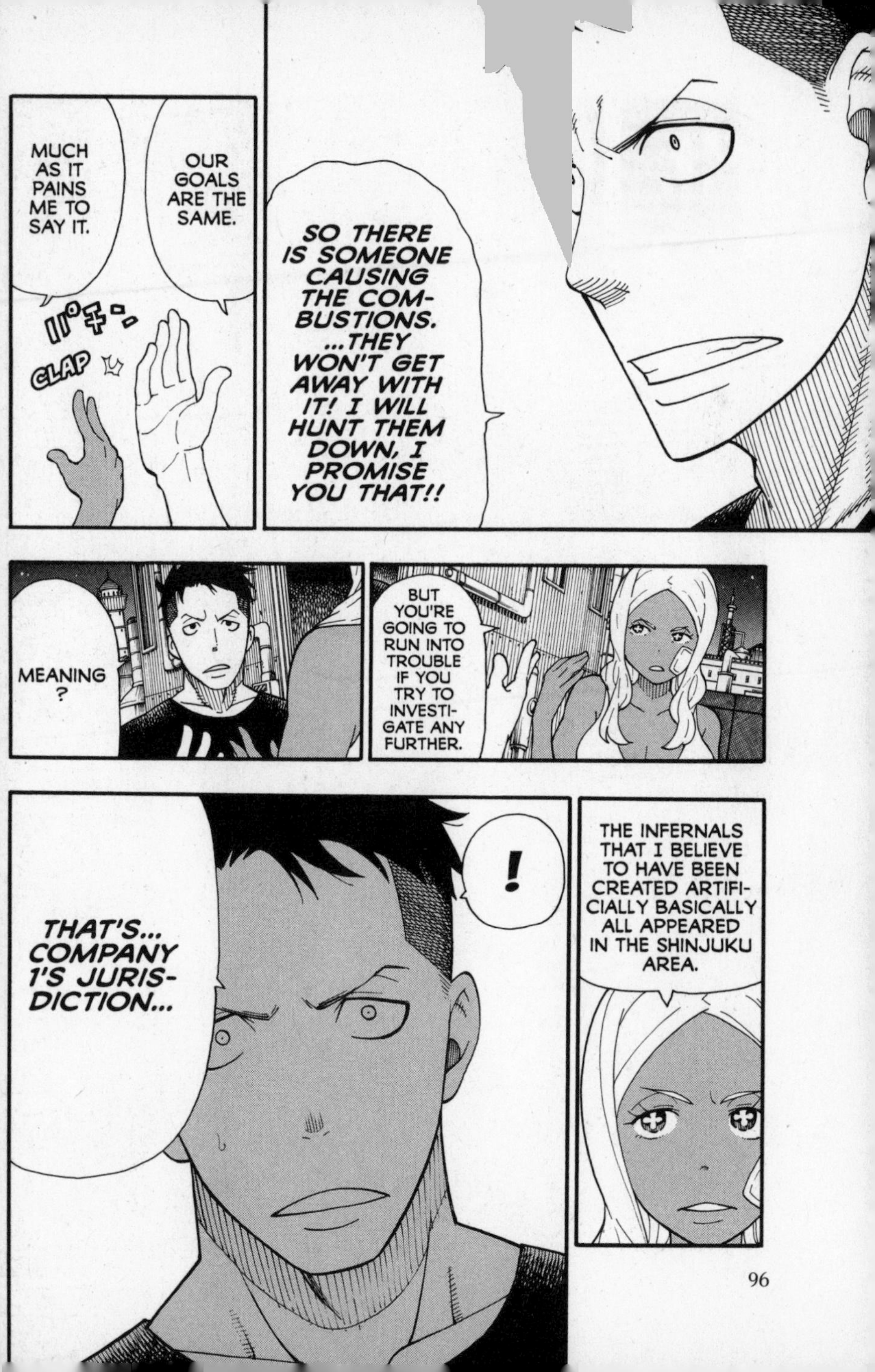
SO THERE IS SOMEONE CAUSING THE COMBUSTIONS. ...THEY WON'T GET AWAY WITH IT! I WILL HUNT THEM DOWN, I PROMISE YOU THAT!!
OUR GOALS ARE THE SAME.
MUCH AS IT PAINS ME TO SAY IT.
CLAP
BUT YOU'RE GOING TO RUN INTO TROUBLE IF YOU TRY TO INVESTIGATE ANY FURTHER.
MEANING?
THE INFERNALS THAT I BELIEVE TO HAVE BEEN CREATED ARTIFICIALLY BASICALLY ALL APPEARED IN THE SHINJUKU AREA.
!
THAT'S... COMPANY 1'S JURISDICTION...

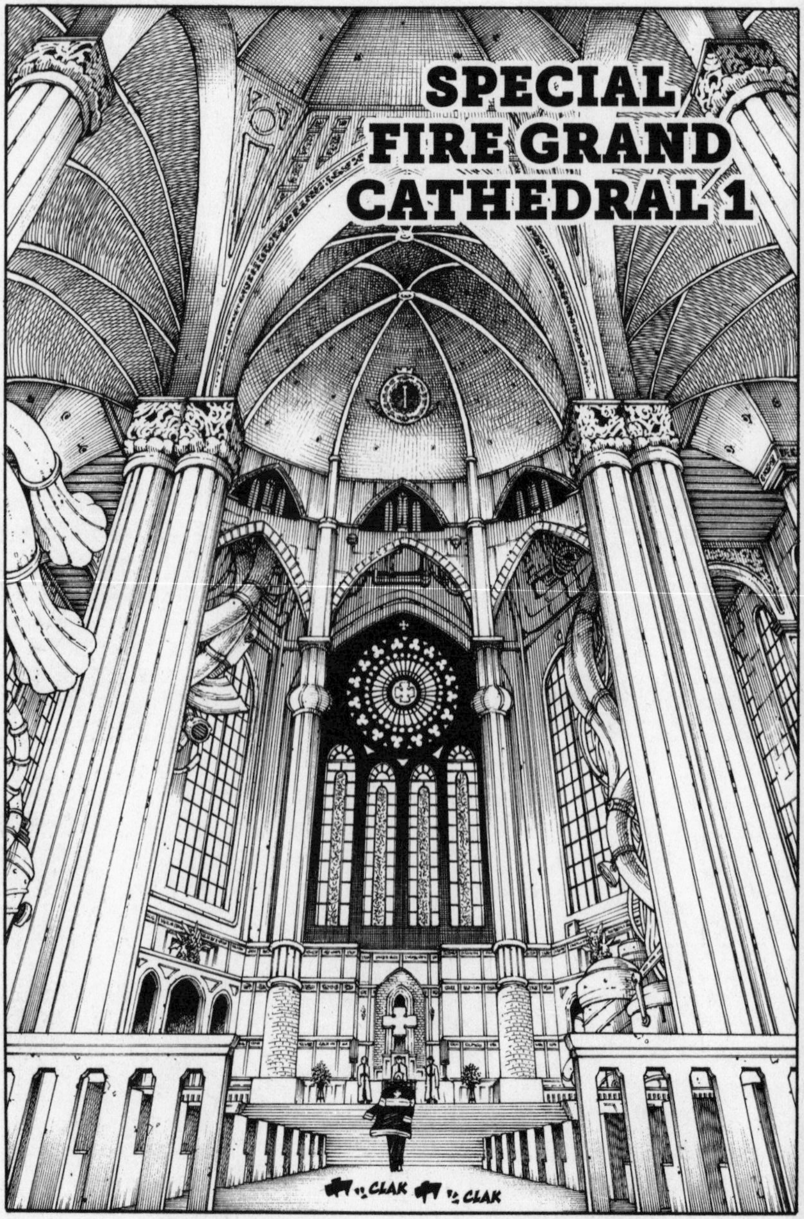
SPECIAL FIRE GRAND CATHEDRAL 1
CLAK
CLAK

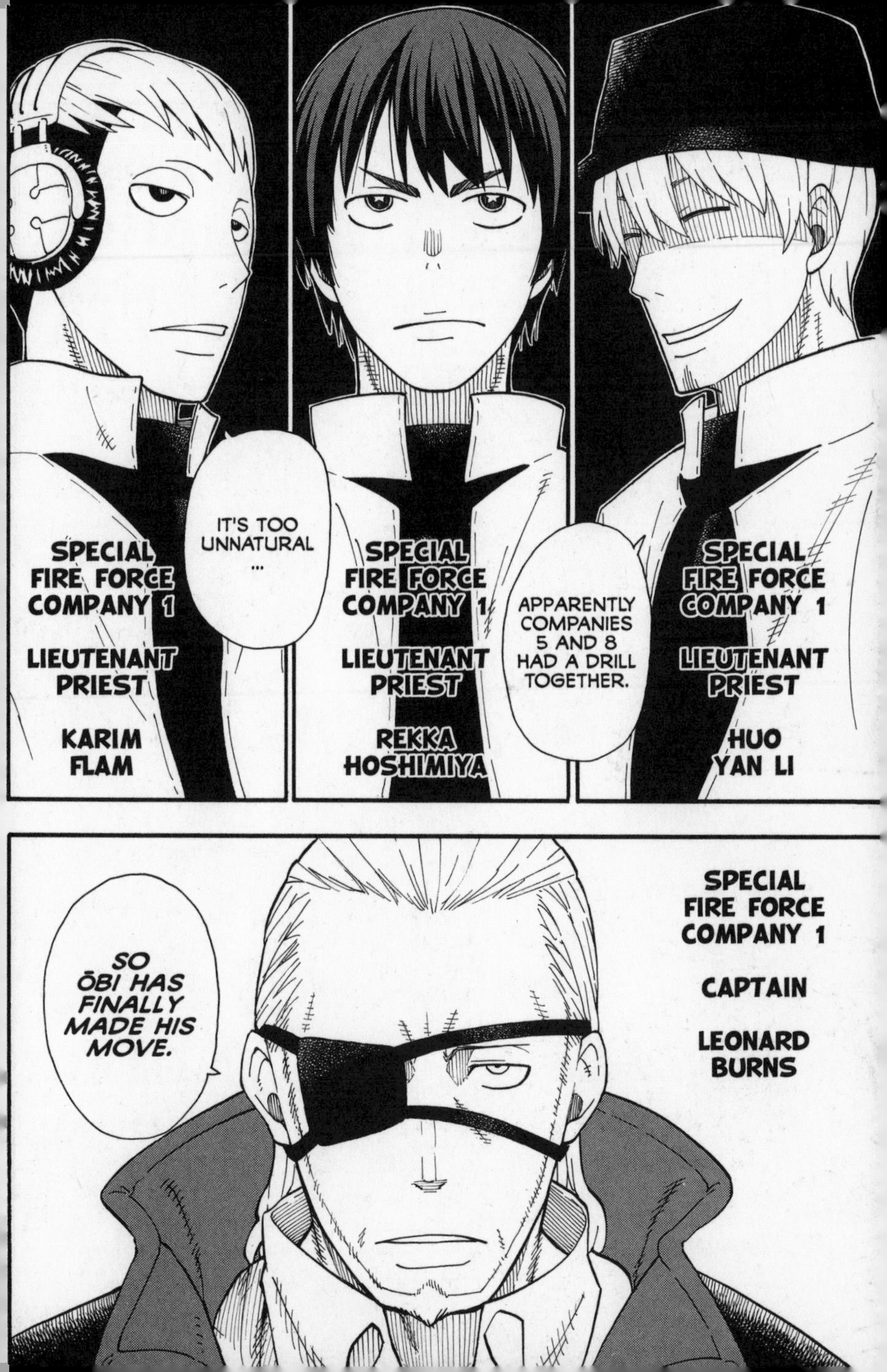
SPECIAL FIRE FORCE COMPANY 1
LIEUTENANT PRIEST
HUO YAN LI
APPARENTLY COMPANIES 5 AND 8 HAD A DRILL TOGETHER.
SPECIAL FIRE FORCE COMPANY 1
LIEUTENANT PRIEST
REKKA HOSHIMIYA
IT'S TOO UNNATURAL...
SPECIAL FIRE FORCE COMPANY 1
LIEUTENANT PRIEST
KARIM FLAM
SPECIAL FIRE FORCE COMPANY 1
CAPTAIN
LEONARD BURNS
SO ŌBI HAS FINALLY MADE HIS MOVE.

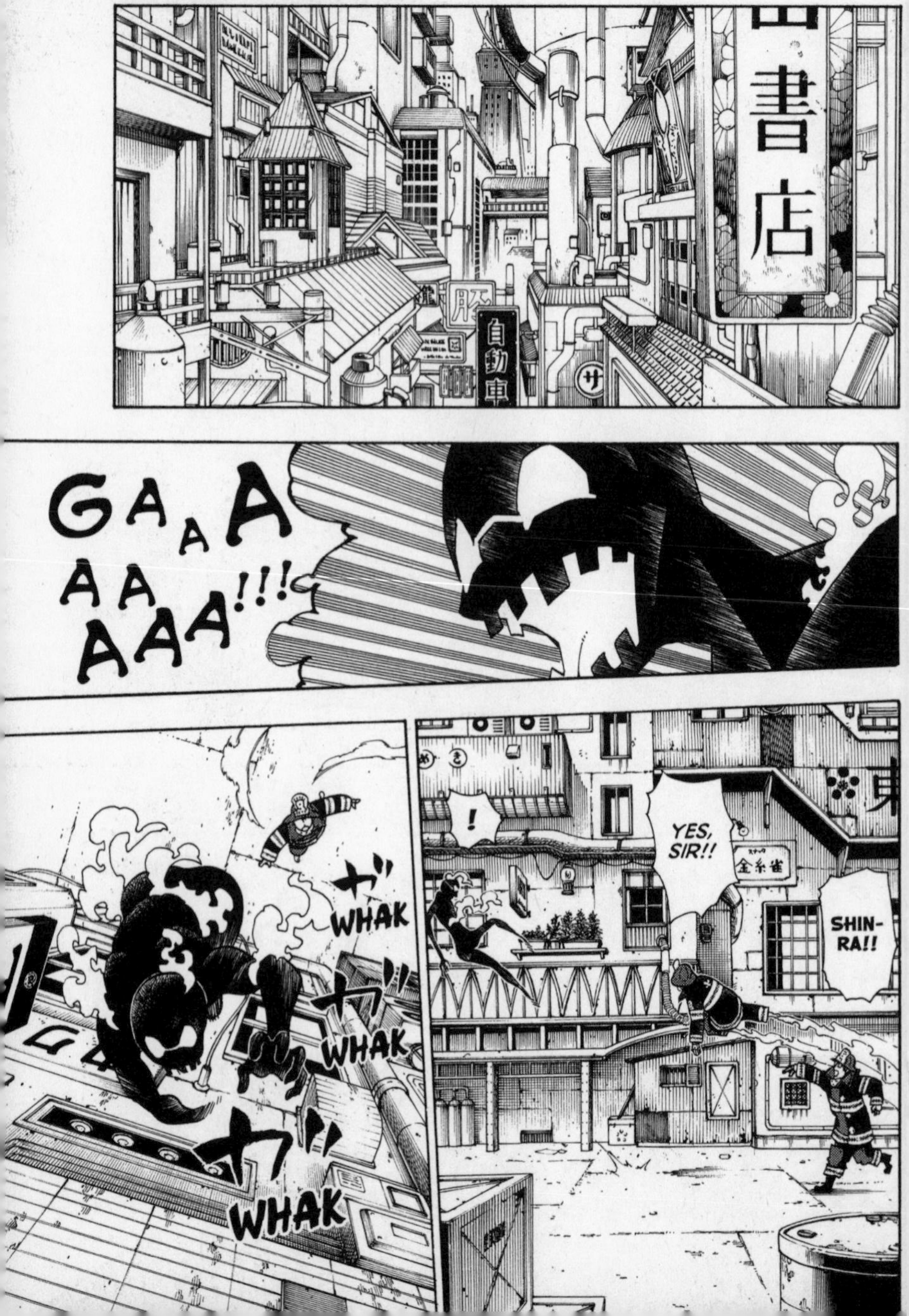
書店
自動車
GAAAAAAAA!!!
SHIN-RA!!
YES, SIR!!
!
WHAK
WHAK
WHAK

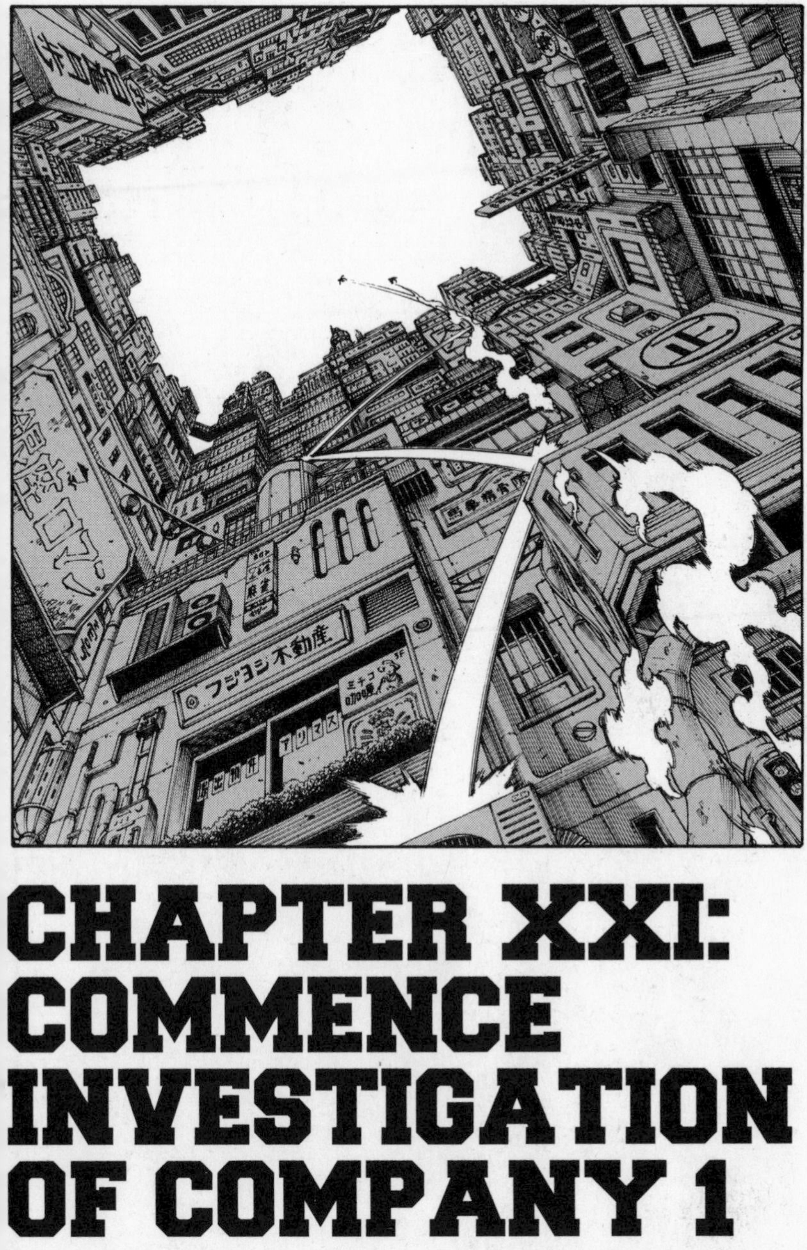
フジヨシ不動産
アリマス

CHAPTER XXI: COMMENCE INVESTIGATION OF COMPANY 1

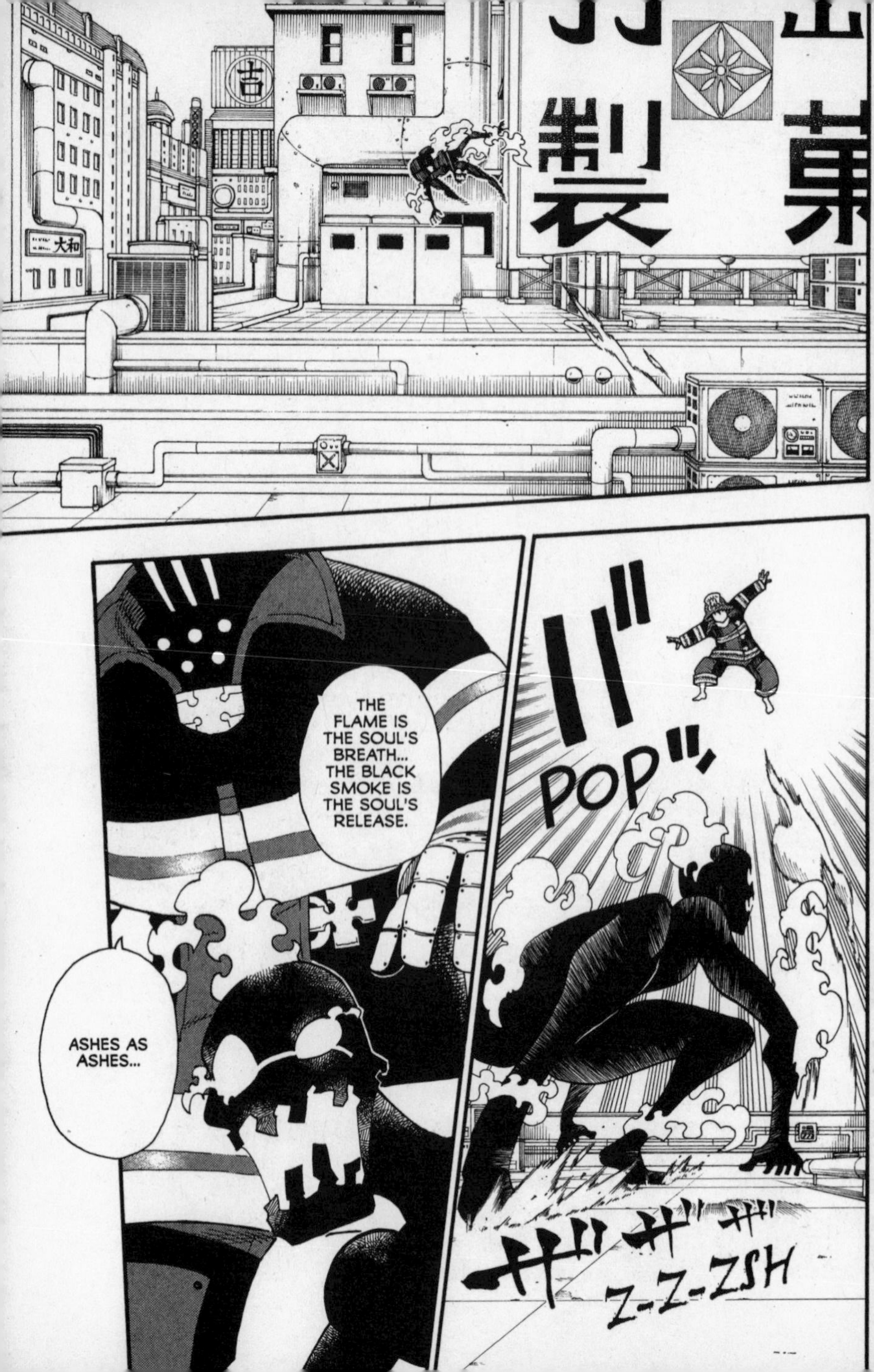
大和
バ
POP
ザザザ
Z-Z-ZSH
THE FLAME IS THE SOUL'S BREATH... THE BLACK SMOKE IS THE SOUL'S RELEASE.
ASHES AS ASHES...

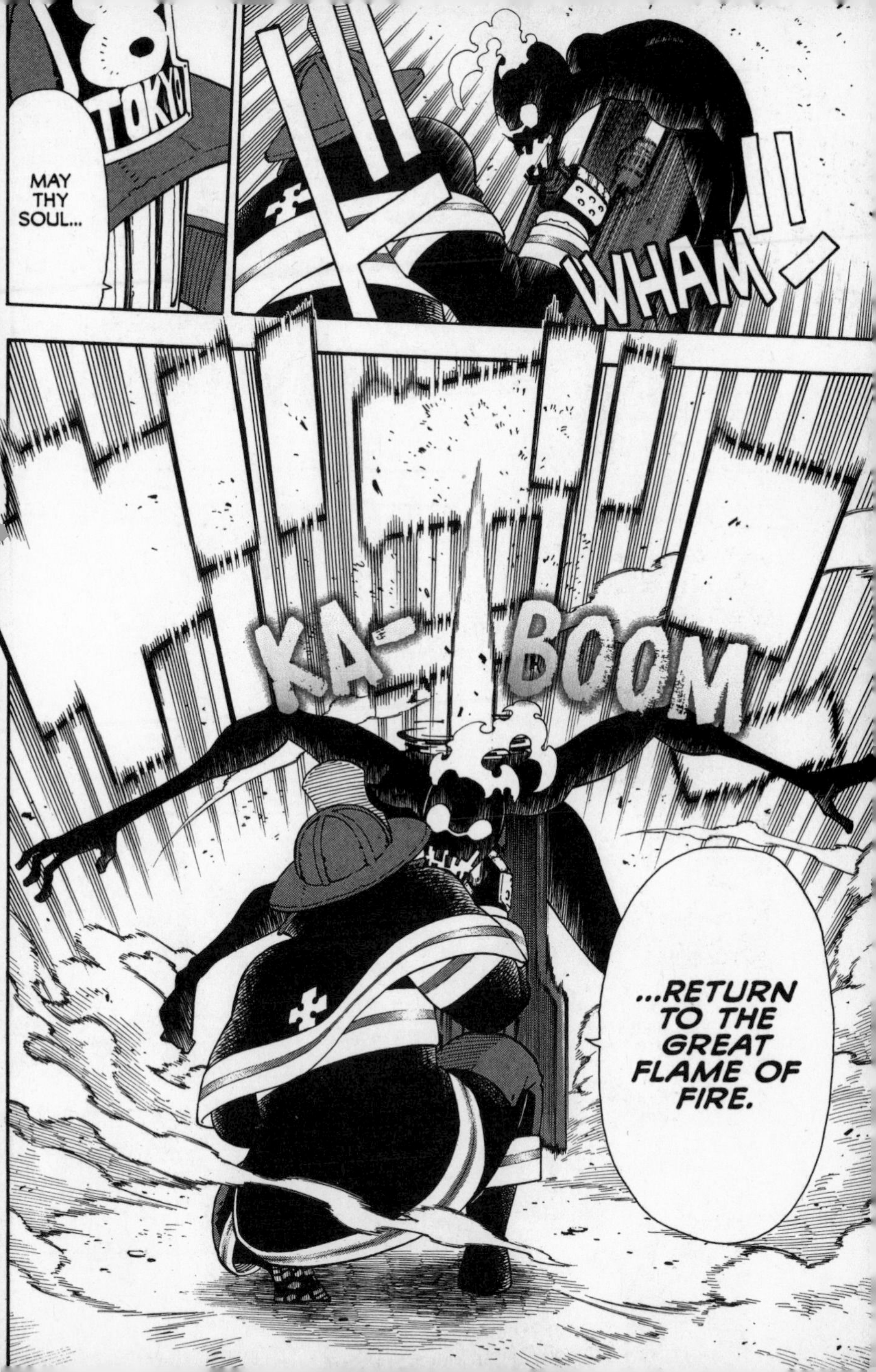
WHAM
8
TOKYO
MAY THY SOUL...
KA-BOOM
...RETURN TO THE GREAT FLAME OF FIRE.

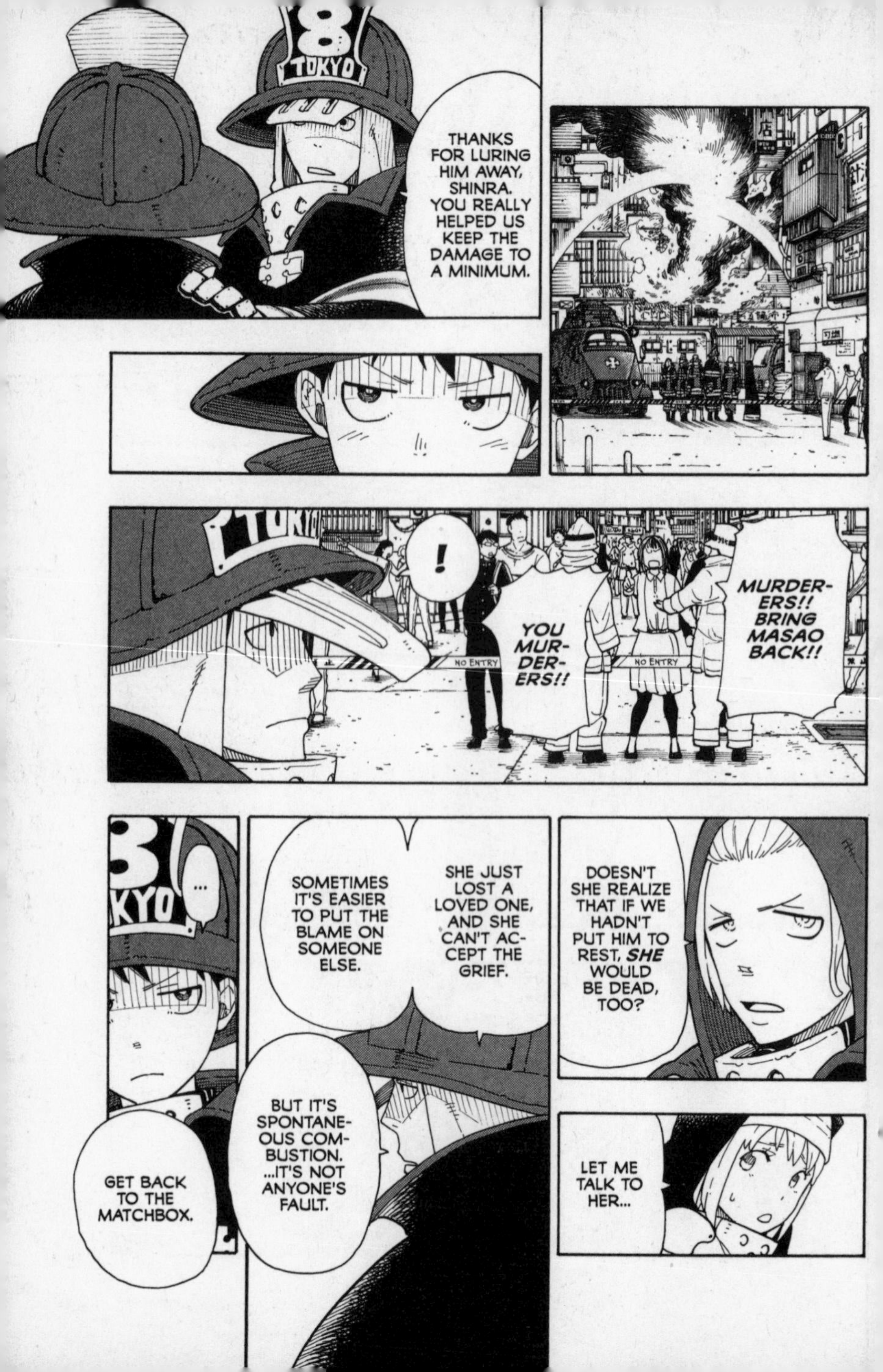
THANKS FOR LURING HIM AWAY, SHINRA. YOU REALLY HELPED US KEEP THE DAMAGE TO A MINIMUM.
MURDERERS!! BRING MASAO BACK!!
YOU MURDERERS!!
!
DOESN'T SHE REALIZE THAT IF WE HADN'T PUT HIM TO REST, *SHE* WOULD BE DEAD, TOO?
LET ME TALK TO HER...
SHE JUST LOST A LOVED ONE, AND SHE CAN'T ACCEPT THE GRIEF.
SOMETIMES IT'S EASIER TO PUT THE BLAME ON SOMEONE ELSE.
BUT IT'S SPONTANEOUS COMBUSTION. ...IT'S NOT ANYONE'S FAULT.
...
GET BACK TO THE MATCHBOX.

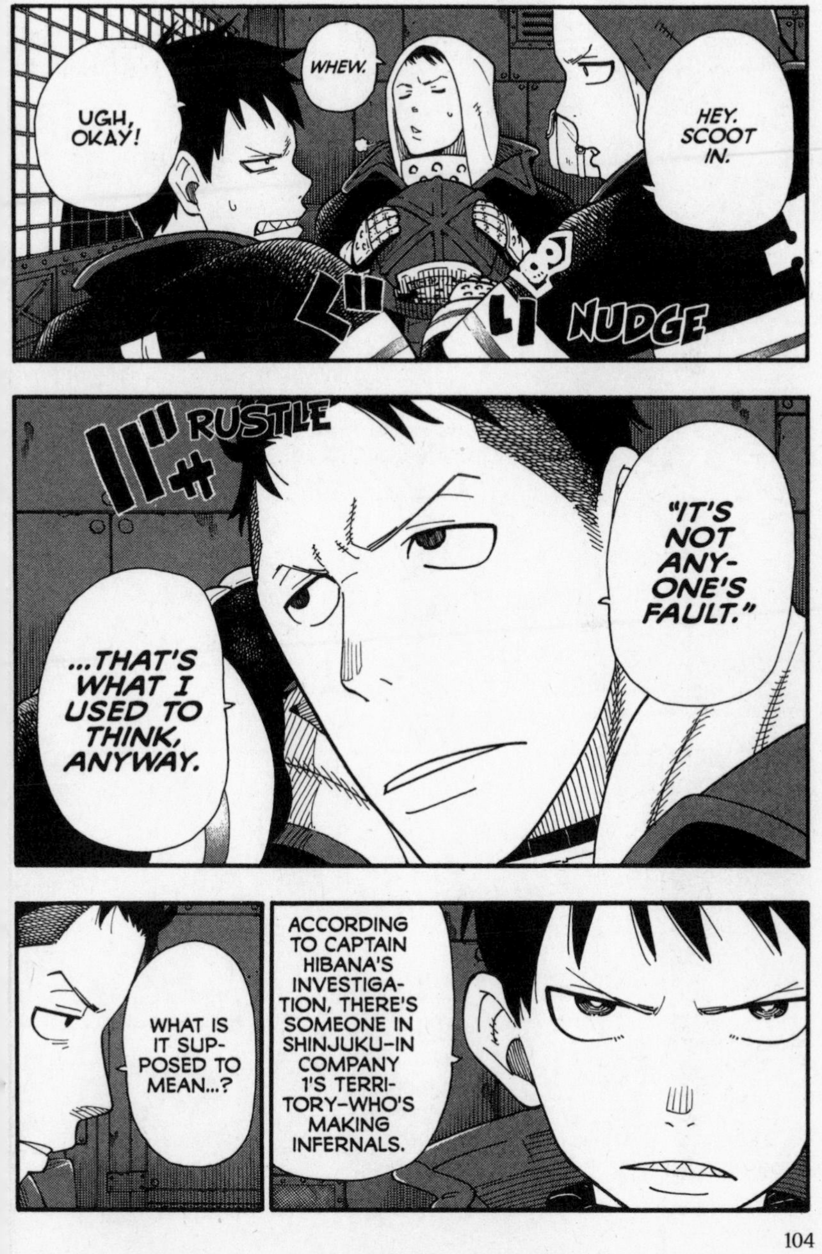
HEY. SCOOT IN.
WHEW.
UGH, OKAY!
NUDGE
"IT'S NOT ANY-ONE'S FAULT."
RUSTLE
...THAT'S WHAT I USED TO THINK, ANYWAY.
ACCORDING TO CAPTAIN HIBANA'S INVESTIGA-TION, THERE'S SOMEONE IN SHINJUKU–IN COMPANY 1'S TERRI-TORY–WHO'S MAKING INFERNALS.
WHAT IS IT SUP-POSED TO MEAN...?

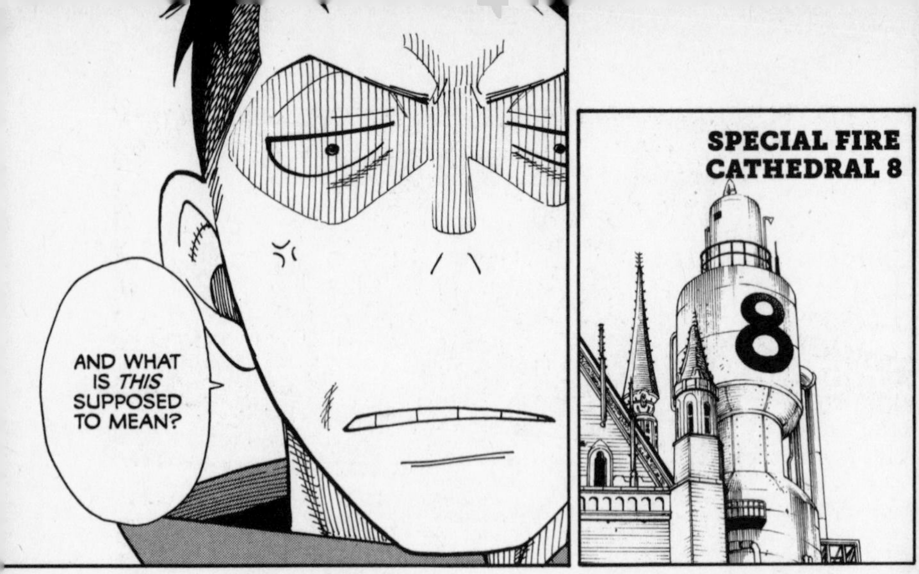
SPECIAL FIRE CATHEDRAL 8
8
AND WHAT IS *THIS* SUPPOSED TO MEAN?

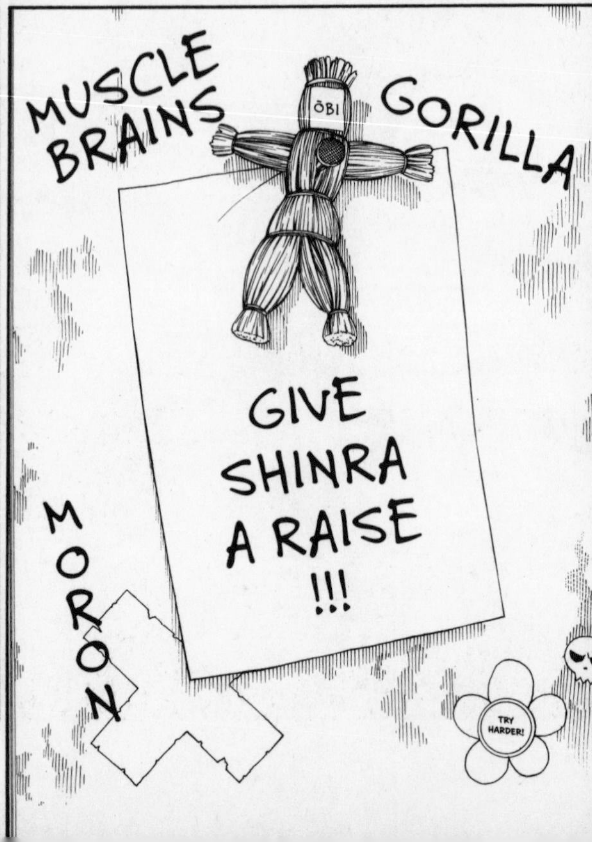
GORILLA
MUSCLE BRAINS
ŌBI
GIVE SHINRA A RAISE !!!
TRY HARDER!
MORON

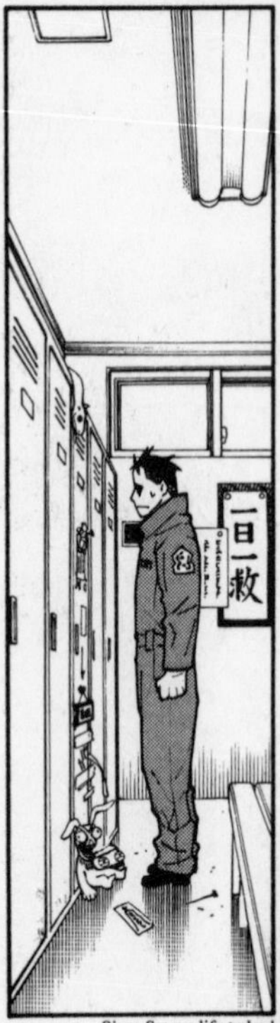
Sign: Save a life today!

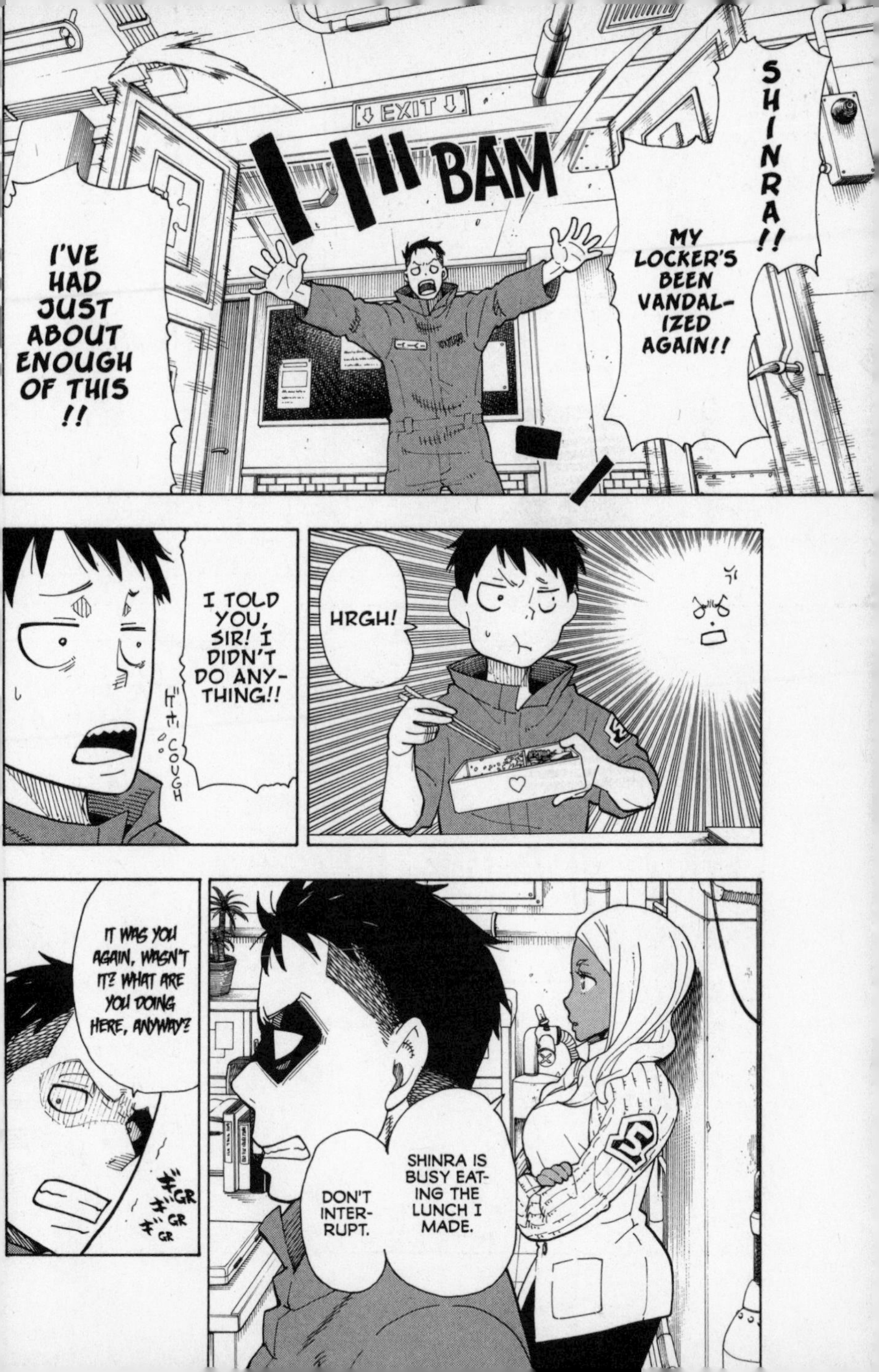
SHINRA!!
MY LOCKER'S BEEN VANDAL-IZED AGAIN!!
EXIT
BAM
I'VE HAD JUST ABOUT ENOUGH OF THIS!!
HRGH!
I TOLD YOU, SIR! I DIDN'T DO ANY-THING!!
COUGH
SHINRA IS BUSY EAT-ING THE LUNCH I MADE.
DON'T INTER-RUPT.
IT WAS YOU AGAIN, WASN'T IT? WHAT ARE YOU DOING HERE, ANYWAY?
GR GR GR

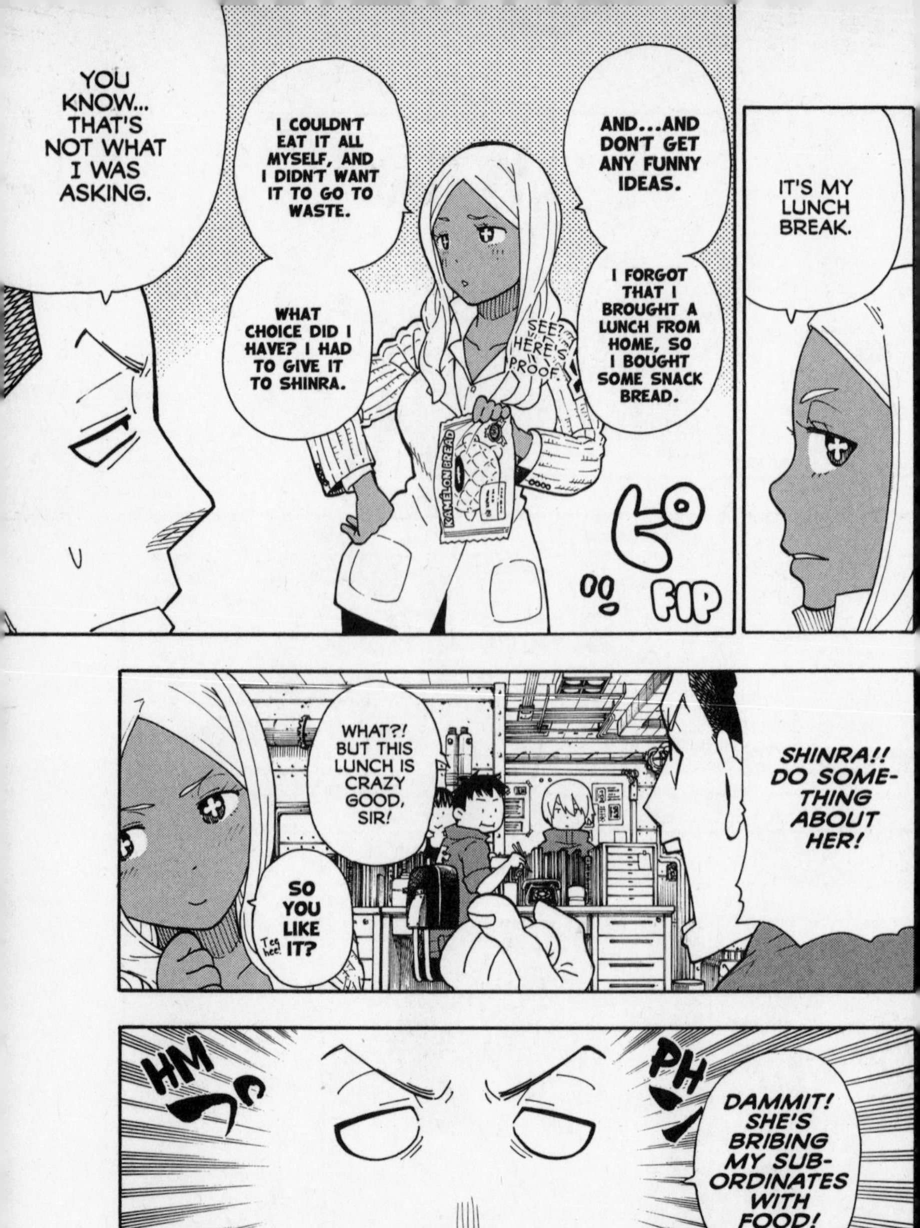
IT'S MY LUNCH BREAK.
AND...AND DON'T GET ANY FUNNY IDEAS.
I FORGOT THAT I BROUGHT A LUNCH FROM HOME, SO I BOUGHT SOME SNACK BREAD.
SEE? HERE'S PROOF.
FIP
I COULDN'T EAT IT ALL MYSELF, AND I DIDN'T WANT IT TO GO TO WASTE.
WHAT CHOICE DID I HAVE? I HAD TO GIVE IT TO SHINRA.
KAMELON BREAD
YOU KNOW... THAT'S NOT WHAT I WAS ASKING.
SHINRA!! DO SOME-THING ABOUT HER!
WHAT?! BUT THIS LUNCH IS CRAZY GOOD, SIR!
SO YOU LIKE IT?
Tee hee!
PH
DAMMIT! SHE'S BRIBING MY SUB-ORDINATES WITH FOOD!
HM

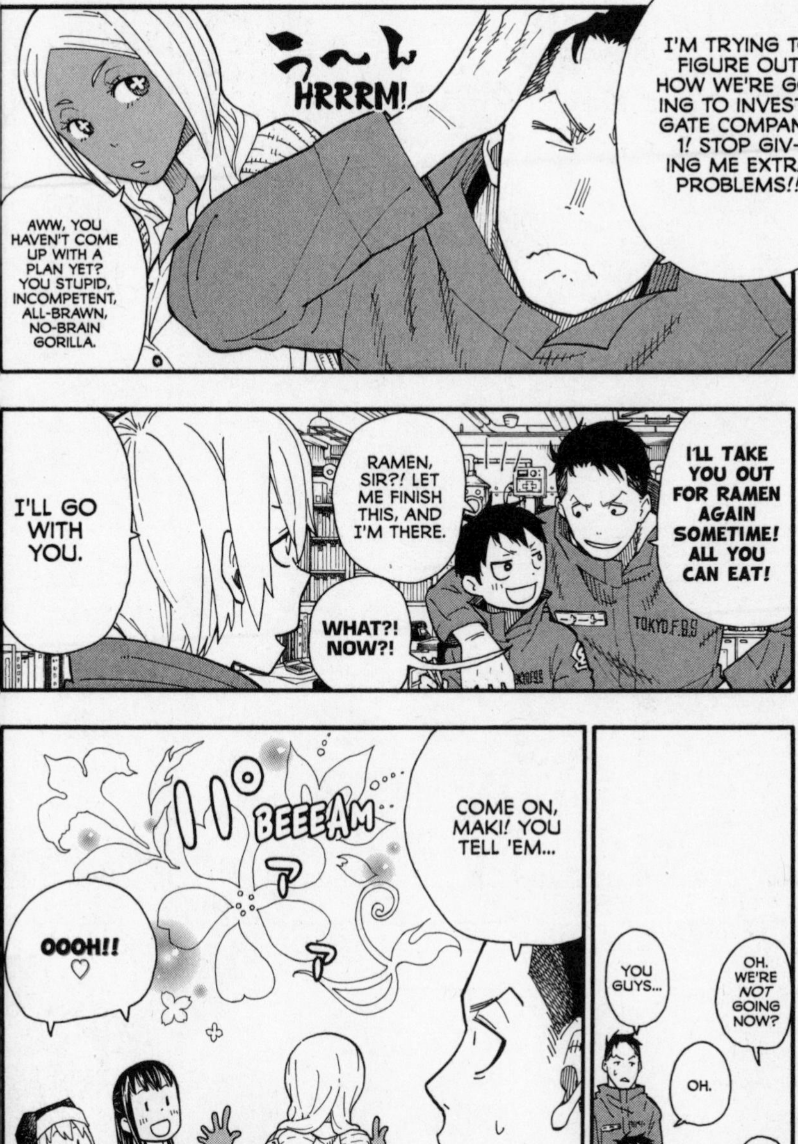
I'M TRYING TO FIGURE OUT HOW WE'RE GO-ING TO INVESTI-GATE COMPANY 1! STOP GIV-ING ME EXTRA PROBLEMS!!
う〜ん
HRRRM!
AWW, YOU HAVEN'T COME UP WITH A PLAN YET? YOU STUPID, INCOMPETENT, ALL-BRAWN, NO-BRAIN GORILLA.
I'LL TAKE YOU OUT FOR RAMEN AGAIN SOMETIME! ALL YOU CAN EAT!
RAMEN, SIR?! LET ME FINISH THIS, AND I'M THERE.
WHAT?! NOW?!
I'LL GO WITH YOU.
OH. WE'RE NOT GOING NOW?
YOU GUYS...
OH.
COME ON, MAKI! YOU TELL 'EM...
BEEEAM
OOOH!! ♡

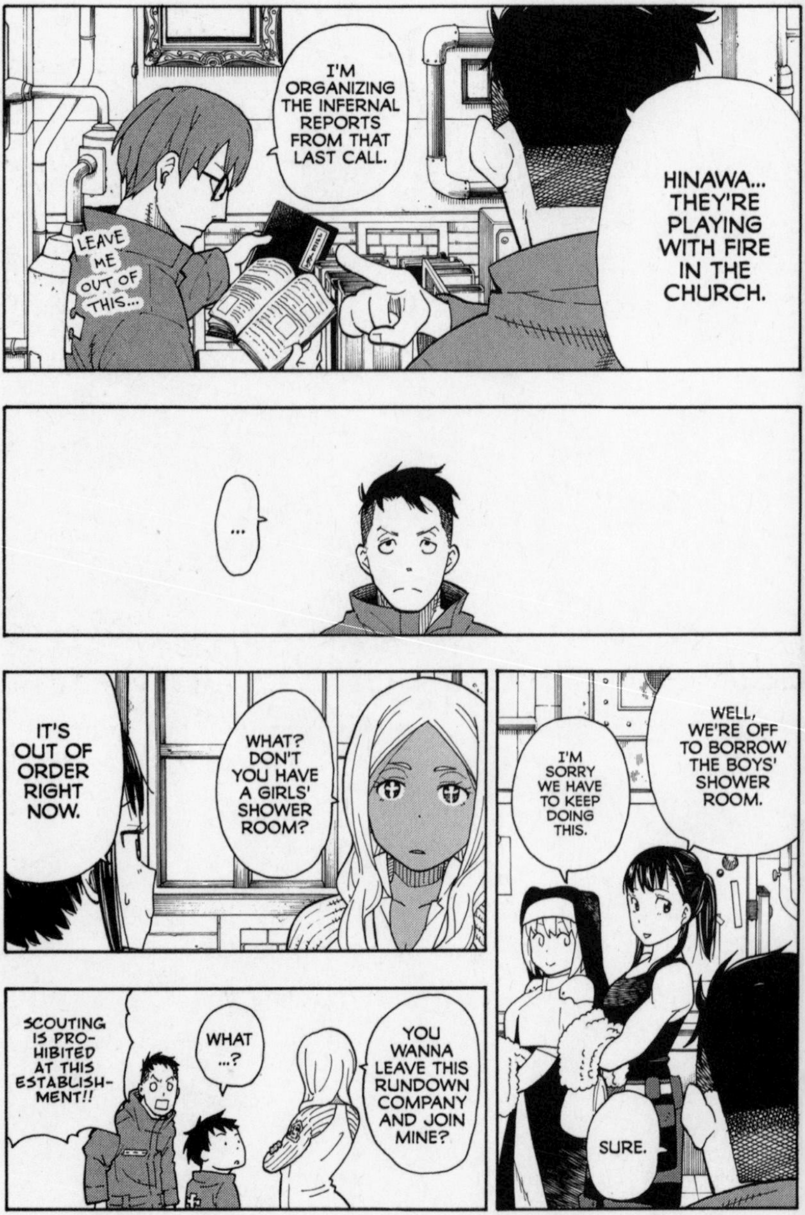
HINAWA... THEY'RE PLAYING WITH FIRE IN THE CHURCH.
I'M ORGANIZING THE INFERNAL REPORTS FROM THAT LAST CALL.
LEAVE ME OUT OF THIS...
...
WELL, WE'RE OFF TO BORROW THE BOYS' SHOWER ROOM.
I'M SORRY WE HAVE TO KEEP DOING THIS.
SURE.
WHAT? DON'T YOU HAVE A GIRLS' SHOWER ROOM?
IT'S OUT OF ORDER RIGHT NOW.
YOU WANNA LEAVE THIS RUNDOWN COMPANY AND JOIN MINE?
WHAT ...?
SCOUTING IS PROHIBITED AT THIS ESTABLISHMENT!!

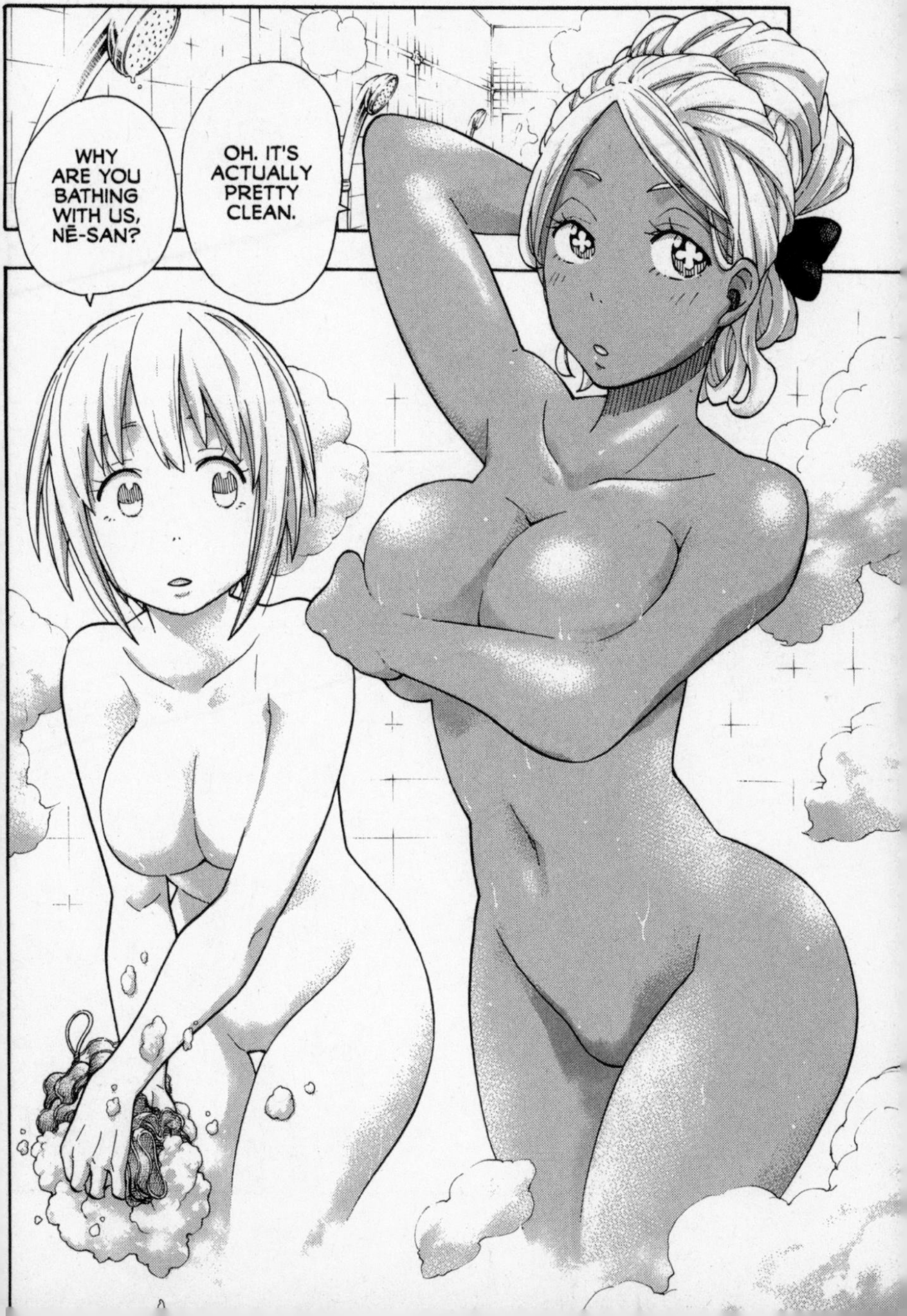
OH. IT'S ACTUALLY PRETTY CLEAN.
WHY ARE YOU BATHING WITH US, NĒ-SAN?

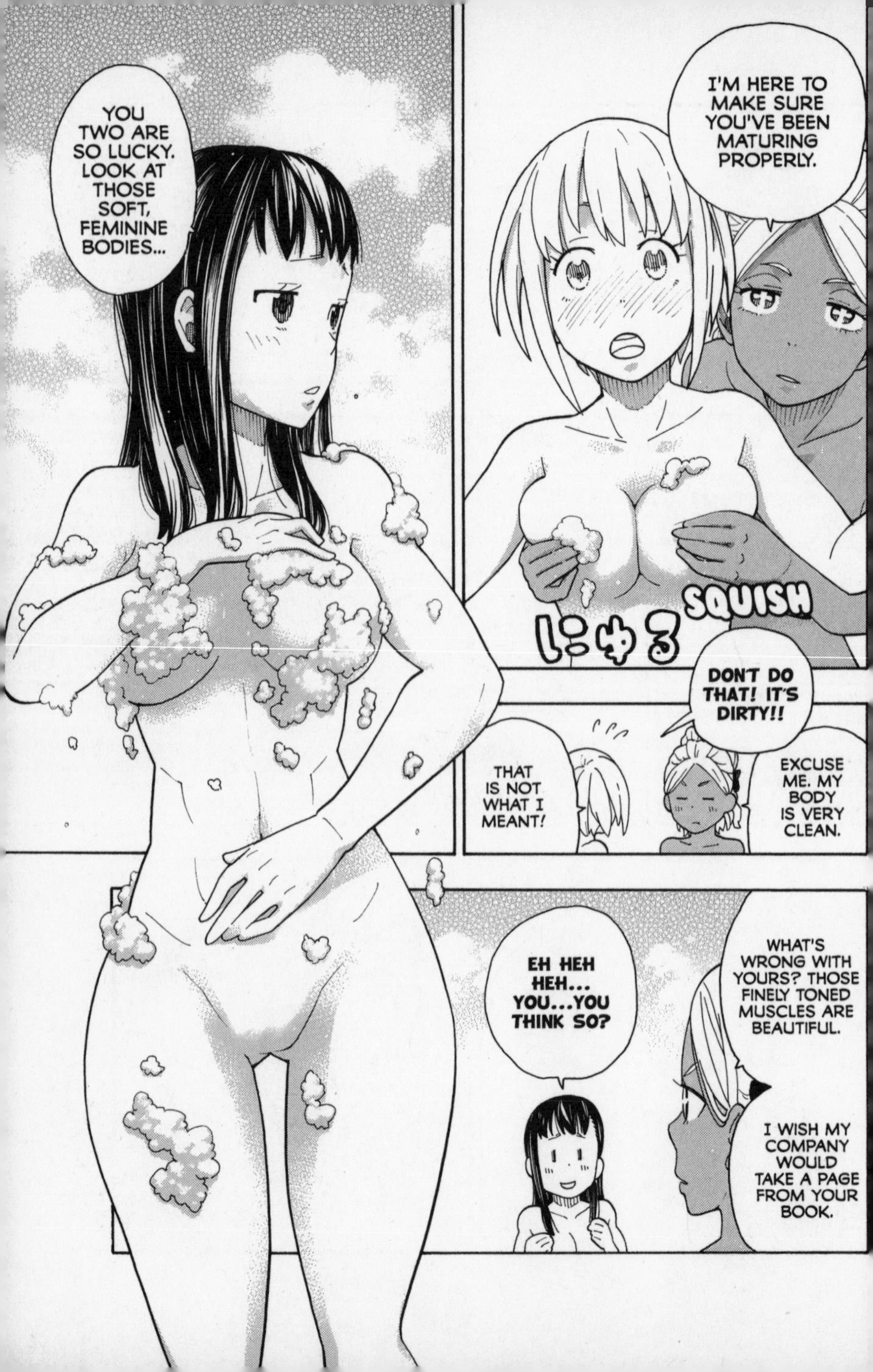
I'M HERE TO MAKE SURE YOU'VE BEEN MATURING PROPERLY.
SQUISH
にゅる
DON'T DO THAT! IT'S DIRTY!!
EXCUSE ME. MY BODY IS VERY CLEAN.
THAT IS NOT WHAT I MEANT!
YOU TWO ARE SO LUCKY. LOOK AT THOSE SOFT, FEMININE BODIES...
WHAT'S WRONG WITH YOURS? THOSE FINELY TONED MUSCLES ARE BEAUTIFUL.
EH HEH HEH... YOU...YOU THINK SO?
I WISH MY COMPANY WOULD TAKE A PAGE FROM YOUR BOOK.

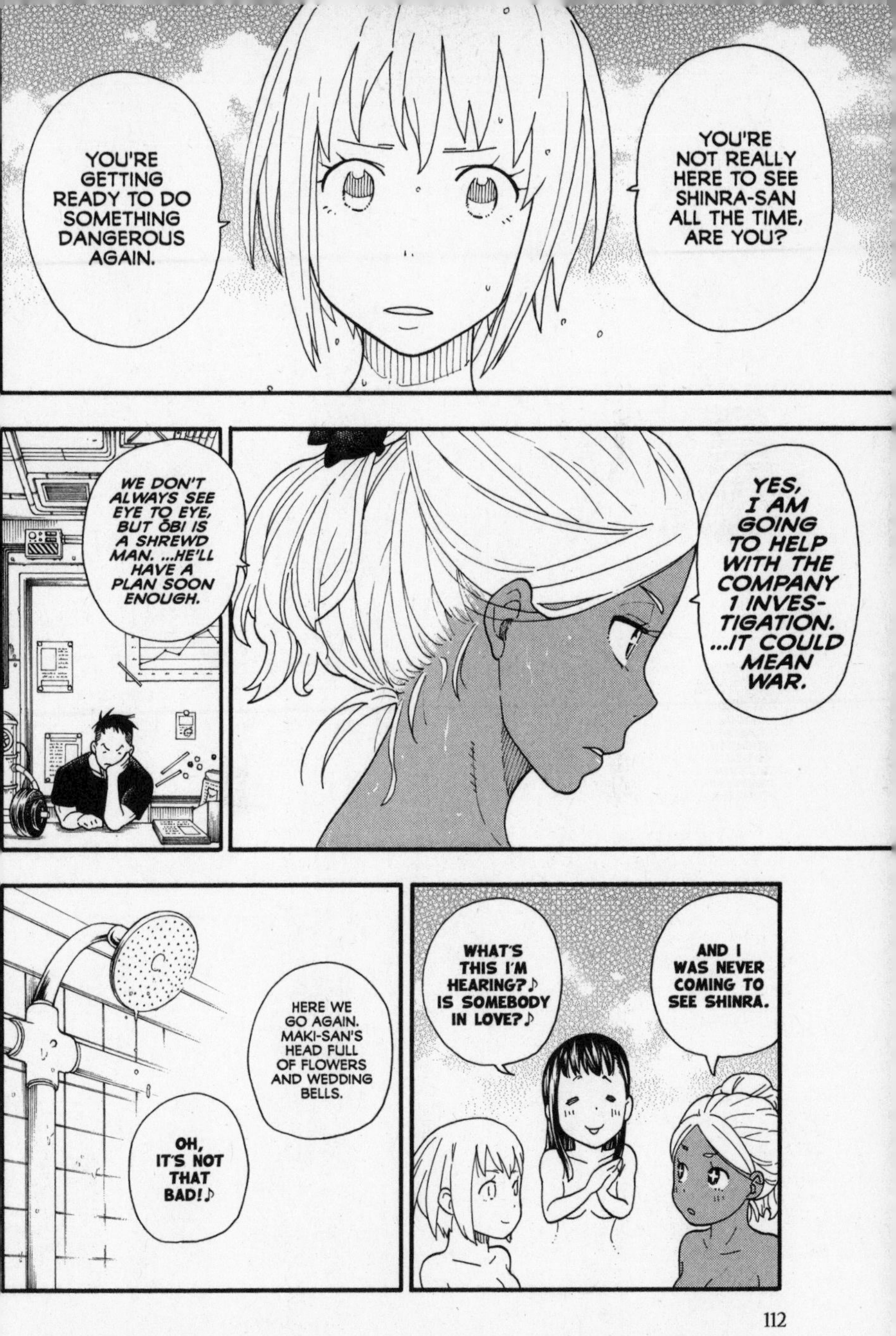
YOU'RE NOT REALLY HERE TO SEE SHINRA-SAN ALL THE TIME, ARE YOU?
YOU'RE GETTING READY TO DO SOMETHING DANGEROUS AGAIN.
YES, I AM GOING TO HELP WITH THE COMPANY 1 INVES-TIGATION. ...IT COULD MEAN WAR.
WE DON'T ALWAYS SEE EYE TO EYE, BUT ŌBI IS A SHREWD MAN. ...HE'LL HAVE A PLAN SOON ENOUGH.
AND I WAS NEVER COMING TO SEE SHINRA.
WHAT'S THIS I'M HEARING?♪ IS SOMEBODY IN LOVE?♪
HERE WE GO AGAIN. MAKI-SAN'S HEAD FULL OF FLOWERS AND WEDDING BELLS.
OH, IT'S NOT THAT BAD!♪

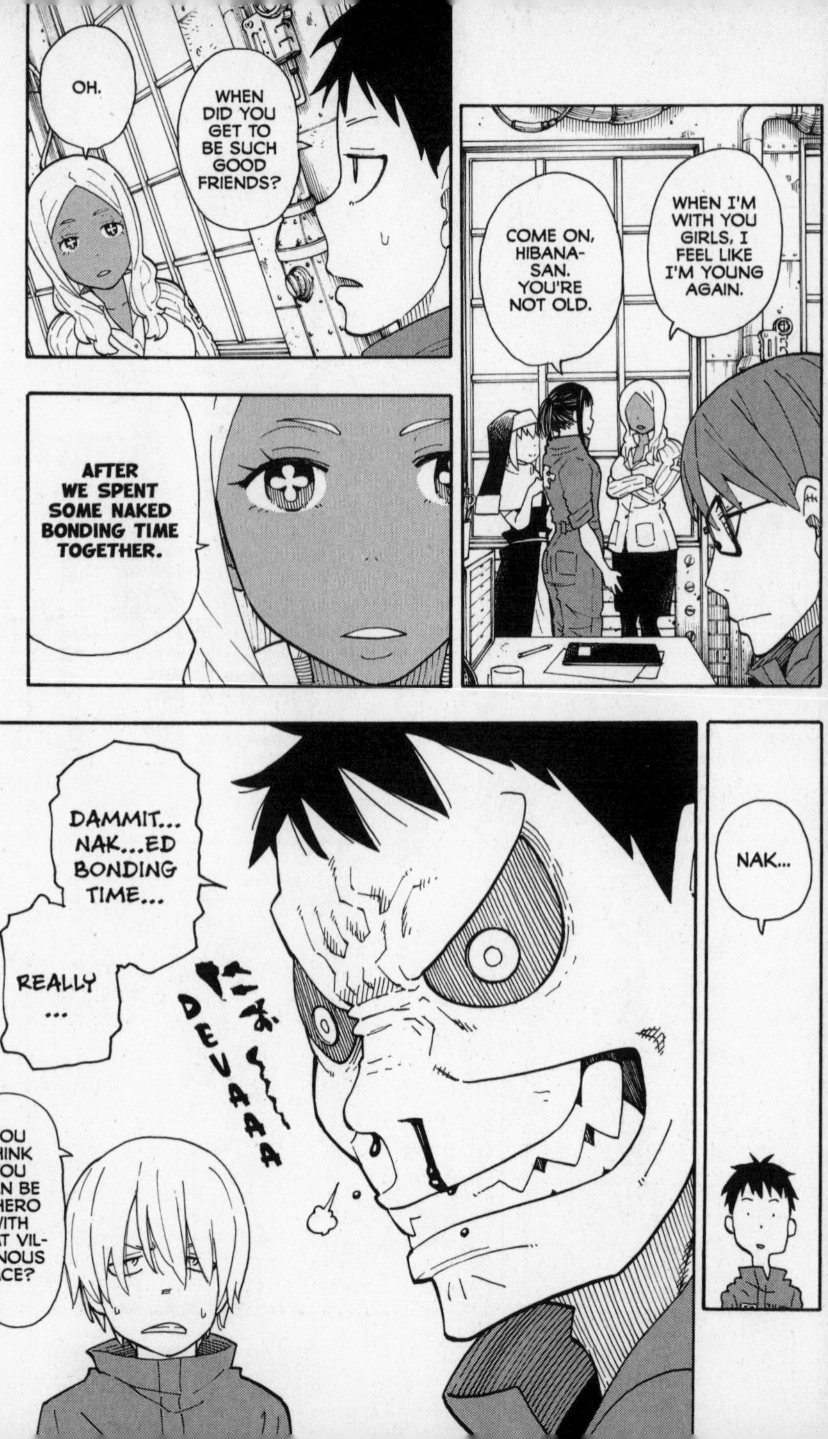
WHEN I'M WITH YOU GIRLS, I FEEL LIKE I'M YOUNG AGAIN.
COME ON, HIBANA-SAN. YOU'RE NOT OLD.
WHEN DID YOU GET TO BE SUCH GOOD FRIENDS?
OH.
AFTER WE SPENT SOME NAKED BONDING TIME TOGETHER.
NAK...
DAMMIT... NAK...ED BONDING TIME...
REALLY ...
DEVAAAA
YOU THINK YOU CAN BE A HERO WITH THAT VIL-LAINOUS FACE?

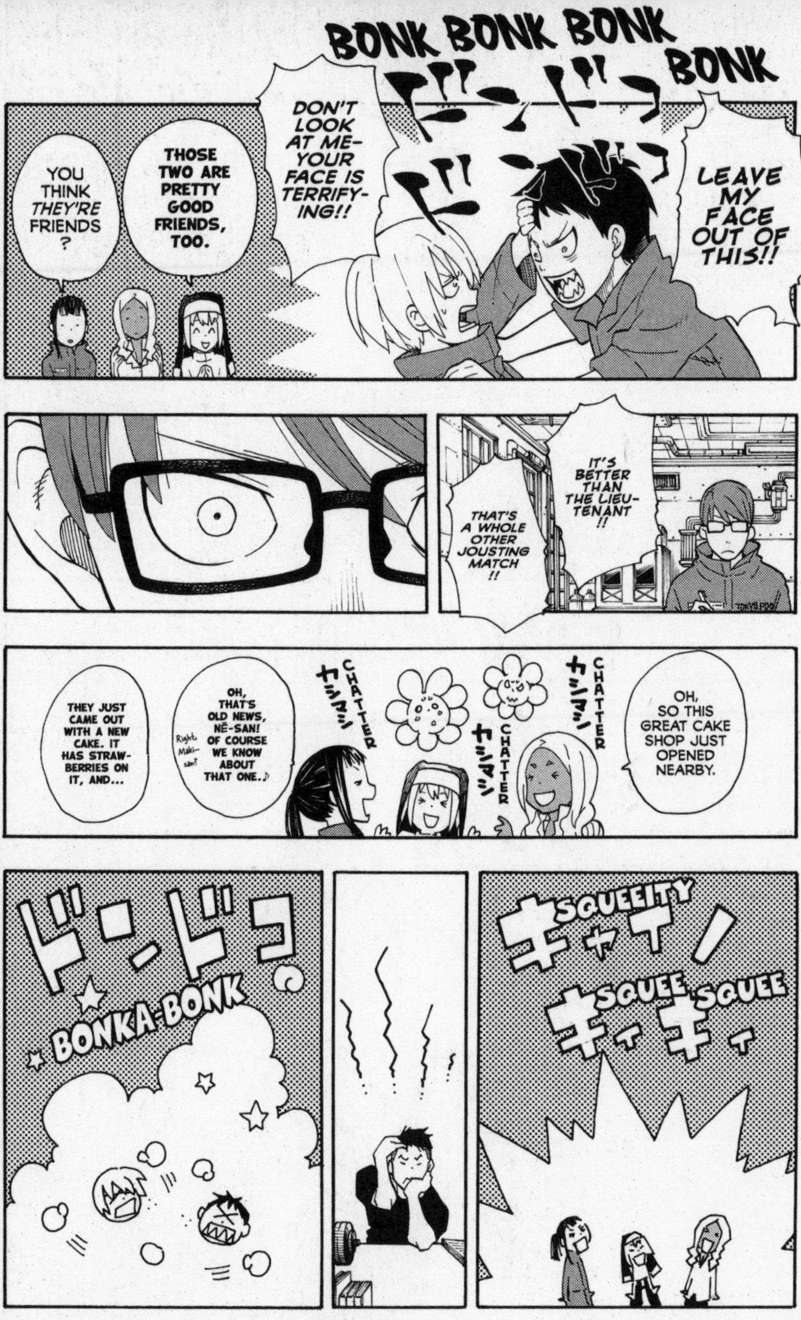

BONK BONK BONK BONK
LEAVE MY FACE OUT OF THIS!!
DON'T LOOK AT ME—YOUR FACE IS TERRIFYING!!
THOSE TWO ARE PRETTY GOOD FRIENDS, TOO.
YOU THINK THEY'RE FRIENDS?
IT'S BETTER THAN THE LIEUTENANT!!
THAT'S A WHOLE OTHER JOUSTING MATCH!!
OH, SO THIS GREAT CAKE SHOP JUST OPENED NEARBY.
カシマシ CHATTER
カシマシ CHATTER
カシマシ CHATTER
OH, THAT'S OLD NEWS, NĒ-SAN! OF COURSE WE KNOW ABOUT THAT ONE.♪
Right, Maki-san?
THEY JUST CAME OUT WITH A NEW CAKE. IT HAS STRAWBERRIES ON IT, AND...
SQUEEEITY
SQUEE SQUEE
BONKA-BONK

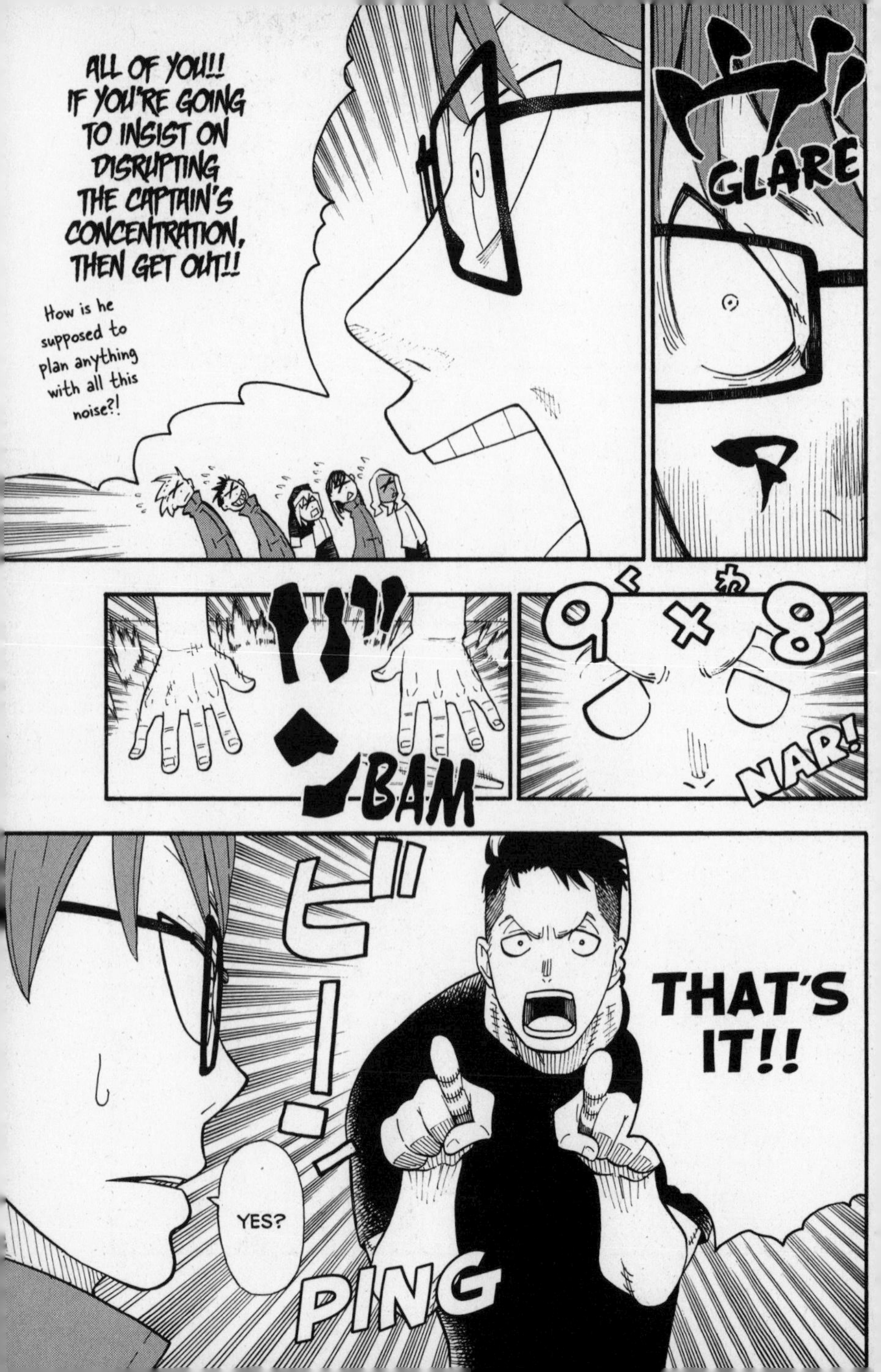
GLARE
ALL OF YOU!! IF YOU'RE GOING TO INSIST ON DISRUPTING THE CAPTAIN'S CONCENTRATION, THEN GET OUT!!
How is he supposed to plan anything with all this noise?!
NAR!
BAM
THAT'S IT!!
YES?
PING

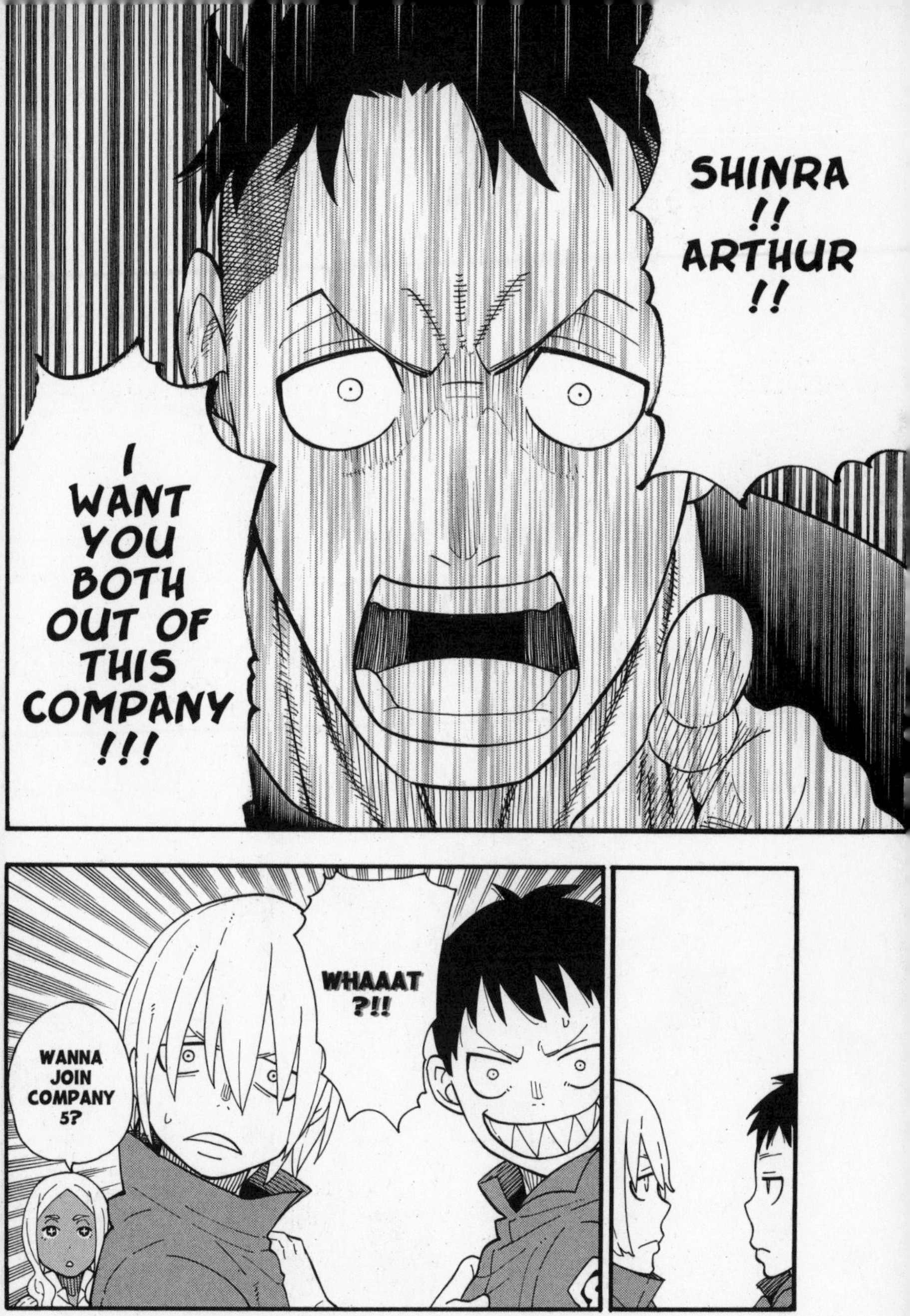
SHINRA!! ARTHUR!!
I WANT YOU BOTH OUT OF THIS COMPANY!!!
WHAAAT?!!
WANNA JOIN COMPANY 5?

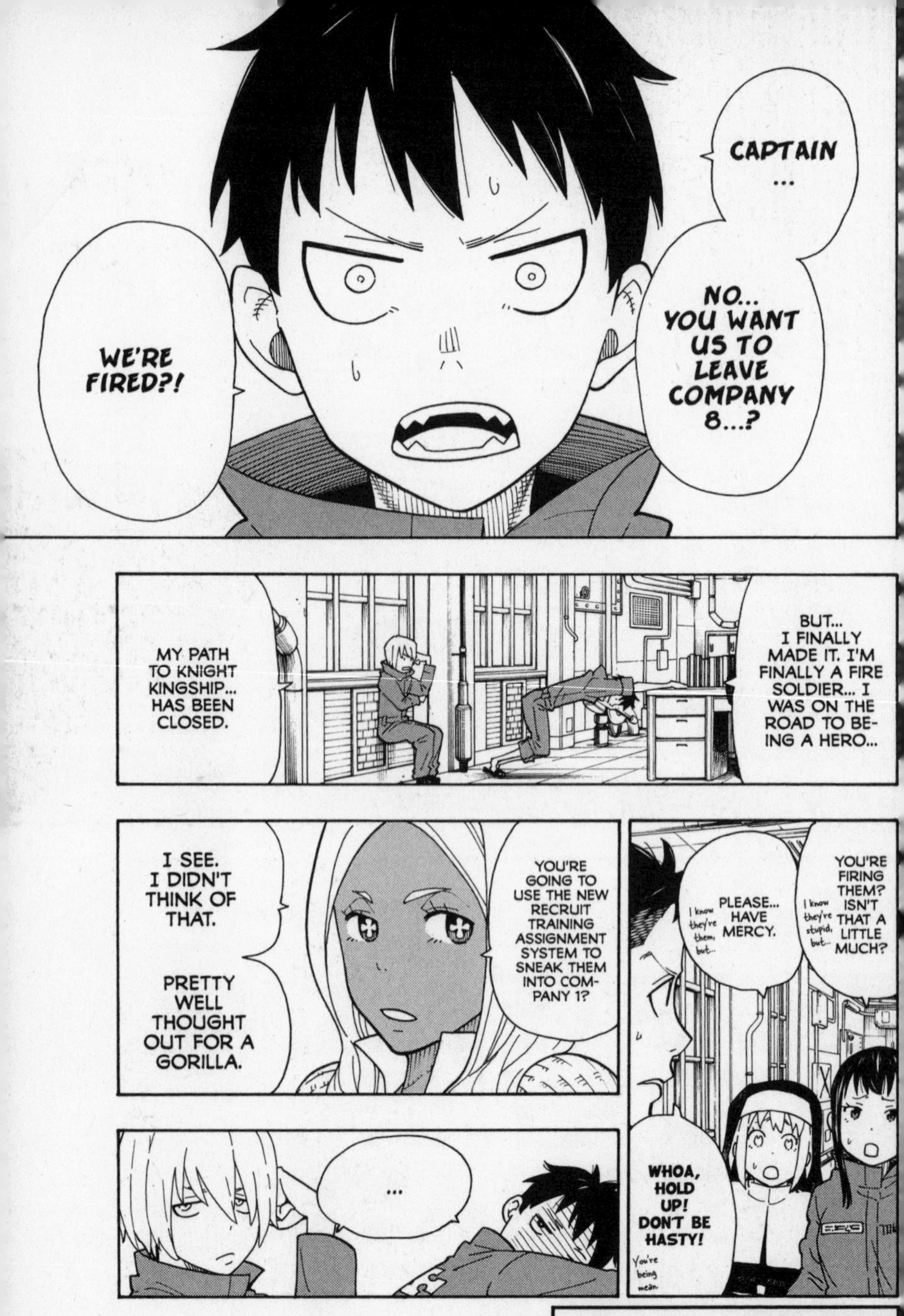
CAPTAIN ...
NO... YOU WANT US TO LEAVE COMPANY 8...?
WE'RE FIRED?!
BUT... I FINALLY MADE IT. I'M FINALLY A FIRE SOLDIER... I WAS ON THE ROAD TO BE-ING A HERO...
MY PATH TO KNIGHT KINGSHIP... HAS BEEN CLOSED.
YOU'RE FIRING THEM? ISN'T THAT A LITTLE MUCH?
I know they're stupid, but...
PLEASE... HAVE MERCY.
I know they're them, but...
WHOA, HOLD UP! DON'T BE HASTY!
You're being mean.
YOU'RE GOING TO USE THE NEW RECRUIT TRAINING ASSIGNMENT SYSTEM TO SNEAK THEM INTO COM-PANY 1?
I SEE. I DIDN'T THINK OF THAT.
PRETTY WELL THOUGHT OUT FOR A GORILLA.
...

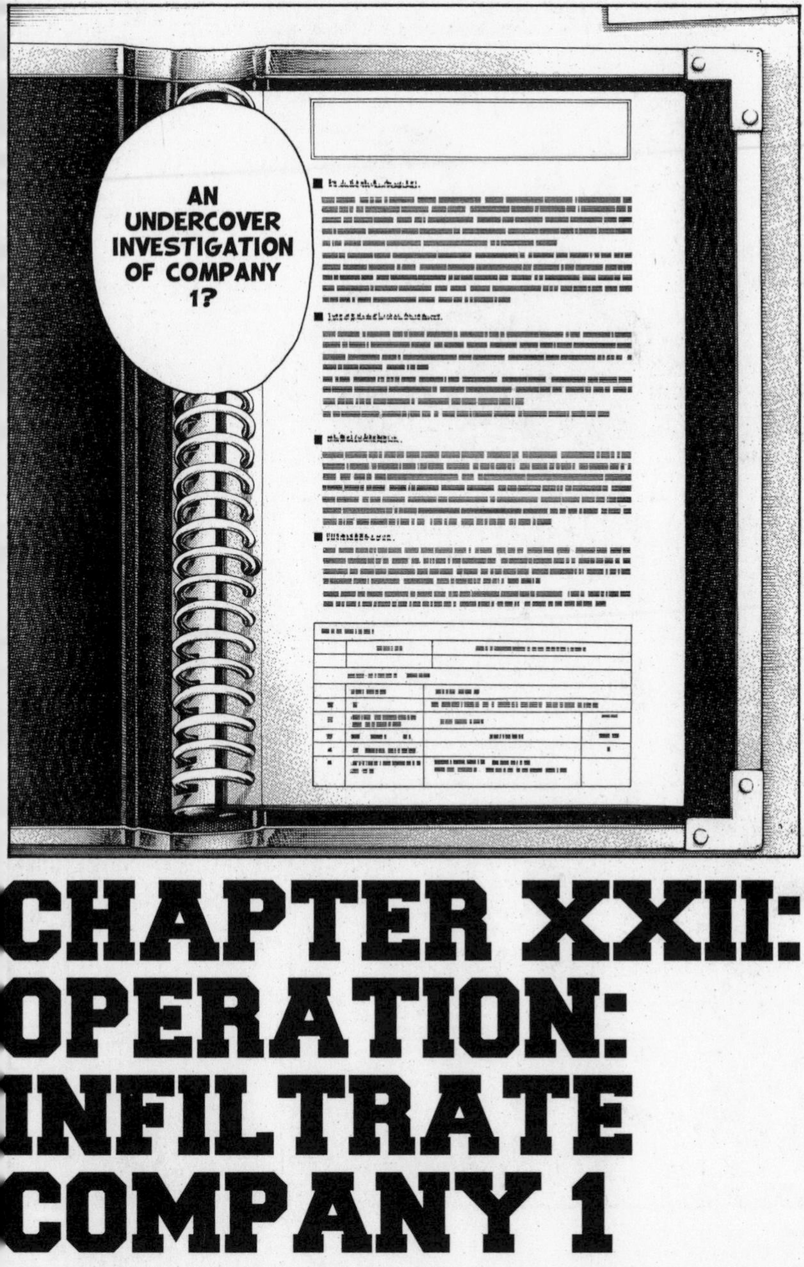
AN UNDERCOVER INVESTIGATION OF COMPANY 1?

CHAPTER XXII: OPERATION: INFILTRATE COMPANY 1

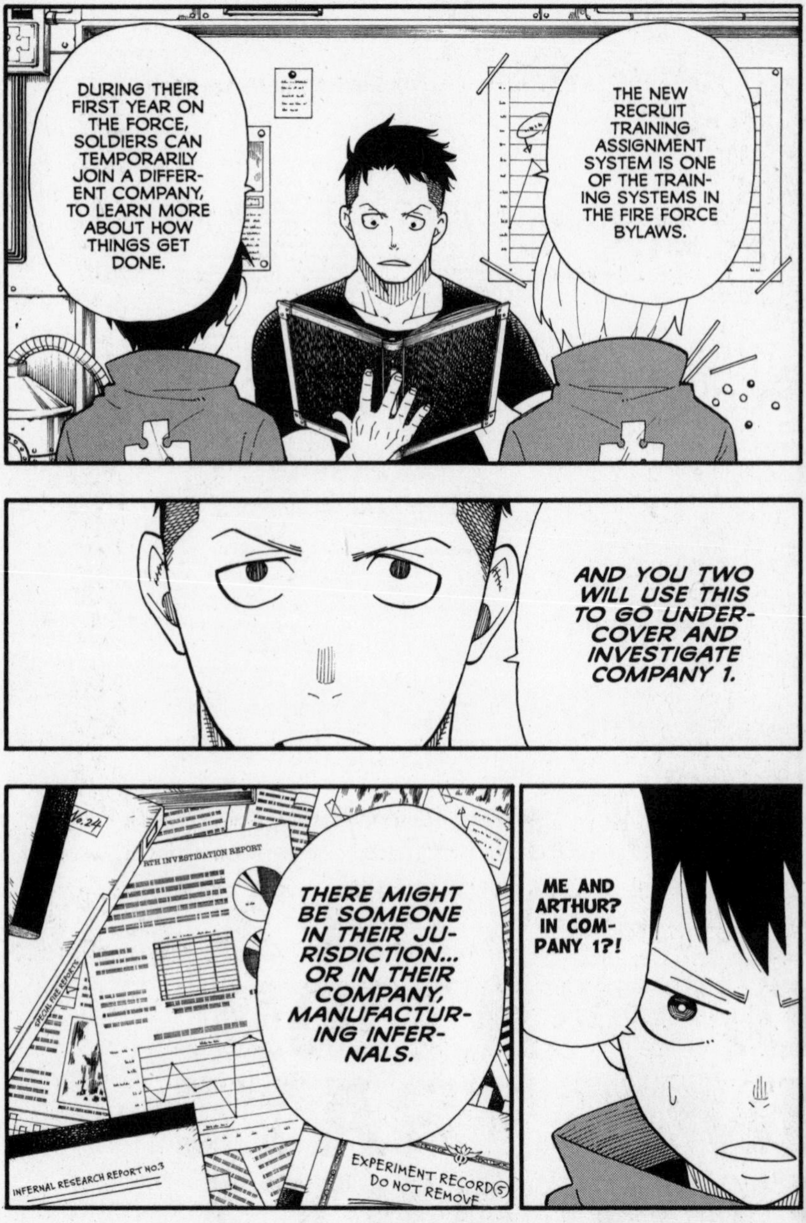
THE NEW RECRUIT TRAINING ASSIGNMENT SYSTEM IS ONE OF THE TRAINING SYSTEMS IN THE FIRE FORCE BYLAWS.
DURING THEIR FIRST YEAR ON THE FORCE, SOLDIERS CAN TEMPORARILY JOIN A DIFFERENT COMPANY, TO LEARN MORE ABOUT HOW THINGS GET DONE.
AND YOU TWO WILL USE THIS TO GO UNDERCOVER AND INVESTIGATE COMPANY 1.
ME AND ARTHUR? IN COMPANY 1?!
No.24
RTH INVESTIGATION REPORT
THERE MIGHT BE SOMEONE IN THEIR JURISDICTION... OR IN THEIR COMPANY, MANUFACTURING INFERNALS.
SPECIAL FIRE REPORTS
INFERNAL RESEARCH REPORT NO.3
EXPERIMENT RECORD 5 DO NOT REMOVE

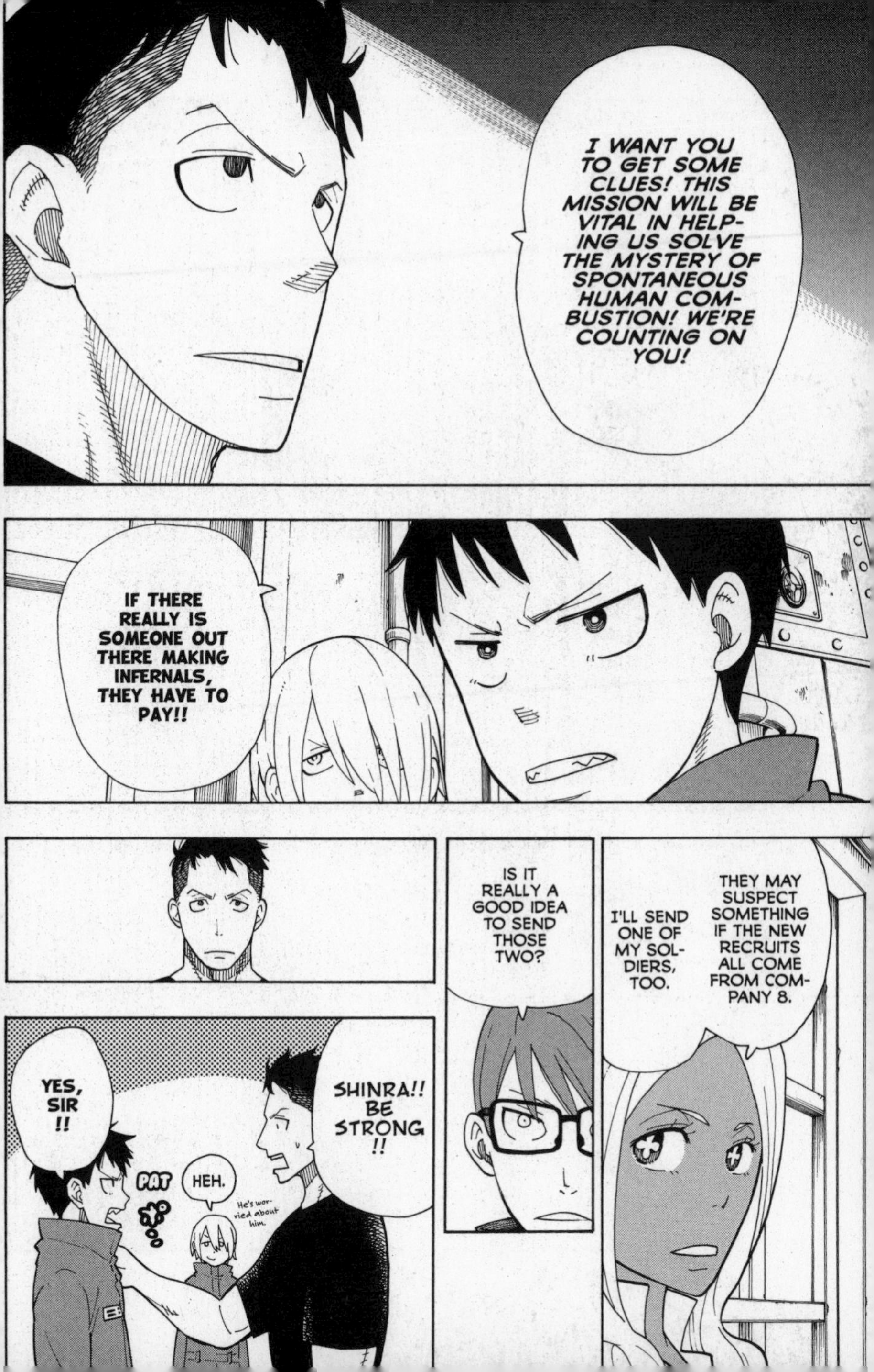
I WANT YOU TO GET SOME CLUES! THIS MISSION WILL BE VITAL IN HELPING US SOLVE THE MYSTERY OF SPONTANEOUS HUMAN COMBUSTION! WE'RE COUNTING ON YOU!
IF THERE REALLY IS SOMEONE OUT THERE MAKING INFERNALS, THEY HAVE TO PAY!!
THEY MAY SUSPECT SOMETHING IF THE NEW RECRUITS ALL COME FROM COMPANY 8.
I'LL SEND ONE OF MY SOLDIERS, TOO.
IS IT REALLY A GOOD IDEA TO SEND THOSE TWO?
SHINRA!! BE STRONG!!
YES, SIR!!
HEH.
PAT
He's worried about him.

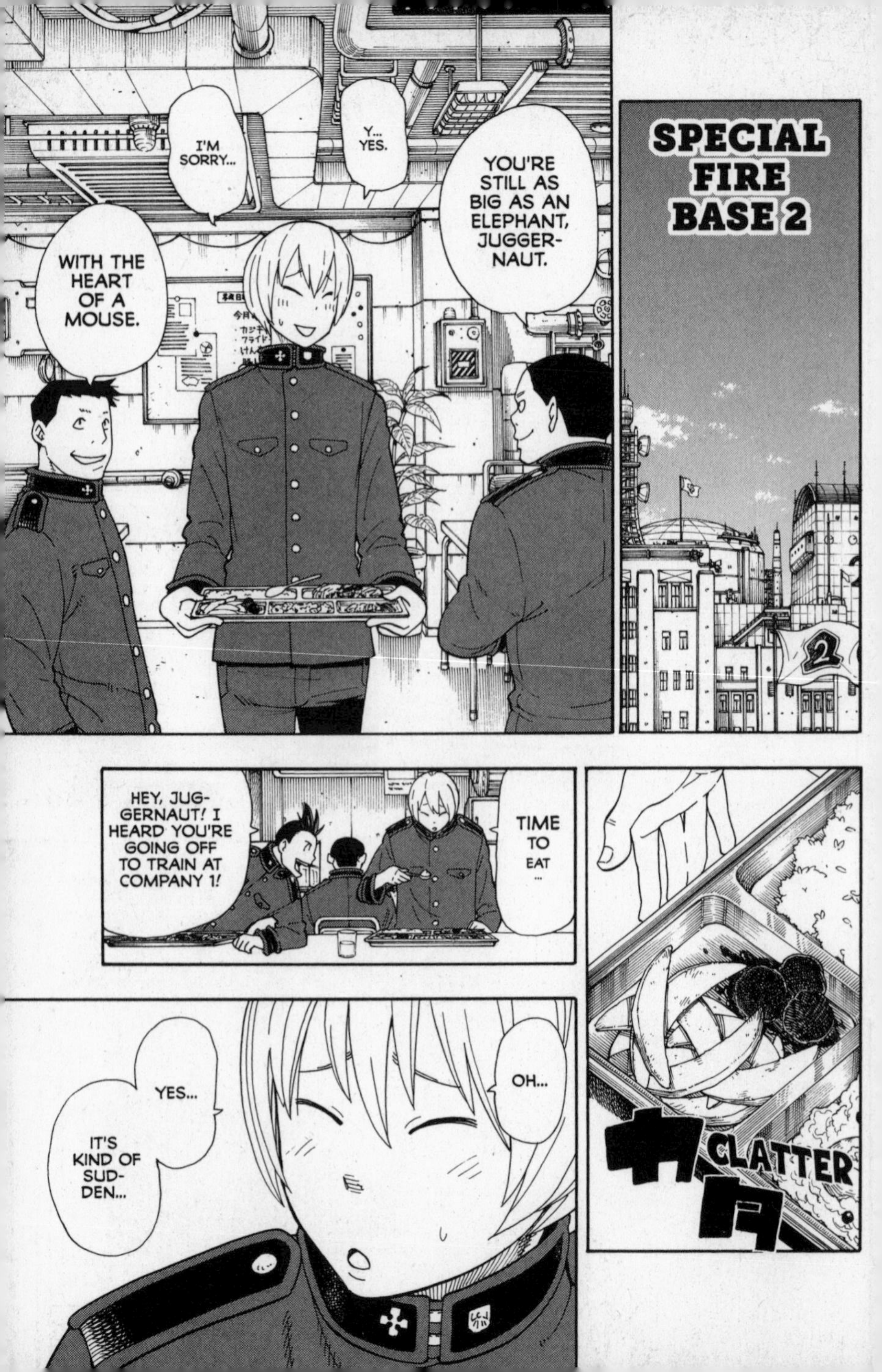
SPECIAL FIRE BASE 2
YOU'RE STILL AS BIG AS AN ELEPHANT, JUGGER-NAUT.
Y... YES.
I'M SORRY...
WITH THE HEART OF A MOUSE.
CLATTER
TIME TO EAT ...
HEY, JUG-GERNAUT! I HEARD YOU'RE GOING OFF TO TRAIN AT COMPANY 1!
OH...
YES...
IT'S KIND OF SUD-DEN...

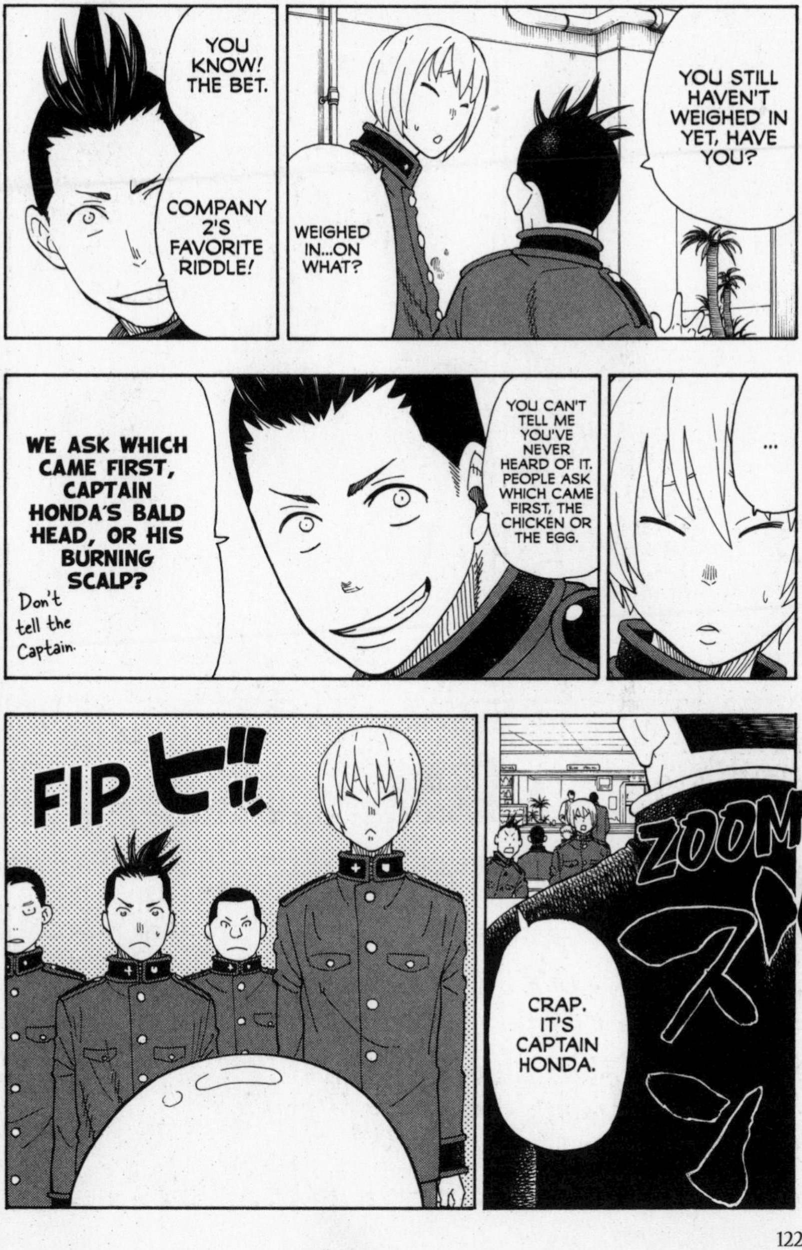
YOU STILL HAVEN'T WEIGHED IN YET, HAVE YOU?
WEIGHED IN...ON WHAT?
YOU KNOW! THE BET.
COMPANY 2'S FAVORITE RIDDLE!
...
YOU CAN'T TELL ME YOU'VE NEVER HEARD OF IT. PEOPLE ASK WHICH CAME FIRST, THE CHICKEN OR THE EGG.
WE ASK WHICH CAME FIRST, CAPTAIN HONDA'S BALD HEAD, OR HIS BURNING SCALP?
Don't tell the Captain.
ZOOM
CRAP. IT'S CAPTAIN HONDA.
FIP

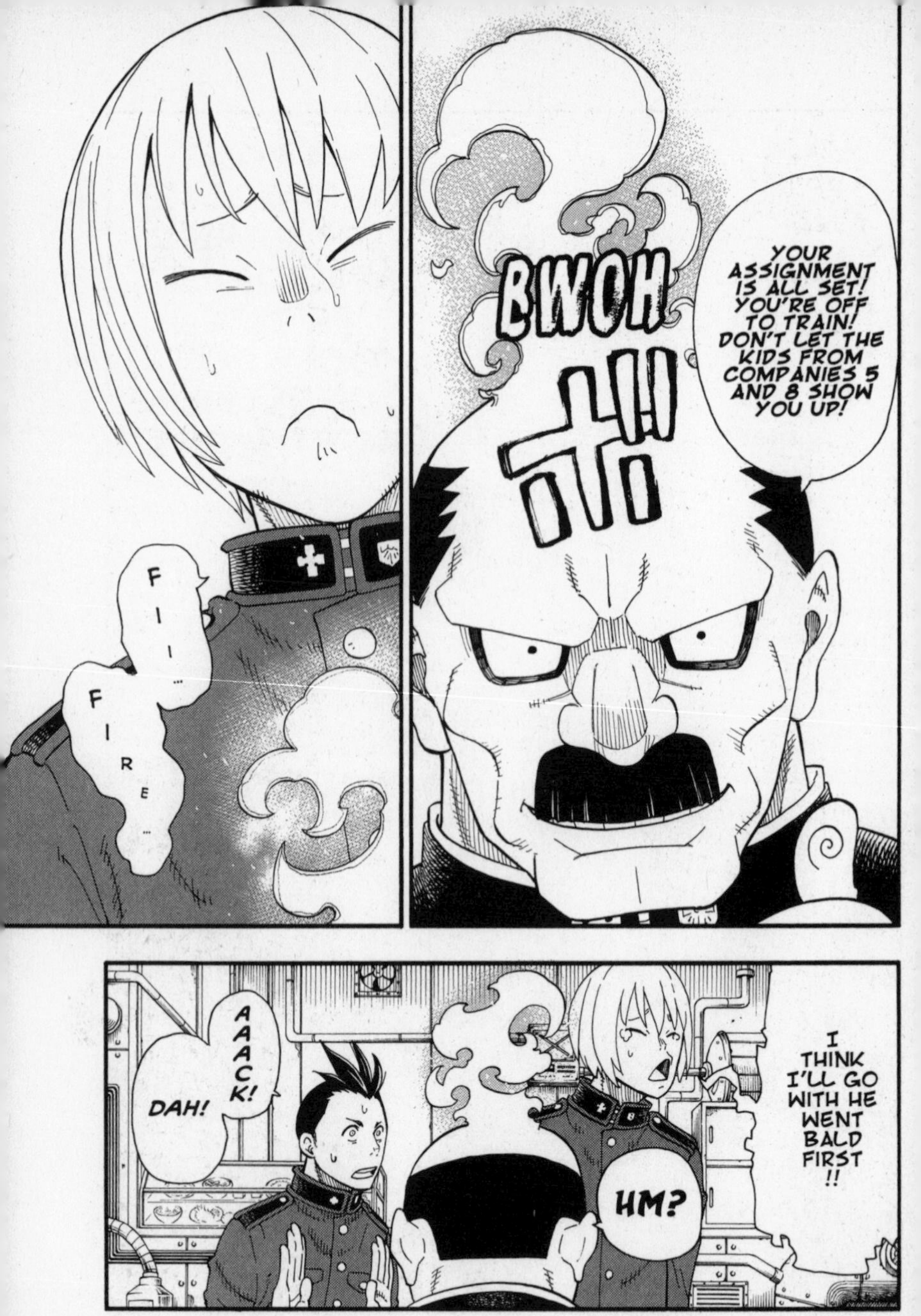
BWOH
YOUR ASSIGNMENT IS ALL SET! YOU'RE OFF TO TRAIN! DON'T LET THE KIDS FROM COMPANIES 5 AND 8 SHOW YOU UP!
FI...
FIRE...
I THINK I'LL GO WITH HE WENT BALD FIRST!!
HM?
AAACK!
DAH!

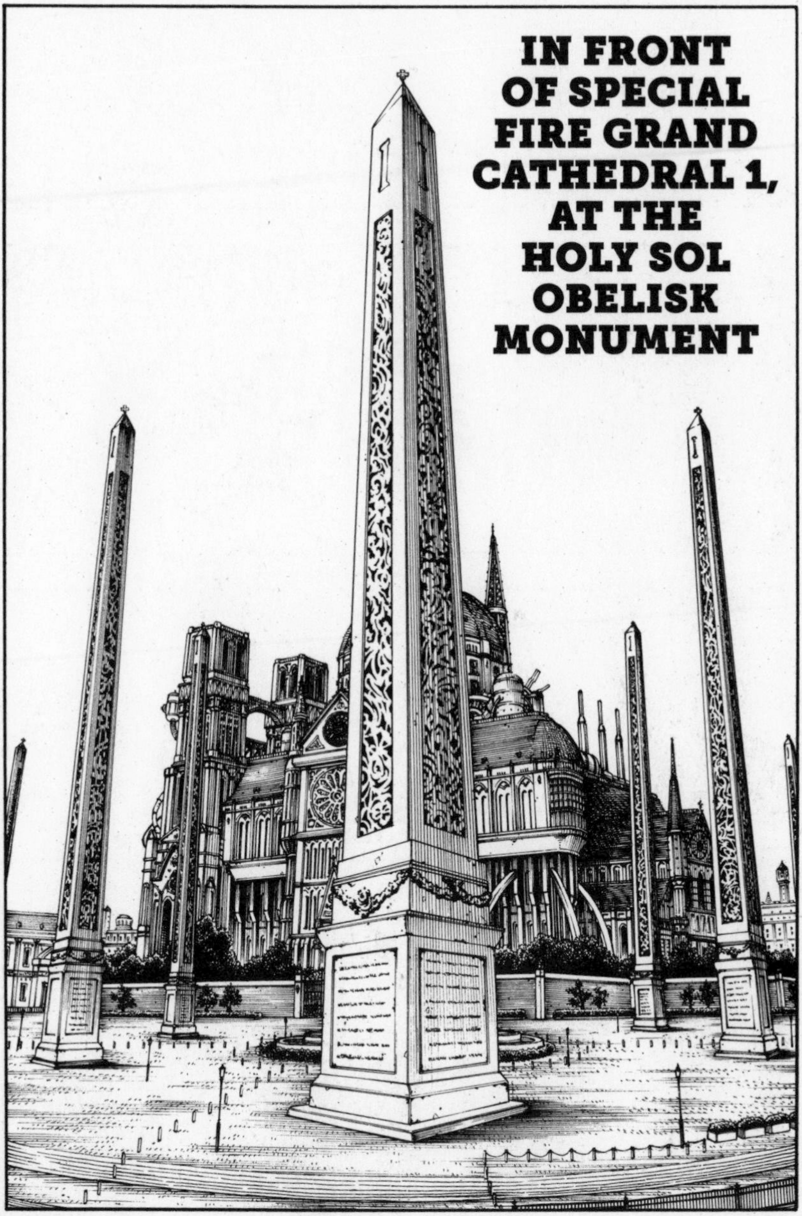
IN FRONT OF SPECIAL FIRE GRAND CATHEDRAL 1, AT THE HOLY SOL OBELISK MONUMENT

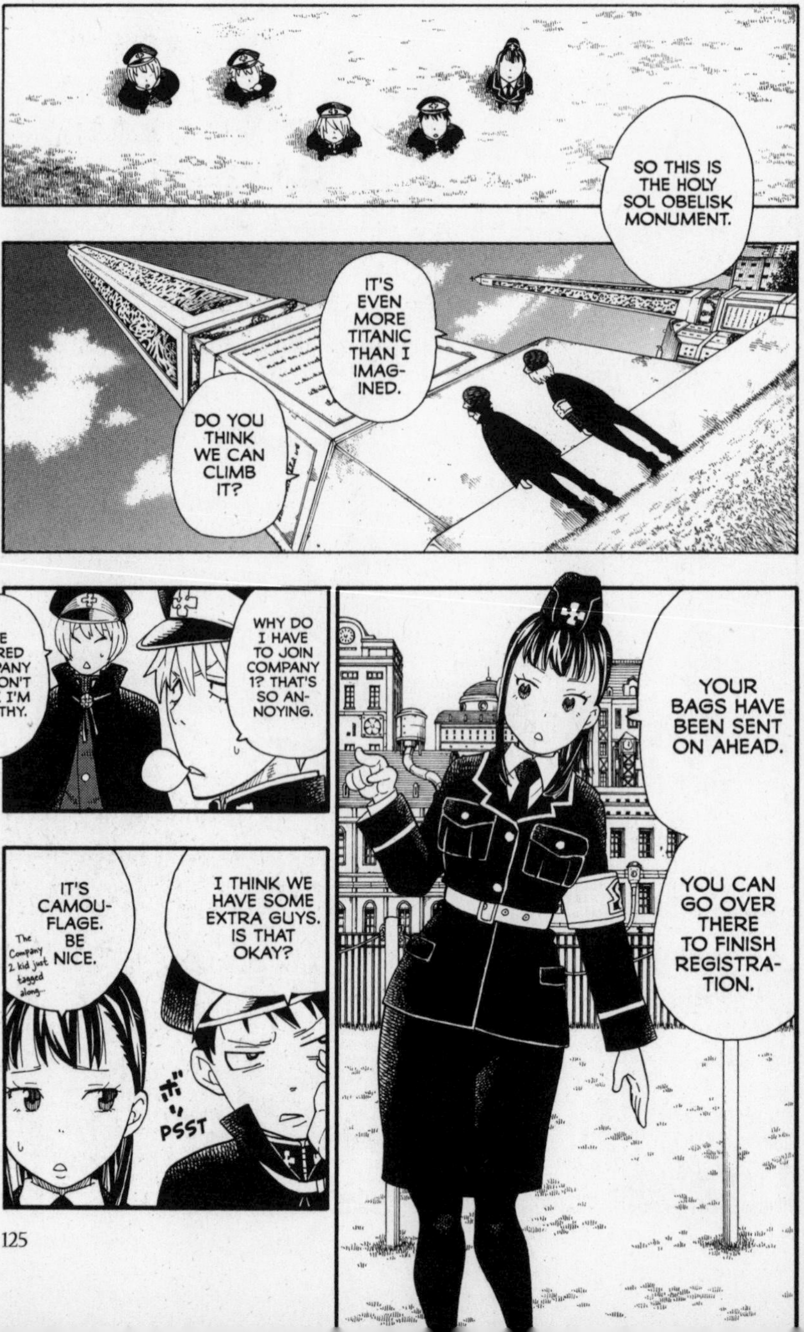
SO THIS IS THE HOLY SOL OBELISK MONUMENT.
IT'S EVEN MORE TITANIC THAN I IMAGINED.
DO YOU THINK WE CAN CLIMB IT?
YOUR BAGS HAVE BEEN SENT ON AHEAD.
YOU CAN GO OVER THERE TO FINISH REGISTRATION.
WHY DO I HAVE TO JOIN COMPANY 1? THAT'S SO ANNOYING.
THE SACRED COMPANY 1...I DON'T THINK I'M WORTHY.
I THINK WE HAVE SOME EXTRA GUYS. IS THAT OKAY?
IT'S CAMOUFLAGE. BE NICE.
The Company 2 kid just tagged along...
PSST

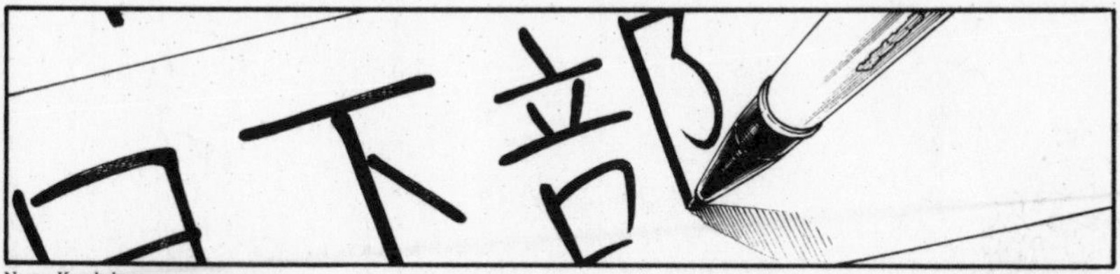

Name: Kusakabe

Sign: Reception

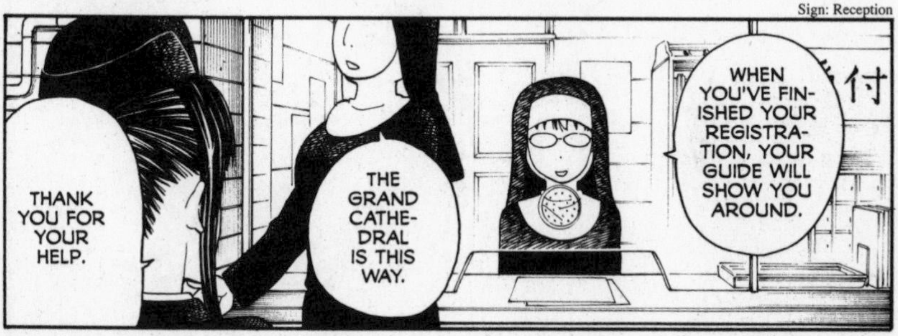
WHEN YOU'VE FIN-ISHED YOUR REGISTRA-TION, YOUR GUIDE WILL SHOW YOU AROUND.
THE GRAND CATHE-DRAL IS THIS WAY.
THANK YOU FOR YOUR HELP.

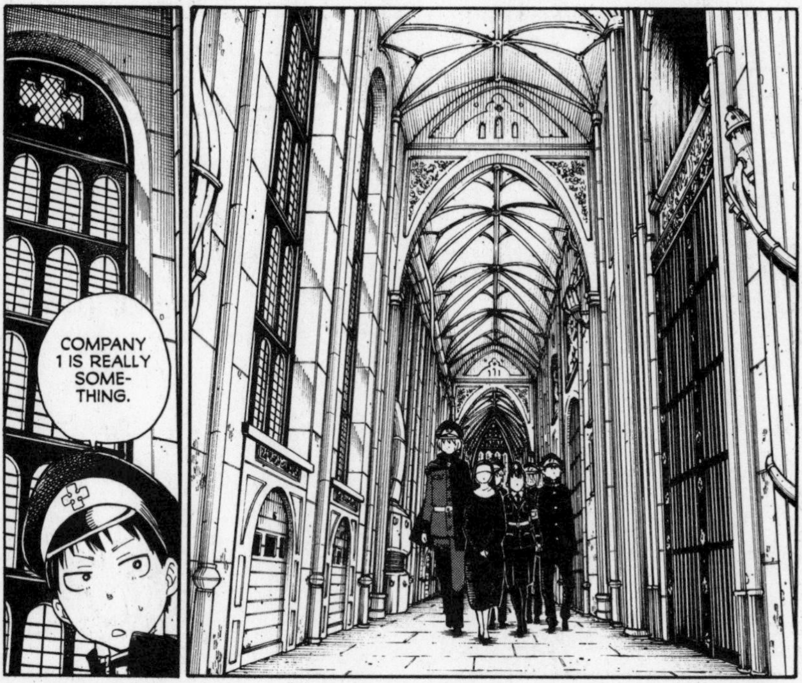
COMPANY 1 IS REALLY SOME-THING.

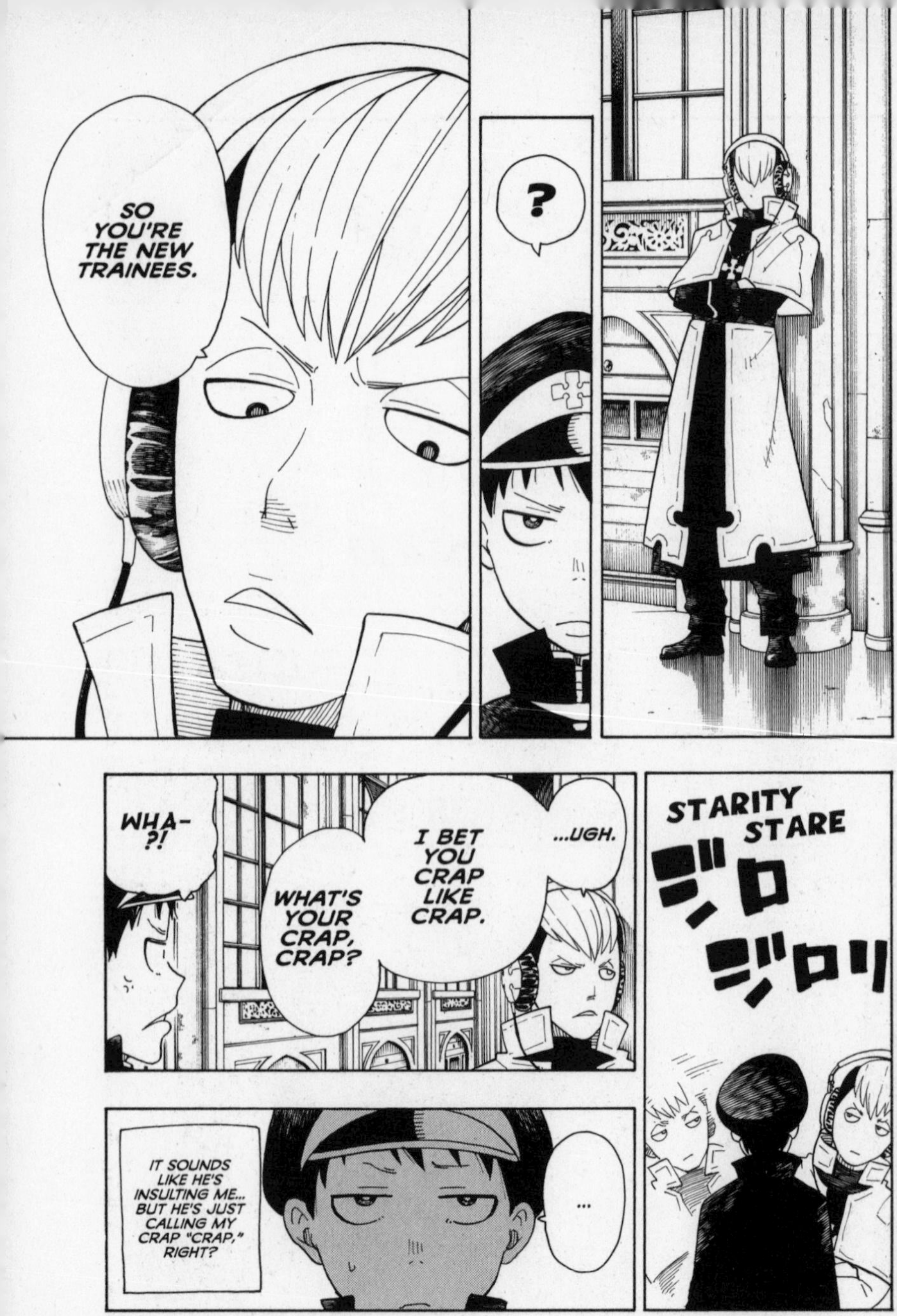
?
SO YOU'RE THE NEW TRAINEES.
STARITY STARE
ジロ
ジロリ
...UGH.
I BET YOU CRAP LIKE CRAP.
WHAT'S YOUR CRAP, CRAP?
WHA-?!
...
IT SOUNDS LIKE HE'S INSULTING ME... BUT HE'S JUST CALLING MY CRAP "CRAP," RIGHT?

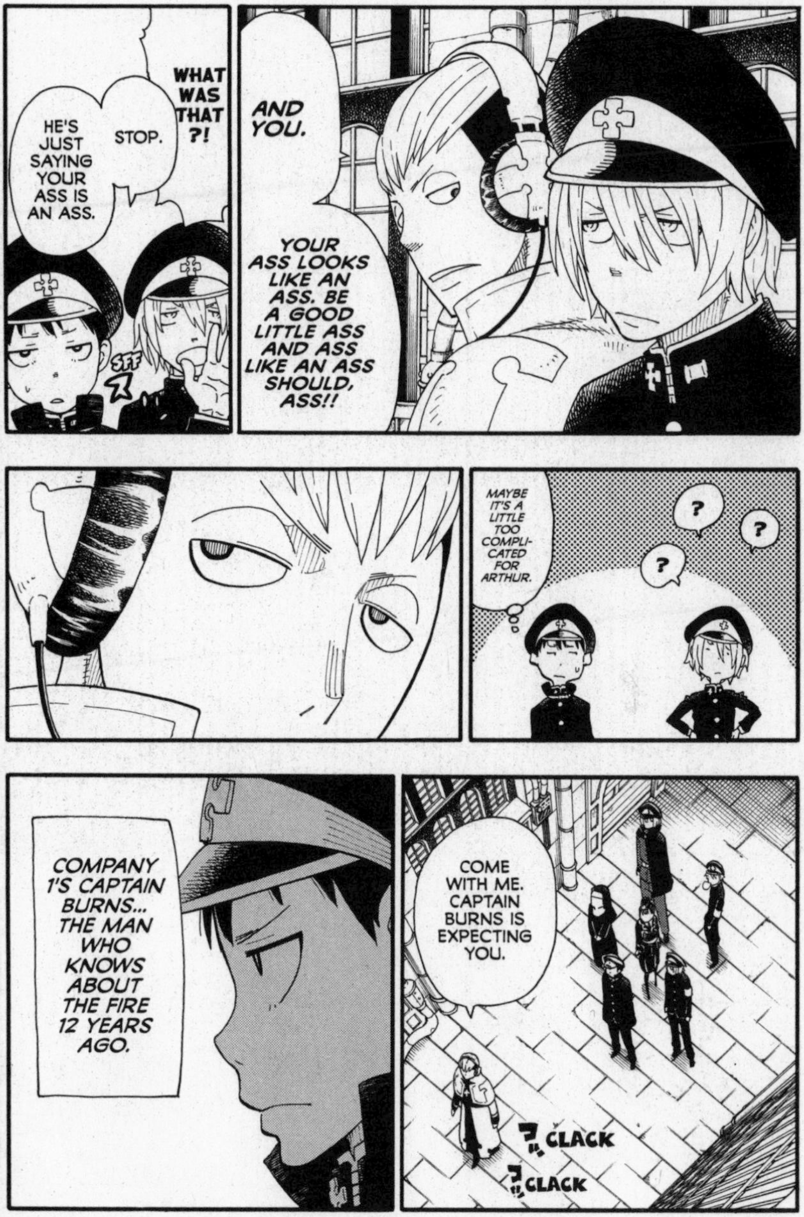
AND YOU.
YOUR ASS LOOKS LIKE AN ASS. BE A GOOD LITTLE ASS AND ASS LIKE AN ASS SHOULD, ASS!!
WHAT WAS THAT?!
STOP.
HE'S JUST SAYING YOUR ASS IS AN ASS.
SFF
?
?
?
MAYBE IT'S A LITTLE TOO COMPLICATED FOR ARTHUR.
COME WITH ME. CAPTAIN BURNS IS EXPECTING YOU.
CLACK
CLACK
COMPANY 1'S CAPTAIN BURNS... THE MAN WHO KNOWS ABOUT THE FIRE 12 YEARS AGO.

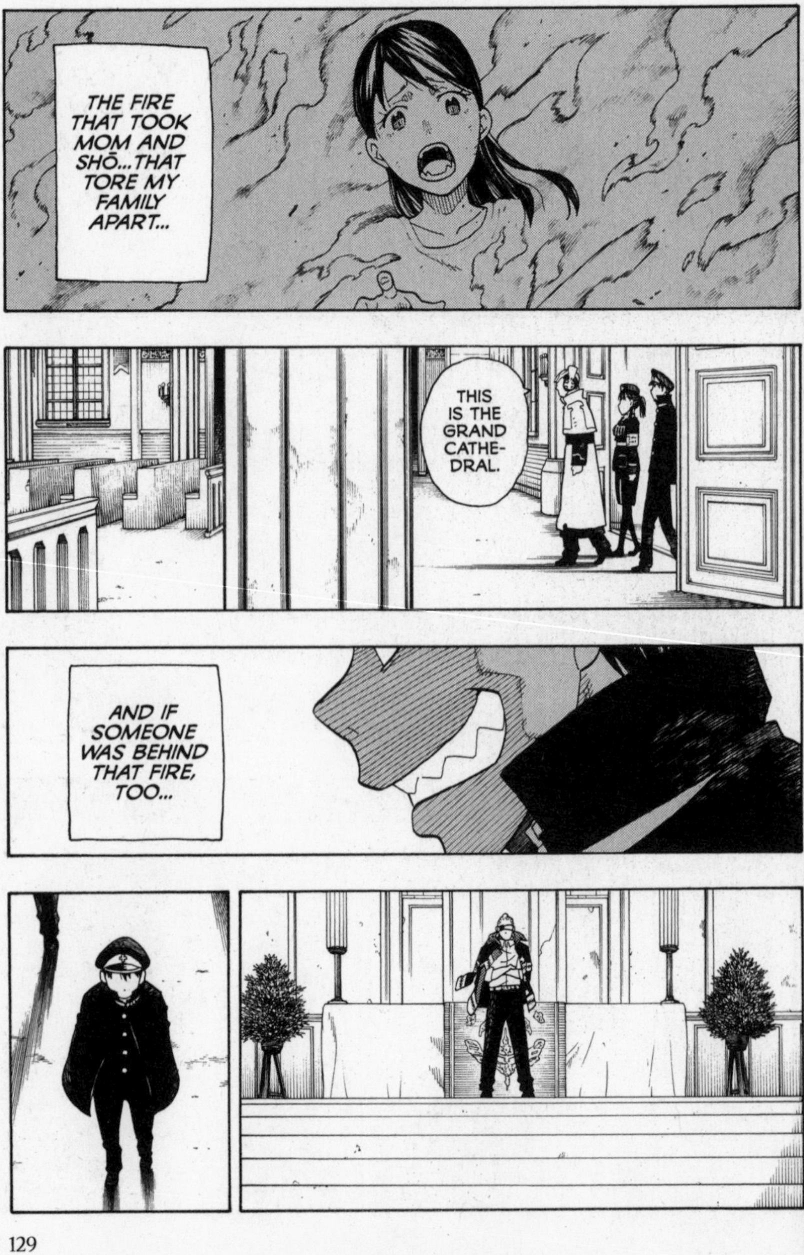
THE FIRE THAT TOOK MOM AND SHŌ...THAT TORE MY FAMILY APART...
THIS IS THE GRAND CATHE-DRAL.
AND IF SOMEONE WAS BEHIND THAT FIRE, TOO...

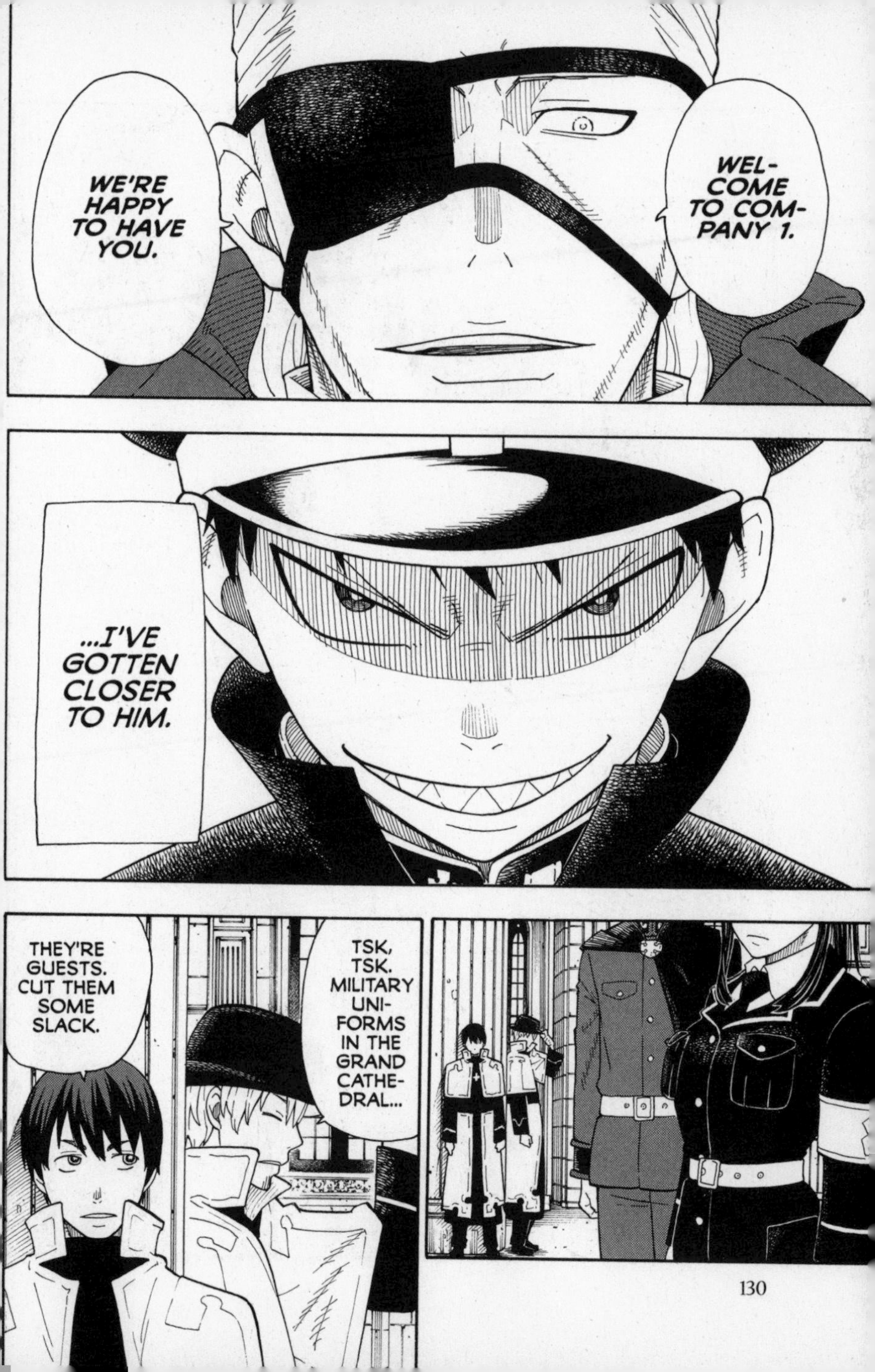
WEL-COME TO COM-PANY 1.
WE'RE HAPPY TO HAVE YOU.
...I'VE GOTTEN CLOSER TO HIM.
TSK, TSK. MILITARY UNI-FORMS IN THE GRAND CATHE-DRAL...
THEY'RE GUESTS. CUT THEM SOME SLACK.

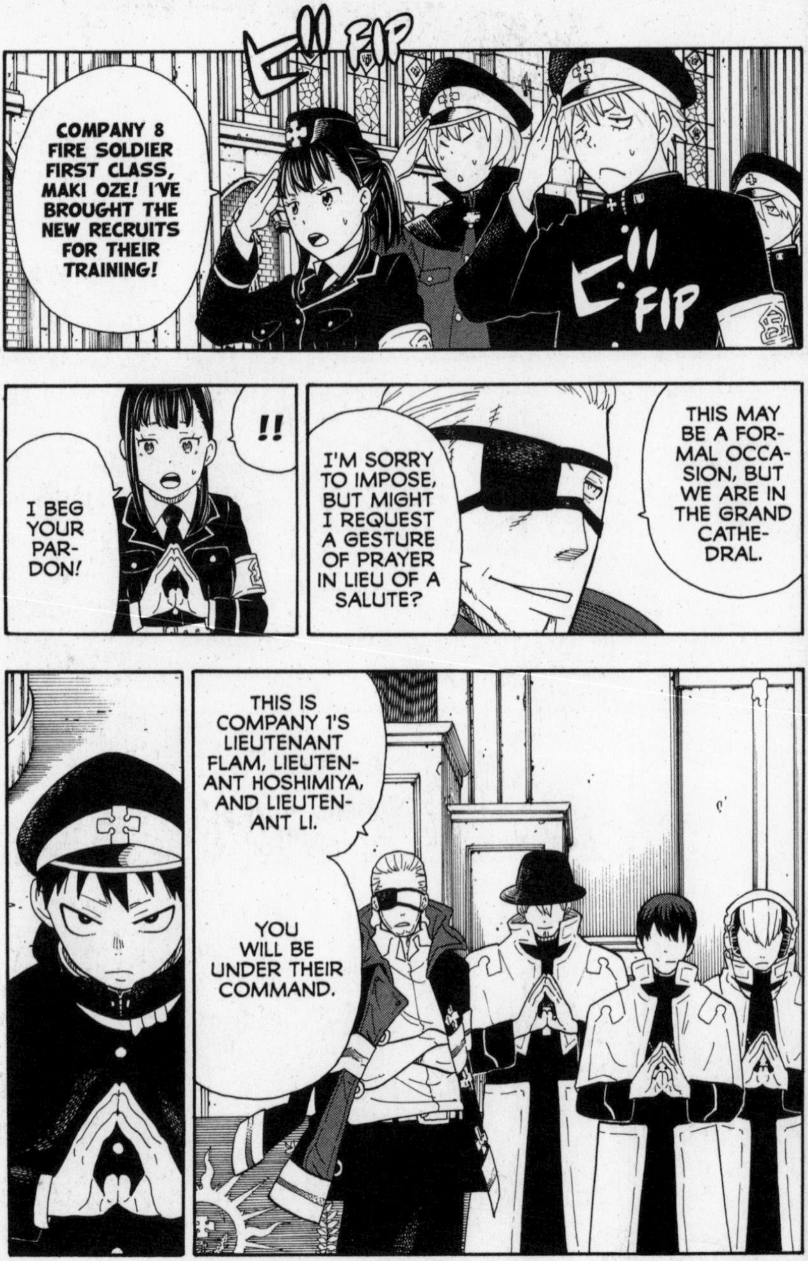

FIP
COMPANY 8 FIRE SOLDIER FIRST CLASS, MAKI OZE! I'VE BROUGHT THE NEW RECRUITS FOR THEIR TRAINING!
FIP
THIS MAY BE A FORMAL OCCASION, BUT WE ARE IN THE GRAND CATHEDRAL.
I'M SORRY TO IMPOSE, BUT MIGHT I REQUEST A GESTURE OF PRAYER IN LIEU OF A SALUTE?
!!
I BEG YOUR PARDON!
THIS IS COMPANY 1'S LIEUTENANT FLAM, LIEUTENANT HOSHIMIYA, AND LIEUTENANT LI.
YOU WILL BE UNDER THEIR COMMAND.

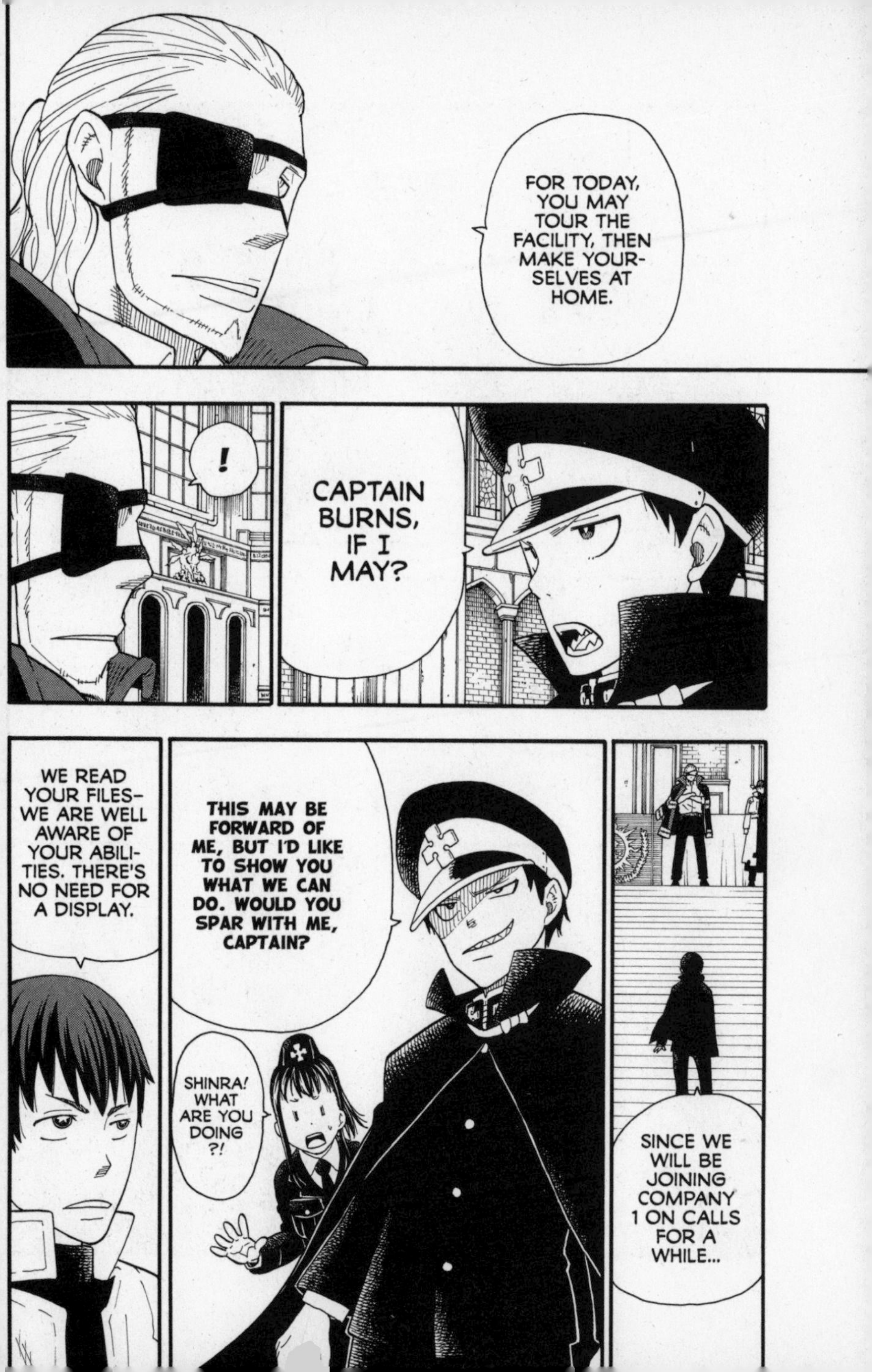
FOR TODAY, YOU MAY TOUR THE FACILITY, THEN MAKE YOUR-SELVES AT HOME.
CAPTAIN BURNS, IF I MAY?
!
SINCE WE WILL BE JOINING COMPANY 1 ON CALLS FOR A WHILE...
THIS MAY BE FORWARD OF ME, BUT I'D LIKE TO SHOW YOU WHAT WE CAN DO. WOULD YOU SPAR WITH ME, CAPTAIN?
SHINRA! WHAT ARE YOU DOING?!
WE READ YOUR FILES—WE ARE WELL AWARE OF YOUR ABILI-TIES. THERE'S NO NEED FOR A DISPLAY.

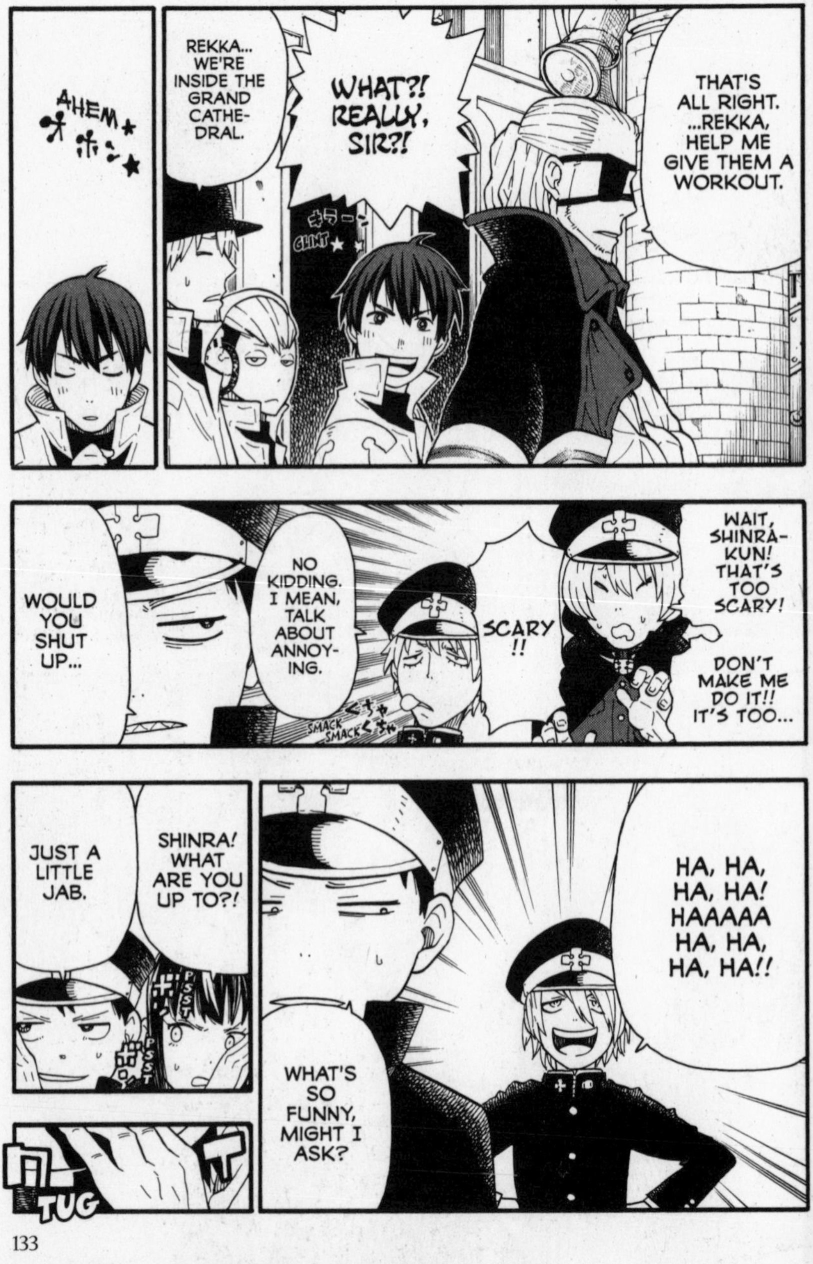
THAT'S ALL RIGHT. ...REKKA, HELP ME GIVE THEM A WORKOUT.
WHAT?! REALLY, SIR?!
REKKA... WE'RE INSIDE THE GRAND CATHEDRAL.
CLINK
AHEM
WAIT, SHINRA-KUN! THAT'S TOO SCARY!
DON'T MAKE ME DO IT!! IT'S TOO...
SCARY!!
NO KIDDING. I MEAN, TALK ABOUT ANNOYING.
SMACK SMACK
WOULD YOU SHUT UP...
HA, HA, HA, HA! HAAAAA HA, HA, HA, HA!!
WHAT'S SO FUNNY, MIGHT I ASK?
SHINRA! WHAT ARE YOU UP TO?!
JUST A LITTLE JAB.
PSST
PSST
TUG

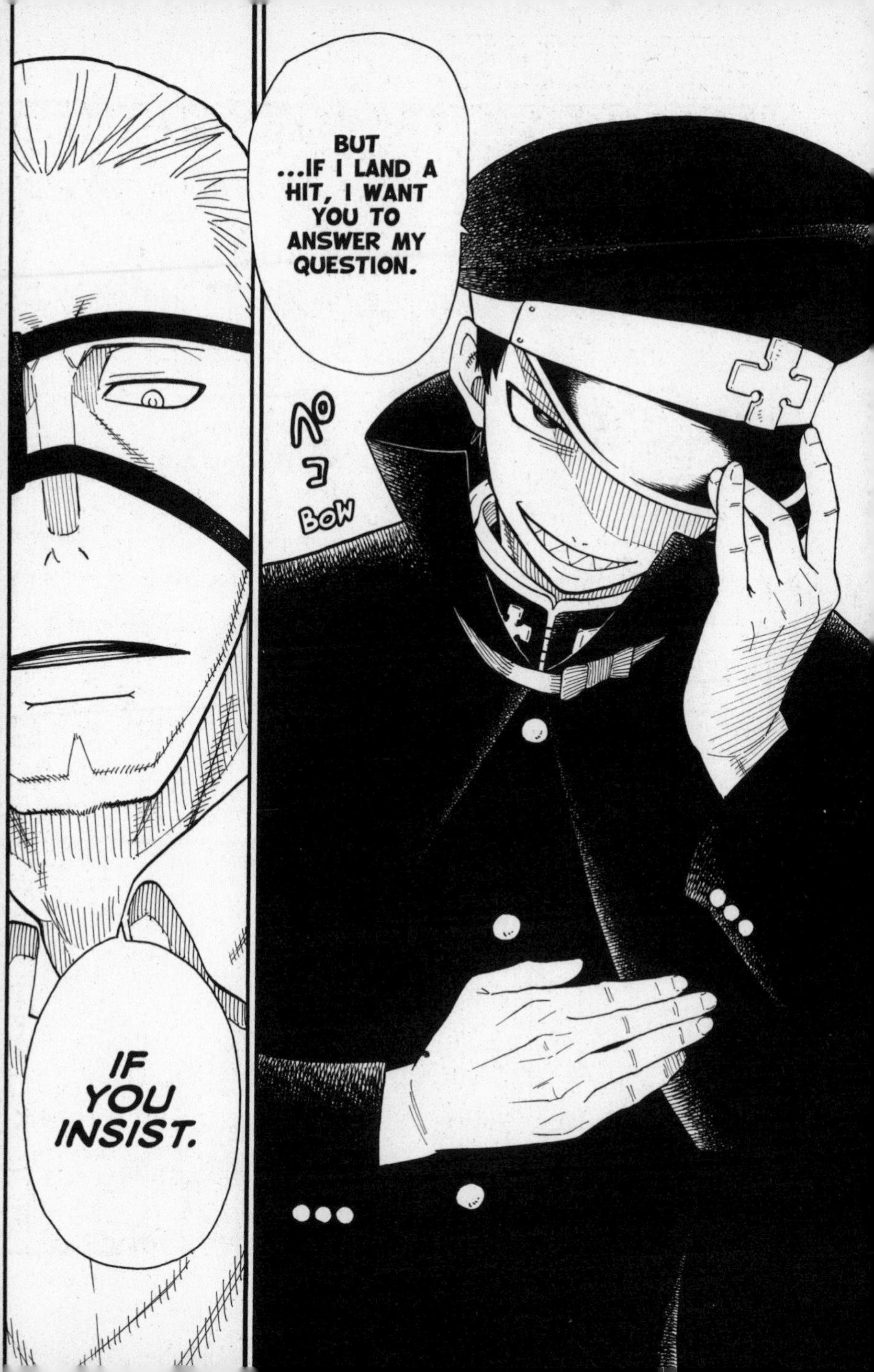
BUT ...IF I LAND A HIT, I WANT YOU TO ANSWER MY QUESTION.
ヘコ
BOW
...
IF YOU INSIST.

FIRE FORCE

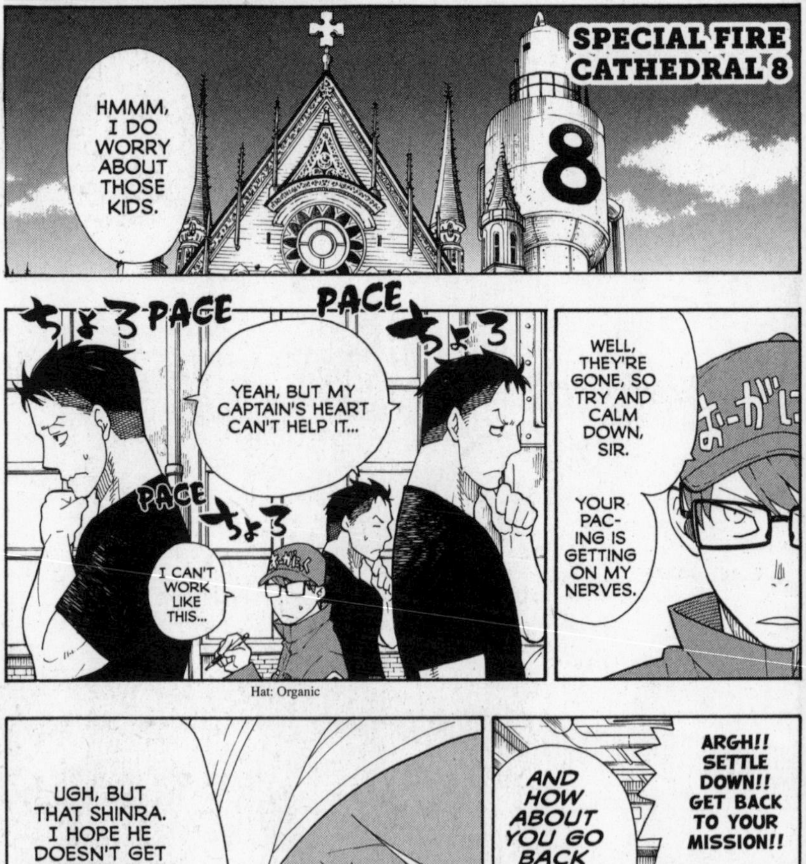
SPECIAL FIRE CATHEDRAL 8
8
HMMM, I DO WORRY ABOUT THOSE KIDS.
WELL, THEY'RE GONE, SO TRY AND CALM DOWN, SIR.
YOUR PAC-ING IS GETTING ON MY NERVES.
PACE
ちょろ
PACE
ちょろ
YEAH, BUT MY CAPTAIN'S HEART CAN'T HELP IT...
PACE
ちょろ
I CAN'T WORK LIKE THIS...

Hat: Organic

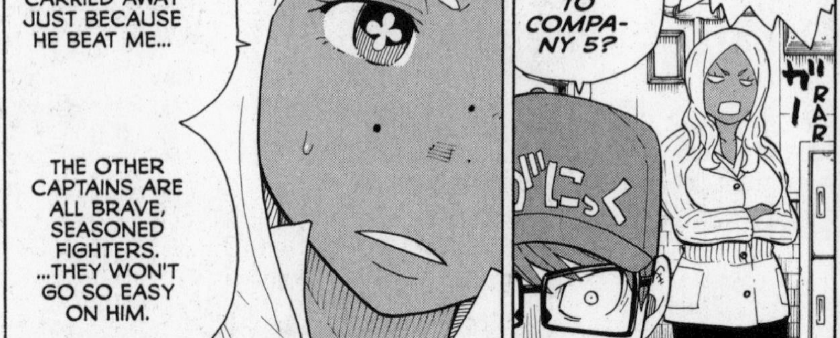
ARGH!! SETTLE DOWN!! GET BACK TO YOUR MISSION!!
AND HOW ABOUT YOU GO BACK TO COMPA-NY 5?
RAR
UGH, BUT THAT SHINRA. I HOPE HE DOESN'T GET CARRIED AWAY JUST BECAUSE HE BEAT ME...
THE OTHER CAPTAINS ARE ALL BRAVE, SEASONED FIGHTERS. ...THEY WON'T GO SO EASY ON HIM.

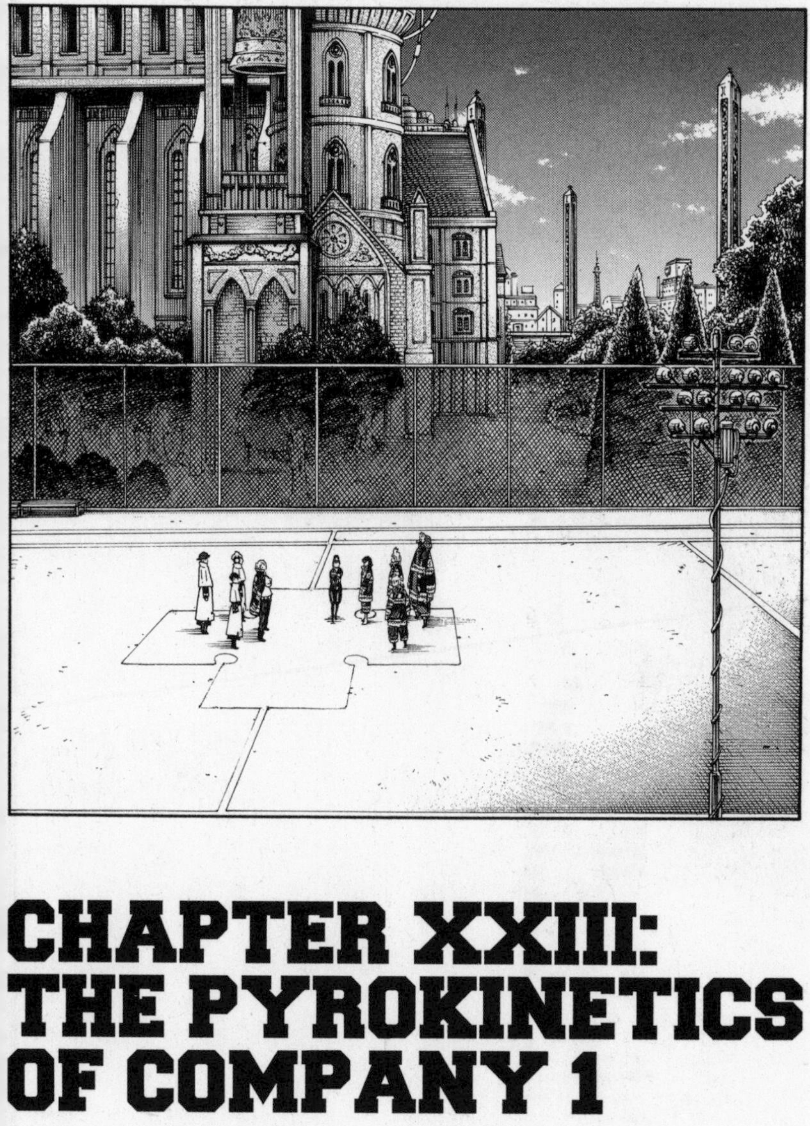

CHAPTER XXIII: THE PYROKINETICS OF COMPANY 1

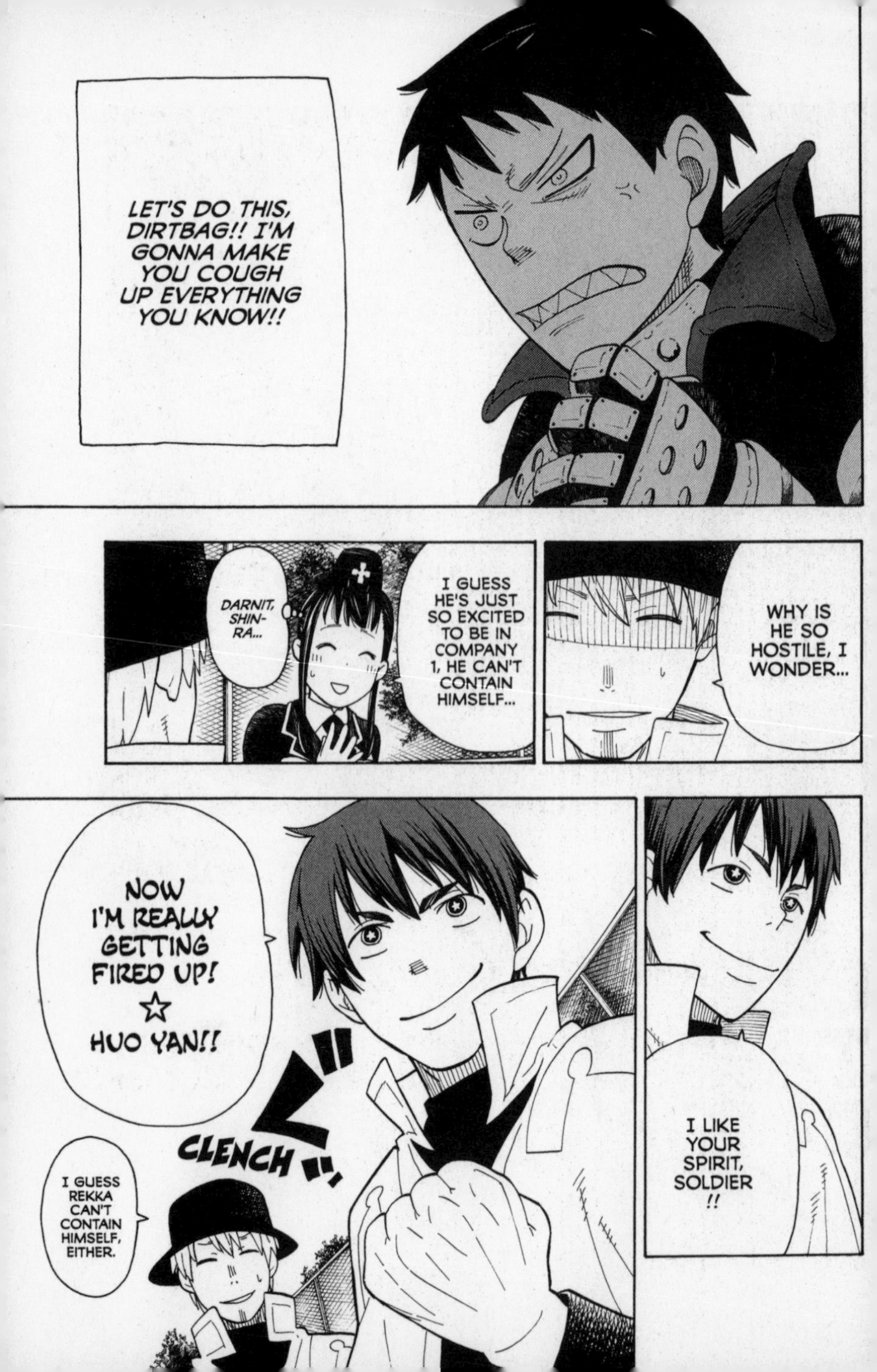
LET'S DO THIS, DIRTBAG!! I'M GONNA MAKE YOU COUGH UP EVERYTHING YOU KNOW!!
WHY IS HE SO HOSTILE, I WONDER...
I GUESS HE'S JUST SO EXCITED TO BE IN COMPANY 1, HE CAN'T CONTAIN HIMSELF...
DARNIT, SHINRA...
I LIKE YOUR SPIRIT, SOLDIER!!
NOW I'M REALLY GETTING FIRED UP! ☆ HUO YAN!!
CLENCH
I GUESS REKKA CAN'T CONTAIN HIMSELF, EITHER.

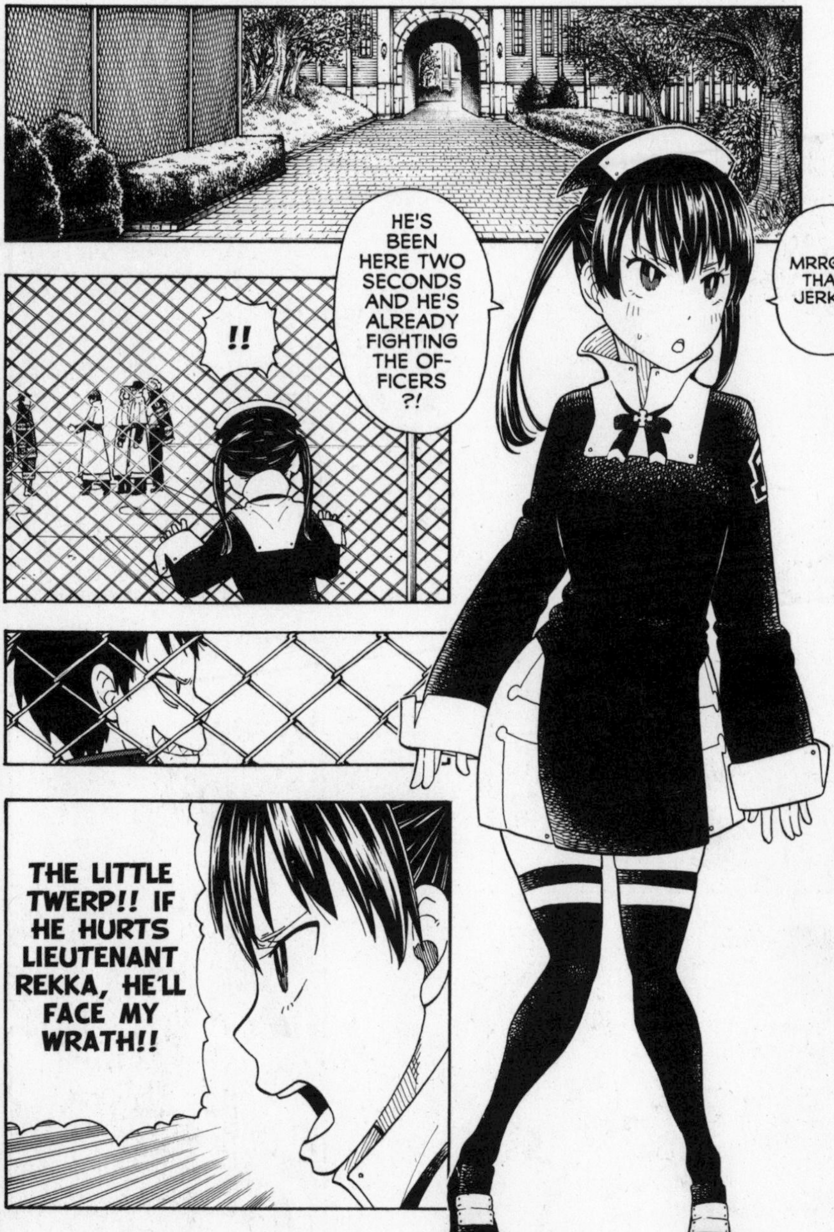
MRRGH, THAT JERK!!
HE'S BEEN HERE TWO SECONDS AND HE'S ALREADY FIGHTING THE OF-FICERS?!
!!
THE LITTLE TWERP!! IF HE HURTS LIEUTENANT REKKA, HE'LL FACE MY WRATH!!

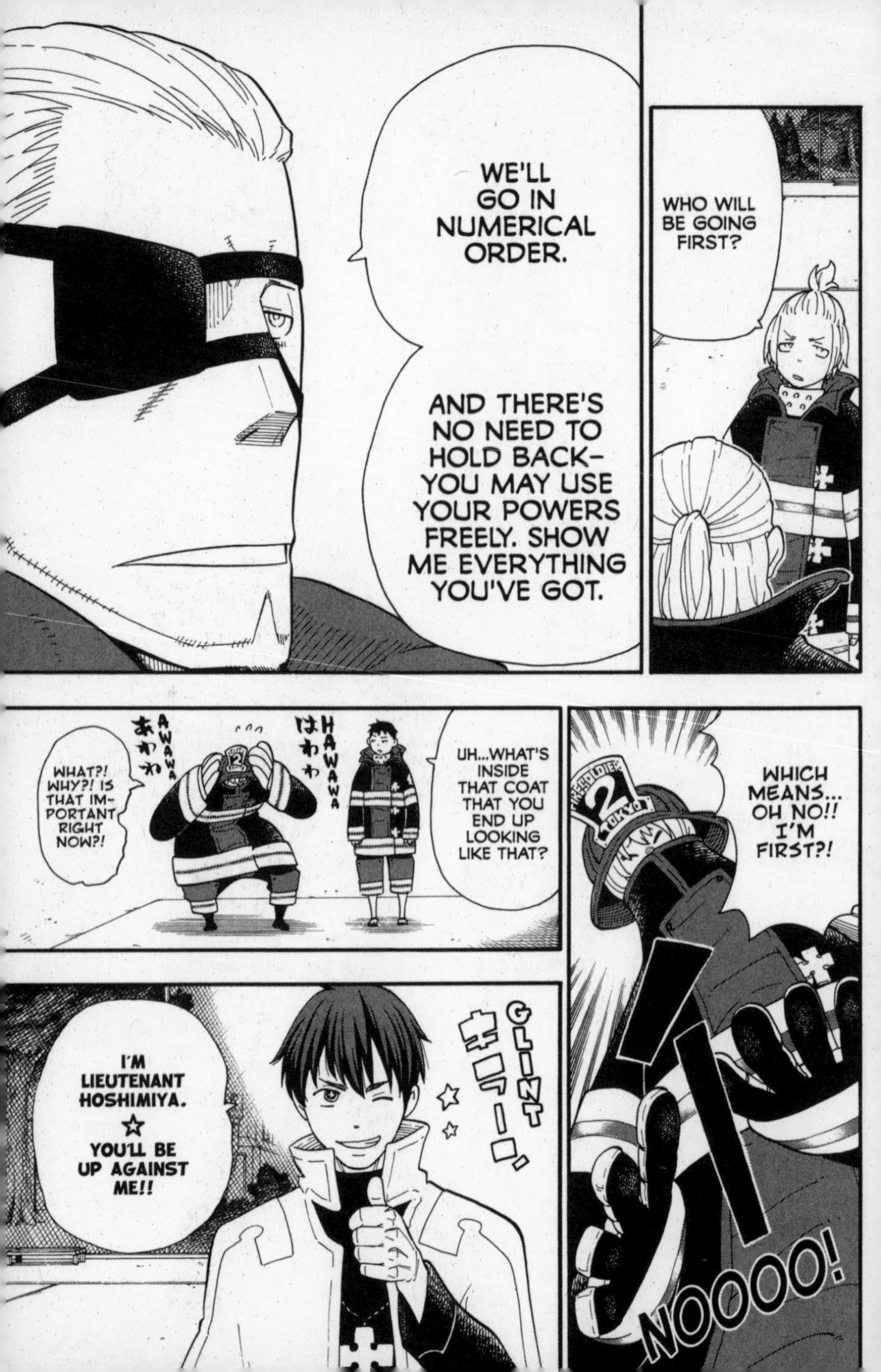
WHO WILL BE GOING FIRST?
WE'LL GO IN NUMERICAL ORDER.
AND THERE'S NO NEED TO HOLD BACK– YOU MAY USE YOUR POWERS FREELY. SHOW ME EVERYTHING YOU'VE GOT.
WHICH MEANS... OH NO!! I'M FIRST?!
NOOOO!
UH...WHAT'S INSIDE THAT COAT THAT YOU END UP LOOKING LIKE THAT?
はわわ HAWAWA
あわわ AWAWA
WHAT?! WHY?! IS THAT IM-PORTANT RIGHT NOW?!
キラーン GLINT
I'M LIEUTENANT HOSHIMIYA. ☆ YOU'LL BE UP AGAINST ME!!

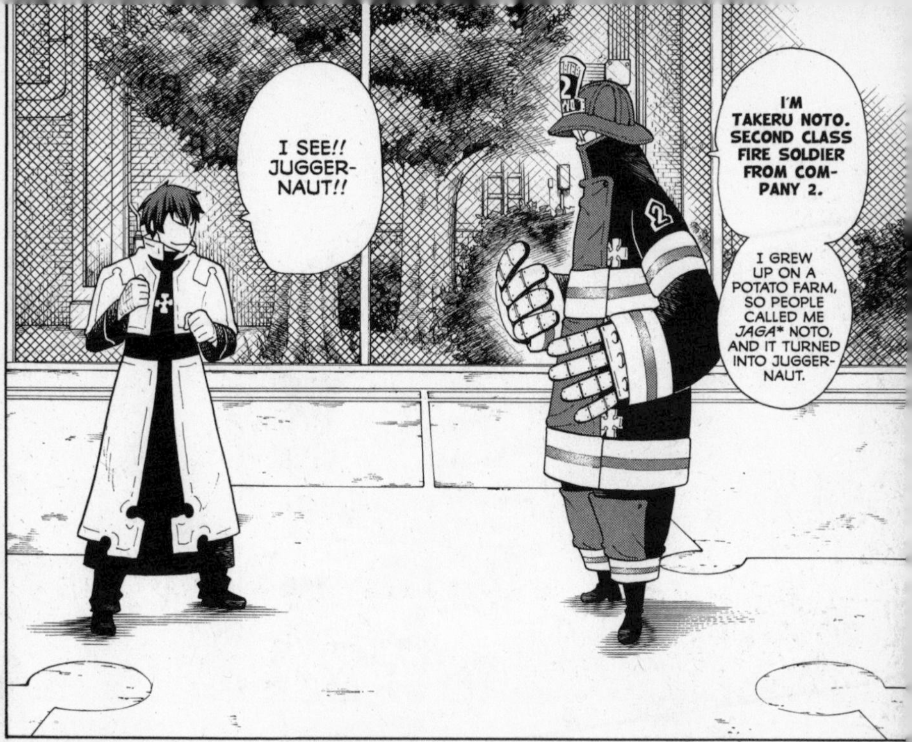
I'M TAKERU NOTO. SECOND CLASS FIRE SOLDIER FROM COMPANY 2.
I GREW UP ON A POTATO FARM, SO PEOPLE CALLED ME *JAGA** NOTO, AND IT TURNED INTO JUGGERNAUT.
I SEE!! JUGGERNAUT!!

*Japanese for "potato."

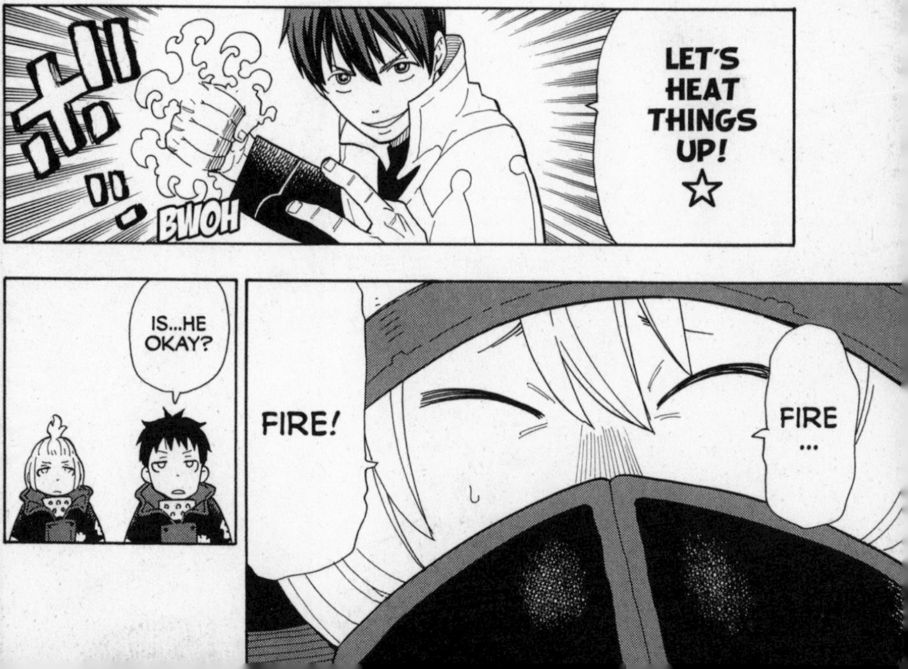
LET'S HEAT THINGS UP! ☆
BWOH
FIRE ...
FIRE!
IS...HE OKAY?

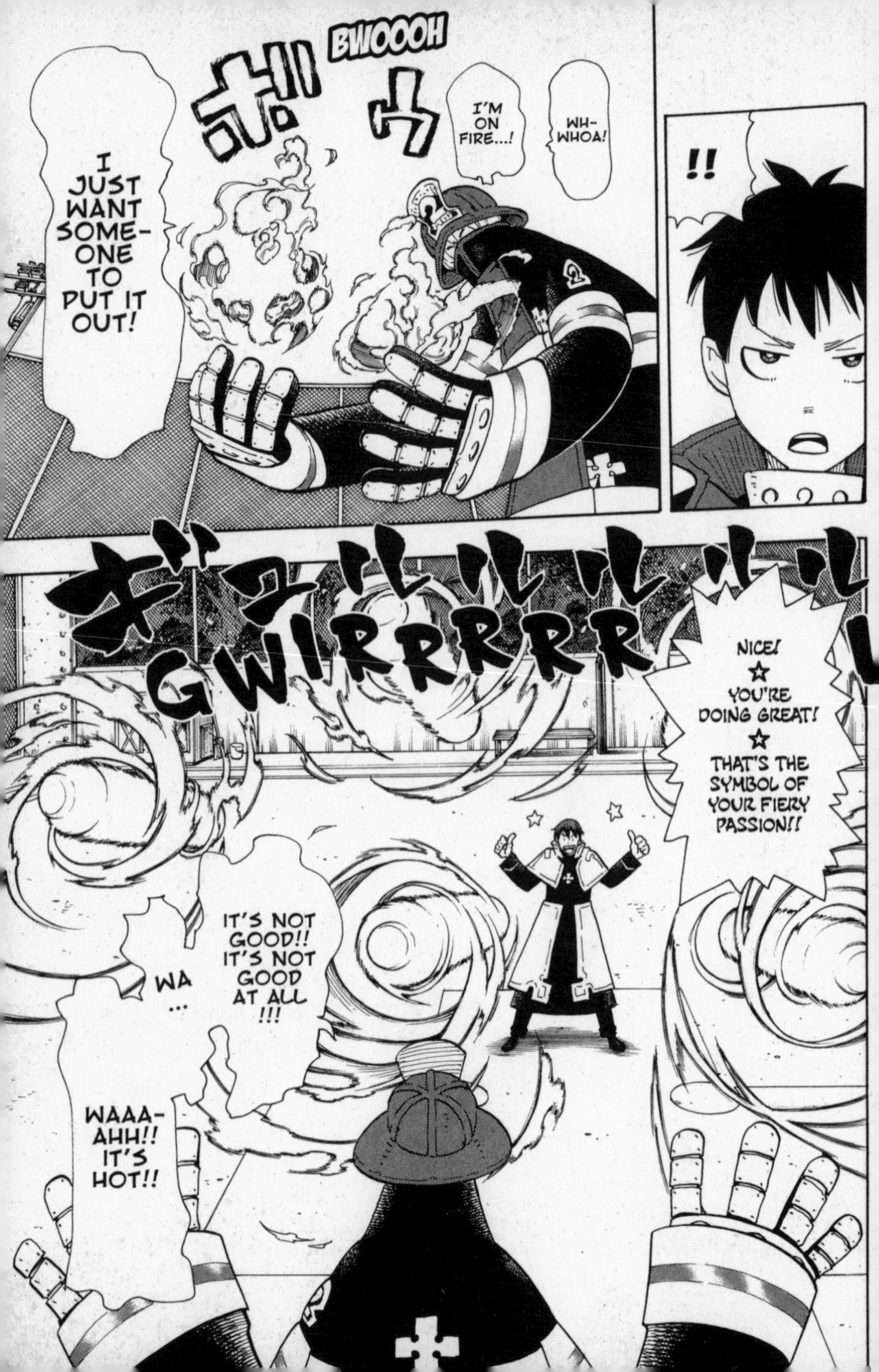
!!
WH-WHOA!
I'M ON FIRE...!
BWOOOH
I JUST WANT SOMEONE TO PUT IT OUT!
GWIRRRRR
NICE! ☆ YOU'RE DOING GREAT! ☆ THAT'S THE SYMBOL OF YOUR FIERY PASSION!!
IT'S NOT GOOD!! IT'S NOT GOOD AT ALL!!!
WA...
WAAAAHH!! IT'S HOT!!

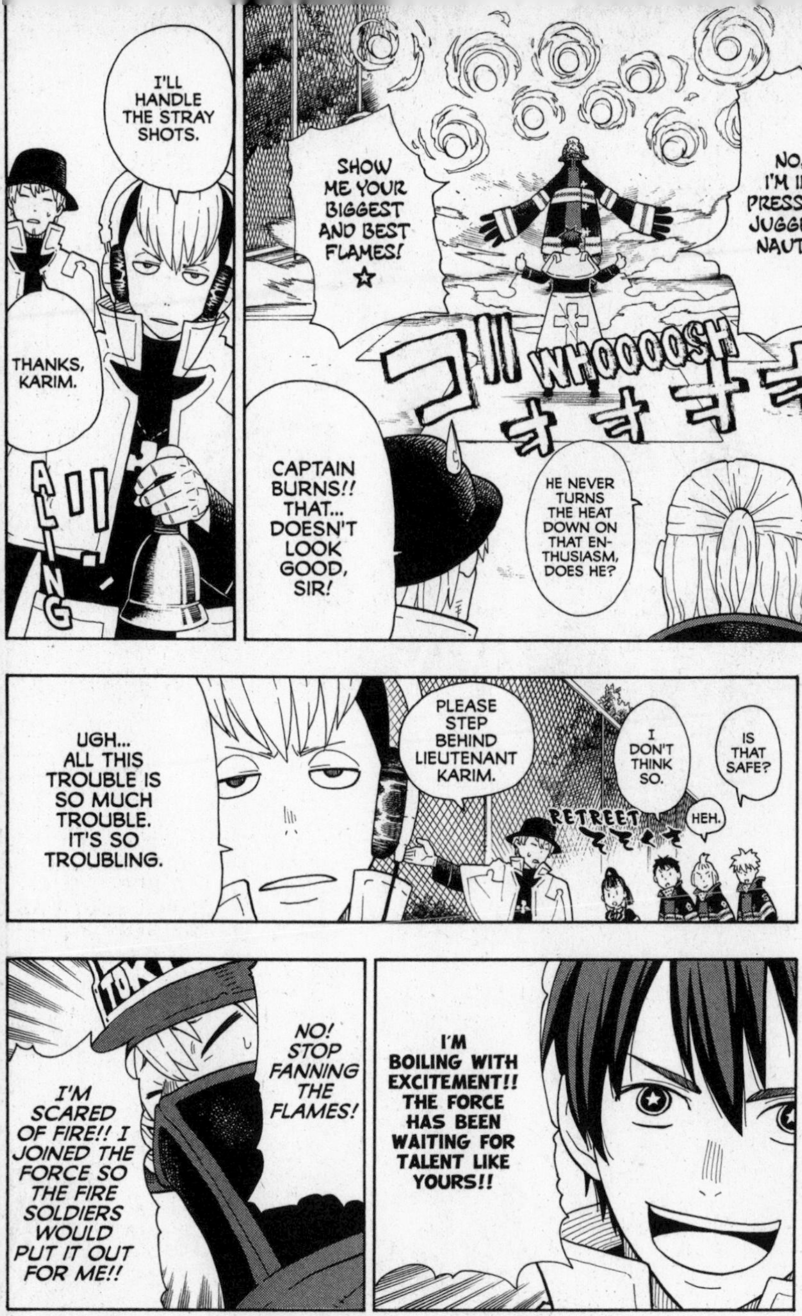
NO, I'M IM-PRESSED, JUGGER-NAUT!!
SHOW ME YOUR BIGGEST AND BEST FLAMES! ☆
WHOOOOSH
HE NEVER TURNS THE HEAT DOWN ON THAT EN-THUSIASM, DOES HE?
CAPTAIN BURNS!! THAT... DOESN'T LOOK GOOD, SIR!
I'LL HANDLE THE STRAY SHOTS.
THANKS, KARIM.
ALING
IS THAT SAFE?
HEH.
I DON'T THINK SO.
PLEASE STEP BEHIND LIEUTENANT KARIM.
RETREET
UGH... ALL THIS TROUBLE IS SO MUCH TROUBLE. IT'S SO TROUBLING.
I'M BOILING WITH EXCITEMENT!! THE FORCE HAS BEEN WAITING FOR TALENT LIKE YOURS!!
NO! STOP FANNING THE FLAMES!
I'M SCARED OF FIRE!! I JOINED THE FORCE SO THE FIRE SOLDIERS WOULD PUT IT OUT FOR ME!!

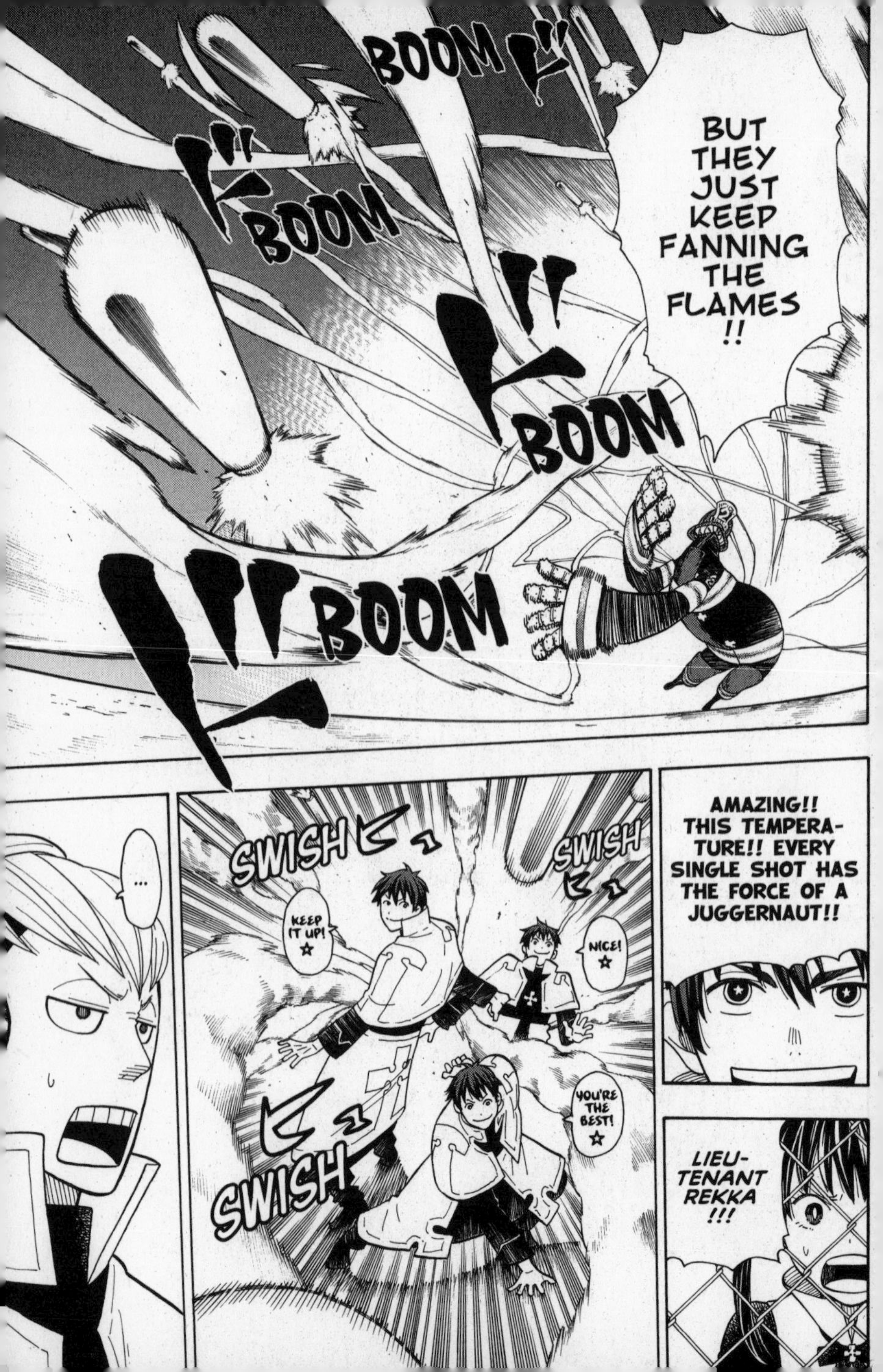
BUT THEY JUST KEEP FANNING THE FLAMES !!
BOOM
BOOM
BOOM
BOOM
AMAZING!! THIS TEMPERA-TURE!! EVERY SINGLE SHOT HAS THE FORCE OF A JUGGERNAUT!!
LIEU-TENANT REKKA !!!
SWISH
SWISH
NICE! ☆
KEEP IT UP! ☆
YOU'RE THE BEST! ☆
SWISH
...

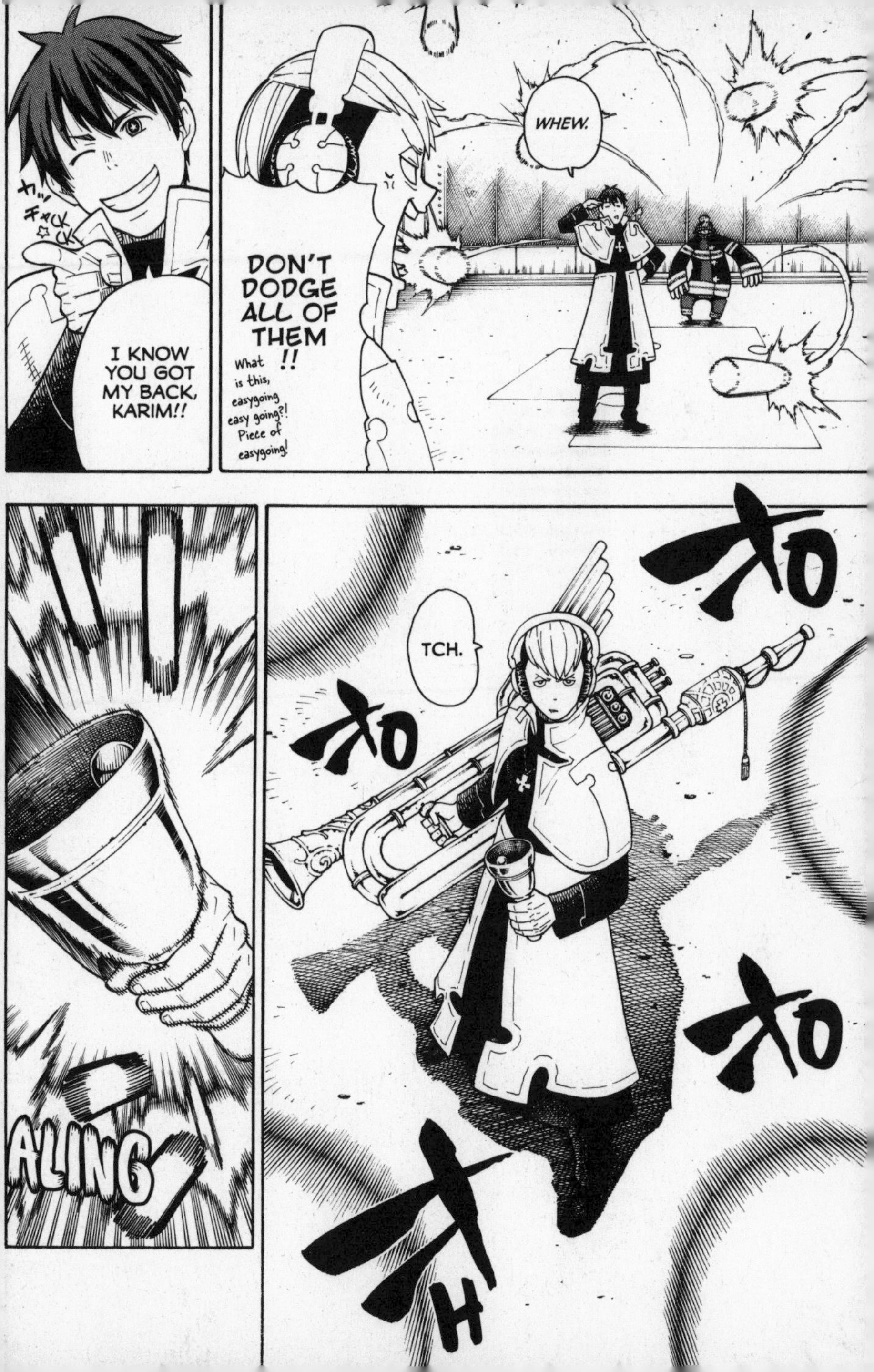
WHEW.
DON'T DODGE ALL OF THEM!!
What is this, easygoing easy going?! Piece of easygoing!
I KNOW YOU GOT MY BACK, KARIM!!
カッチャ☆
CK CK
TCH.
ALING

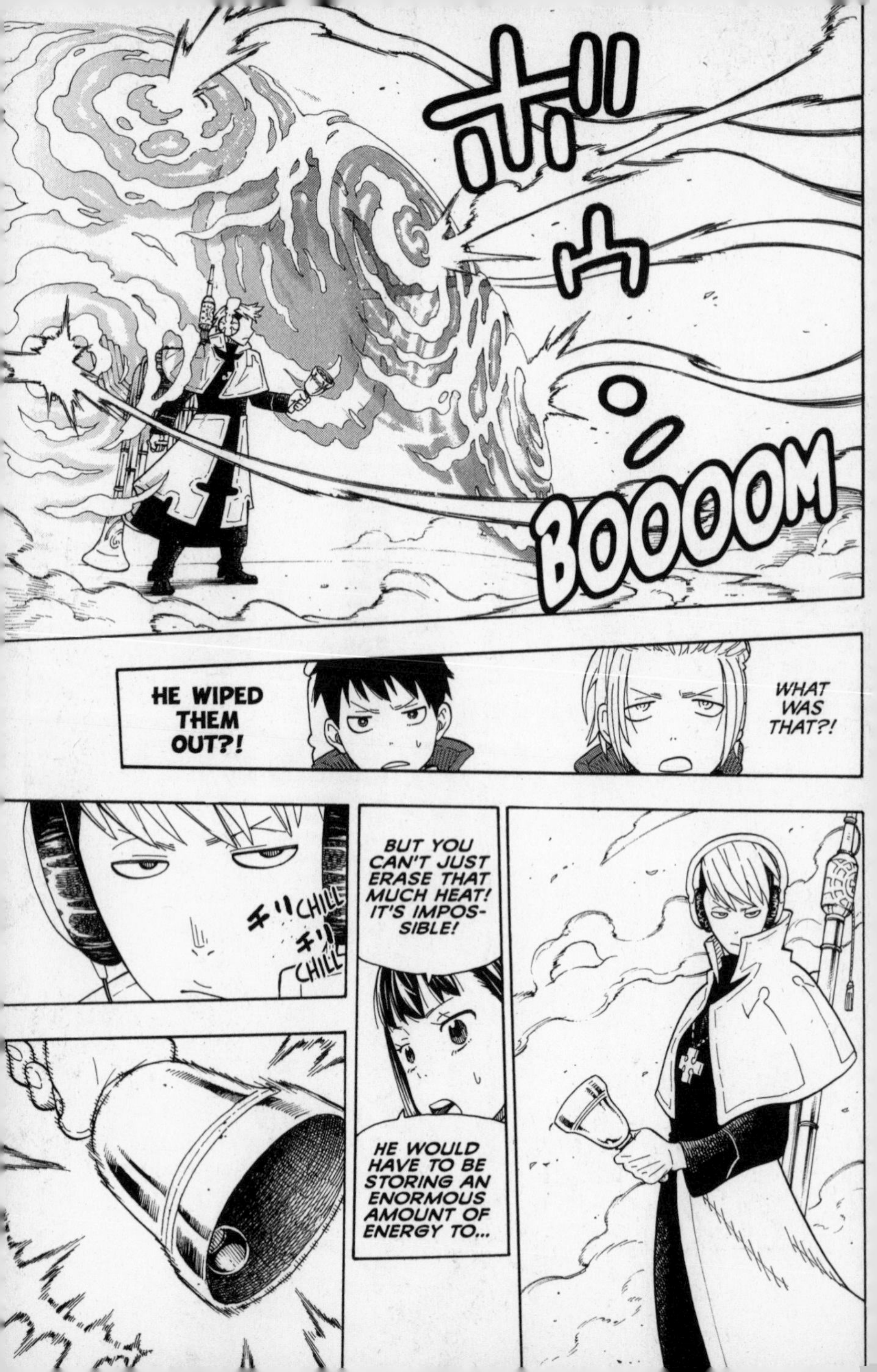
ボウッ
BOOOOM
WHAT WAS THAT?!
HE WIPED THEM OUT?!
BUT YOU CAN'T JUST ERASE THAT MUCH HEAT! IT'S IMPOSSIBLE!
HE WOULD HAVE TO BE STORING AN ENORMOUS AMOUNT OF ENERGY TO...
チリ CHILL
チリ CHILL

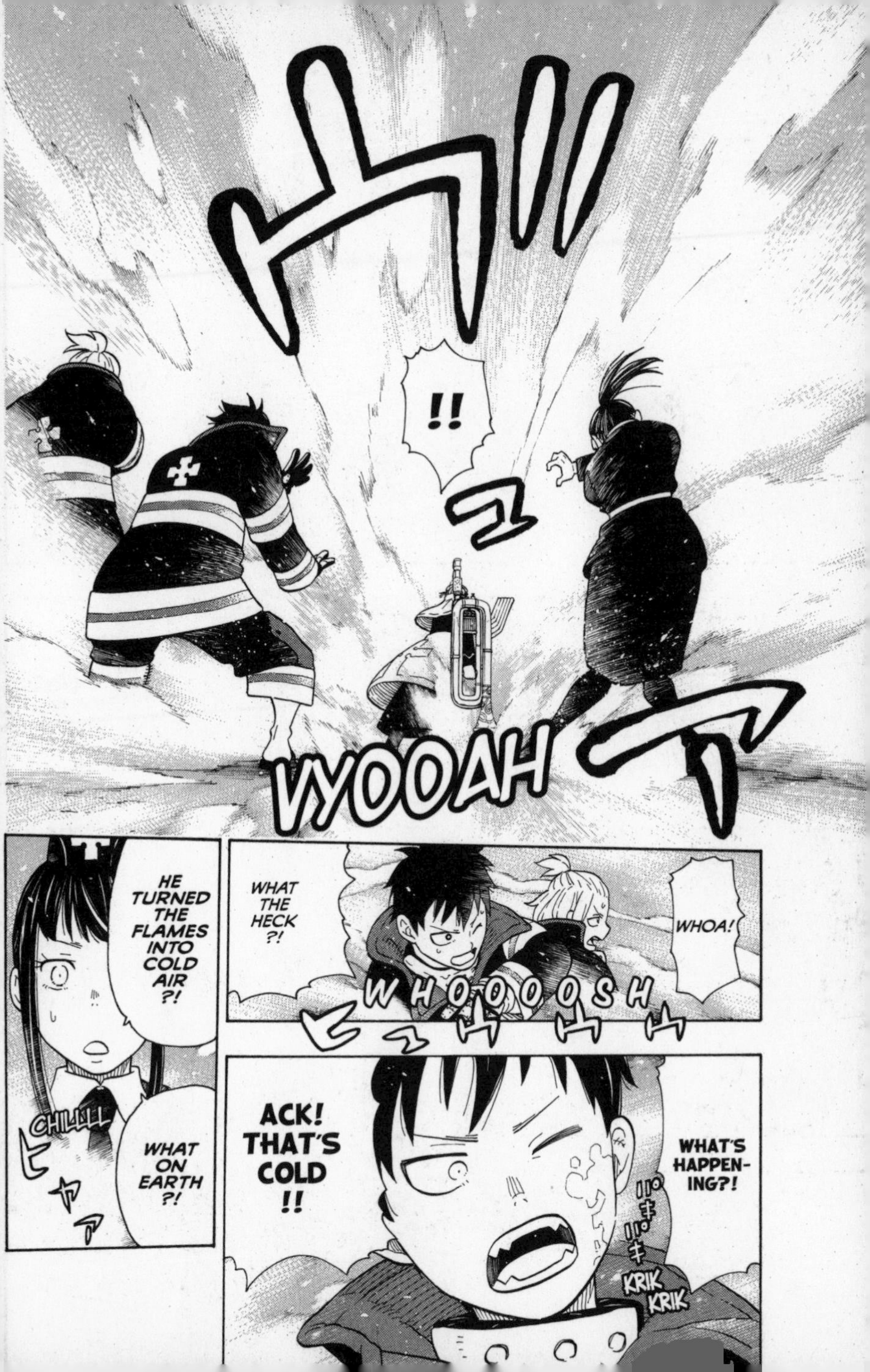
!!
VYOOAH
WHOA!
WHAT THE HECK?!
WHOOOOOSH
WHAT'S HAPPENING?!
ACK! THAT'S COLD!!
KRIK KRIK
HE TURNED THE FLAMES INTO COLD AIR?!
WHAT ON EARTH?!
CHILLLL

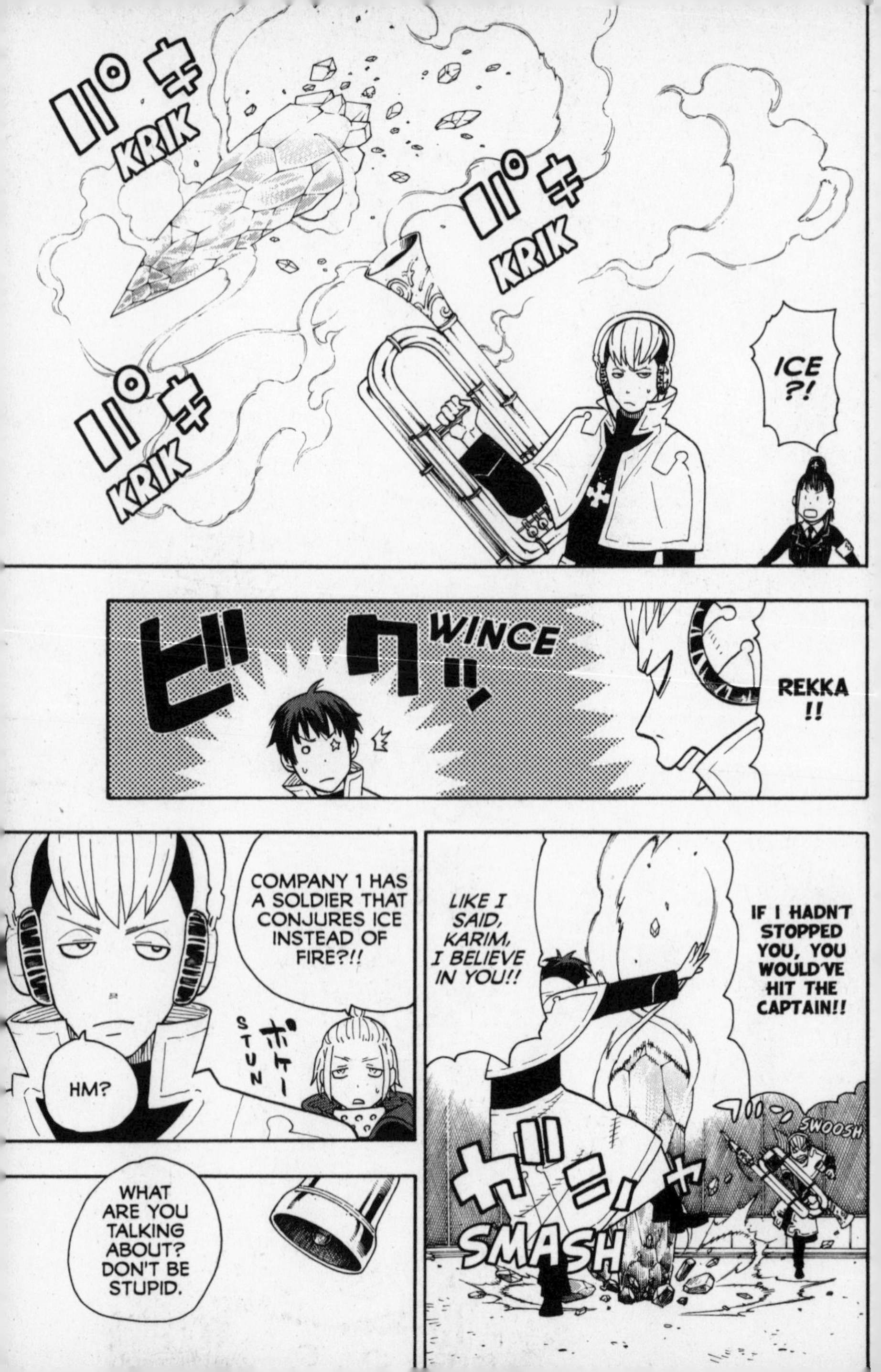
KRIK
KRIK
KRIK
ICE ?!
REKKA !!
WINCE
IF I HADN'T STOPPED YOU, YOU WOULD'VE HIT THE CAPTAIN!!
LIKE I SAID, KARIM, I BELIEVE IN YOU!!
SWOOSH
SMASH
COMPANY 1 HAS A SOLDIER THAT CONJURES ICE INSTEAD OF FIRE?!!
STUN
HM?
WHAT ARE YOU TALKING ABOUT? DON'T BE STUPID.

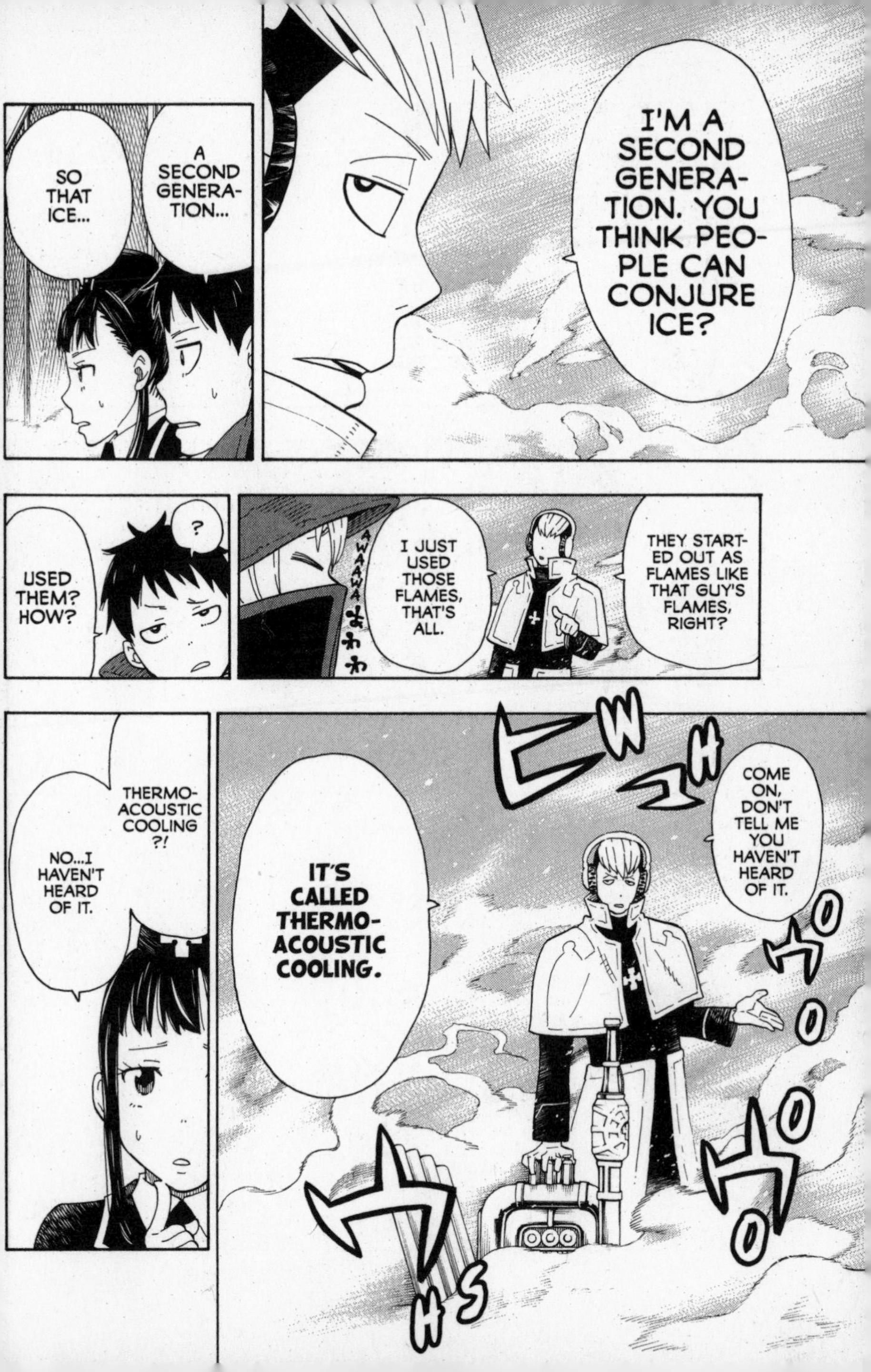
I'M A SECOND GENERATION. YOU THINK PEOPLE CAN CONJURE ICE?
A SECOND GENERATION...
SO THAT ICE...
THEY STARTED OUT AS FLAMES LIKE THAT GUY'S FLAMES, RIGHT?
I JUST USED THOSE FLAMES, THAT'S ALL.
AWAAWA
?
USED THEM? HOW?
WH
COME ON, DON'T TELL ME YOU HAVEN'T HEARD OF IT.
OOOOO
IT'S CALLED THERMO-ACOUSTIC COOLING.
SH
THERMO-ACOUSTIC COOLING?!
NO...I HAVEN'T HEARD OF IT.

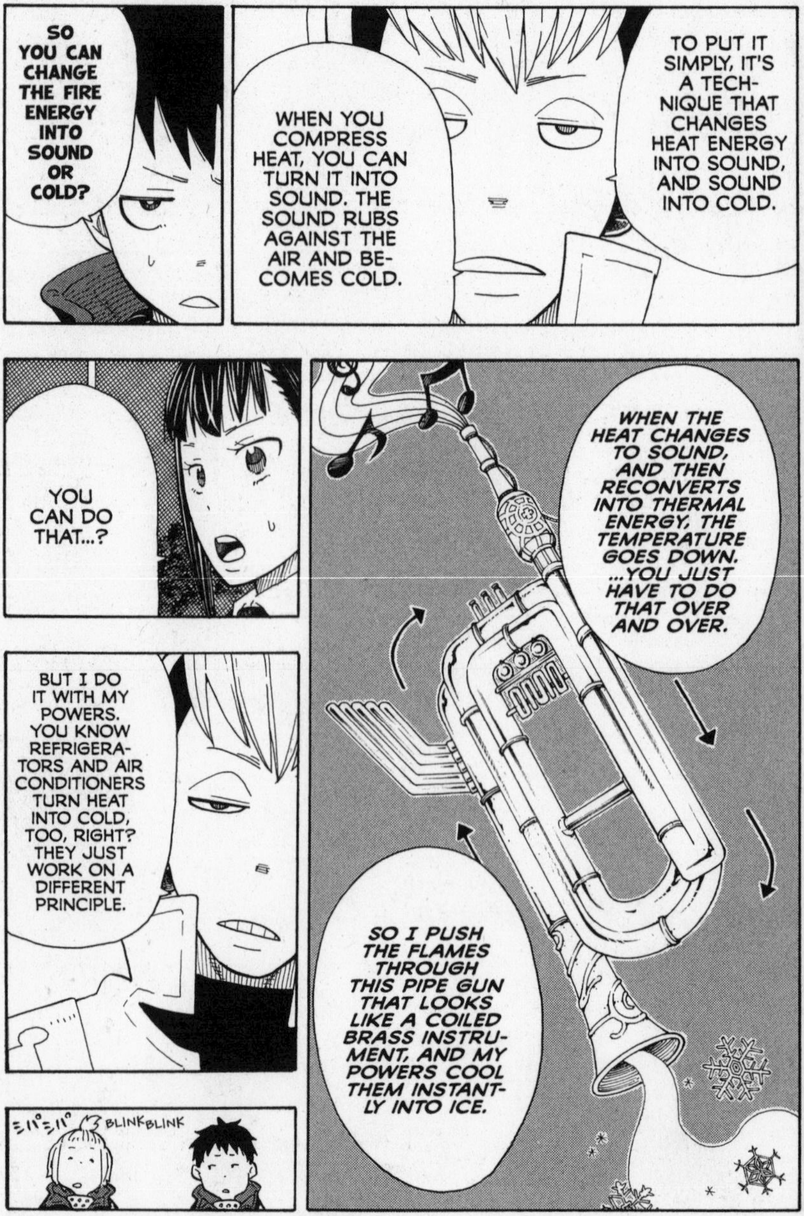
TO PUT IT SIMPLY, IT'S A TECHNIQUE THAT CHANGES HEAT ENERGY INTO SOUND, AND SOUND INTO COLD.
WHEN YOU COMPRESS HEAT, YOU CAN TURN IT INTO SOUND. THE SOUND RUBS AGAINST THE AIR AND BECOMES COLD.
SO YOU CAN CHANGE THE FIRE ENERGY INTO SOUND OR COLD?
WHEN THE HEAT CHANGES TO SOUND, AND THEN RECONVERTS INTO THERMAL ENERGY, THE TEMPERATURE GOES DOWN. ...YOU JUST HAVE TO DO THAT OVER AND OVER.
SO I PUSH THE FLAMES THROUGH THIS PIPE GUN THAT LOOKS LIKE A COILED BRASS INSTRUMENT, AND MY POWERS COOL THEM INSTANTLY INTO ICE.
YOU CAN DO THAT...?
BUT I DO IT WITH MY POWERS. YOU KNOW REFRIGERATORS AND AIR CONDITIONERS TURN HEAT INTO COLD, TOO, RIGHT? THEY JUST WORK ON A DIFFERENT PRINCIPLE.
シパシパ
BLINKBLINK

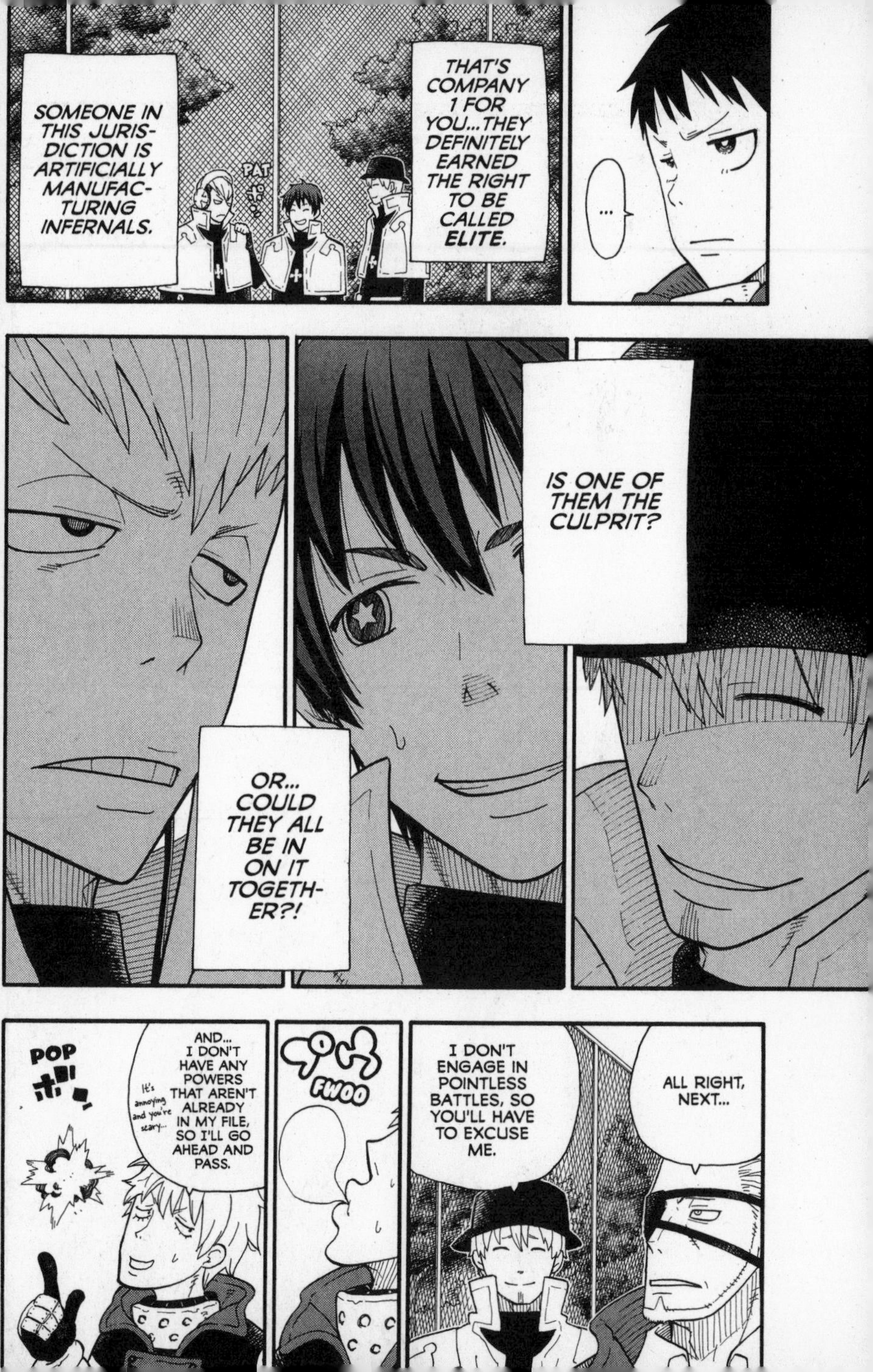
...
THAT'S COMPANY 1 FOR YOU...THEY DEFINITELY EARNED THE RIGHT TO BE CALLED ELITE.
PAT
SOMEONE IN THIS JURIS-DICTION IS ARTIFICIALLY MANUFAC-TURING INFERNALS.
IS ONE OF THEM THE CULPRIT?
OR... COULD THEY ALL BE IN ON IT TOGETH-ER?!
ALL RIGHT, NEXT...
I DON'T ENGAGE IN POINTLESS BATTLES, SO YOU'LL HAVE TO EXCUSE ME.
FWOO
AND... I DON'T HAVE ANY POWERS THAT AREN'T ALREADY IN MY FILE, SO I'LL GO AHEAD AND PASS.
It's annoying and you're scary...
POP

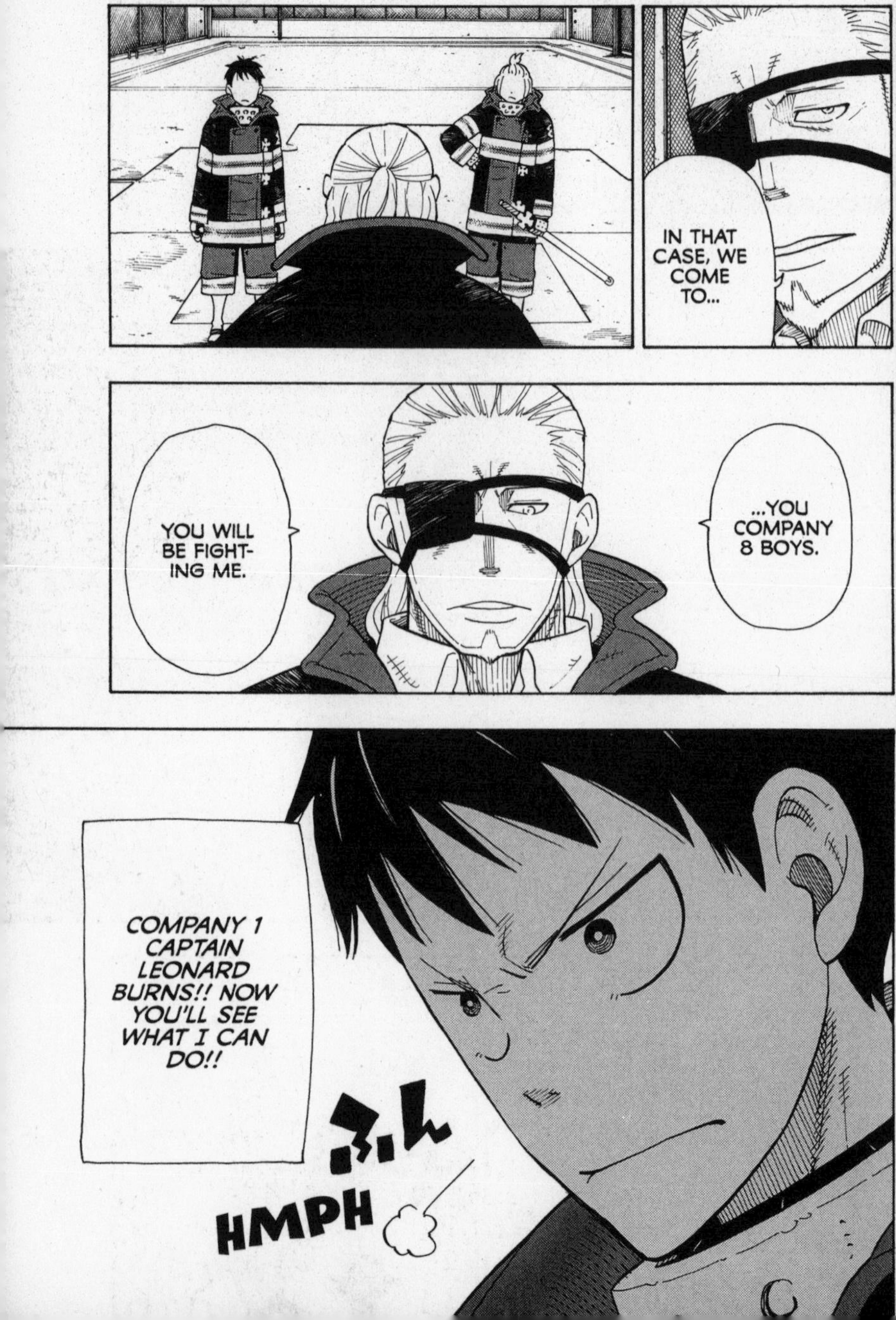
IN THAT CASE, WE COME TO...
...YOU COMPANY 8 BOYS.
YOU WILL BE FIGHTING ME.
COMPANY 1 CAPTAIN LEONARD BURNS!! NOW YOU'LL SEE WHAT I CAN DO!!
ふん
HMPH

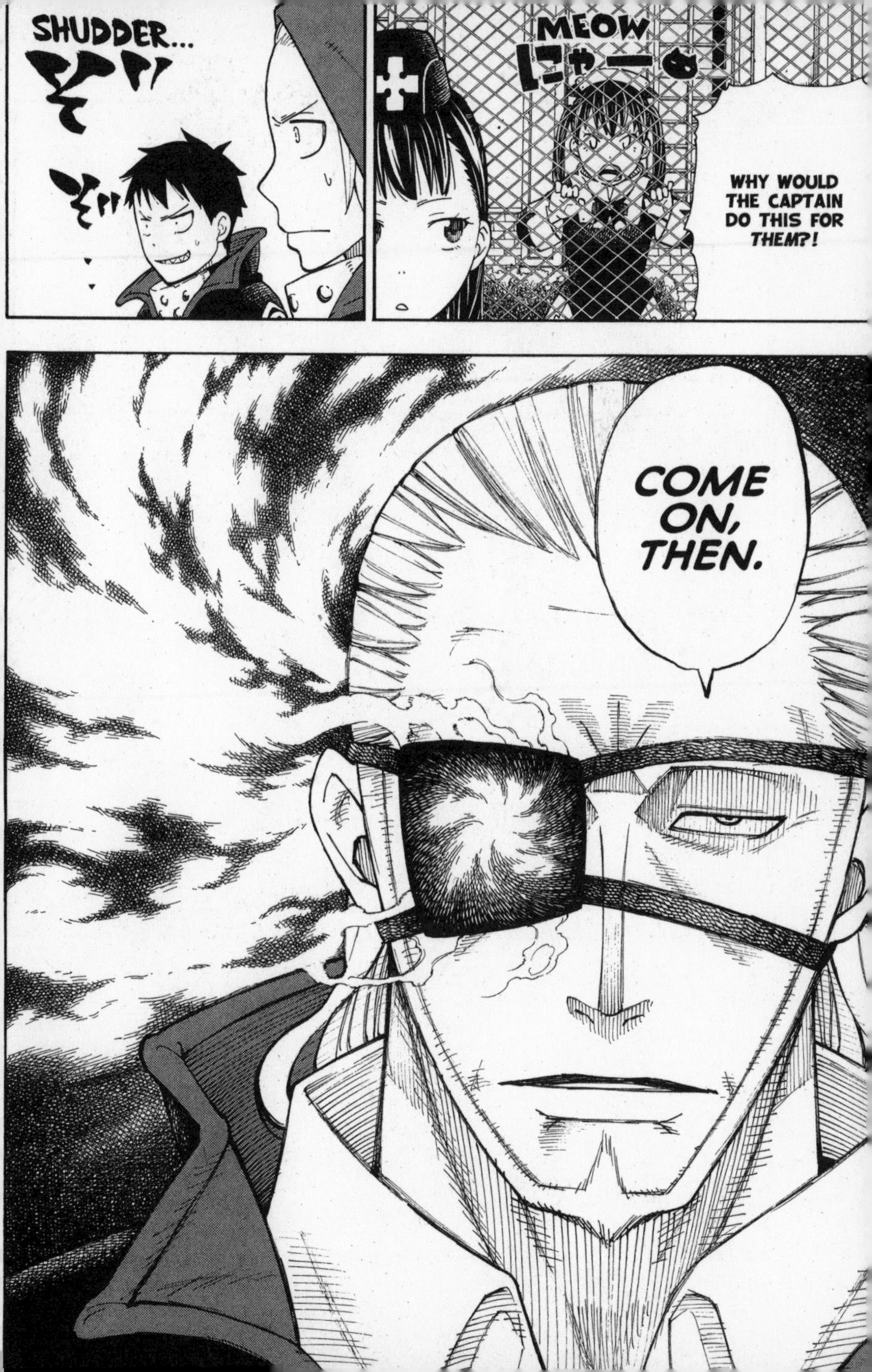
MEOW
にゃー
WHY WOULD THE CAPTAIN DO THIS FOR THEM?!
SHUDDER...
COME ON, THEN.

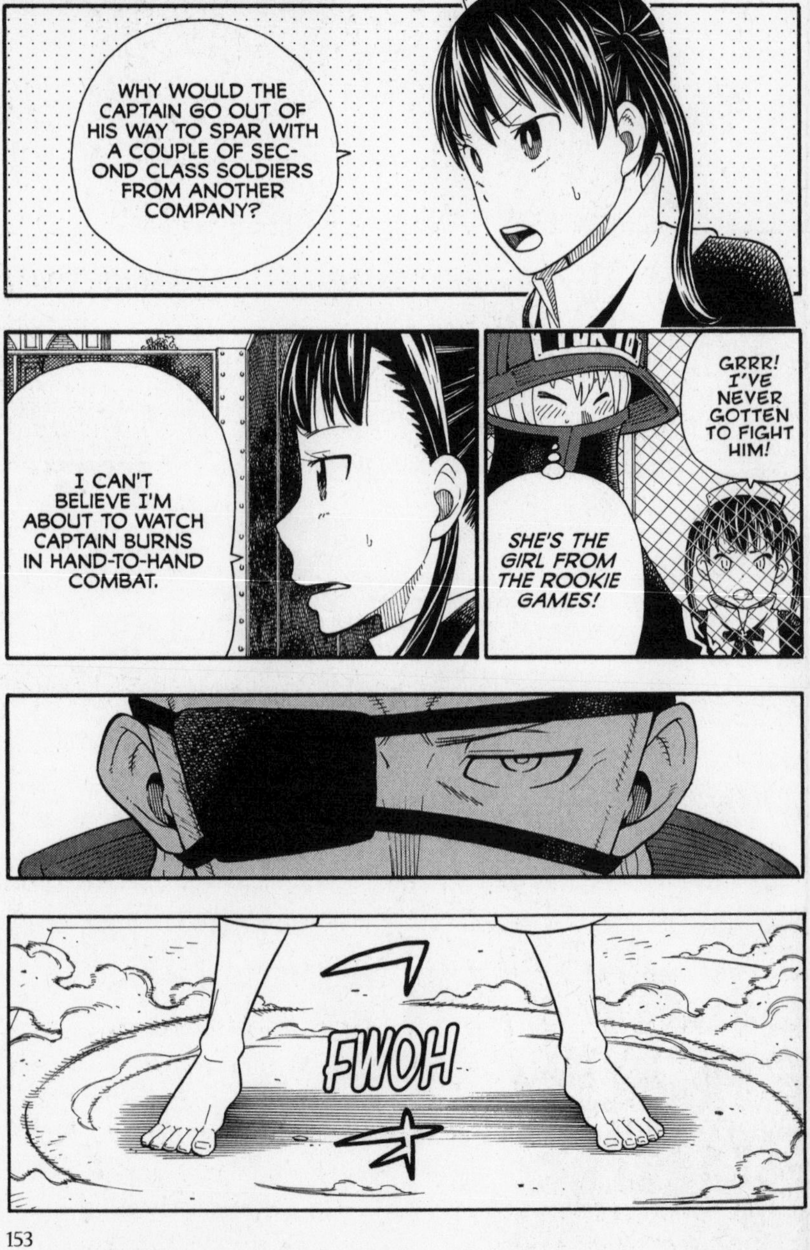
WHY WOULD THE CAPTAIN GO OUT OF HIS WAY TO SPAR WITH A COUPLE OF SEC- OND CLASS SOLDIERS FROM ANOTHER COMPANY?
GRRR! I'VE NEVER GOTTEN TO FIGHT HIM!
SHE'S THE GIRL FROM THE ROOKIE GAMES!
I CAN'T BELIEVE I'M ABOUT TO WATCH CAPTAIN BURNS IN HAND-TO-HAND COMBAT.
FWOH

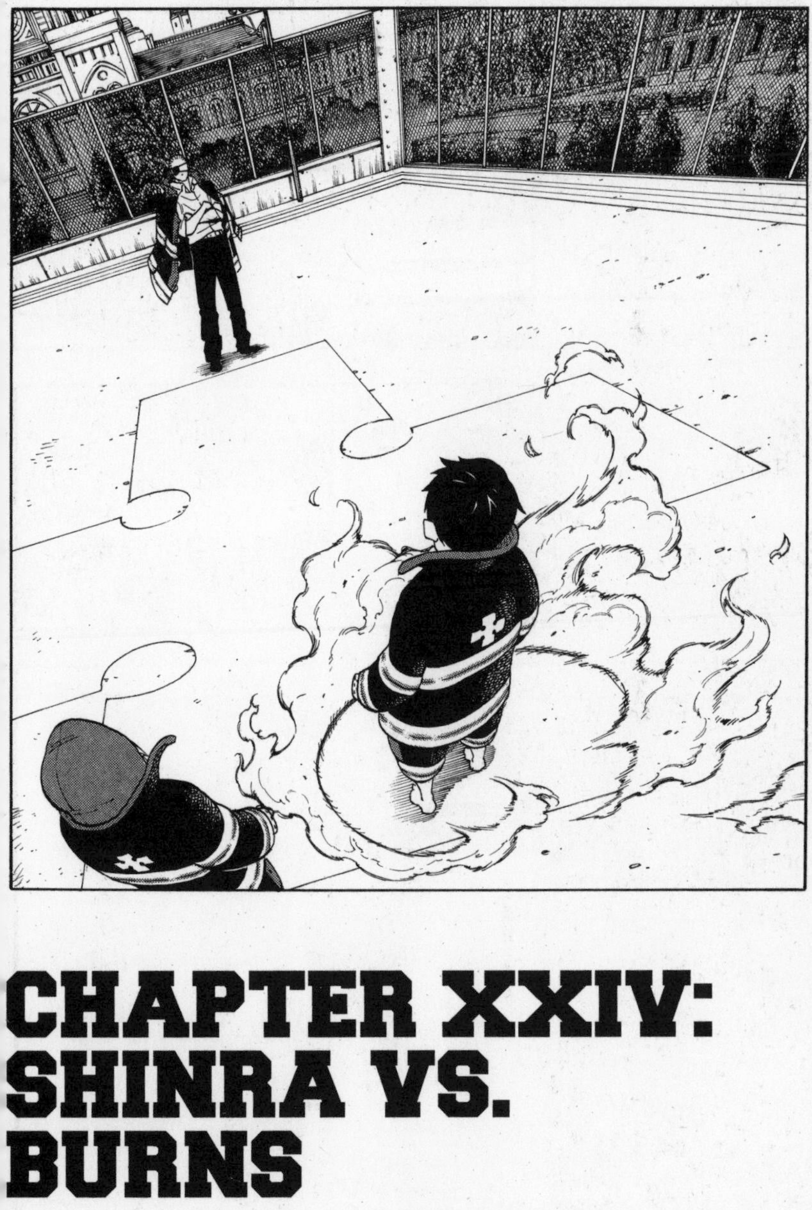

CHAPTER XXIV: SHINRA VS. BURNS

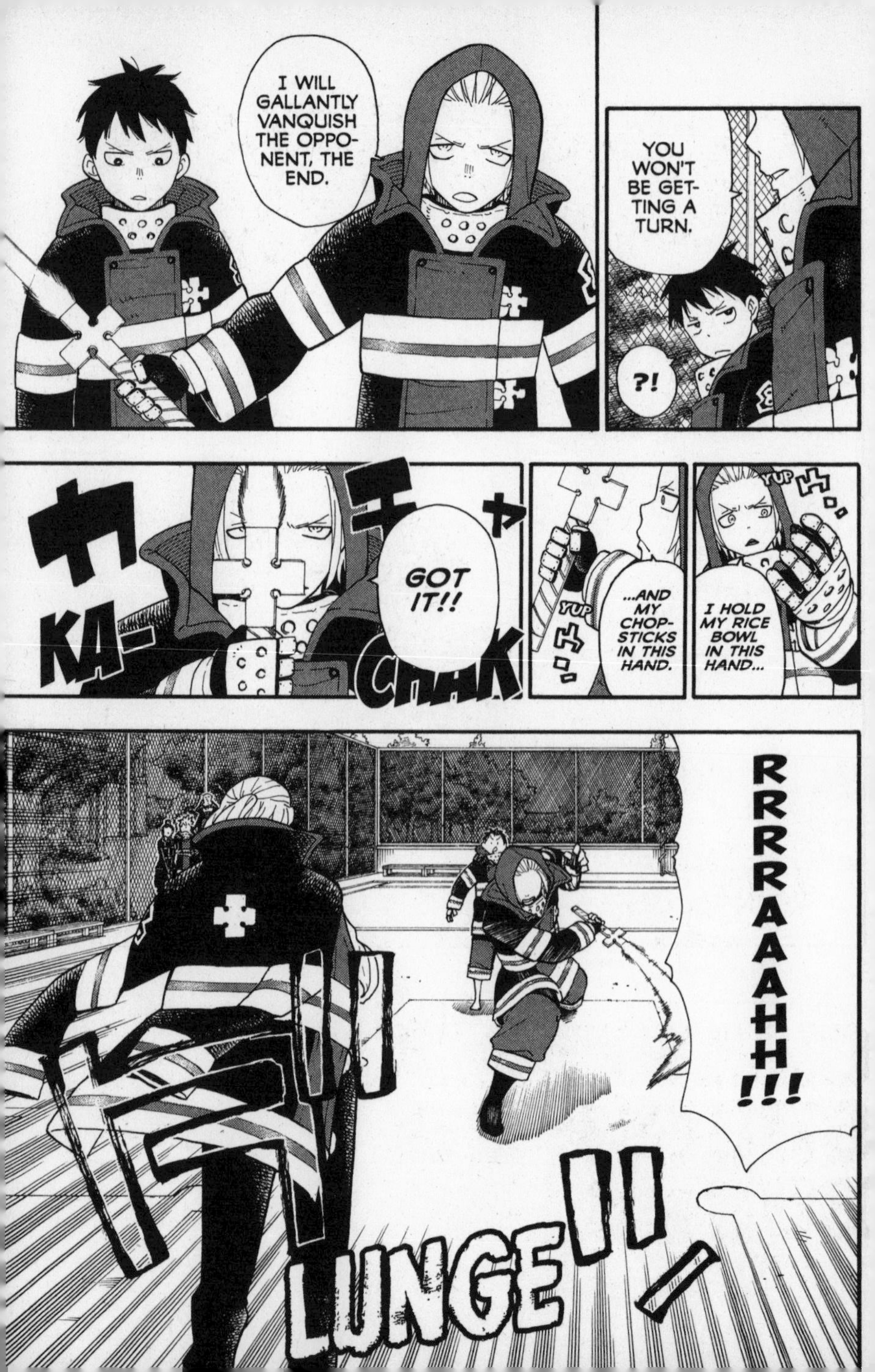
YOU WON'T BE GETTING A TURN.
?!
I WILL GALLANTLY VANQUISH THE OPPONENT, THE END.
YUP
I HOLD MY RICE BOWL IN THIS HAND...
YUP
...AND MY CHOPSTICKS IN THIS HAND.
GOT IT!!
KA-
CHAK
RRRRAAAAHH!!!
LUNGE!!

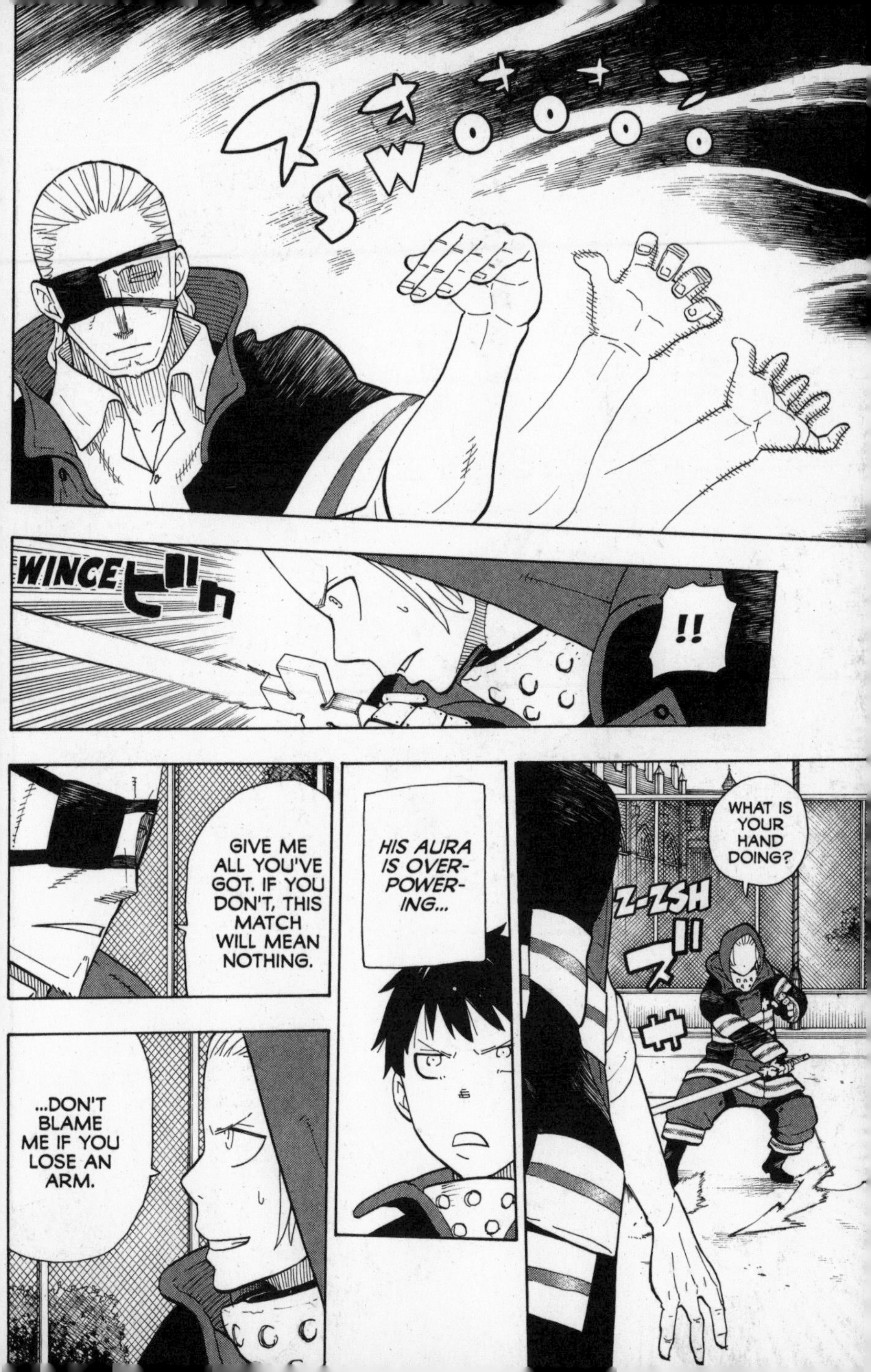
SWOOOOO
WINCE
!!
WHAT IS YOUR HAND DOING?
Z-ZSH
HIS AURA IS OVER-POWERING...
GIVE ME ALL YOU'VE GOT. IF YOU DON'T, THIS MATCH WILL MEAN NOTHING.
...DON'T BLAME ME IF YOU LOSE AN ARM.

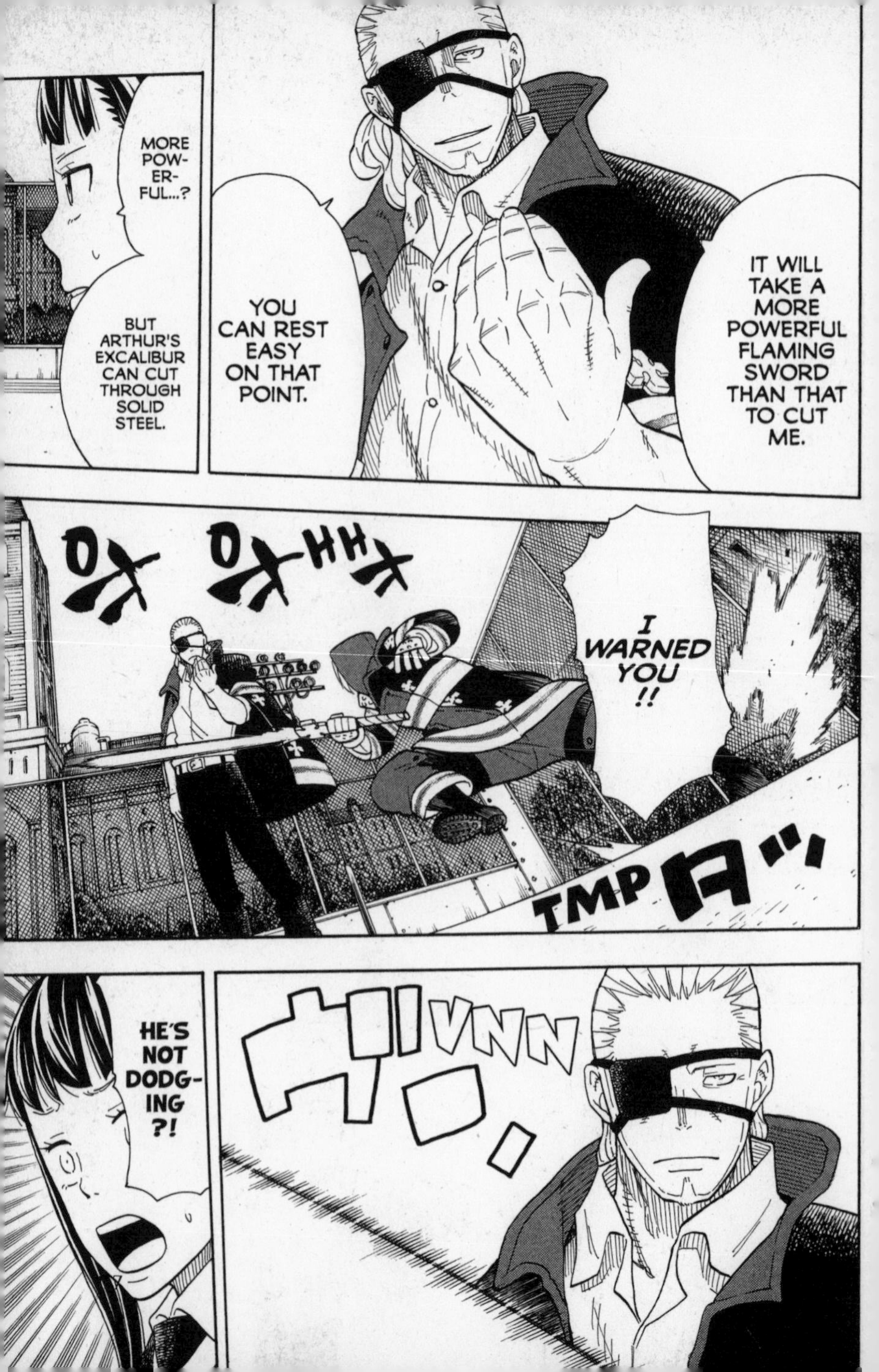
IT WILL TAKE A MORE POWERFUL FLAMING SWORD THAN THAT TO CUT ME.
YOU CAN REST EASY ON THAT POINT.
MORE POW-ER-FUL...?
BUT ARTHUR'S EXCALIBUR CAN CUT THROUGH SOLID STEEL.
I WARNED YOU!!
TMP
VNN
HE'S NOT DODG-ING?!

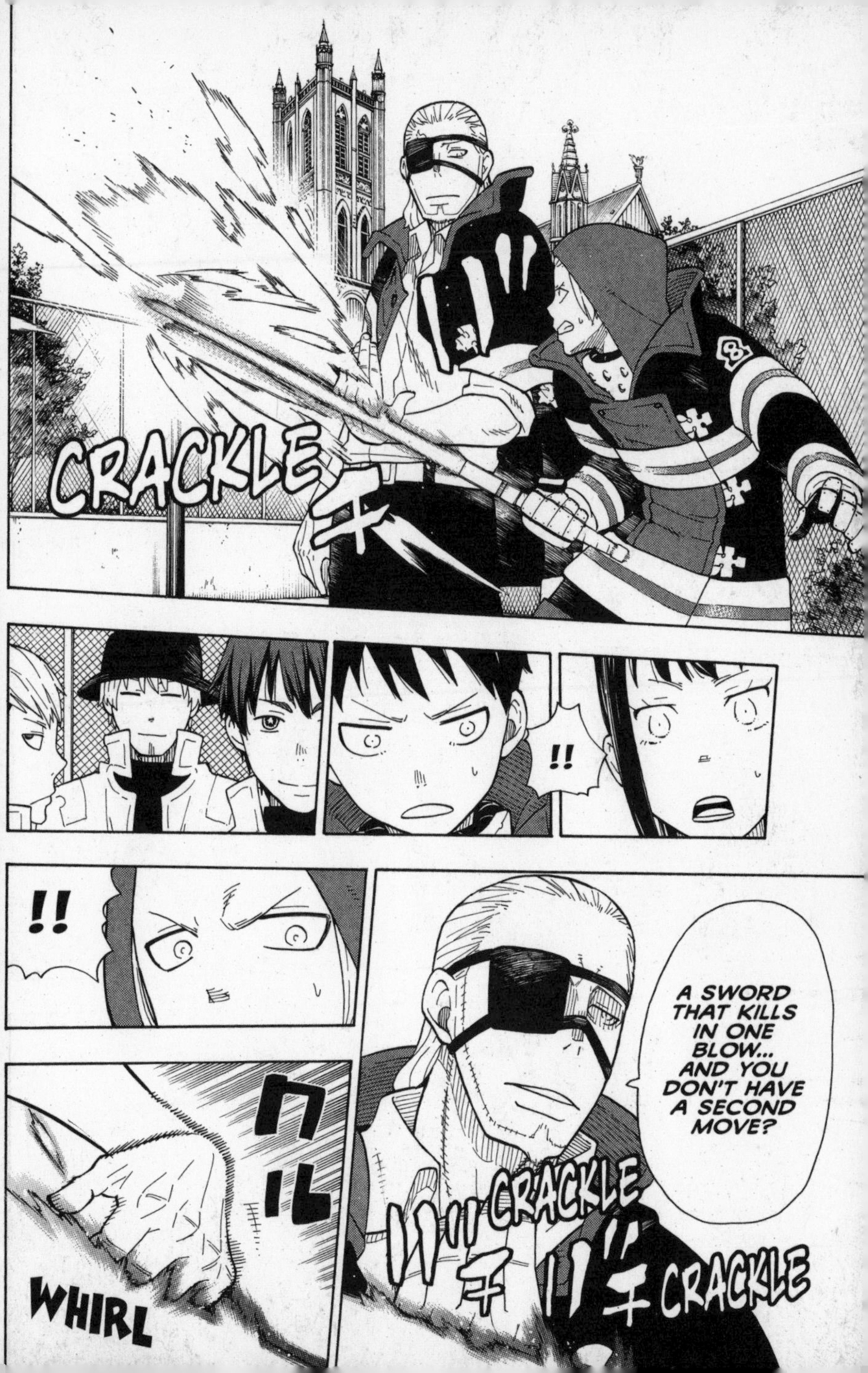
CRACKLE
!!
A SWORD THAT KILLS IN ONE BLOW... AND YOU DON'T HAVE A SECOND MOVE?
CRACKLE
CRACKLE
!!
WHIRL

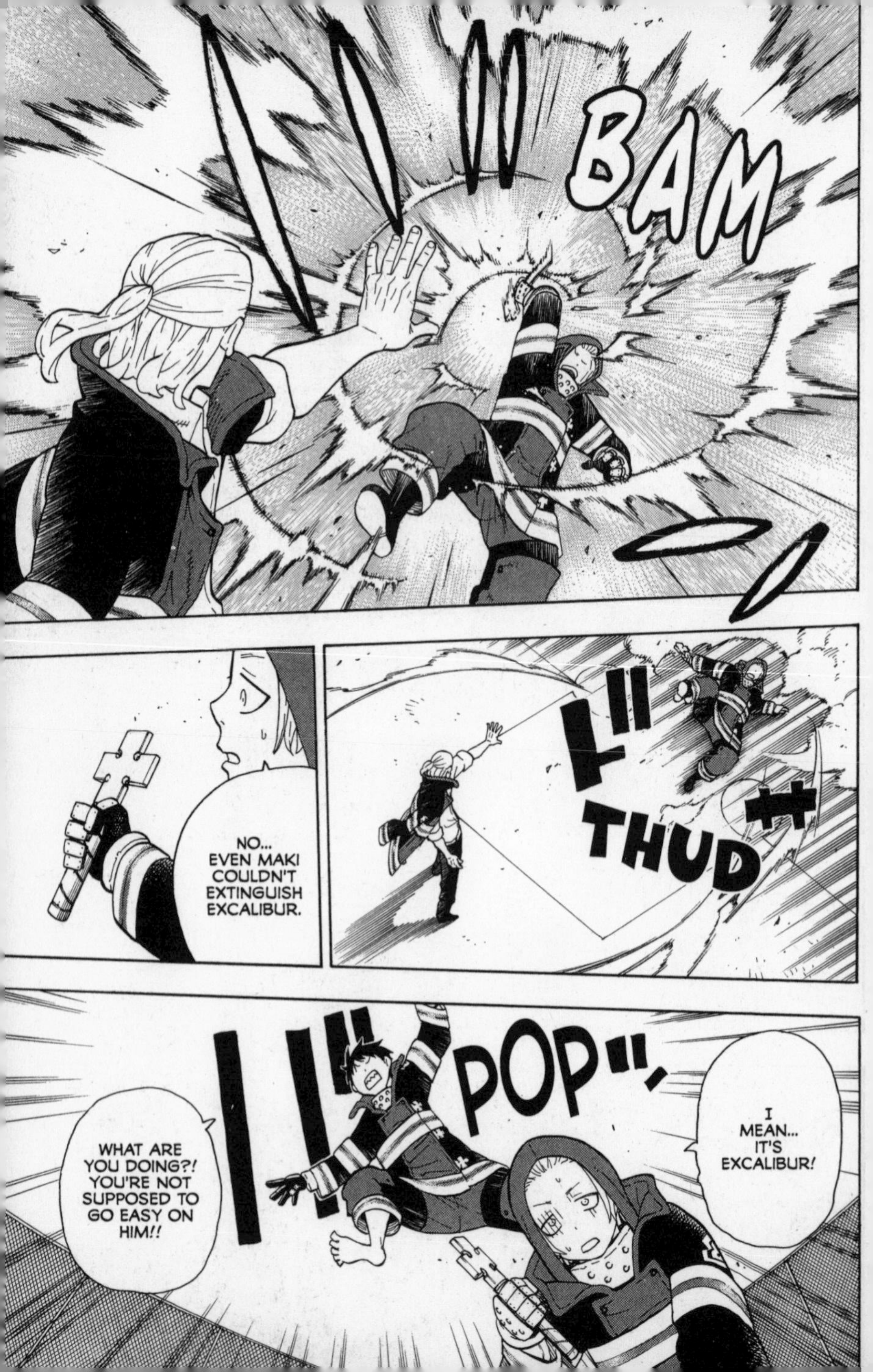
BAM
THUD
NO... EVEN MAKI COULDN'T EXTINGUISH EXCALIBUR.
POP
I MEAN... IT'S EXCALIBUR!
WHAT ARE YOU DOING?! YOU'RE NOT SUPPOSED TO GO EASY ON HIM!!

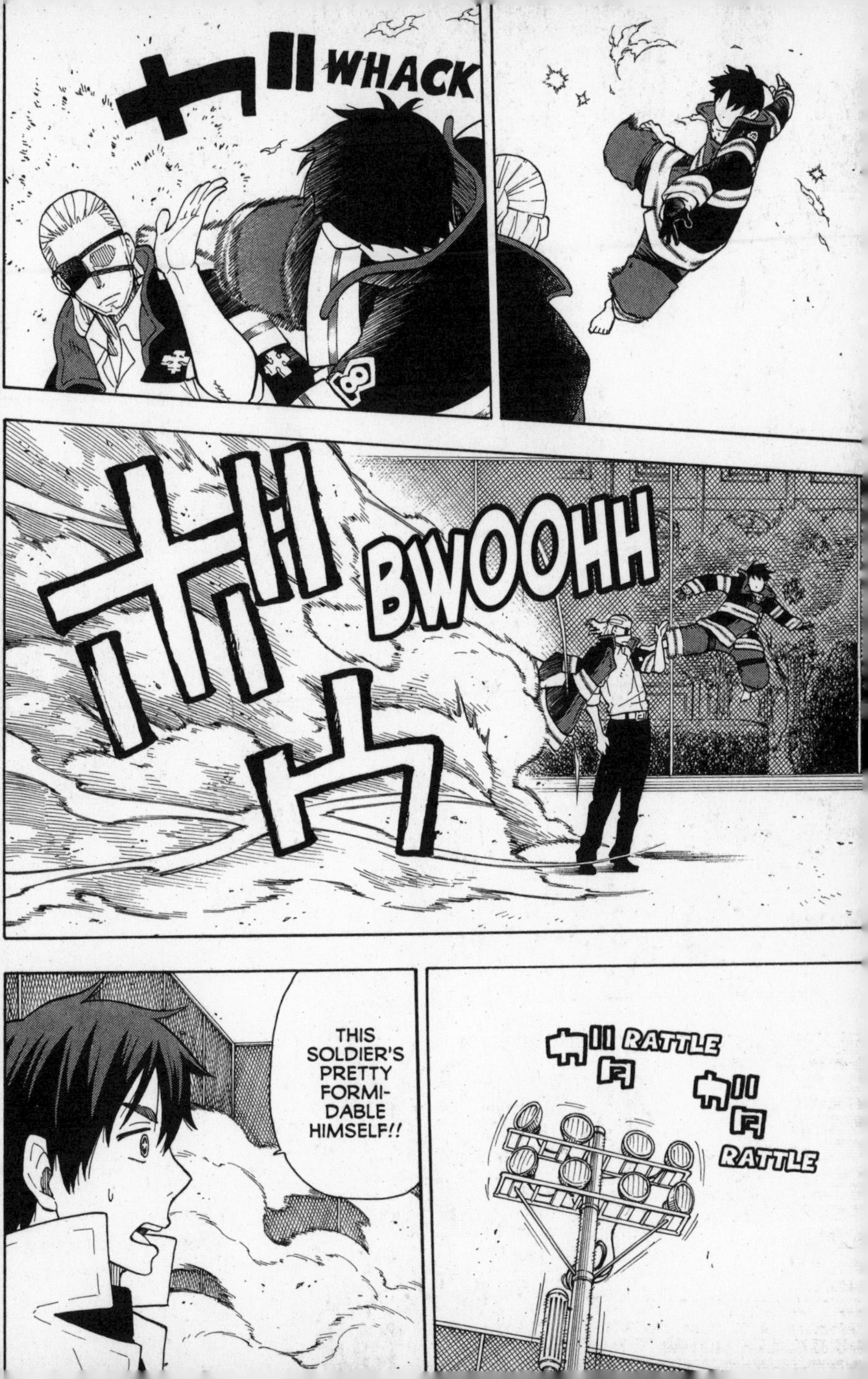
WHACK
BWOOHH
RATTLE
RATTLE
THIS SOLDIER'S PRETTY FORMI-DABLE HIMSELF!!

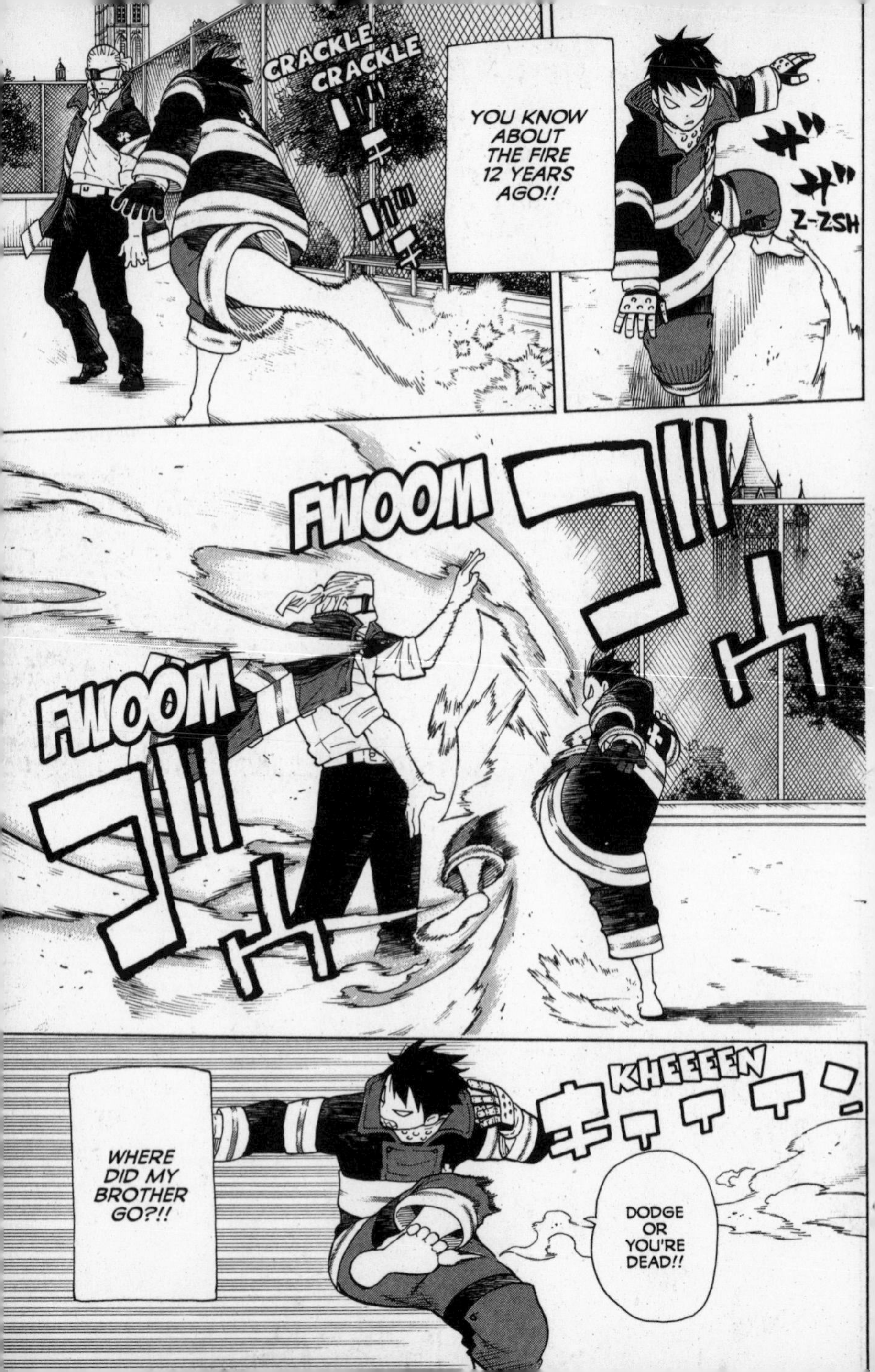
YOU KNOW ABOUT THE FIRE 12 YEARS AGO!!
Z-ZSH
CRACKLE CRACKLE
FWOOM
FWOOM
KHEEEEN
DODGE OR YOU'RE DEAD!!
WHERE DID MY BROTHER GO?!!

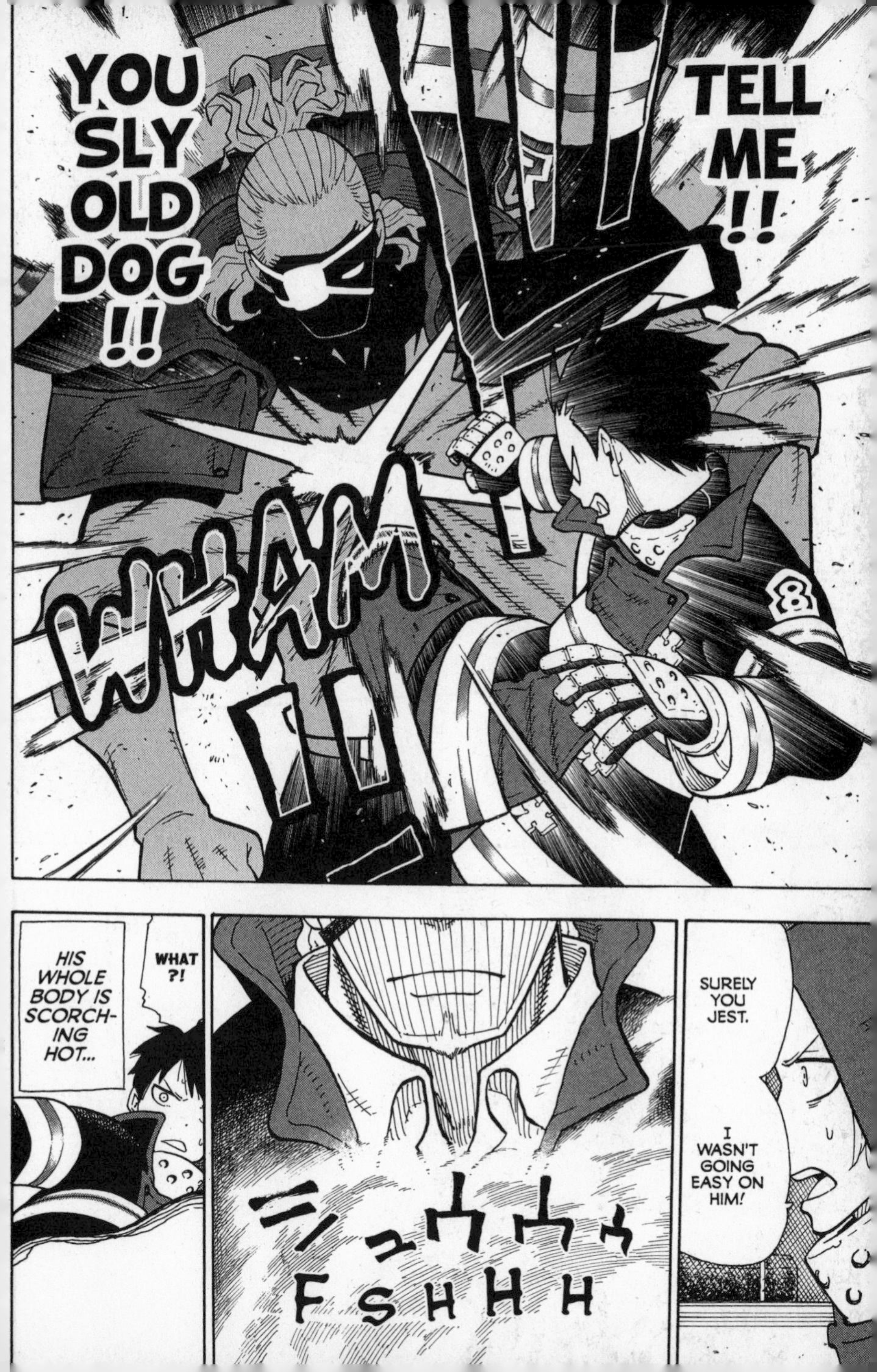
TELL ME!!
YOU SLY OLD DOG!!
WHAM!!
SURELY YOU JEST.
I WASN'T GOING EASY ON HIM!
FSHHH
WHAT?!
HIS WHOLE BODY IS SCORCHING HOT...

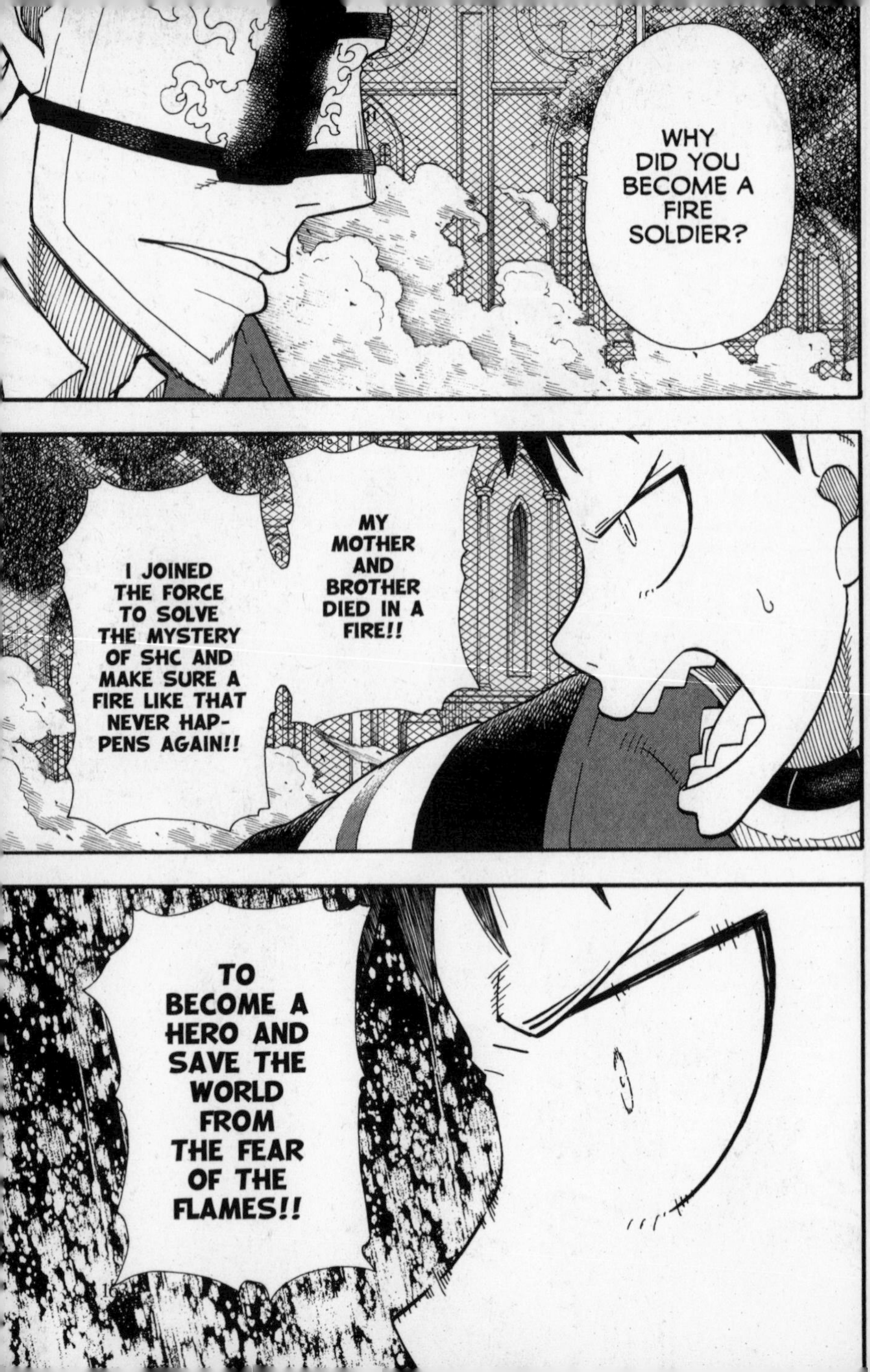
WHY DID YOU BECOME A FIRE SOLDIER?
MY MOTHER AND BROTHER DIED IN A FIRE!!
I JOINED THE FORCE TO SOLVE THE MYSTERY OF SHC AND MAKE SURE A FIRE LIKE THAT NEVER HAP-PENS AGAIN!!
TO BECOME A HERO AND SAVE THE WORLD FROM THE FEAR OF THE FLAMES!!

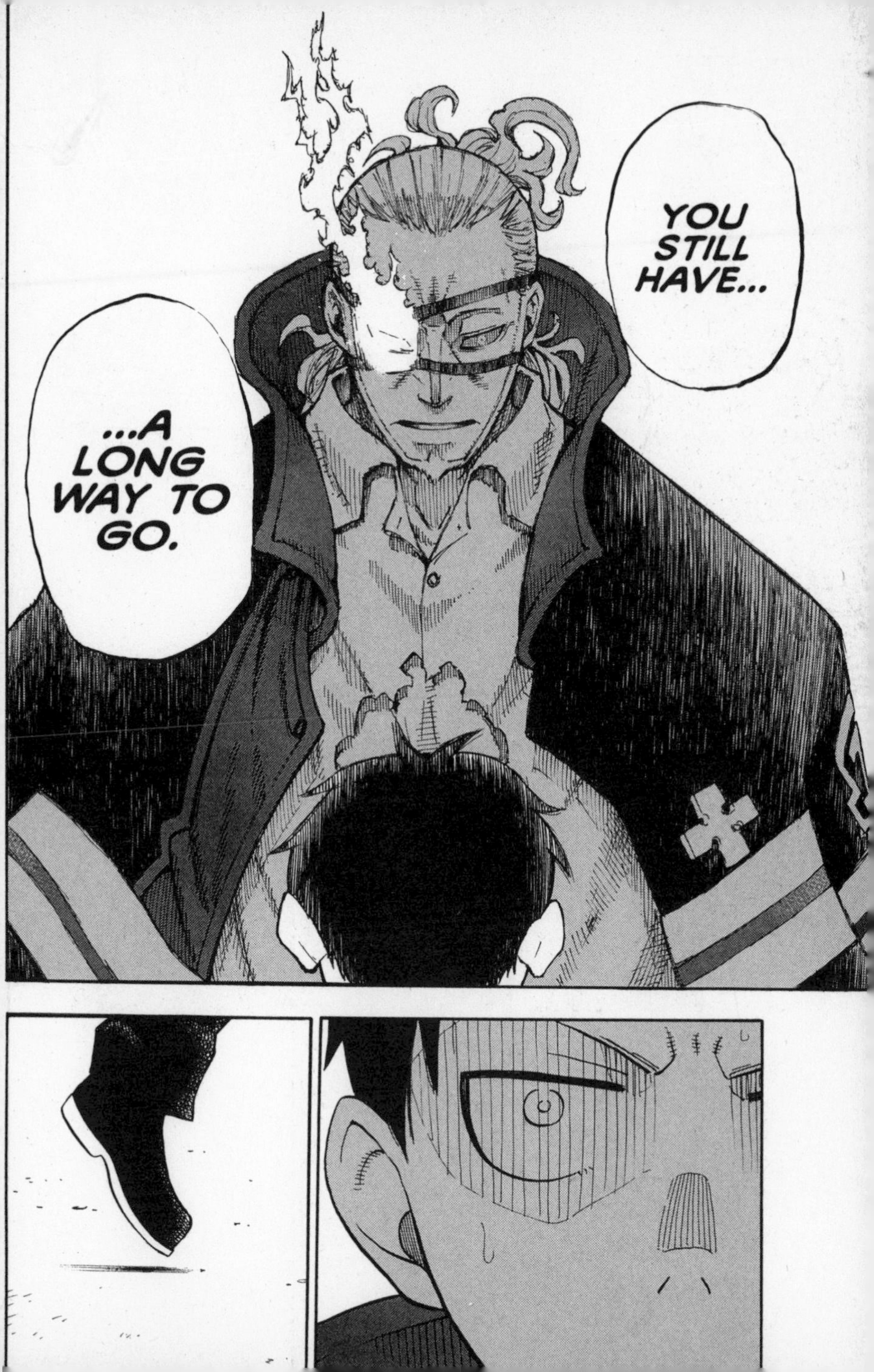
YOU STILL HAVE...
...A LONG WAY TO GO.

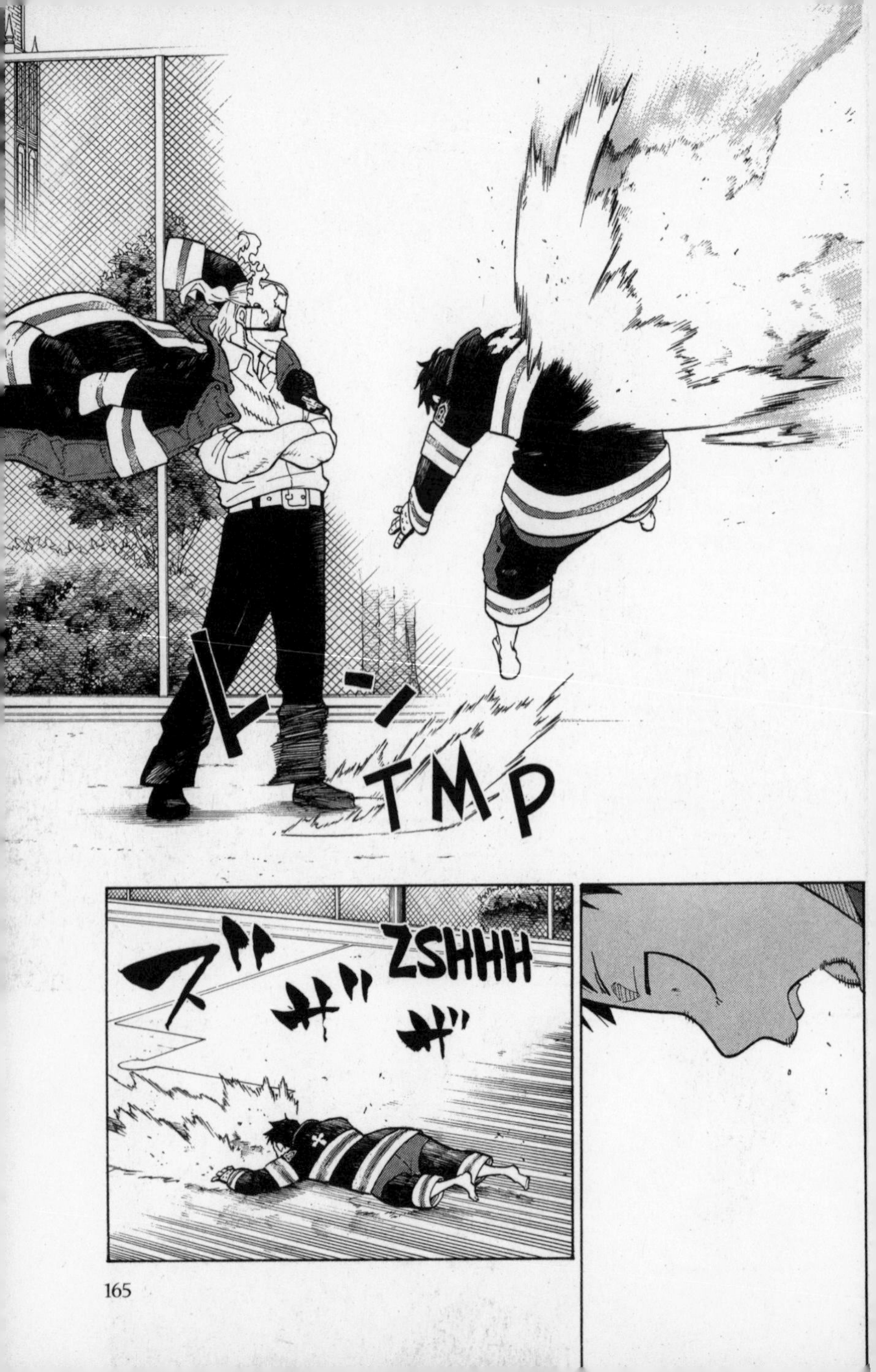
TMP
ZSHHH

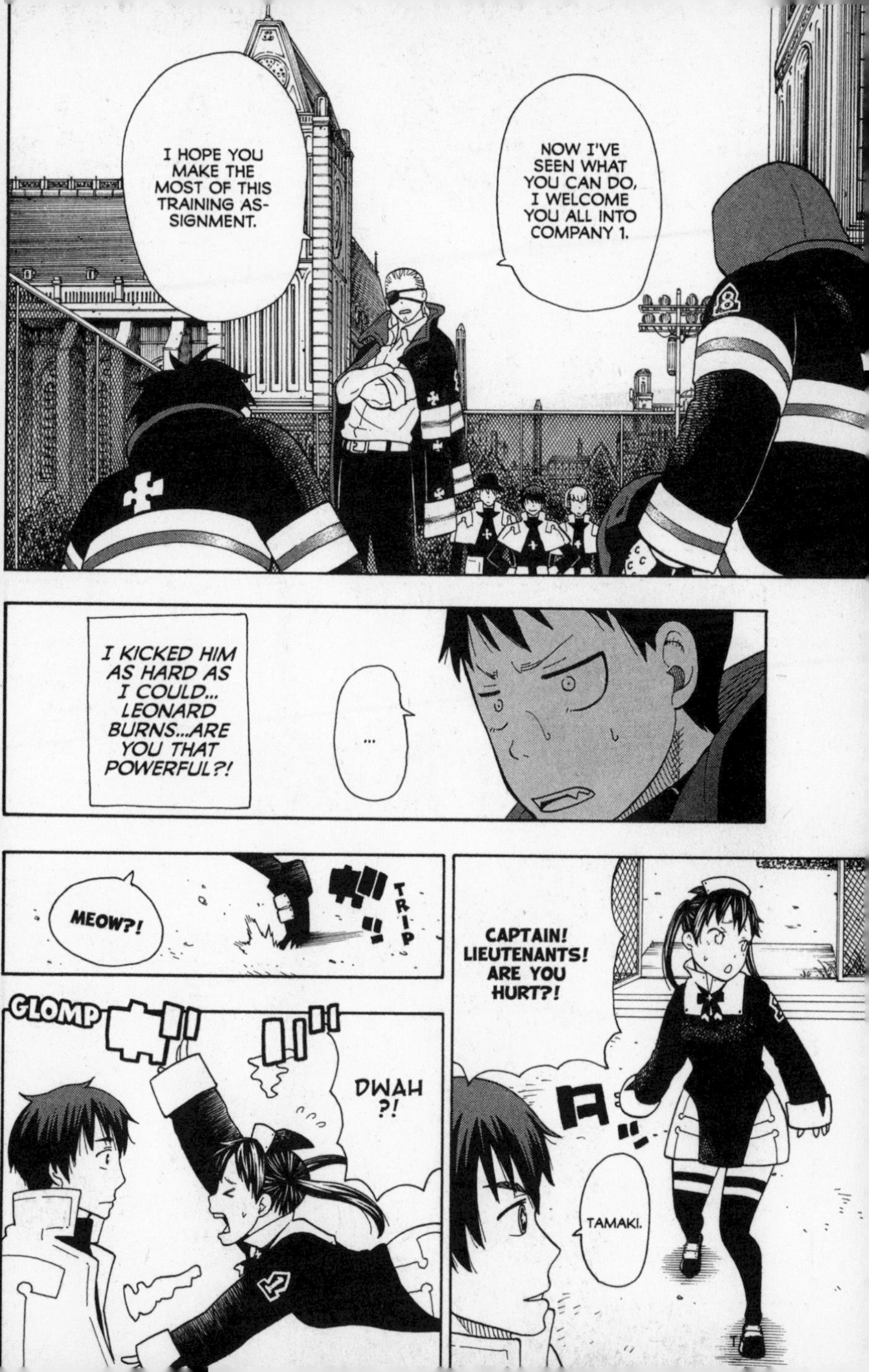
NOW I'VE SEEN WHAT YOU CAN DO, I WELCOME YOU ALL INTO COMPANY 1.
I HOPE YOU MAKE THE MOST OF THIS TRAINING AS-SIGNMENT.
...
I KICKED HIM AS HARD AS I COULD... LEONARD BURNS...ARE YOU THAT POWERFUL?!
CAPTAIN! LIEUTENANTS! ARE YOU HURT?!
TAMAKI.
TRIP
MEOW?!
GLOMP
DWAH ?!

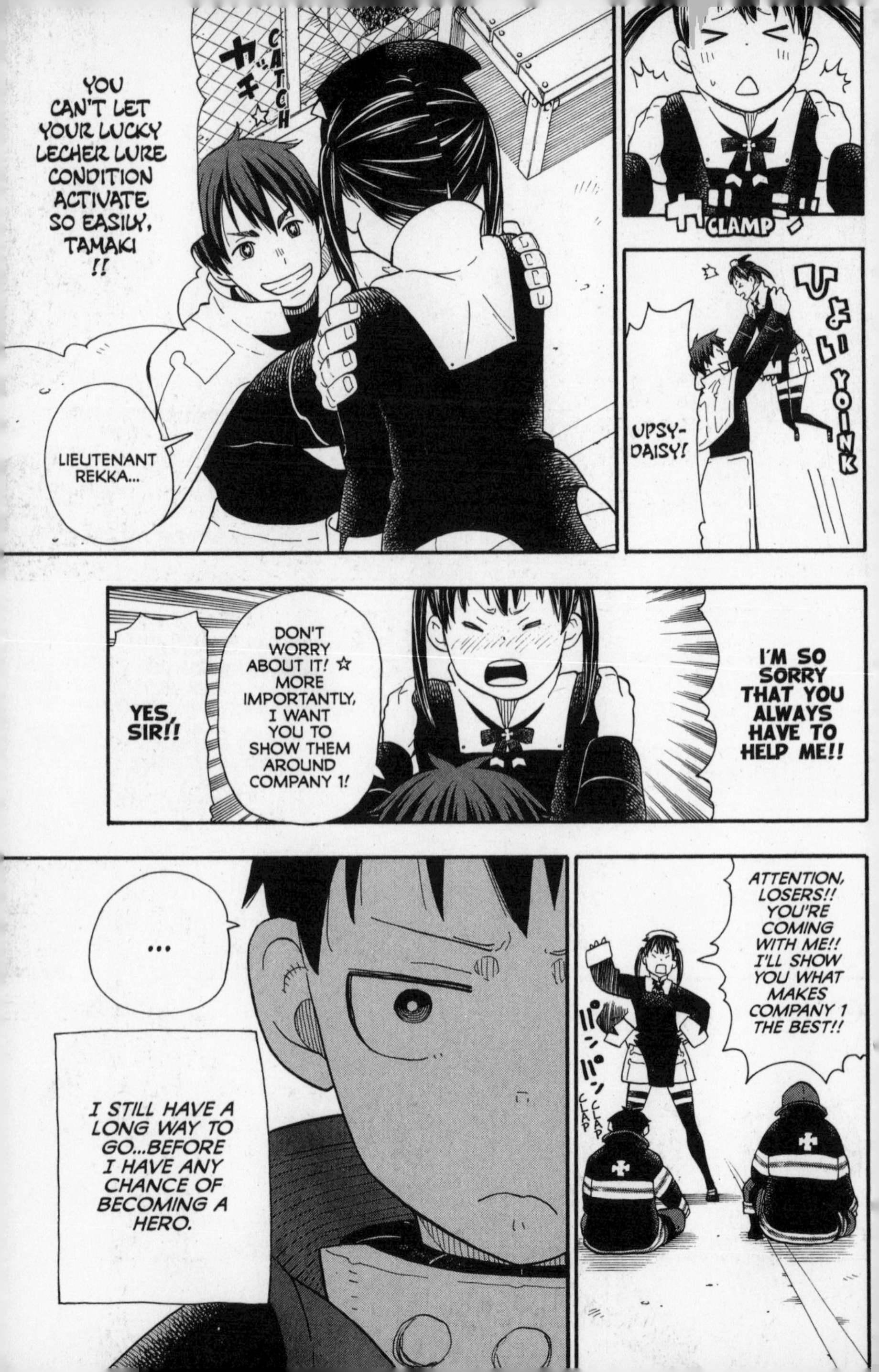
CLAMP
UPSY-DAISY!
YOINK
CATCH
YOU CAN'T LET YOUR LUCKY LECHER LURE CONDITION ACTIVATE SO EASILY, TAMAKI!!
LIEUTENANT REKKA...
I'M SO SORRY THAT YOU ALWAYS HAVE TO HELP ME!!
DON'T WORRY ABOUT IT! ☆ MORE IMPORTANTLY, I WANT YOU TO SHOW THEM AROUND COMPANY 1!
YES, SIR!!
ATTENTION, LOSERS!! YOU'RE COMING WITH ME!! I'LL SHOW YOU WHAT MAKES COMPANY 1 THE BEST!!
CLAP CLAP
...
I STILL HAVE A LONG WAY TO GO...BEFORE I HAVE ANY CHANCE OF BECOMING A HERO.

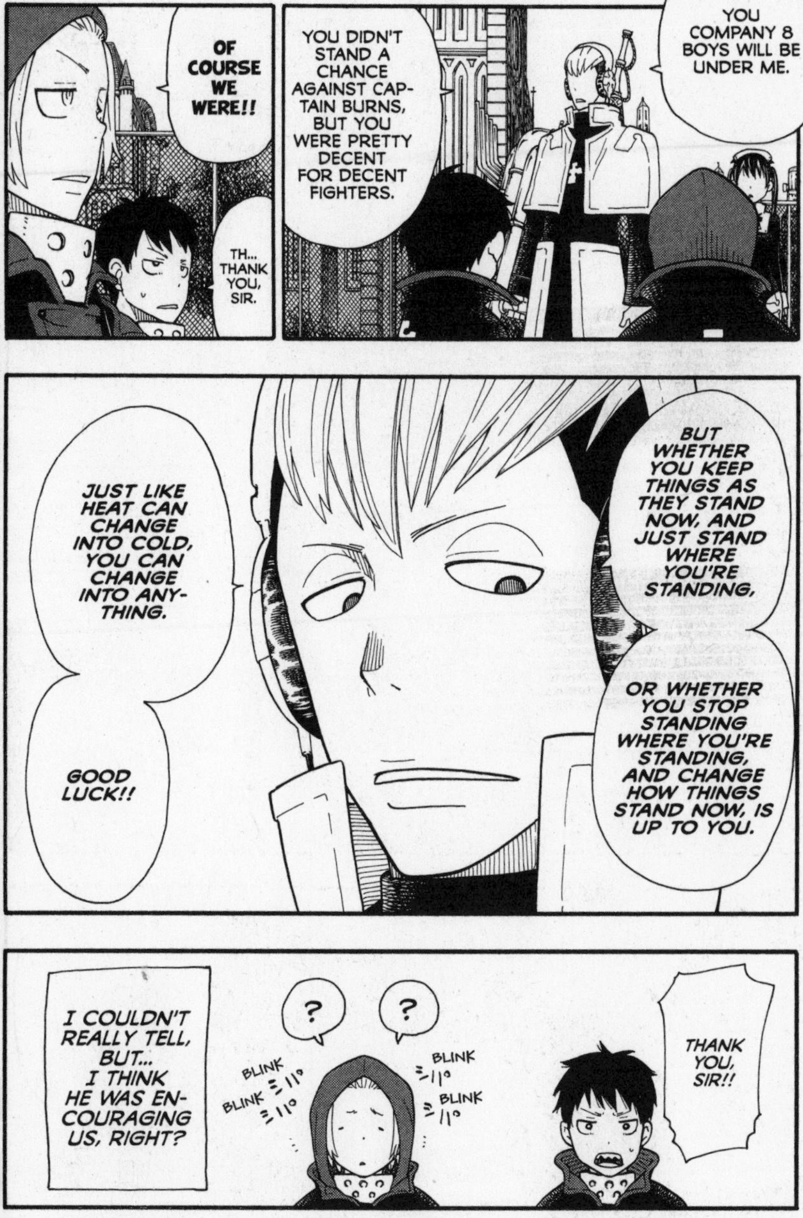
YOU COMPANY 8 BOYS WILL BE UNDER ME.
YOU DIDN'T STAND A CHANCE AGAINST CAP-TAIN BURNS, BUT YOU WERE PRETTY DECENT FOR DECENT FIGHTERS.
OF COURSE WE WERE!!
TH... THANK YOU, SIR.
BUT WHETHER YOU KEEP THINGS AS THEY STAND NOW, AND JUST STAND WHERE YOU'RE STANDING,
OR WHETHER YOU STOP STANDING WHERE YOU'RE STANDING, AND CHANGE HOW THINGS STAND NOW, IS UP TO YOU.
JUST LIKE HEAT CAN CHANGE INTO COLD, YOU CAN CHANGE INTO ANY-THING.
GOOD LUCK!!
THANK YOU, SIR!!
?
?
BLINK
BLINK
BLINK
BLINK
I COULDN'T REALLY TELL, BUT... I THINK HE WAS EN-COURAGING US, RIGHT?

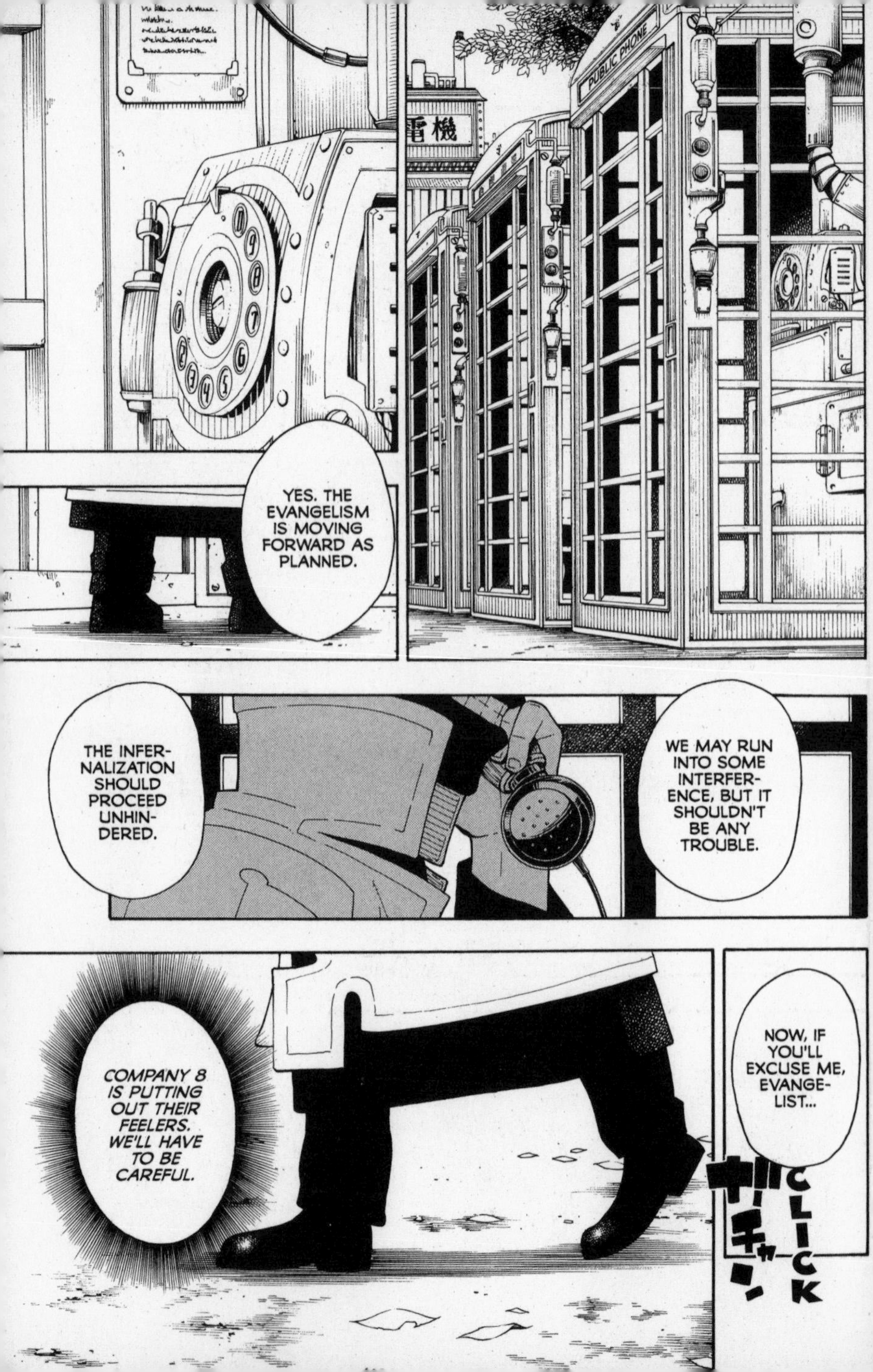
PUBLIC PHONE
YES. THE EVANGELISM IS MOVING FORWARD AS PLANNED.
WE MAY RUN INTO SOME INTERFER-ENCE, BUT IT SHOULDN'T BE ANY TROUBLE.
THE INFER-NALIZATION SHOULD PROCEED UNHIN-DERED.
NOW, IF YOU'LL EXCUSE ME, EVANGE-LIST...
ガチャン
CLICK
COMPANY 8 IS PUTTING OUT THEIR FEELERS. WE'LL HAVE TO BE CAREFUL.

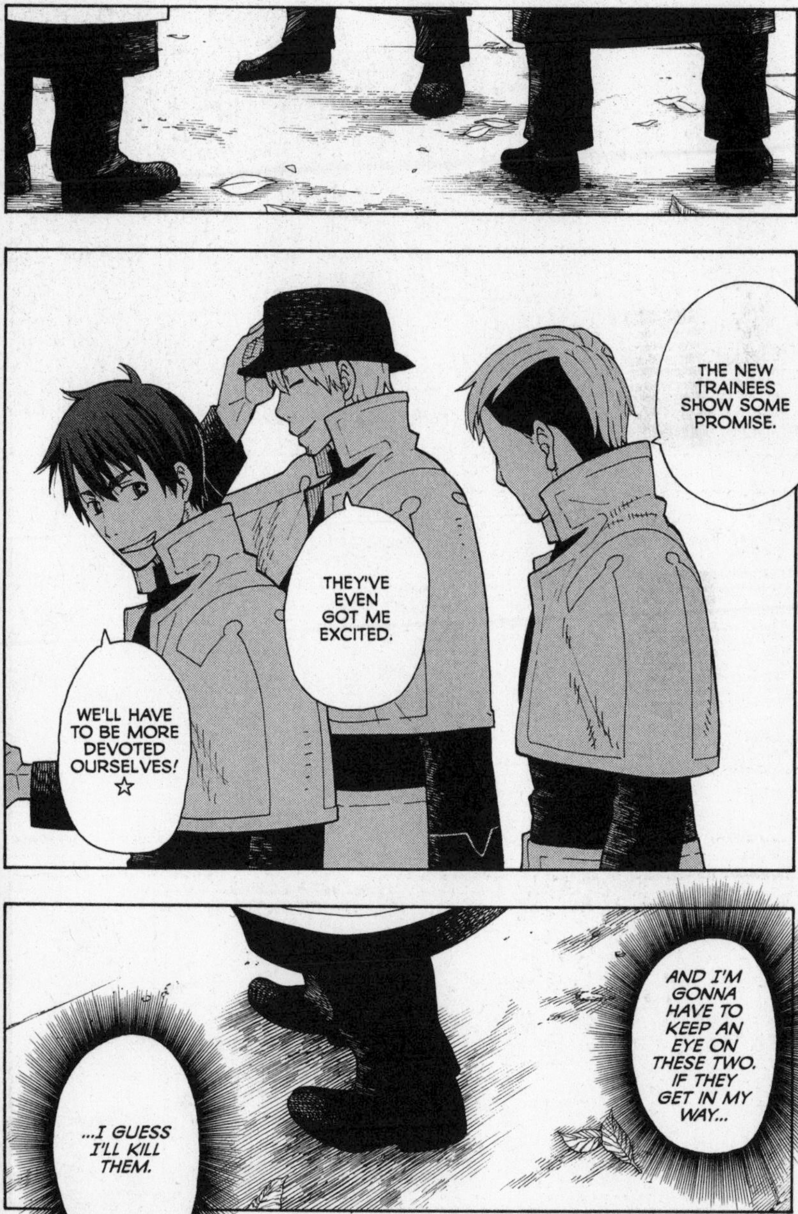
THE NEW TRAINEES SHOW SOME PROMISE.
THEY'VE EVEN GOT ME EXCITED.
WE'LL HAVE TO BE MORE DEVOTED OURSELVES! ☆
AND I'M GONNA HAVE TO KEEP AN EYE ON THESE TWO. IF THEY GET IN MY WAY...
...I GUESS I'LL KILL THEM.

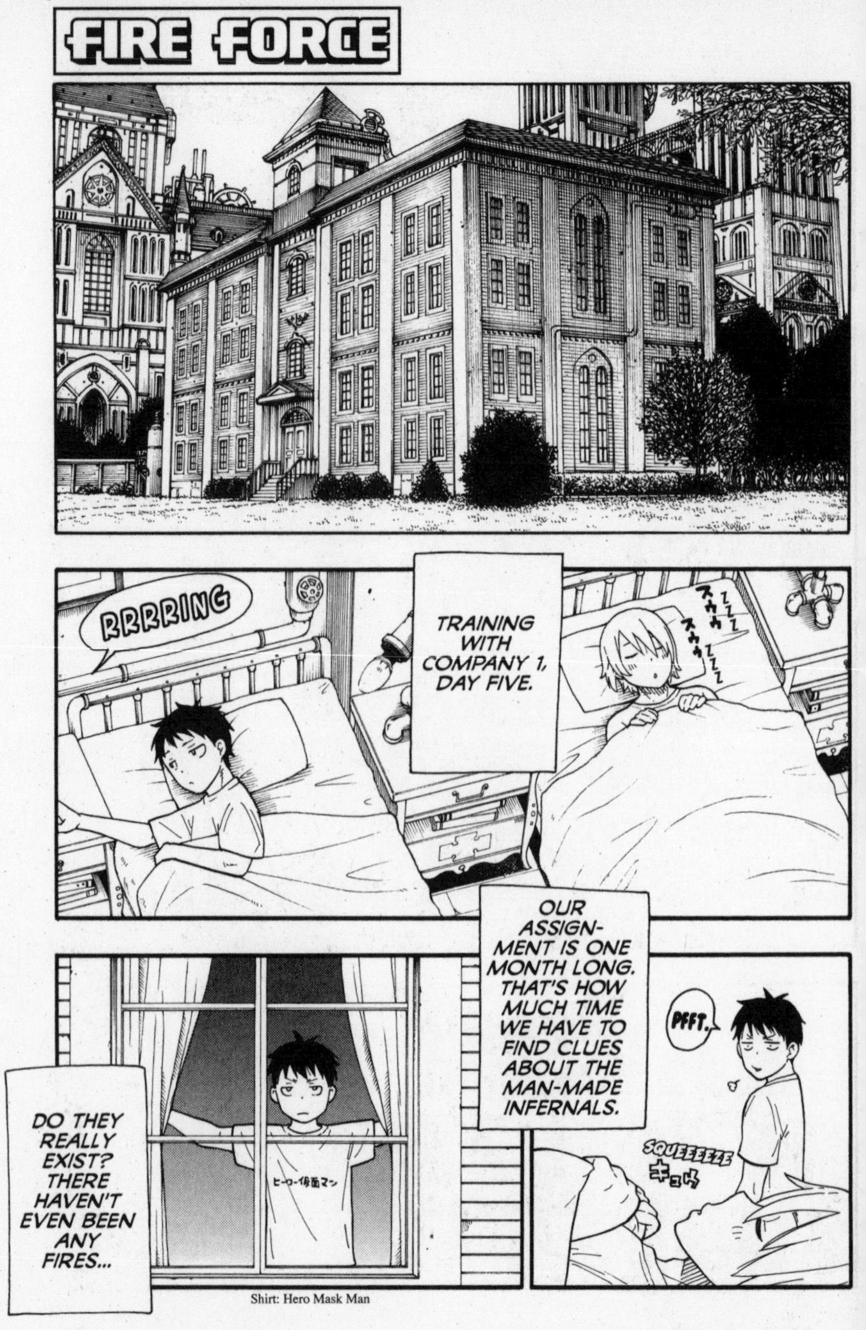
スゥゥ ZZZ スゥゥ ZZZ
TRAINING WITH COMPANY 1, DAY FIVE.
RRRRING
OUR ASSIGNMENT IS ONE MONTH LONG. THAT'S HOW MUCH TIME WE HAVE TO FIND CLUES ABOUT THE MAN-MADE INFERNALS.
PFFT.
SQUEEEEEZE
キュッ
DO THEY REALLY EXIST? THERE HAVEN'T EVEN BEEN ANY FIRES...
ヒーロー仮面マン

Shirt: Hero Mask Man

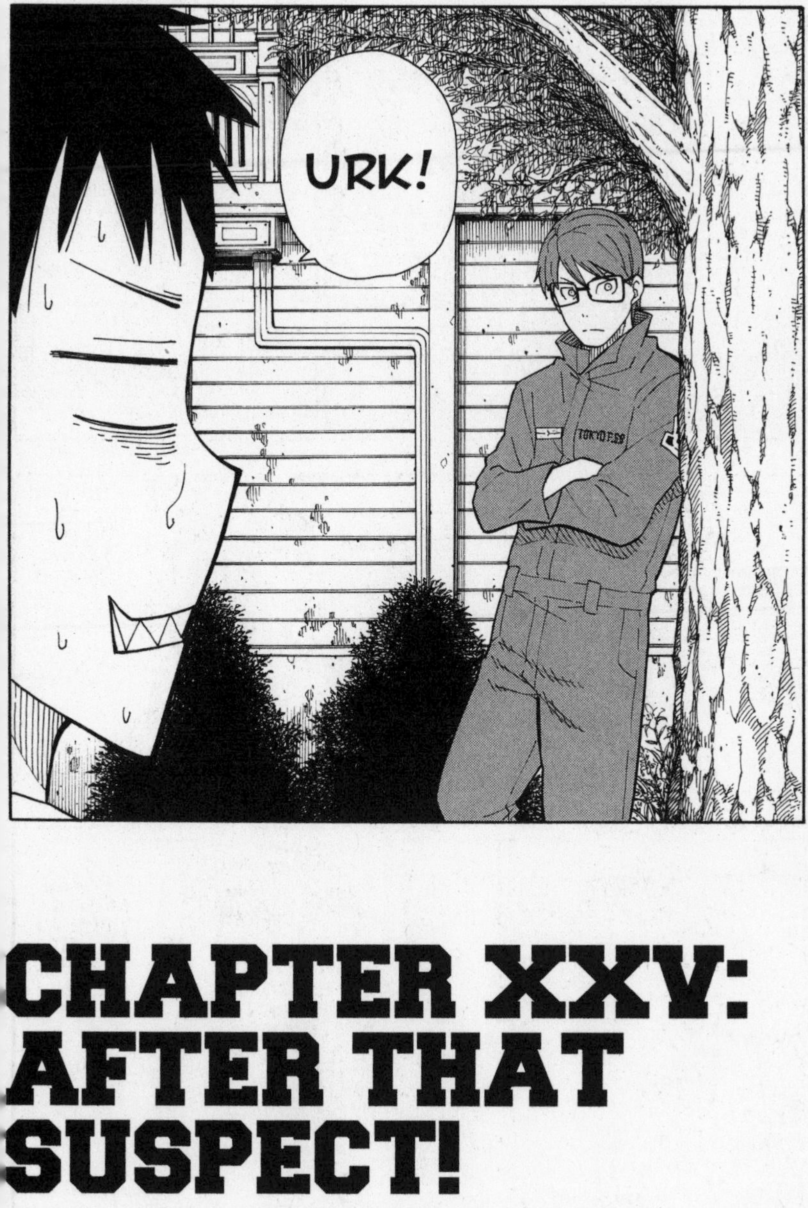
URK!

CHAPTER XXV: AFTER THAT SUSPECT!

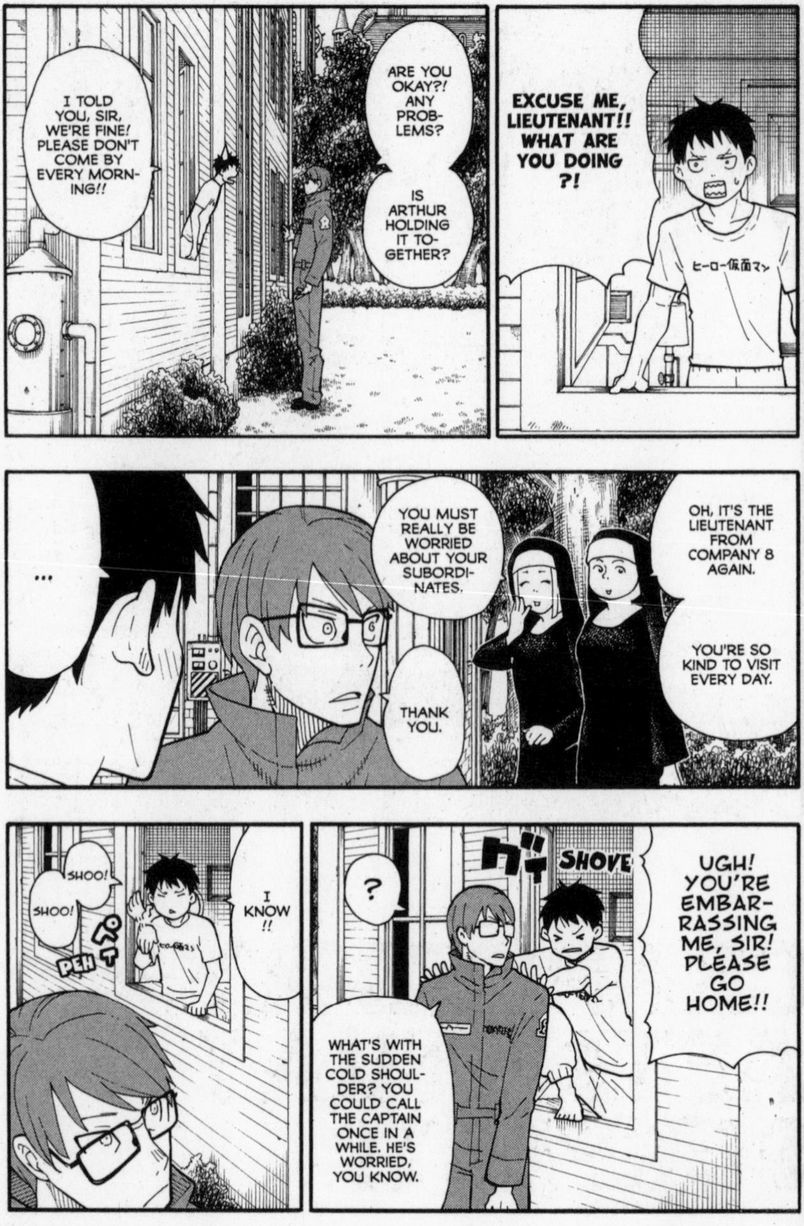
EXCUSE ME, LIEUTENANT!! WHAT ARE YOU DOING?!
ヒーロー仮面マン
ARE YOU OKAY?! ANY PROBLEMS?
IS ARTHUR HOLDING IT TOGETHER?
I TOLD YOU, SIR, WE'RE FINE! PLEASE DON'T COME BY EVERY MORNING!!
OH, IT'S THE LIEUTENANT FROM COMPANY 8 AGAIN.
YOU'RE SO KIND TO VISIT EVERY DAY.
YOU MUST REALLY BE WORRIED ABOUT YOUR SUBORDINATES.
THANK YOU.
...
UGH! YOU'RE EMBARRASSING ME, SIR! PLEASE GO HOME!!
SHOVE
?
WHAT'S WITH THE SUDDEN COLD SHOULDER? YOU COULD CALL THE CAPTAIN ONCE IN A WHILE. HE'S WORRIED, YOU KNOW.
I KNOW!!
SHOO!
SHOO!
PEH

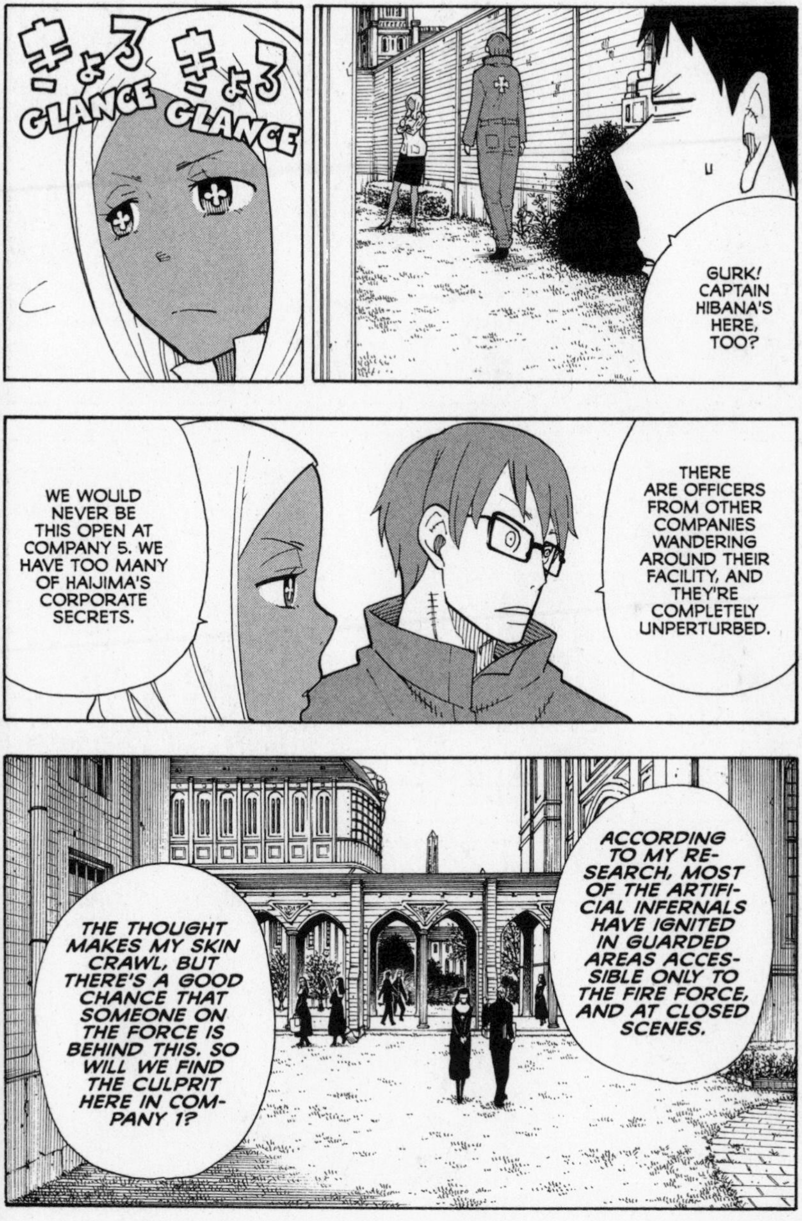
GURK! CAPTAIN HIBANA'S HERE, TOO?
きょろ きょろ
GLANCE GLANCE
THERE ARE OFFICERS FROM OTHER COMPANIES WANDERING AROUND THEIR FACILITY, AND THEY'RE COMPLETELY UNPERTURBED.
WE WOULD NEVER BE THIS OPEN AT COMPANY 5. WE HAVE TOO MANY OF HAIJIMA'S CORPORATE SECRETS.
ACCORDING TO MY RE-SEARCH, MOST OF THE ARTIFI-CIAL INFERNALS HAVE IGNITED IN GUARDED AREAS ACCES-SIBLE ONLY TO THE FIRE FORCE, AND AT CLOSED SCENES.
THE THOUGHT MAKES MY SKIN CRAWL, BUT THERE'S A GOOD CHANCE THAT SOMEONE ON THE FORCE IS BEHIND THIS. SO WILL WE FIND THE CULPRIT HERE IN COM-PANY 1?

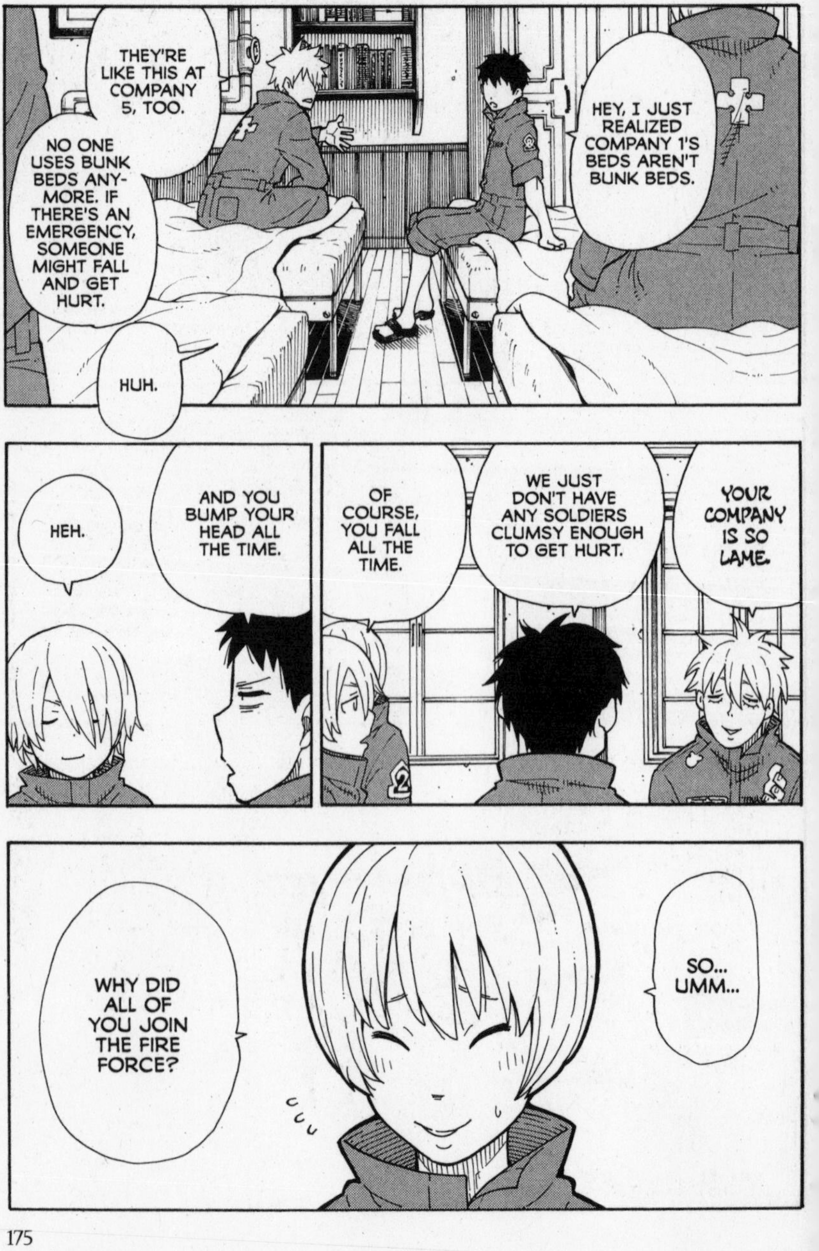
HEY, I JUST REALIZED COMPANY 1'S BEDS AREN'T BUNK BEDS.
THEY'RE LIKE THIS AT COMPANY 5, TOO.
NO ONE USES BUNK BEDS ANY-MORE. IF THERE'S AN EMERGENCY, SOMEONE MIGHT FALL AND GET HURT.
HUH.
YOUR COMPANY IS SO LAME.
WE JUST DON'T HAVE ANY SOLDIERS CLUMSY ENOUGH TO GET HURT.
OF COURSE, YOU FALL ALL THE TIME.
AND YOU BUMP YOUR HEAD ALL THE TIME.
HEH.
SO... UMM...
WHY DID ALL OF YOU JOIN THE FIRE FORCE?

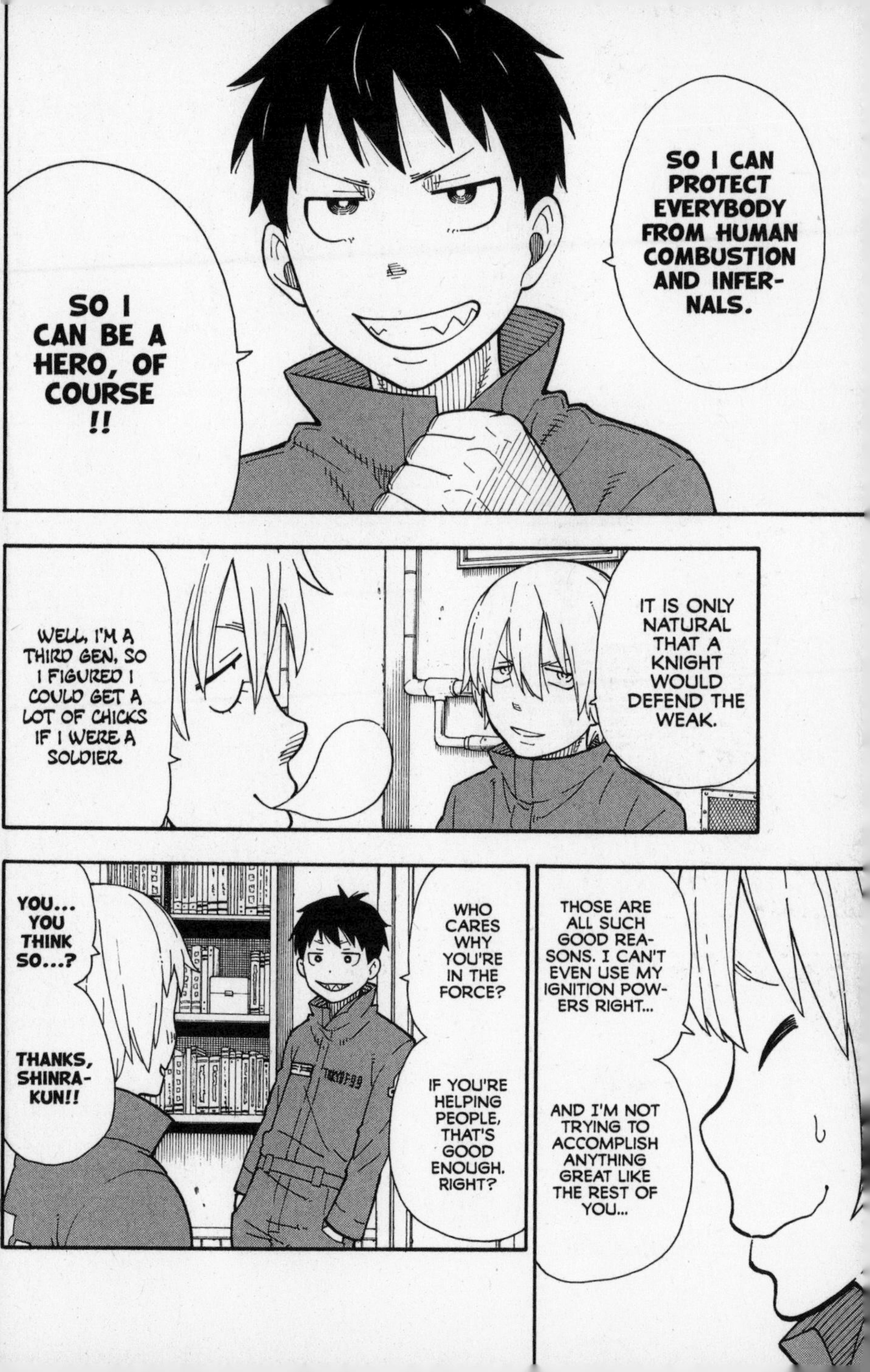
SO I CAN PROTECT EVERYBODY FROM HUMAN COMBUSTION AND INFERNALS.
SO I CAN BE A HERO, OF COURSE!!
IT IS ONLY NATURAL THAT A KNIGHT WOULD DEFEND THE WEAK.
WELL, I'M A THIRD GEN, SO I FIGURED I COULD GET A LOT OF CHICKS IF I WERE A SOLDIER.
THOSE ARE ALL SUCH GOOD REASONS. I CAN'T EVEN USE MY IGNITION POWERS RIGHT...
AND I'M NOT TRYING TO ACCOMPLISH ANYTHING GREAT LIKE THE REST OF YOU...
WHO CARES WHY YOU'RE IN THE FORCE?
IF YOU'RE HELPING PEOPLE, THAT'S GOOD ENOUGH. RIGHT?
YOU... YOU THINK SO...?
THANKS, SHINRA-KUN!!

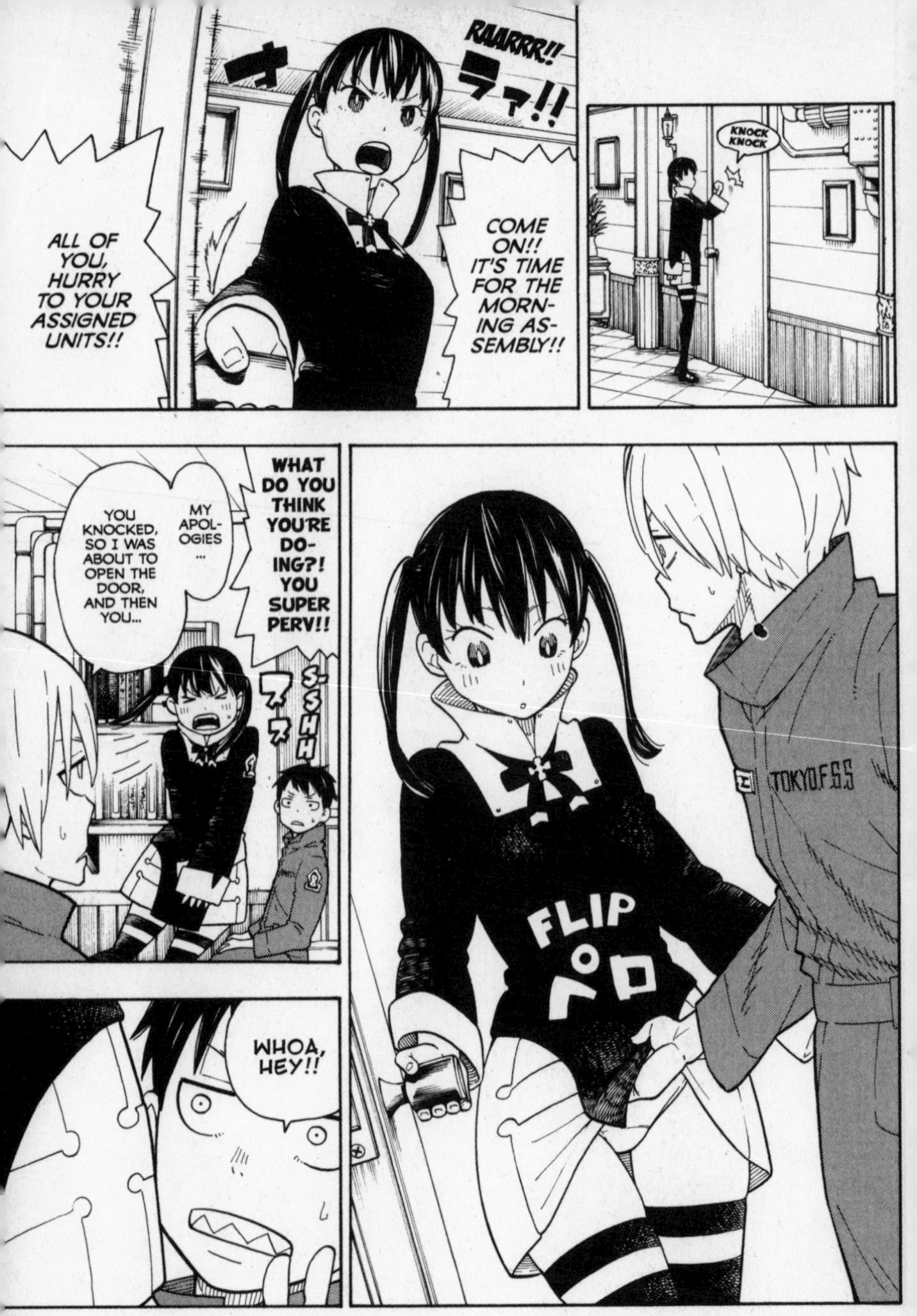
KNOCK KNOCK
RAARRR!!
オラァ!!
COME ON!! IT'S TIME FOR THE MORNING ASSEMBLY!!
ALL OF YOU, HURRY TO YOUR ASSIGNED UNITS!!
TOKYO F.S.S
FLIP
WHAT DO YOU THINK YOU'RE DOING?! YOU SUPER PERV!!
MY APOLOGIES...
YOU KNOCKED, SO I WAS ABOUT TO OPEN THE DOOR, AND THEN YOU...
S-SHH
WHOA, HEY!!

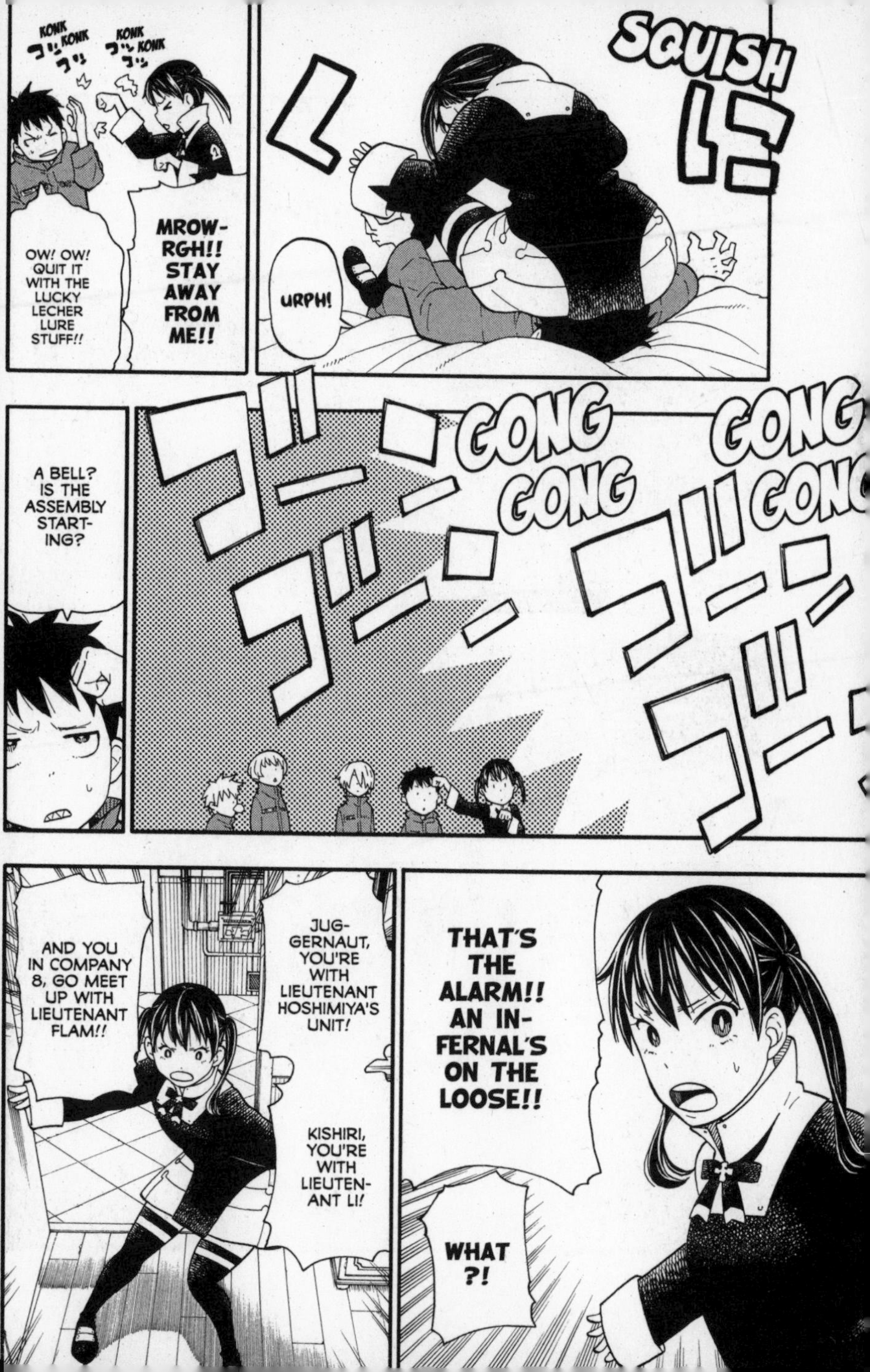
SQUISH
URPH!
KONK KONK
KONK KONK
MROW-RGH!! STAY AWAY FROM ME!!
OW! OW! QUIT IT WITH THE LUCKY LECHER LURE STUFF!!
GONG GONG
GONG GONG
A BELL? IS THE ASSEMBLY START-ING?
THAT'S THE ALARM!! AN IN-FERNAL'S ON THE LOOSE!!
WHAT?!
JUG-GERNAUT, YOU'RE WITH LIEUTENANT HOSHIMIYA'S UNIT!
KISHIRI, YOU'RE WITH LIEUTEN-ANT LI!
AND YOU IN COMPANY 8, GO MEET UP WITH LIEUTENANT FLAM!!

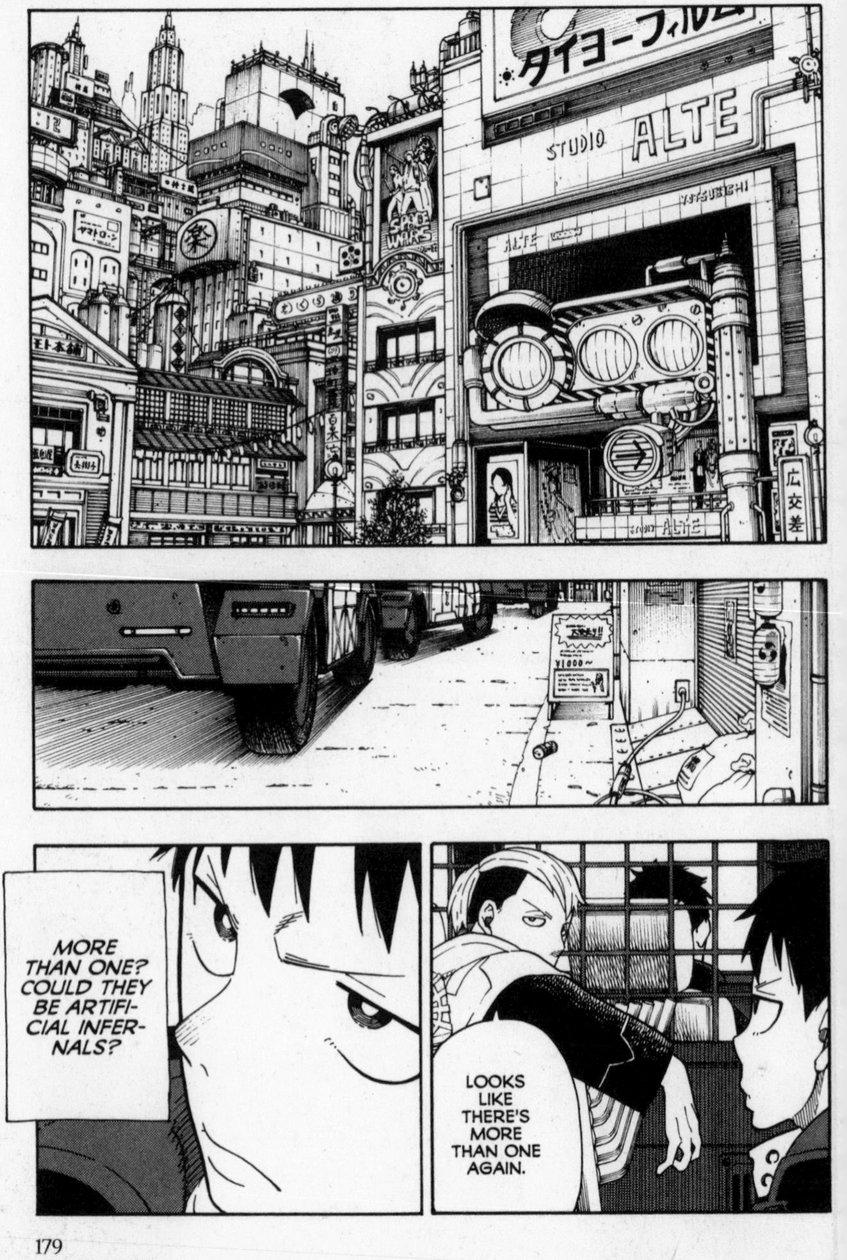
タイヨーフィルム
STUDIO ALTE
SPACE WARS
広交差
¥1000~
LOOKS LIKE THERE'S MORE THAN ONE AGAIN.
MORE THAN ONE? COULD THEY BE ARTIFICIAL INFERNALS?

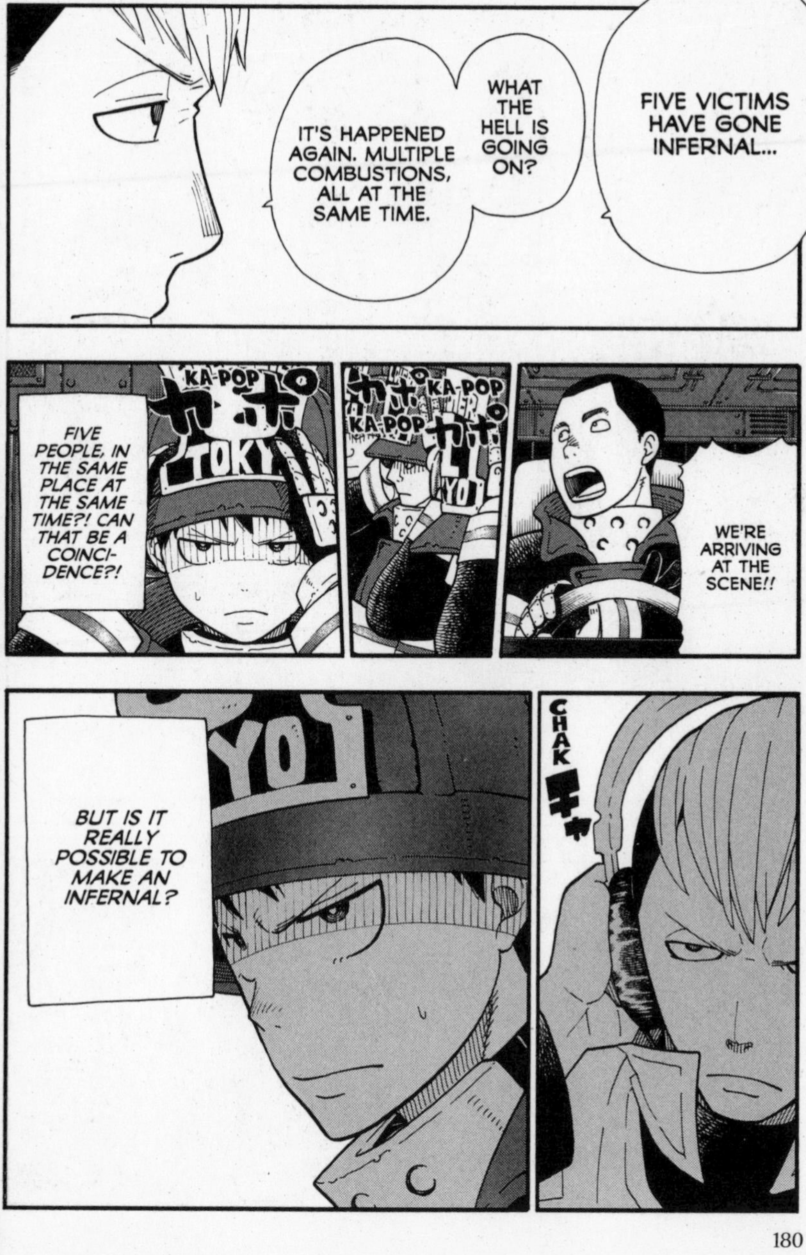
FIVE VICTIMS HAVE GONE INFERNAL...
WHAT THE HELL IS GOING ON?
IT'S HAPPENED AGAIN. MULTIPLE COMBUSTIONS, ALL AT THE SAME TIME.
WE'RE ARRIVING AT THE SCENE!!
KA-POP
KA-POP
KA-POP
FIVE PEOPLE, IN THE SAME PLACE AT THE SAME TIME?! CAN THAT BE A COINCI-DENCE?!
CHAK
BUT IS IT REALLY POSSIBLE TO MAKE AN INFERNAL?

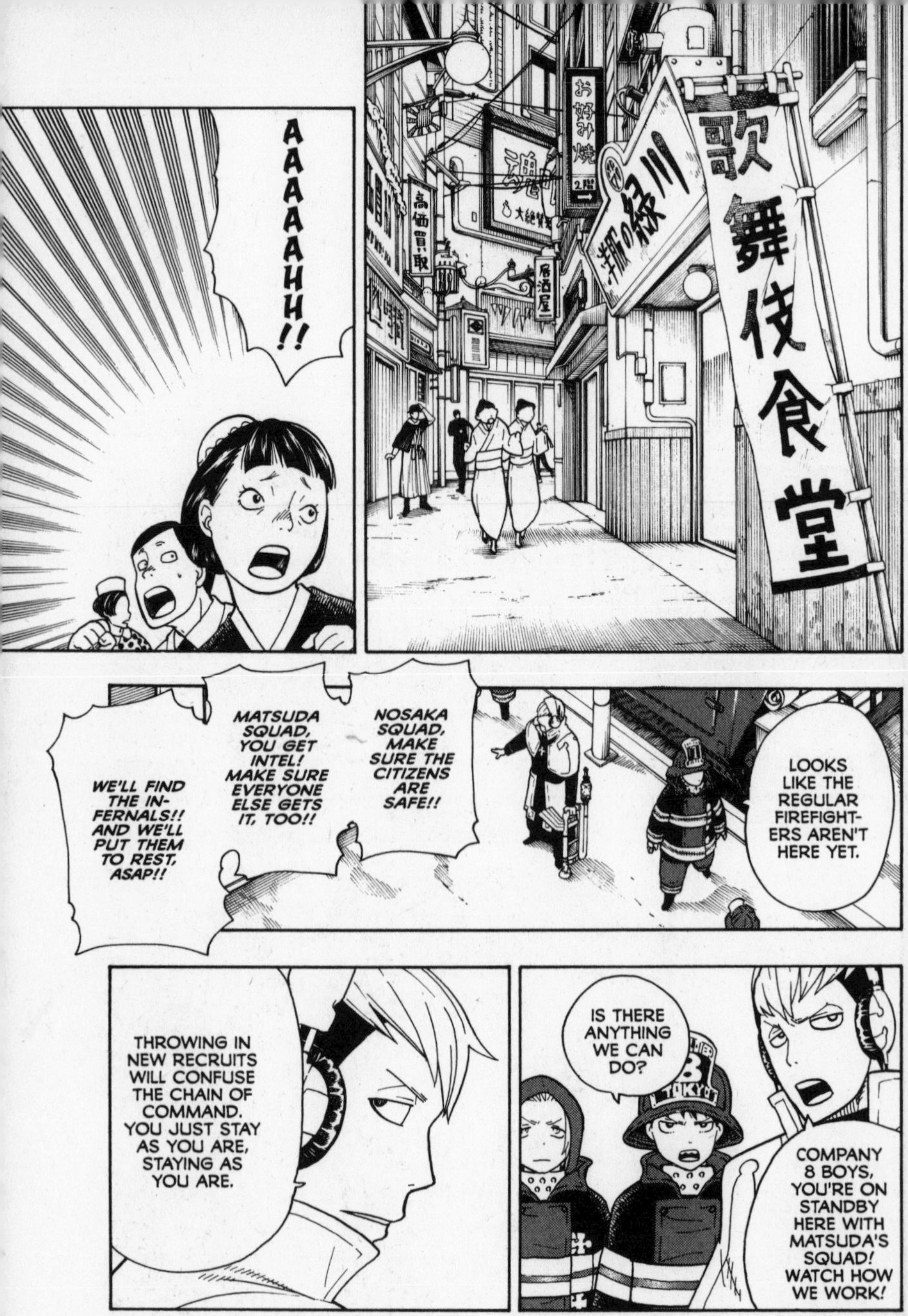
歌舞伎食堂
お好み焼
高価買取
居酒屋
AAAAAAHH!!
LOOKS LIKE THE REGULAR FIREFIGHTERS AREN'T HERE YET.
NOSAKA SQUAD, MAKE SURE THE CITIZENS ARE SAFE!!
MATSUDA SQUAD, YOU GET INTEL! MAKE SURE EVERYONE ELSE GETS IT, TOO!!
WE'LL FIND THE INFERNALS!! AND WE'LL PUT THEM TO REST, ASAP!!
IS THERE ANYTHING WE CAN DO?
COMPANY 8 BOYS, YOU'RE ON STANDBY HERE WITH MATSUDA'S SQUAD! WATCH HOW WE WORK!
THROWING IN NEW RECRUITS WILL CONFUSE THE CHAIN OF COMMAND. YOU JUST STAY AS YOU ARE, STAYING AS YOU ARE.

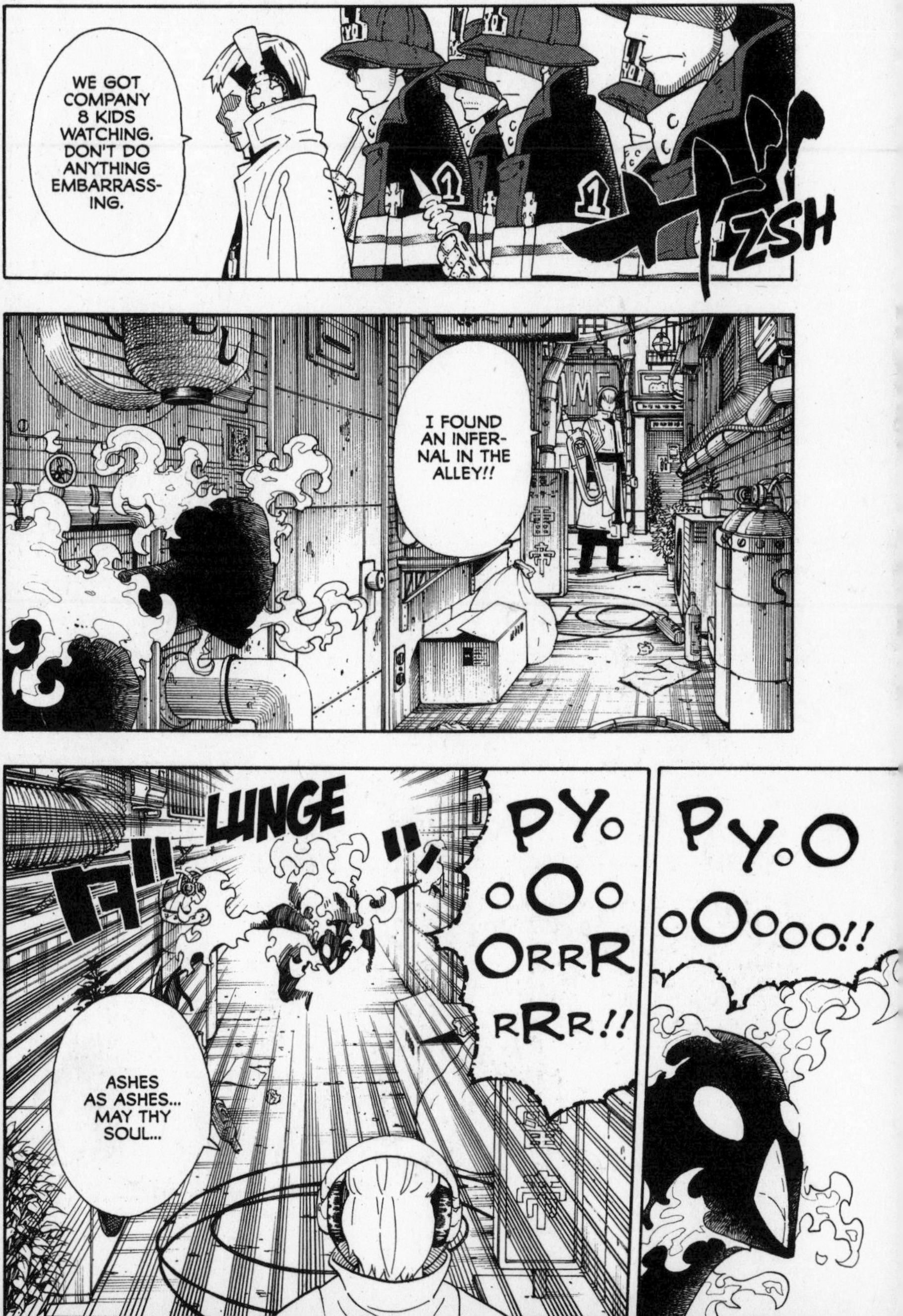
ZSH
WE GOT COMPANY 8 KIDS WATCHING. DON'T DO ANYTHING EMBARRASS-ING.
I FOUND AN INFER-NAL IN THE ALLEY!!
PY.O oOoooo!!
PY.o oOo ORRR rRr!!
LUNGE
ASHES AS ASHES... MAY THY SOUL...

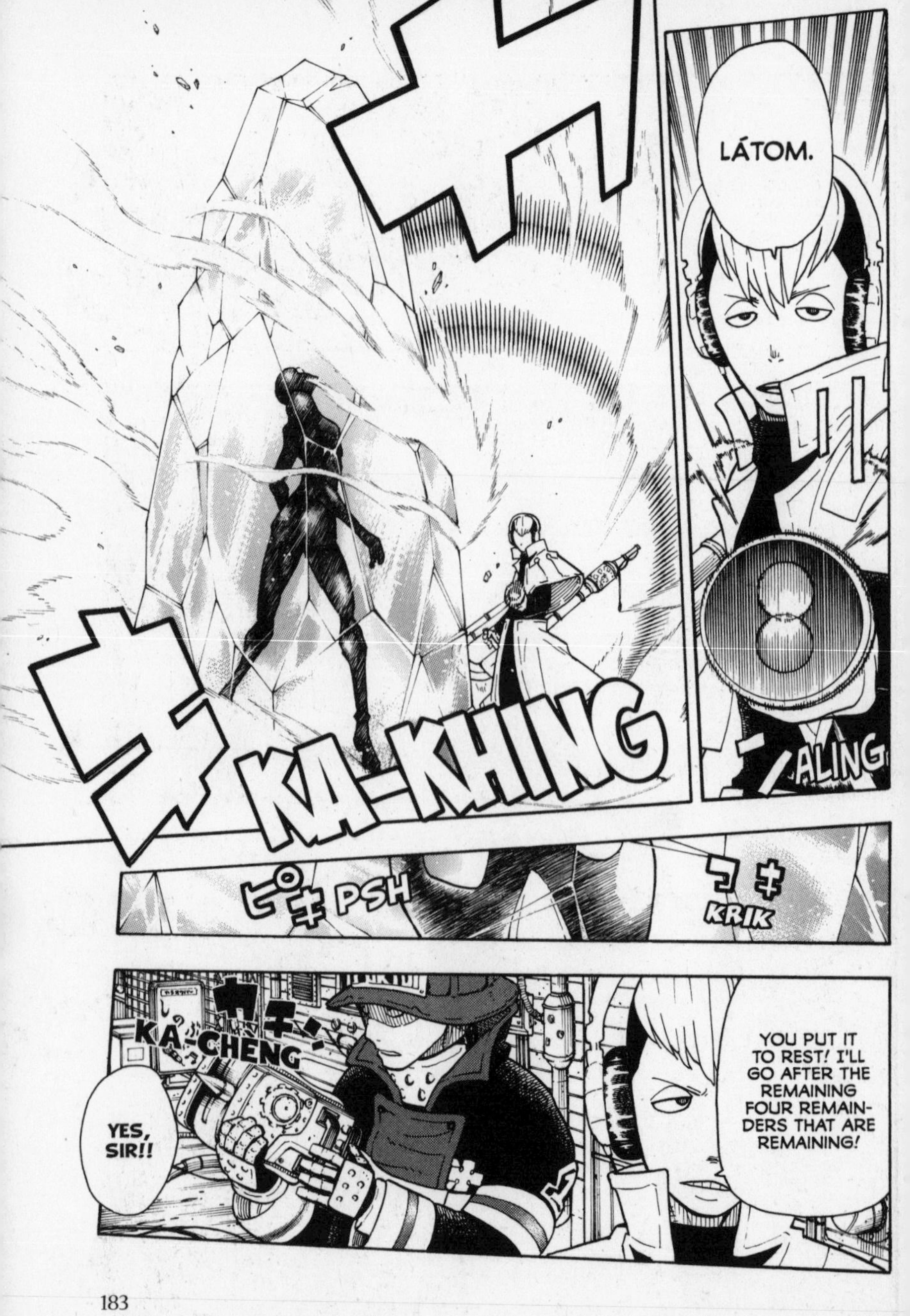
LÁTOM.
ALING
KA-KHING
コキ KRIK
ピキ PSH
YOU PUT IT TO REST! I'LL GO AFTER THE REMAINING FOUR REMAINDERS THAT ARE REMAINING!
KA-CHENG
YES, SIR!!

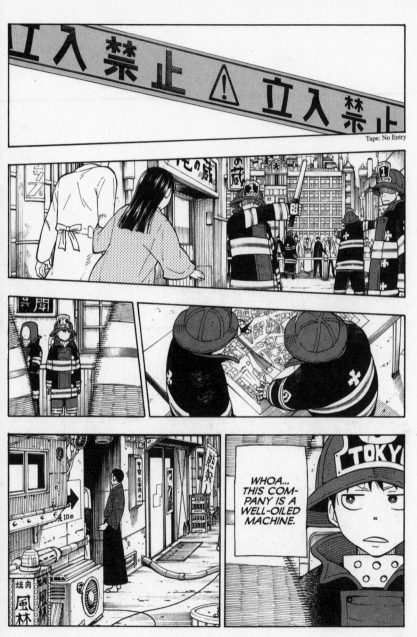

Tape: No Entry

WHOA...
THIS COM-
PANY IS A
WELL-OILED
MACHINE.

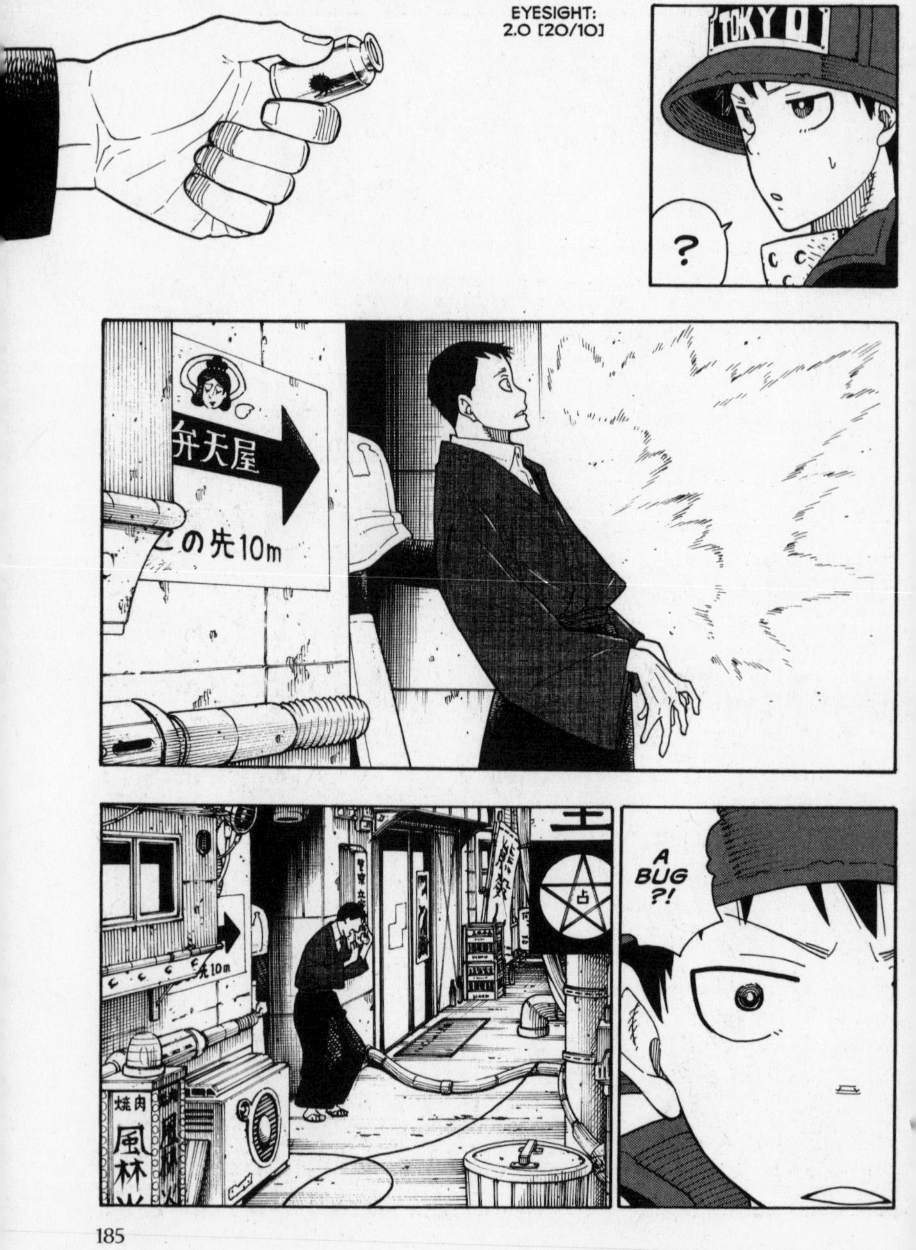
?
EYESIGHT:
2.0 [20/10]
弁天屋
この先10m
A BUG ?!
占
焼肉
風林

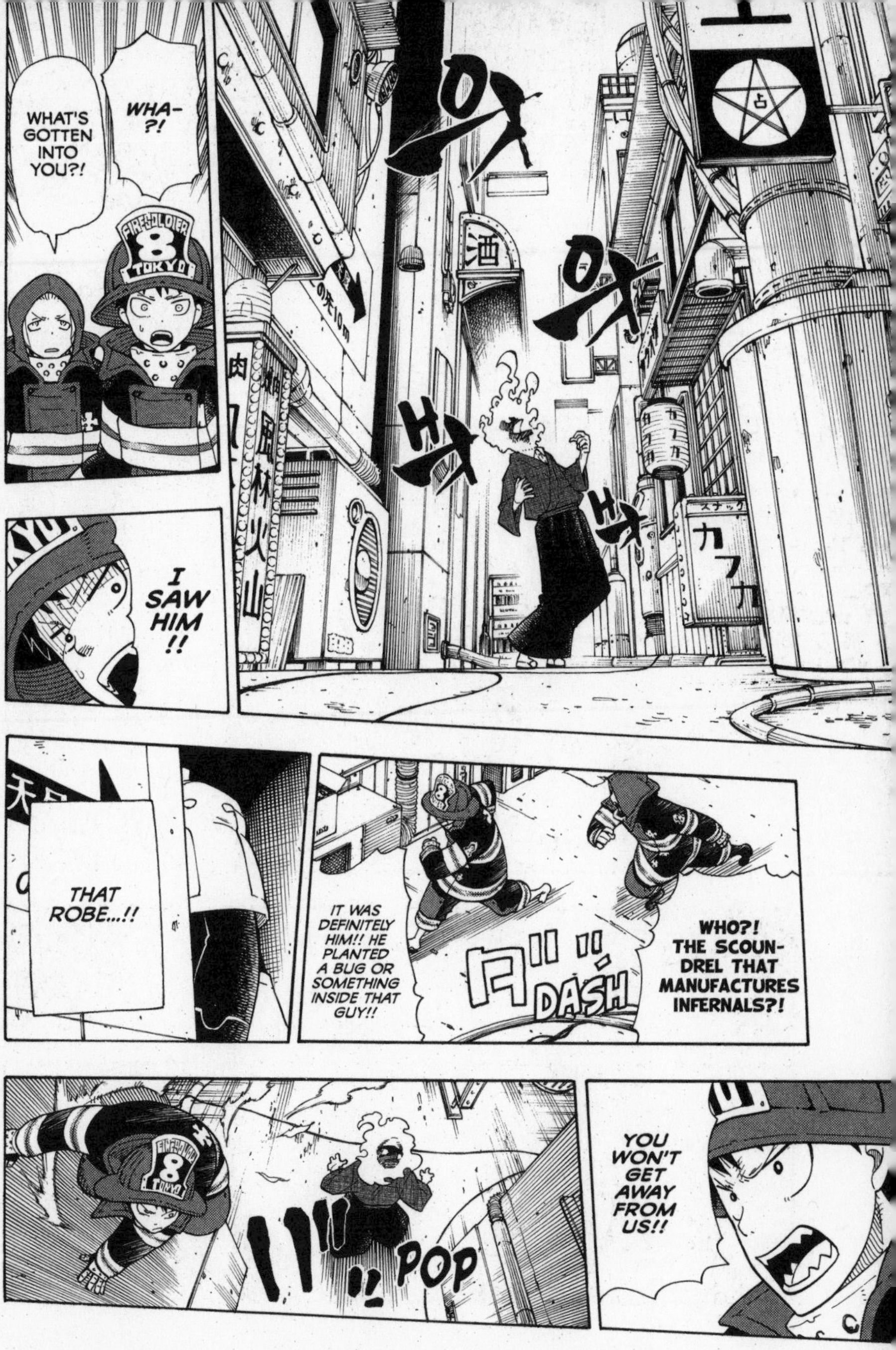
WHA-?!
WHAT'S GOTTEN INTO YOU?!
FIRE SOLDIER 8 TOKYO
I SAW HIM!!
WHO?! THE SCOUN-DREL THAT MANUFACTURES INFERNALS?!
DASH
IT WAS DEFINITELY HIM!! HE PLANTED A BUG OR SOMETHING INSIDE THAT GUY!!
THAT ROBE...!!
YOU WON'T GET AWAY FROM US!!
POP

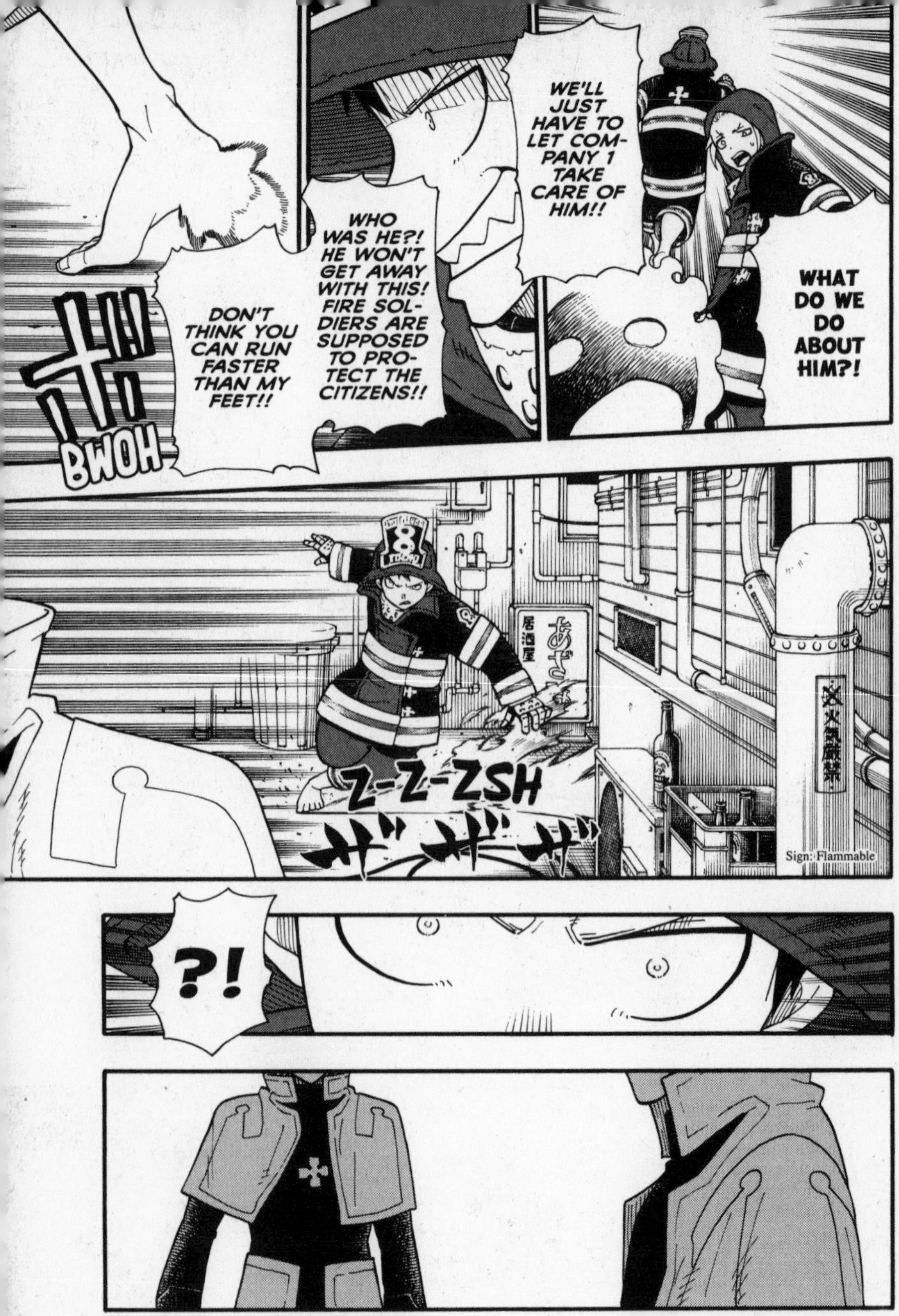

WHAT DO WE DO ABOUT HIM?!
WE'LL JUST HAVE TO LET COMPANY 1 TAKE CARE OF HIM!!
WHO WAS HE?! HE WON'T GET AWAY WITH THIS! FIRE SOLDIERS ARE SUPPOSED TO PROTECT THE CITIZENS!!
DON'T THINK YOU CAN RUN FASTER THAN MY FEET!!
BWOH
居酒屋
火気厳禁
Z-Z-ZSH
ザザザ
Sign: Flammable
?!

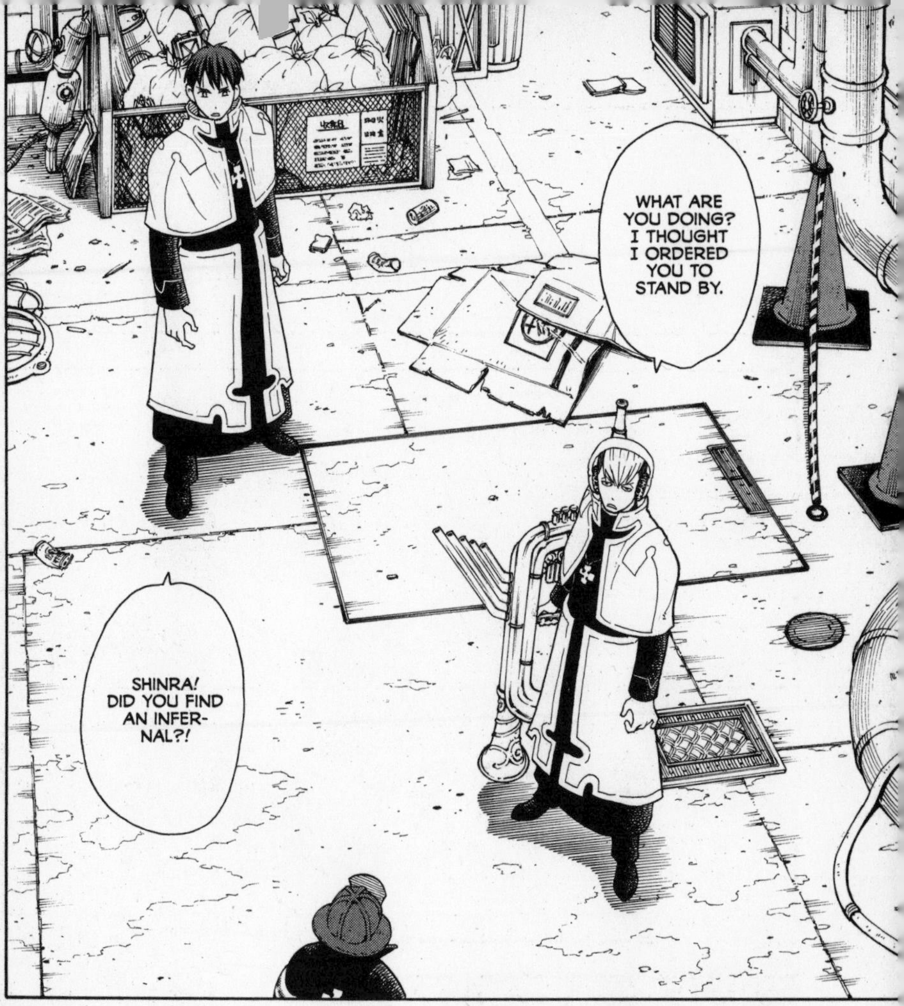
WHAT ARE YOU DOING? I THOUGHT I ORDERED YOU TO STAND BY.
SHINRA! DID YOU FIND AN INFERNAL?!

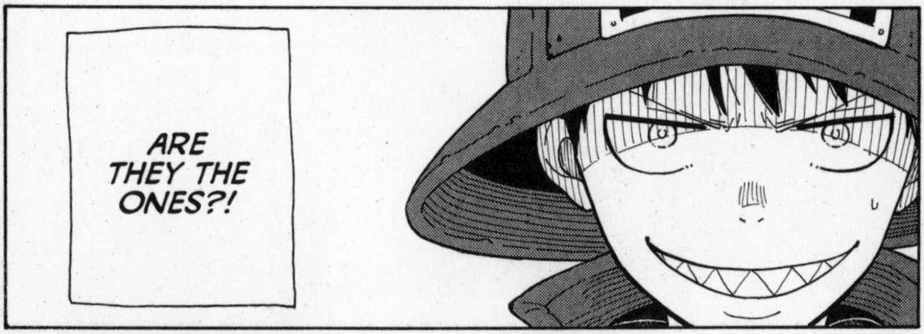
ARE THEY THE ONES?!

TO BE CONTINUED IN VOLUME 4!!

AFTERWORD MANGA: ATSUSHIYA

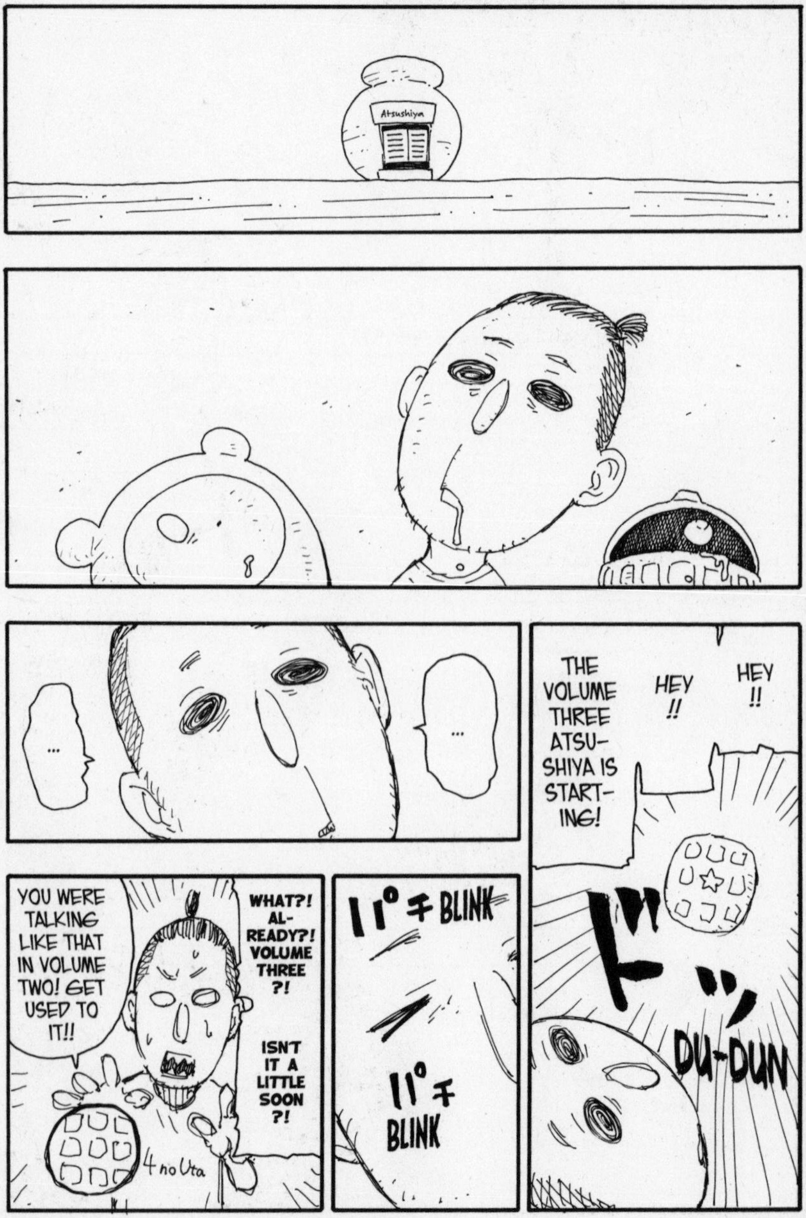

Atsushiya
HEY !!
HEY !!
THE VOLUME THREE ATSUSHIYA IS STARTING!
ドッ
DU-DUN
...
...
パチ BLINK
パチ BLINK
WHAT?! ALREADY?! VOLUME THREE ?!
ISN'T IT A LITTLE SOON ?!
YOU WERE TALKING LIKE THAT IN VOLUME TWO! GET USED TO IT!!
4 no Uta

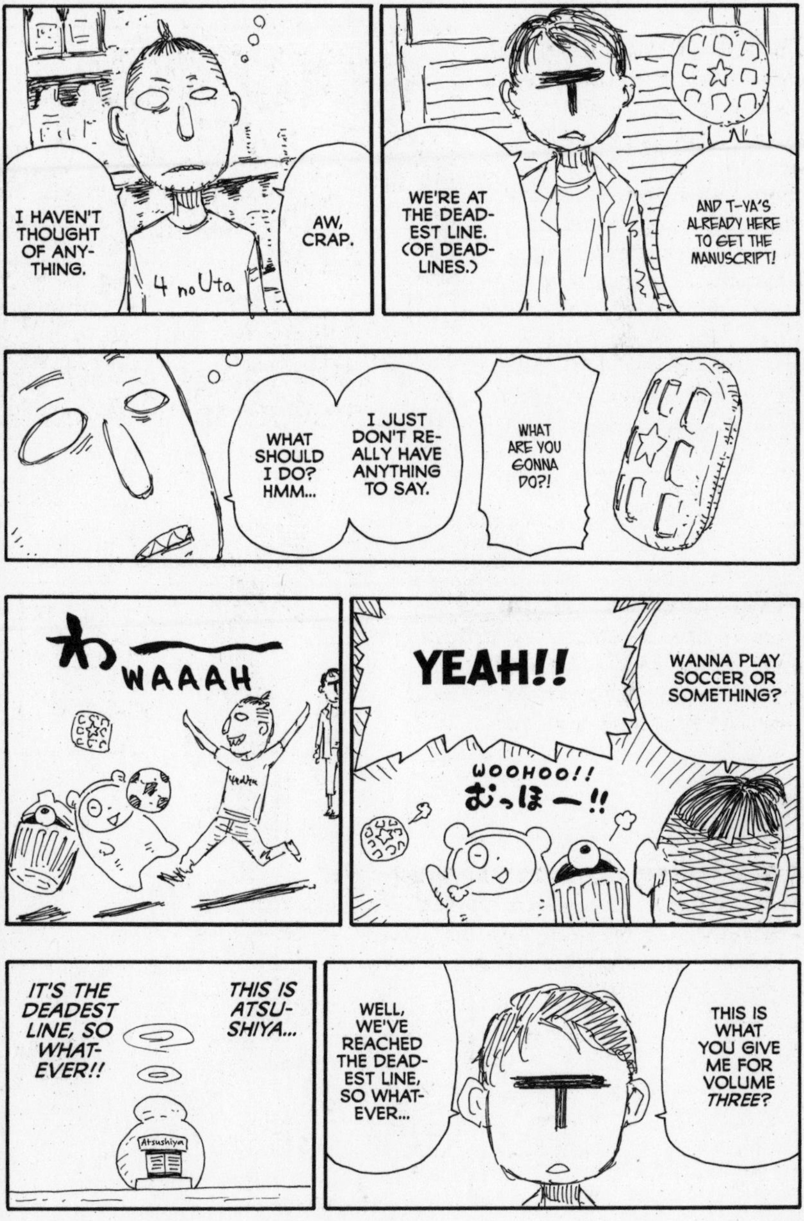
WE'RE AT THE DEADEST LINE. (OF DEADLINES.)
AND T-YA'S ALREADY HERE TO GET THE MANUSCRIPT!
AW, CRAP.
I HAVEN'T THOUGHT OF ANYTHING.
4 no Uta
WHAT ARE YOU GONNA DO?!
I JUST DON'T REALLY HAVE ANYTHING TO SAY.
WHAT SHOULD I DO? HMM...
WANNA PLAY SOCCER OR SOMETHING?
YEAH!!
WOOHOO!!
むっほー!!
わー
WAAAH
THIS IS WHAT YOU GIVE ME FOR VOLUME *THREE*?
WELL, WE'VE REACHED THE DEADEST LINE, SO WHATEVER...
THIS IS ATSUSHIYA...
IT'S THE DEADEST LINE, SO WHATEVER!!
Atsushiya

Translation Notes:

Violet Flash, page 21

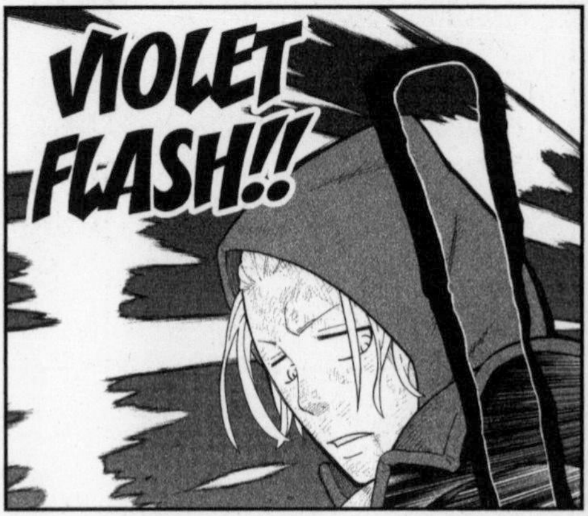
VIOLET FLASH!!

A more literal translation of this move's name would be "violet electric single flash." The Japanese name is shiden issen, where shiden literally means "purple lightning," but it can also refer to the flash of light reflected off of a sword or other blade as it is swung at an enemy. The translators simplified the name of the attack in an attempt to choose the coolest and edgiest wording.

A lily, please, page 79

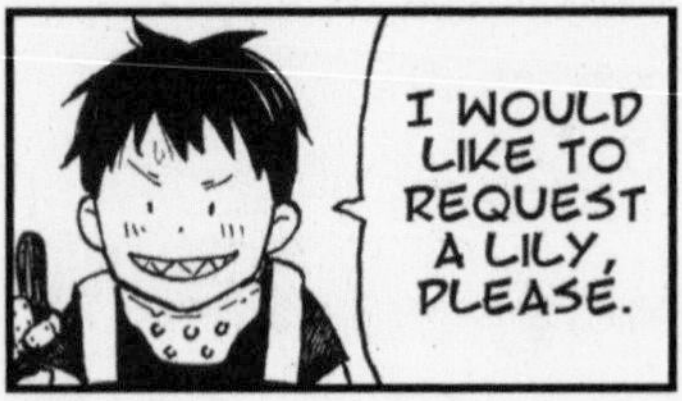
I WOULD LIKE TO REQUEST A LILY, PLEASE.

In answer to Hibana's question, the reason Shinra might request a lily is that the Japanese word for lily, *yuri*, also refers to romance between two women.

Stop being so formal,page 91

When speaking to Hibana, Captain Ōbi uses a polite form of Japanese. Because they are the same rank and Hibana is younger, this normally would not be required, but Ōbi defers to her as someone who has been in the Fire Force longer.

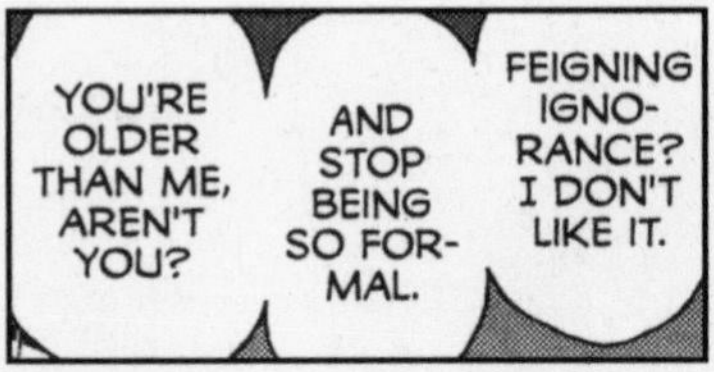
FEIGNING IGNO- RANCE? I DON'T LIKE IT.
AND STOP BEING SO FOR- MAL.
YOU'RE OLDER THAN ME, AREN'T YOU?

Kamélon bread, page 107

A common type of bread eaten as a snack (or a quick substitute for lunch) in Japan is melon bread, named for its melon shape. It has a hard, crispy shell, and a soft inside. As the reader can see, this particular piece of bread looks more like a turtle, and so is named Kamélon—a combination of melon and *kamé*, meaning turtle.

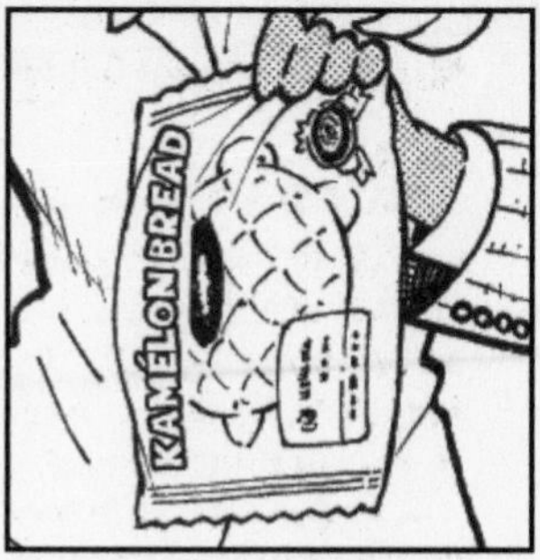
KAMÉLON BREAD

Deva, page 113

Shinra is apparently making the sound of Niō, two deva kings who are often seen guarding the gates of Buddhist temples, frightening off intruders with their wrathful countenances—countenances not unlike Shinra's face here.

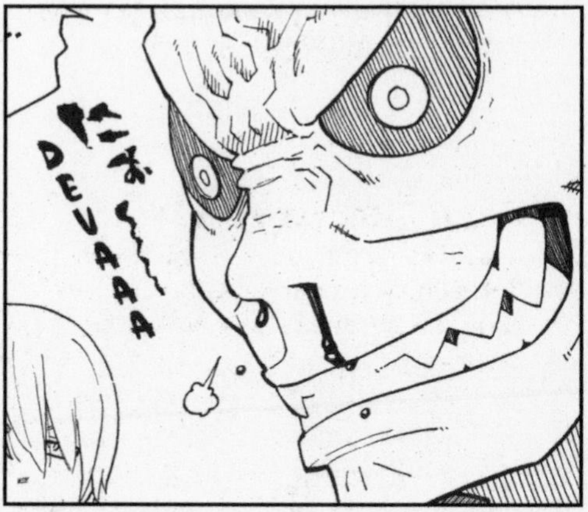
DEVAAA

Nar, page 115

Readers may be wondering what the 9 and the 8 are doing in this panel. The answer is that they are spelling the sound effect. Because Japanese numbers have so many different pronunciations, sometimes it can be fun to spell out words using those pronunciations. For example, *yoroshiku* (roughly translated as "nice to meet you") can be spelled 4649, where 4 is both *yo* and *shi*. In the case of this sound effect, the 9 and the 8 are used to spell *kuwa*, which the sound of a violent burst of emotion, such as inspiration or rage. The mathematical symbol may also be a symbol of the mind at work. In a desperate attempt to replicate this effect, the translators resorted to using Medieval number abbreviations, where the N represents 90 and R is 80. These "numbers" were chosen partially because they include nine and eight, but also because they work together to make a reasonable substitute for the *kuwa* sound.

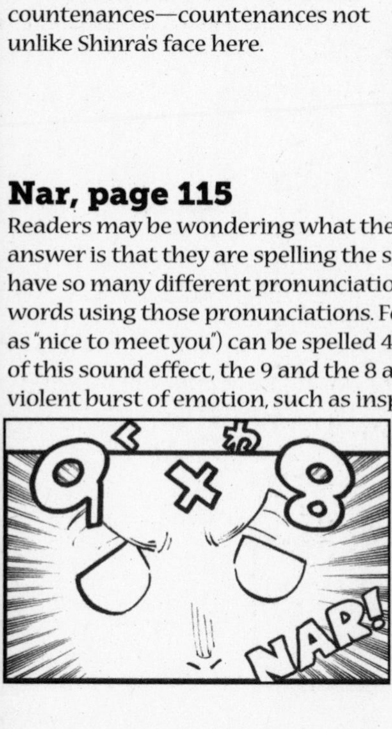
9 × 8
NAR!

Soul Eater, big hit, page 181

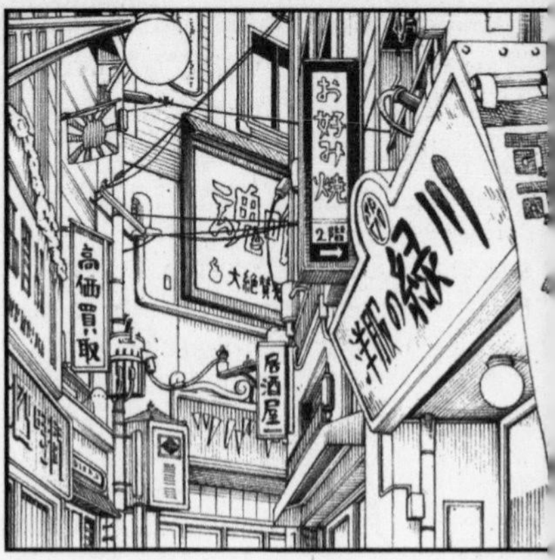
洋服の緑川
お好み焼
2階
魂
高価買取
居酒屋

Though many of the signs in this manga are left untranslated, as they're mostly atmospheric (ads for bars, automobile retailers, film companies, etc), Ohkubo-sensei inserted an ad that was a nod to his last manga, *Soul Eater*. The sign simply says "Soul Eater, Big Hit." The bar directly below the sign is named Tsubaki—another character from the manga.

4 *no Uta*, page 189

Translated as "Song of 4," this is the title of a song performed by the world's cutest heavy metal group, Babymetal. The song is a tribute to the number four, a number which may or may not have been chosen because one Japanese pronunciation for "four," *shi*, can also mean "death."

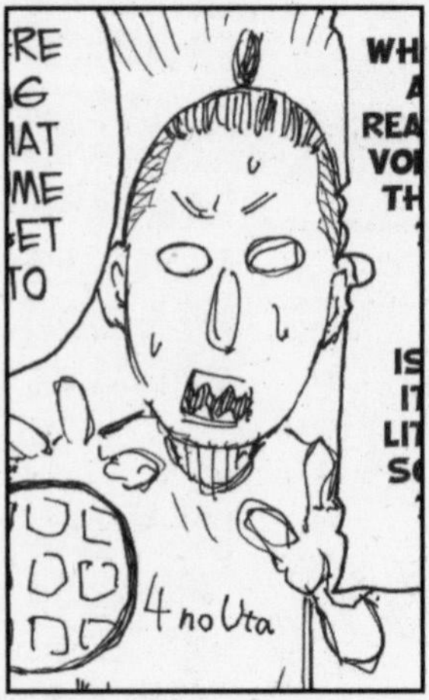
4 no Uta

SISTER IRIS

FIRE FORCE

AFFILIATION:
SPECIAL FIRE
FORCE COMPANY 8

RANK:
NUN

ABILITY:
NONE

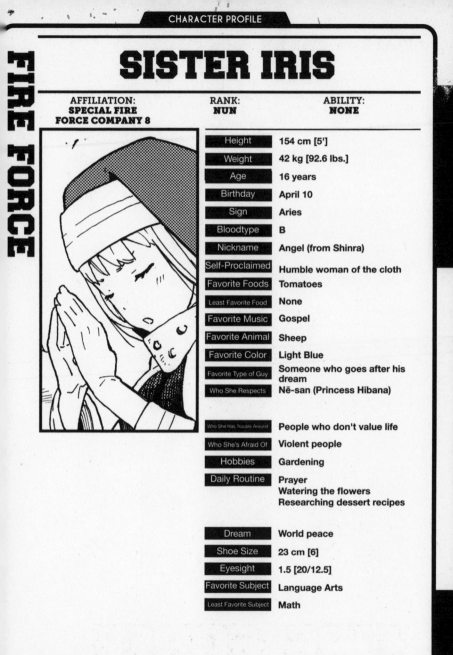

Height	154 cm [5']
Weight	42 kg [92.6 lbs.]
Age	16 years
Birthday	April 10
Sign	Aries
Bloodtype	B
Nickname	Angel (from Shinra)
Self-Proclaimed	Humble woman of the cloth
Favorite Foods	Tomatoes
Least Favorite Food	None
Favorite Music	Gospel
Favorite Animal	Sheep
Favorite Color	Light Blue
Favorite Type of Guy	Someone who goes after his dream
Who She Respects	Nē-san (Princess Hibana)
Who She Has Trouble Around	People who don't value life
Who She's Afraid Of	Violent people
Hobbies	Gardening
Daily Routine	Prayer Watering the flowers Researching dessert recipes
Dream	World peace
Shoe Size	23 cm [6]
Eyesight	1.5 [20/12.5]
Favorite Subject	Language Arts
Least Favorite Subject	Math

FIRE FORCE

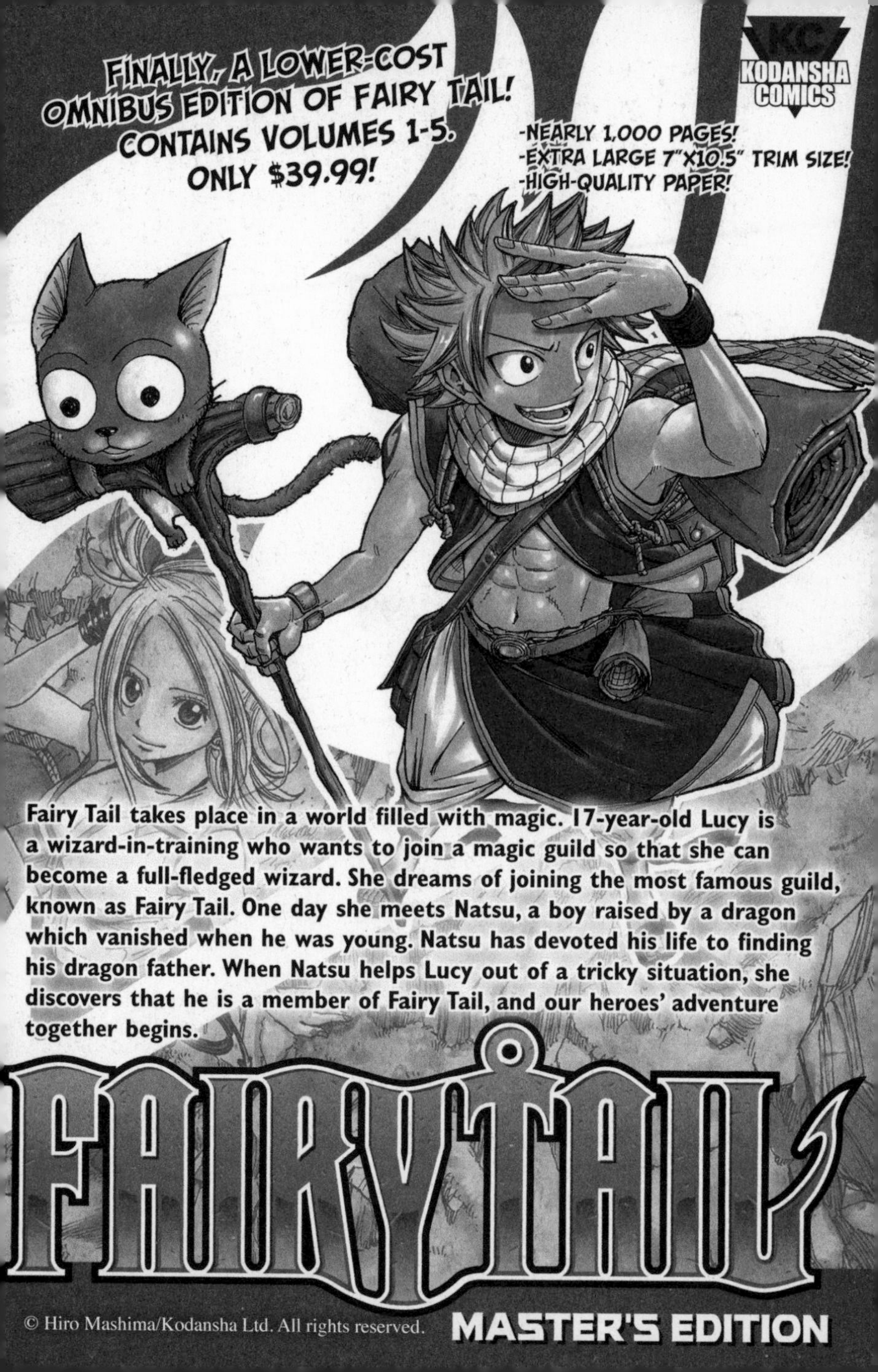
FINALLY, A LOWER-COST OMNIBUS EDITION OF FAIRY TAIL! CONTAINS VOLUMES 1-5. ONLY $39.99!
KODANSHA COMICS
-NEARLY 1,000 PAGES!
-EXTRA LARGE 7"X10.5" TRIM SIZE!
-HIGH-QUALITY PAPER!
Fairy Tail takes place in a world filled with magic. 17-year-old Lucy is a wizard-in-training who wants to join a magic guild so that she can become a full-fledged wizard. She dreams of joining the most famous guild, known as Fairy Tail. One day she meets Natsu, a boy raised by a dragon which vanished when he was young. Natsu has devoted his life to finding his dragon father. When Natsu helps Lucy out of a tricky situation, she discovers that he is a member of Fairy Tail, and our heroes' adventure together begins.
FAIRY TAIL
MASTER'S EDITION
© Hiro Mashima/Kodansha Ltd. All rights reserved.

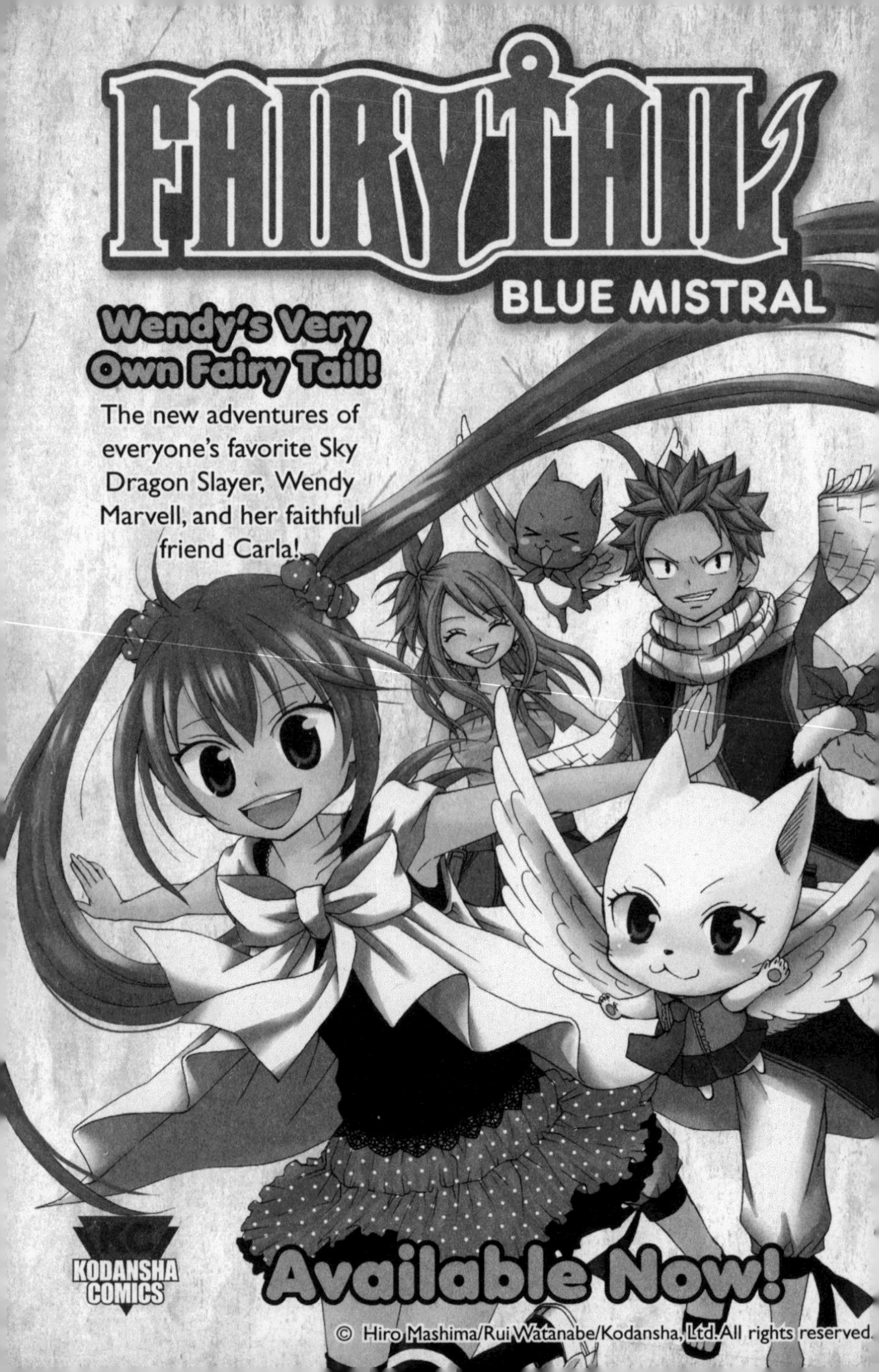
FAIRY TAIL
BLUE MISTRAL
Wendy's Very Own Fairy Tail!
The new adventures of everyone's favorite Sky Dragon Slayer, Wendy Marvell, and her faithful friend Carla!
KODANSHA COMICS
Available Now!
© Hiro Mashima/Rui Watanabe/Kodansha, Ltd. All rights reserved.

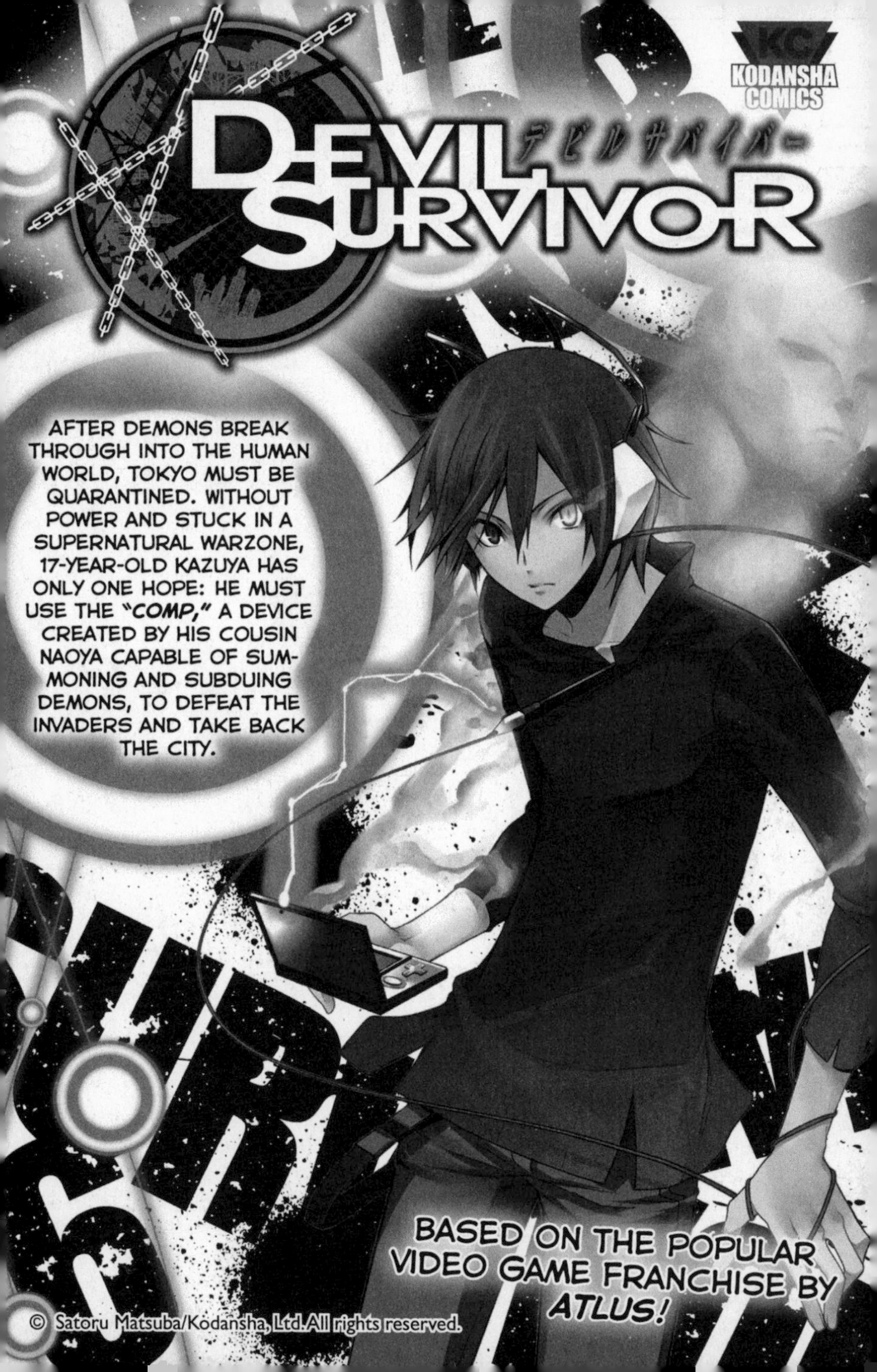
KC
KODANSHA COMICS
DEVIL SURVIVOR
デビルサバイバー
AFTER DEMONS BREAK THROUGH INTO THE HUMAN WORLD, TOKYO MUST BE QUARANTINED. WITHOUT POWER AND STUCK IN A SUPERNATURAL WARZONE, 17-YEAR-OLD KAZUYA HAS ONLY ONE HOPE: HE MUST USE THE "COMP," A DEVICE CREATED BY HIS COUSIN NAOYA CAPABLE OF SUM-MONING AND SUBDUING DEMONS, TO DEFEAT THE INVADERS AND TAKE BACK THE CITY.
BASED ON THE POPULAR VIDEO GAME FRANCHISE BY ATLUS!
© Satoru Matsuba/Kodansha, Ltd. All rights reserved.

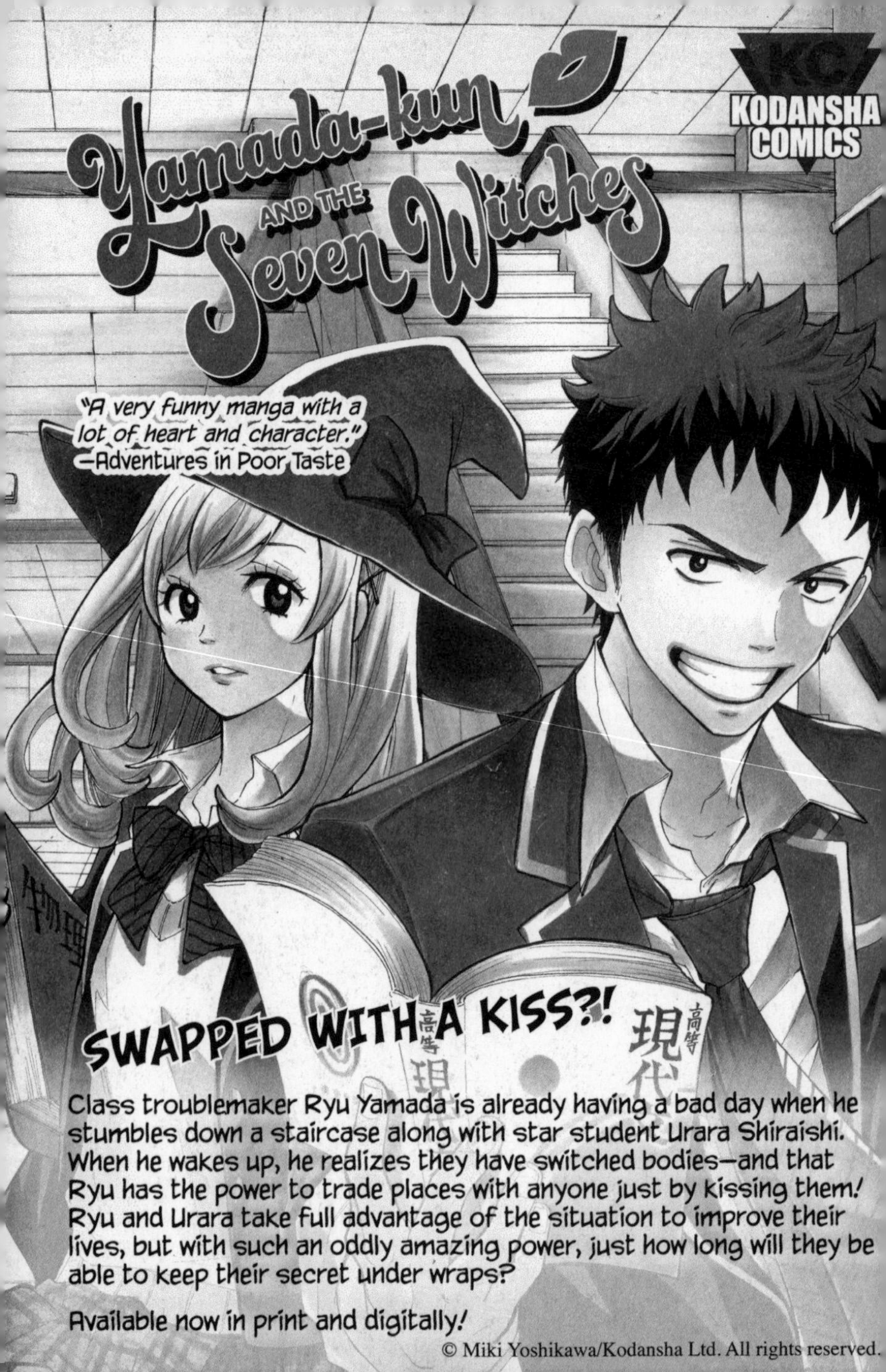
KC
KODANSHA COMICS
Yamada-kun AND THE Seven Witches
"A very funny manga with a lot of heart and character."
—Adventures in Poor Taste
SWAPPED WITH A KISS?!
Class troublemaker Ryu Yamada is already having a bad day when he stumbles down a staircase along with star student Urara Shiraishi. When he wakes up, he realizes they have switched bodies—and that Ryu has the power to trade places with anyone just by kissing them! Ryu and Urara take full advantage of the situation to improve their lives, but with such an oddly amazing power, just how long will they be able to keep their secret under wraps?
Available now in print and digitally!

DON'T MISS THE MOST ACCLAIMED ACTION MANGA OF 2013!

"Gripping doesn't begin to describe Vinland Saga. 5 stars."
—ICv2

"Deeply engrossing... If you have any interest at all in Vikings, the Medieval period, or pirates, this is not a series you want to miss."
—Anime News Network

"The art is gorgeous, a combination of beautiful cartooning and realistic backgrounds. Yukimura is also a master of pacing, both in frenetic battle scenes and charged emotional moments."
—Faith Erin Hicks, *Friends With Boys*

"For those who love Berserk, you'll love this too... Worth the long wait."
—A Case Suitable for Treatment

"It will be impossible to stop watching this story unfold."
—Japan Media Arts Awards jury

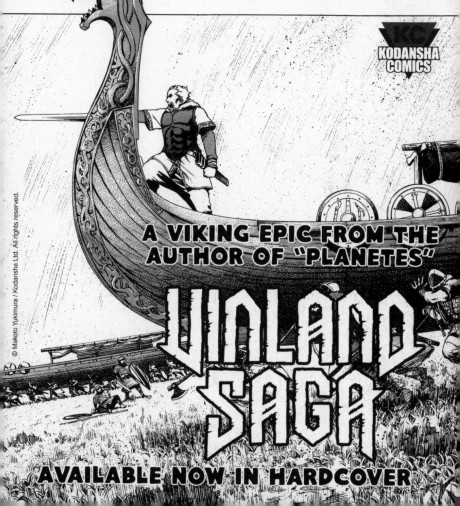

KC KODANSHA COMICS

A VIKING EPIC FROM THE AUTHOR OF "PLANETES"

VINLAND SAGA

AVAILABLE NOW IN HARDCOVER

INUYASHIKI

A superhero like none you've ever seen, from the creator of "Gantz"!

ICHIRO INUYASHIKI IS DOWN ON HIS LUCK. HE LOOKS MUCH OLDER THAN HIS 58 YEARS, HIS CHILDREN DESPISE HIM, AND HIS WIFE THINKS HE'S A USELESS COWARD. SO WHEN HE'S DIAGNOSED WITH STOMACH CANCER AND GIVEN THREE MONTHS TO LIVE, IT SEEMS THE ONLY ONE WHO'LL MISS HIM IS HIS DOG.

THEN A BLINDING LIGHT FILLS THE SKY, AND THE OLD MAN IS KILLED... ONLY TO WAKE UP LATER IN A BODY HE ALMOST RECOGNIZES AS HIS OWN. CAN IT BE THAT ICHIRO INUYASHIKI IS NO LONGER HUMAN?

COMES IN EXTRA-LARGE EDITIONS WITH COLOR PAGES!

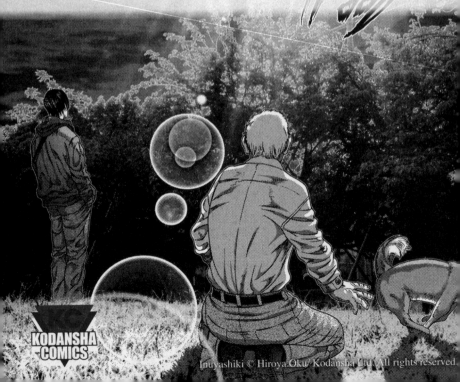

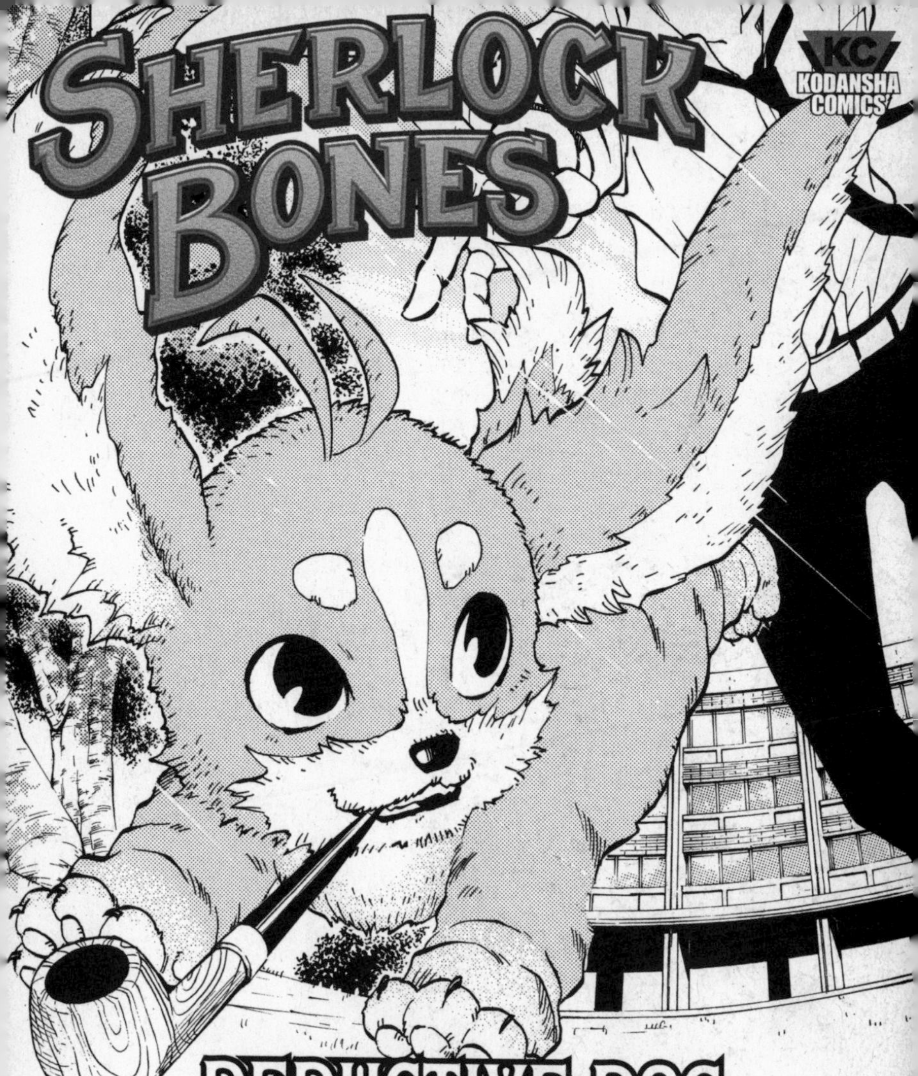
SHERLOCK BONES
KC
KODANSHA COMICS

DEDUCTIVE DOG DETECTIVE

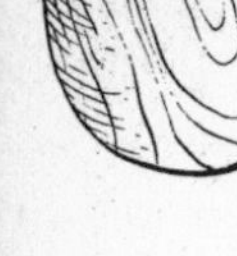

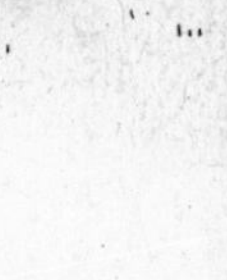

When Takeru adopts a new pet, he's in for a surprise—the dog is none other than the reincarnation of Sherlock Holmes. With no one else able to communicate with Holmes, Takeru is roped into becoming Sherdog's assistant, John Watson. Using his sleuthing skills, Holmes uncovers clues to solve the trickiest crimes.

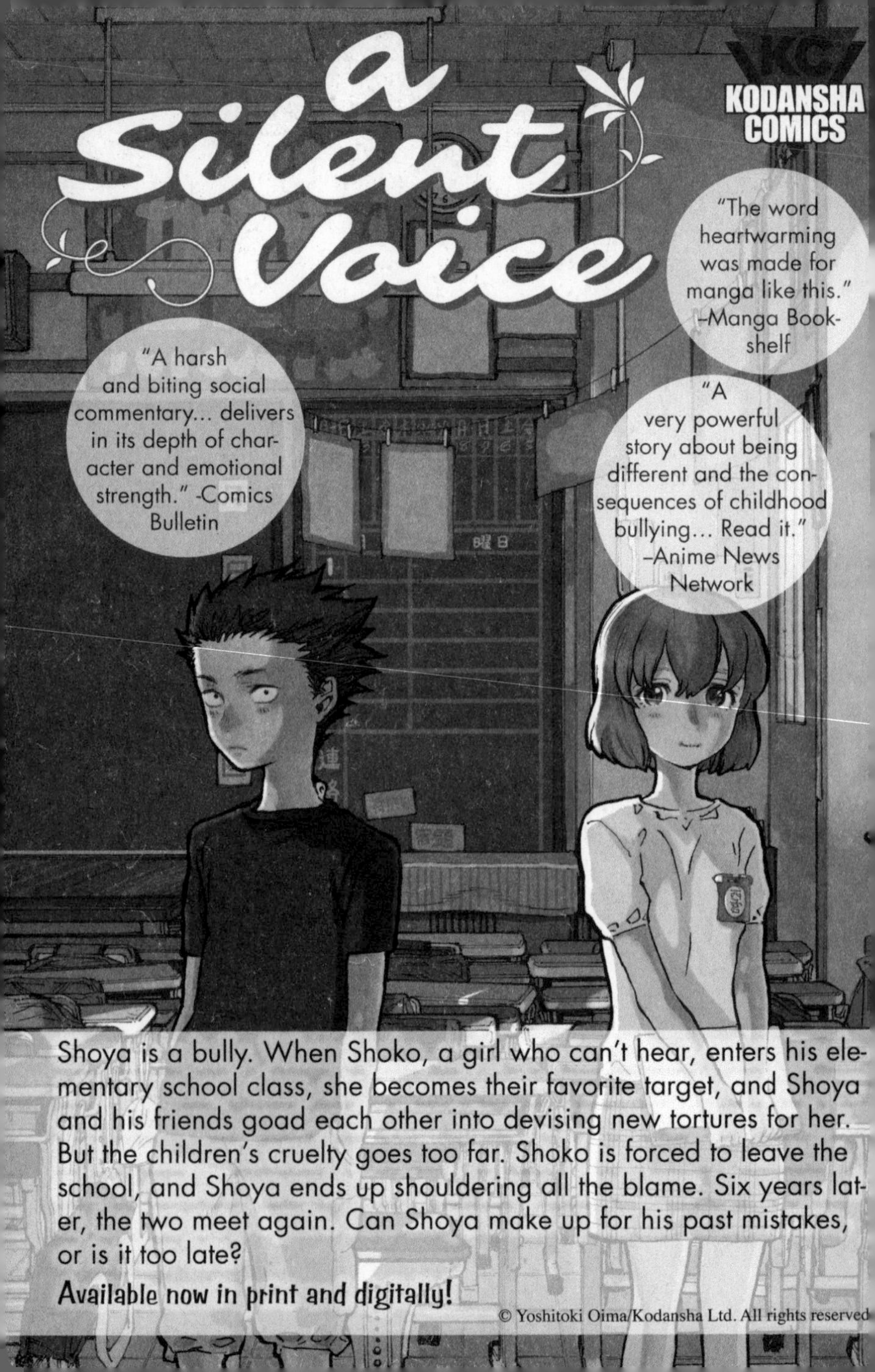
KODANSHA COMICS
a Silent Voice
"The word heartwarming was made for manga like this." –Manga Bookshelf
"A harsh and biting social commentary... delivers in its depth of character and emotional strength." -Comics Bulletin
"A very powerful story about being different and the consequences of childhood bullying... Read it." –Anime News Network
Shoya is a bully. When Shoko, a girl who can't hear, enters his elementary school class, she becomes their favorite target, and Shoya and his friends goad each other into devising new tortures for her. But the children's cruelty goes too far. Shoko is forced to leave the school, and Shoya ends up shouldering all the blame. Six years later, the two meet again. Can Shoya make up for his past mistakes, or is it too late?
Available now in print and digitally!
© Yoshitoki Oima/Kodansha Ltd. All rights reserved

My Little Monster

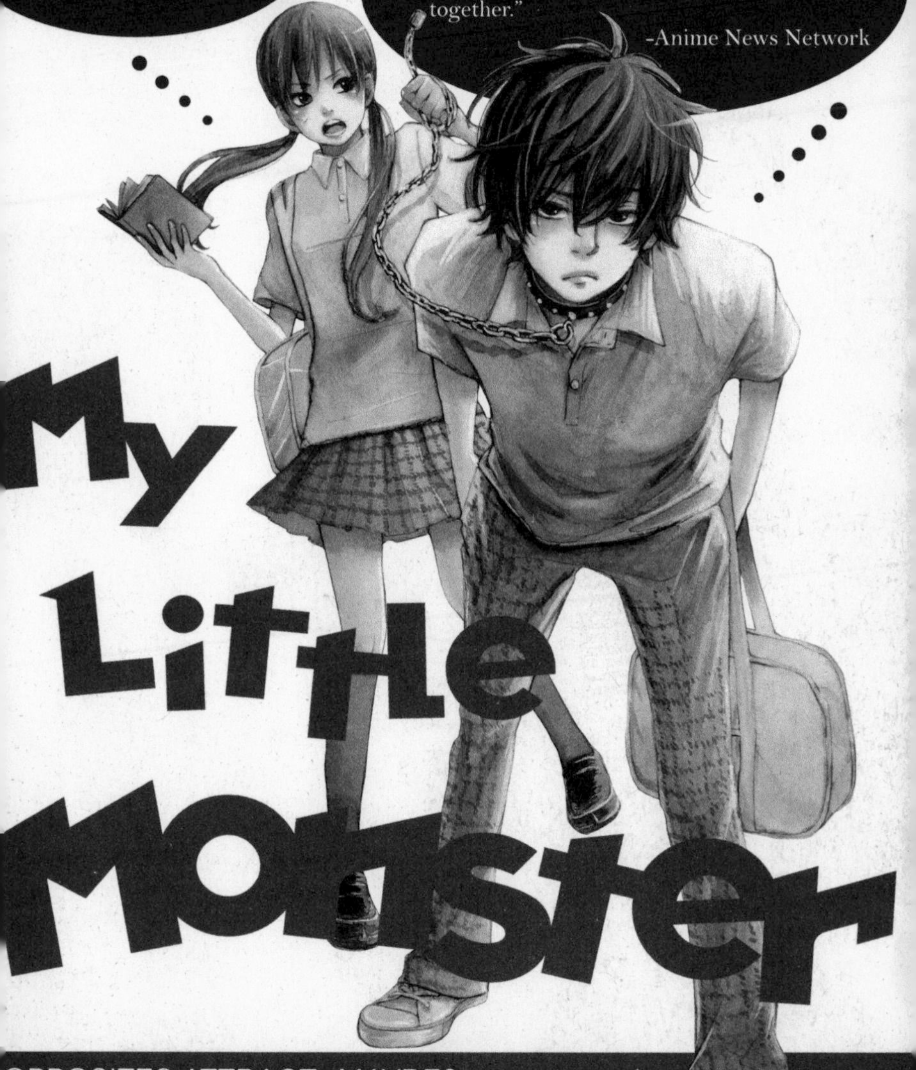

OPPOSITES ATTRACT...MAYBE?

Haru Yoshida is feared as an unstable and violent "monster." Mizutani Shizuku is a grade-obsessed student with no friends. Fate brings these two together to form the most unlikely pair. Haru firmly believes he's in love with Mizutani and she firmly believes he's insane.

KC
KODANSHA
COMICS

Say I Love You.

KC
KODANSHA
COMICS

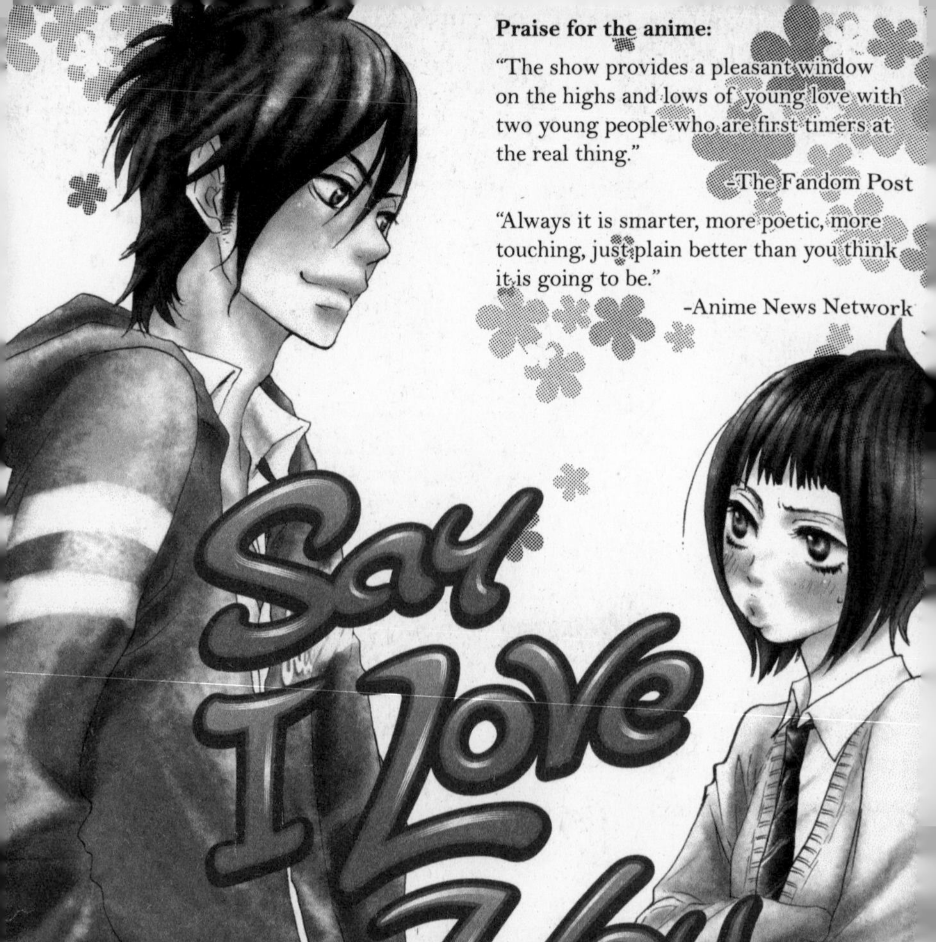

Mei Tachibana has no friends — and says she doesn't need them!
But everything changes when she accidentally roundhouse kicks the most popular boy in school! However, Yamato Kurosawa isn't angry in the slightest— in fact, he thinks his ordinary life could use an unusual girl like Mei. But winning Mei's trust will be a tough task. How long will she refuse to say, "I love you"?

P9-CMX-514

A Kodansha Comics Trade Paperback Original.

Fire Force volume 3 copyright © 2016 Atsushi Ohkubo
English translation copyright © 2017 Atsushi Ohkubo

Published in the United States by Kodansha Comics, an imprint of Kodansha USA Publishing, LLC, New York.

Publication rights for this English edition arranged through Kodansha Ltd., Tokyo.

First published in Japan in 2016 by Kodansha Ltd., Tokyo.

ISBN 978-1-63236-378-7

Printed in the United States of America.

www.kodanshacomics.com

9 8 7 6 5 4 3 2 1

Translation: Alethea Nibley & Athena Nibley
Lettering: AndWorld Design
Editing: Lauren Scanlan
Kodansha Comics edition cover design: Phil Balsman